PR 131 GAU

SCOTTISH STUDIES INTERNATIONAL

PUBLICATIONS OF THE SCOTTISH STUDIES CENTRE
OF THE JOHANNES GUTENBERG UNIVERSITÄT MAINZ
IN GERMERSHEIM

General Editor: Horst W. Drescher

Vol./Bd. 37

PETER LANG

Frankfurt am Main · Berlin · Bern · Bruxelles · New York · Oxford · Wien

Gauti Kristmannsson

Literary Diplomacy I

The Role of Translation in the Construction of National Literatures in Britain and Germany 1750 – 1830

PETER LANG

Europäischer Verlag der Wissenschaften

Bibliographic Information published by Die Deutsche Bibliothek
Die Deutsche Bibliothek lists this publication in the Deutsche Nationalbibliografie; detailed bibliographic data is available in the internet at <http://dnb.ddb.de>.

Zugl.: Mainz, Univ., Diss., 2001

Printed with support of the
University of Iceland.

D 77
ISSN 1430-9572
ISBN 3-631-39130-7
US-ISBN 0-8204-5485-0

© Peter Lang GmbH
Europäischer Verlag der Wissenschaften
Frankfurt am Main 2005
All rights reserved.

Printed in Germany 1 2 3 4   6 7

www.peterlang.de

TABLE OF CONTENTS

PREFACE

These two volumes have been distilled out of what originally was a doctoral dissertation submitted to the Johannes Gutenberg-University in Mainz / Germersheim and naturally they bear some marks of these origins. At first, the intention was to write a comparison of translation and national literatures in Germany and Scotland in the latter part of the eighteenth century, but as such intentions go, this changed considerably during research and writing. It is a commonplace now that translation influences national literatures and after the theoretical work of the polysystem theorists such as Itamar Even-Zohar, André Lefevere, along with Susan Bassnett and many others, such influences have a solid theoretical basis on which more detailed translation theories can be based on.

The same can be said about the *Skopos* theories of the functionalist theorists such as Katharina Reiss and Hans J. Vermeer, Paul Kußmaul, Hans Hönig, Mary Snell-Hornby and Christiane Nord, to name the main representatives; theories which, although sometimes strongly dismissed and disputed, certainly widened the definition of the concept of translation and thus opened several new directions in the field of translation studies.

On the other hand, different theorists with a postmodern slant such as Lawrence Venuti, Edwin Gentzler, Anthony Pym and Douglas Robinson, for example, have supported and drawn out new and different facets of translation theory, such as ideology and the philosophy of language, and same can be said about the so-called Manipulation School and the descriptive and empirical approaches of scholars like Wolfram Wilss, Peter Newmark, Gideon Toury and James Holmes.

Other useful approaches can be recounted, such as Radegundis Stolze's hermeneutic theory, Rainer Kohlmayer's concept of empathy, or Michael Schreiber's of invariance, but in the end, I took the decision to avoid theory with a little theory, so to speak, that is I did not write on theory specifically, particularly since the quest for method in translation theory seemed repetitive, and, in fact, convinced me that many theories in translation studies end up in the dual dead end street of free versus literal, whatever each of these concepts can be made to mean.

Hence I attempted a kind of kaleidoscope of responses to the presence of theories I often accept and reject simultaneously, theories I need to be able to talk at all and which at the same time I cannot use at all for my own purposes. This kaleidoscope represents the first part of the first volume and makes no pretence of being a theory of its own.

The second part of volume I focuses on the British part of the story, for although it was Scotland and Scottish literature which gave me the initial "shove", to lean a little freely on Heidegger's term, it soon became apparent that the "inter-national" literary rivalry of the British regions (in BBC jargon) was at the core of the fragmentation of what may be seen as one of the first attempts to create a nation state. All the experts will note instantly that not a fraction of the possible material has been covered, but I answer that my focus on translation has probably been outside of most treatments of the subjects discussed anyway.

The third part on Germany was indeed a logical step to take from Britain, both in terms of material and theoretical conception. The wholesale import of all things British in the latter part of the eighteenth century was a remarkable process in itself, in particular since it can be said that at the end of that century German culture was at, if not Europe's, then at least its own zenith, and that despite the fact that it was a fragmented cluster of small states lacking a centrifugal metropolitan drive of large states such as Britain and France. The major impact was probably due to three literary figures, Shakespeare, James Macpherson and Thomas Percy. I do not, however, attempt write a history of the reception of their works, but much rather reflect on the theoretical application of such influences, in particular through translation.[1]

The second volume has a more philosophical slant with a view towards how major Enlightenment thinkers reshaped their own thought with each other's thoughts. It is mostly divided between Adam Smith and Johann Gottfried Herder, both of whose works are haunted by the spectre of Rousseau; the most important common feature of this trio is the fact that all wrote on the origin of language.

One result of the work is a simple paradox: translation without an original, not in the Lacanian sense of metalanguage, but rather in the intended transformation of the foreign into an original of one's own.[2] This transformation can take on many forms, but the most important one may be the translation of forms and genres between cultures, without original texts in between, which very often represents an attempt by the translating culture to achieve the same aesthetic standards as the culture translated from.

Another and very related result is an observation of a movement, not a religious one, although partly based in religon, a movement that systematically makes the native language, the national language the preferred mode of communication. This took several hundred years in Western Europe, but native lan-

---

[1] For a seminal work on the Ossianic reception in Germany the very recent four volumes by Wolf Gerhard Schmidt represent a comprehensive overview. It consists of a two volume dissertation on the subject and the other two volumes include almost all important German texts in this respect: >Homer des Nordens< und >Mutter der Romantik<. James Macphersons Ossian und seine Rezeption in der deutschsprachigen Literatur. 4. vols. Co-ed. of vol. 4 Howard Gaskill. Berlin, New York: Walter de Gruyter, 2004.

[2] See my "Ossian: a Case of Celtic Tribalism or a Translation without an Original?" Transfer: Übersetzen – Dolmetschen – Interkulturalität. Ed. Horst W. Drescher. Frankfurt/Main: Peter Lang, 1997. 451 – 462.

guage ideology certainly has been at the core of many nationalist movements, be they large or small, malignant or benign.[3]

I have many people to thank for their assistance and support during the conception and writing of this text. First of all, I would like to thank my supervisor, professor Horst W. Drescher, for his support through the years. His co-supervisor, professor Andreas F. Kelletat, I thank for his guidance and help on the German side. Without grants from the Johannes Gutenberg-University and the *Landesgraduiertenförderung Rheinland-Pfalz* this project would not have been possible and I thank the committees and professor Walter Bisang for their support. The two people who encouraged me initially, Julian M. D'Arcy at the University of Iceland and Ian Campbell at the University of Edinburgh I have a lot to thank, for I would not have begun this work without them. Fiona Stafford at Somerville College in Oxford I thank for giving me an early opportunity to give a paper at the James Macpherson Bicentenary Conference in Oxford and taking the time to read a draft of what is now a chapter of this dissertation. Katherine O'Connor and Jóhann R. Kristjánsson I thank for their dedicated proofreading, and I am grateful to my colleagues Susanne Hagemann, Klaus Schmidt and Pétur Knútsson for reading chapters for me and Viðar Þorsteinsson for preparing the lay-out. For her help with the index I thank Kristín Vilhjálms-dóttir. Thanks also to Marion Lerner and Torfi H. Tulinius for reading German and French passages, respectively, and Svavar Hrafn Svavarsson I thank for his help with the Greek. [4] I am particularly grateful to all the friends who have done more than can be expected to support me. Philippe Laplace, Álfrún Gunnlaugs-dóttir, Böðvar Leós, Şebnem Bahadır, Dilek Dizdar, Ahmed Farouk, Litsa Chat-ziioannou, and especially Karim Berzig and Ron Walker, you have all shown me what friendship is and I will always remember that. My children, Fjóla, Jakob and Selma, who have all had to suffer through different phases of this project I thank for their often unrequited patience. You, who has given me every-thing I needed, I can never thank enough, but this is still dedicated to you, Sabine, Sabine.

Gauti Kristmannsson

---

3   Not to be confused with native language ideology as it has been referred to in anthro-pological research on native American tribes.

4   Primary languages are English and German, originals in other languages are in footnotes. The bibliography is at the end of the second volume and abbreviations used are in their alphabetical order with their respective titles in the bibliography.

Part I
Translation

The idea of an original was defined through translation, was a translation. Originally, there was only experience and imitation and imitation of an imitation. The difference between the acts of imitation and interpretation was only one of language, not of action. When language became corporeal through writing, a corpus of fixed imitations and interpretations developed. Enlarged, the corpus became valuable as property and traditions developed, defining the propriety of action. In this state it could embody the power of a culture and define the difference between cultures. The others are barbarians and when they realise this they feel their inferiority. They now need translation in addition to interpretation. The difference of language is now physical and the lack of property, tradition and propriety is manifested in the act of translation, which is not an act of understanding anymore, but an act of achieving power, to become level with the superior culture.

Christoph Marschall[4]

1   OPENING

To begin with, the classical disclaimer: This is not a history, simply an observation of a paradox. A seeming paradox of translation locked in a dialectic of originals and translations, which, in turn, created the paradox of translation, simultaneously derivative and new. But although this is not a history, I will not hesitate to use history, or rather historical "moments", the claim to an exhaustive treatment having already been dismissed. Certainly, most of the texts I will discuss made history in both senses of the phrase, but many of them, translations, did so by being startlingly original in their time, absolutely ahistorical, disrupting traditional modes of thought by presenting something – not necessarily a text – from outside the tradition, something that disturbed and deconstructed it from within once the translation had been made, thus contributing to a new tradition while at the same time being dismissed due to their "secondary" nature.

Even if this text is not a history it has to begin somewhere in time and space. The arbitrary decision has been taken to confine the bulk of it to the latter part of the eighteenth century in Britain, more particularly Scotland, and Germany. But then again, the notoriously indefinable idea of *nation* in the modern

---

[4]   My translation.

sense probably has an earlier origin and a geographically different place of birth than these parameters offer. One of the most famous definitions of nation is Benedict Anderson's notion of the "imagined community", a coinage which reminds me of Isaiah Berlin's "imaginary *Gemeinschaft*" in the essay "Nationalism" (*Current* 337). Berlin distinguishes between *nationalism* and *national consciousness,* the latter of which he considers to be a much older phenomenon than the former. For Berlin, as for most of the latter-day scholars dealing with the subject, nationalism has its origins in the eighteenth century.[5] The differences lie in the definition of the concept and in what the nation and nationalism are seen to encompass. Like Anthony D. Smith, Berlin thinks that nations have what Smith refers to as an "ethnic" origin, but both see modern nationalism, and thus the modern interpretation of the nation, as a relatively new development. Ernest Gellner and Hugh Seton-Watson take a more radical view and see nations as inventions where none existed previously, and almost indefinable objects in themselves, merely products of nationalism. Anderson follows this line, taking a more Marxist and hence materialist angle. According to him, nationality and nationalism are "cultural artefacts of a particular kind" (4). Anderson's definition is an attempt to avoid the pitfalls of the crude racial, linguistic and religious definitions of nation, not by rejecting the nation as a myth, but taking it seriously as a construct of the imagination with real force in modern societies. This, in essence, dual perspective, which discards the traditional historical and genealogical or organic notions of nation, and at the same time accepts their powerful historical and familial relevance, is in fact common to many of the modern scholars who have dealt with this most difficult concept of identity in modernity.

Antonio Negri and Michael Hardt have criticised Anderson's conception along these lines in their *Empire*:

> It may be true, as Benedict Anderson says, that a nation should be understood as an imagined community—but here we should recognize that the claim is inverted so that *the nation becomes the only way to imagine community!* Every imagination of a community becomes overcoded as a nation, and hence our conception of community is severely impoverished. Just as in the context of the dominant countries, here too the multiplicity and singularity of the multitude are negated in the straitjacket of the identity and homogeneity of the people. Once again, the unifying power of the subaltern nation is a double-edged sword, at once progressive and reactionary (107).

Nationalism, it must be admitted, despite its savagery and ideologically fraudulent drawbacks, has been one of the major driving forces of the Western

---

[5] Eric Hobsbawm puts the moment at around 1780 in his critique of the ethnic origins of nationalism. The collection of essays he edited, *The Invention of Tradition,* examined several inventions of nation, although Hugh Trevor-Roper does not hesitate to apply a prehistorical ethnic argument in his essay in the volume "The Invention of Tradition: The Highland Tradition of Scotland".

world for the last three centuries, an indispensable element not only in the repression of the multitudes at home and abroad, but also in the democratic and intellectual achievements which have taken place.

In German discourse the rise of modern nationalism has, until recently, not been seen as a part of the age of Enlightenment and the so-called *Weimarer Klassik*. This seems to be changing now as a recent issue of *Aufklärung*, with the subtitle *Nationalismus vor dem Nationalismus*, edited by Eckhart Hellmuth and Reinhard Stauber, bears witness to. More recently, Hans-Martin Blitz argued in his *Aus Liebe zum Vaterland. Die deutsche Nation im 18. Jahrhundert* that eighteenth-century nationalism in Germany was de-nationalised after 1945 to rescue the greats of the Enlightenment from the shadow of national ideology (9-10). He seems to have touched a nerve, for the reviews by Harro Zimmermann in *Die Zeit* (April 19, 2000) and Christian Geulen in the *Süddeutsche Zeitung* (April 29, 2000) were harsh and the latter criticised the author for failing to "move" the beginnings of modern German nationalism to a date previous to the watershed events of 1789 and 1806. This raises the question of whether or not the cosmopolitan Germans of the Enlightenment were aware of the nationalist movements in other countries.[6]

Henry Kissinger, on the other hand, sets the origins of the nation state much earlier than 1789. As a diplomat, scholar and statesman who has wielded political power on the global stage, he sees Cardinal Richelieu, who during the Thirty Years War applied his doctrine of *raison d'état* and acted purely in the national interest, irrespective of religion or moral codes, as the first nationalist politician (56-77).[7]

The development was of a different nature in seventeenth-century Britain: the civil war and religious and political struggles made their mark *within* the country in a tug of war between particular political interests, but these events also contributed to the national identification processes of religious groups such as the Scottish Covenanters. The solutions after the decapitation of (attempted) absolute rule were both pragmatic and in the "national" interest: the Restoration of Charles II, the Glorious Revolution; the Union of 1707, and, finally, the placing of the Hanoverian dynasty on the throne. In all cases, however, there was a strengthening of the state as a political and national entity, a development that precedes modern nationalist politics *and* in the end defines the goal of most latter day nationalist movements.

The development of the nation state may be one of the reasons for the dilemma Scottish nationalism has faced since 1707. As long as Scottish interests

---

[6]   In his *Nation und Nationalismus in Deutschland* Otto Dann sets the starting point at 1770, around the time that *Sturm und Drang* started to make its mark in German letters. He also discusses briefly the preceding development.

[7]   Richelieu's role in the foundation of the *Académie française* also indicates a desire for cultural nationalism.

were undeniably commensurate with those of the British state, Scottish nationalism never became as radical as nationalism in many other countries, perhaps because the Scots attempted more than the English to identify with the British state. Time and again in the twentieth century the question of Scottish nationhood was raised, and even more forcefully in works published recently, Robert Crawford's *Devolving English Literature,* with its focus on linguistic cleansing and the establishment of chairs in literature for the native language being a case in point. Scottish scholars have been very industrious lately: William Ferguson's *The Identity of the Scottish Nation,* with the frank subtitle *An Historic Quest,* goes back to the misty ethnic origins of the Scots as Gaels and narrates the historiographical development of their story;[8] T.M. Devine's title for his ambitious work *The Scottish Nation 1700-2000* shows how important and self-evident Scottish nationhood has become for Scottish intellectuals, whereas Colin Kidd has examined the fragmentary political, ideological, literary and indeed theological discourses that inform and support national identity building in his *Subverting Scotland's Past* and more recently in his *British Identities before Nationalism.* Michael Fry has written in his *The Scottish Empire* on the great part Scots played in building a British Empire, and argues that this experience was among those that shaped the modern Scottish nation. Murray Pittock argues in his *Scottish Nationality* for an ethnic nationality and a nationalism that extends at least as far back as the Declaration of Arbroath in 1320, whereas Neil Davidson's *The Origins of Scottish Nationhood* claims there was no Scottish nation as late as 1707. These works and many others reflect the major current orientations on the subject of nationalism: the ethnic, the materialist and the discursive.

It may be argued that Benedict Anderson's work, along with Tom Nairn's influential *The Break-Up of Britain,* became the driving intellectual forces behind the enlightened Scottish nationalism of the last two or three decades, a movement of both intellectuals and the people of Scotland generally, neither militant nor violent, which finally achieved the goal of re-establishing a parliament in Edinburgh. At the same time, it must be kept in mind that just across the Irish Sea, and a few thousand kilometres south-east of Scotland, nationalism has continued to cause the shedding of blood through the murderous rage and madness that only nationalism seems to be capable of producing. It is in the light of this dialectic of achievement and insanity that the subject of nationalism needs to be discussed. My primary concern, however, is not with nationalism as such, but with one of its major pillars, national literature, and its ideological function. I will attempt in what follows to show that the literature of "modernity" (i.e., of

---

[8]   To support his ethnic version of history, Ferguson claims that Adrian Hastings has "exploded" Hobsbawm's theory that "nationhood and nationalism cannot pre-date 1780" (301). Hastings' *The Construction of Nationhood* shows well the problem of definition when he takes religion into the equation and moves the time frame back to the Middle Ages.

roughly the last three hundred years) has deeper roots in the act of translation than the ideology of originality is ready to admit.[9]

But first it is necessary to go briefly beyond the time frame and consider other beginnings and concepts. My decision to look briefly at fragments of the history of translation, for example in ancient Rome, during the Renaissance, or early biblical translation, is perhaps as unoriginal and arbitrary as any other, but I base this choice on the simple fact of the growing use of native language, an increase which had both political and ideological ramifications and which was given additional impetus by the onset of "print capitalism" to once again use Anderson's terminology. The use of native language may have been strongly influenced by the laws of the market and the fact that it was possible to "reproduce" (Benjamin) literary works of art, but translation also influenced the native languages greatly and, arguably, gave them the form they took, which they needed to become literary, comparable to the high cultures that written culture propagates and perpetuates through the strength of canonisation and thus survival.[10] The moment native languages became the ideological carriers in works of, for example, Dante, Luther and Descartes (names too well known to be dropped in both senses of the word), they slowly but surely started displacing the dead languages they were referring to. It is in that combination of referral and displacement that translation plays a decisive role in the construction of national literature, one of the main pillars of any culture aspiring to become one of the collective national subjects of the world – with a name and a family, with a history and genealogy, with its own flag and a poetic tradition strong enough to compete in the Olympic arena of world literature.

---

[9] "Modernity" is also one of the indefinables; in Western literature the candidates for its first author might range from Dante to Joyce. It will be exciting to see who will get the honour of being called the "last". Fiona Stafford provides an interesting literary survey on these sorts of myths in her *The Last of the Race*.

[10] Which is of course also Benjamin's thesis in "Die Aufgabe des Übersetzers".

2 KEY CONCEPTS

2.1 Translation and Definition

It is perhaps appropriate to begin by discussing a few terms. At least since Kant, academics have considered it their duty to define the terms of their discourse with as much precision as possible.[11] Self-evident as it may seem, this has wider implications in academic discourse. Firstly, it has served and still serves to give the impression that the discourse offered is objective, and scientific with a capital "S". In the humanities, a paper must be *wissenschaftlich*; otherwise it has no justification.

Although not exclusively German, this primarily methodological approach seems to me to be more important in German academic discourse than elsewhere, perhaps due to a lingering positivist *Angst* that one cannot be "scientific" in the humanities.[12] The second reason for this approach to terminological definition is one which is closer to the subject of many disciplines in the humanities and certainly that of this book, namely the dread and destruction of ambiguity. Despite the considerable onslaught of post-structuralist and deconstructivist discourses, the demand for a stylistically clear and unambiguous message based on empirical detail retains its hold on the mainstream, and that of course not only in Germany.[13]

It is not my intention to embark on a deconstruction of German and/or British academic discourse, but merely to point out the first problem this or any

---

[11]   See Kant's *Kritik der reinen Vernunft* "Methodenlehre 1. Hauptstück. 1. Abschnitt" (744-754).

[12]   This kind of *Angst* may well be behind the tendency in the humanities to apply mathematical equations and other paraphernalia from the natural sciences, as Alan Sokal has so memorably shown with his famous hoax in *Social Text* and in the book *Intellectual Impostures.* On the other hand, his colleagues in the natural sciences seem to be unafraid to use terms from the humanities and redefine them for their own purposes. Modern genetics uses a host of terms that could derive from modern translation studies or linguistics (or medieval theology for that matter). The terms translation and transcription are, for example, used in genetics without a blush and it would be easy to prove that this metaphorical usage was initially not entered in any comprehensive dictionary. The natural sciences can, it seems, use language freely and give extant terms a new meaning, whereas mathematical equations are unambiguous (are they for everybody?) and not to be used by scholars in the humanities. The question of what Sokal would say to a poet who had used $E=mc^2$ as a title for a poem remains unanswered. The literary critic would simply call it a cliché. Cf. "Translation as genetic metaphor" below. See also Isaiah Berlin "The Divorce between the Sciences and the Humanities" in *Against the Current* for an example of an attempt to consider the causes of this dialectic of the "body" and "soul" of knowledge (80-110).

[13]   See also Deleuze and Guattari's discussion of the creative term or concept in their *Q'est-ce que la philosophie?* (*Was ist Philosophie?* in the German translation).

work on translation and nation has to deal with before these subjects themselves can be discussed. On the one hand, there is the necessity of defining the concepts clearly; on the other, both defy definition. The problem of defining "nation" and "nationalism" has already been touched upon in the opening and it is one that is plainly detectable in the centuries-old debate on what makes a translation, and indeed in the absolute certainties some people hold with regard to these concepts. The difficulty of defining the concept of translation has to do with its wide-ranging meaning and implications; apart from such definitions as those applied to the nomination of Catholic bishops, the act of translation has not only moved political and theological, literary and linguistic discourses, but is also an ethical concept in itself, making the translator in her no-man's land a moral agent through the potentialities of faithfulness and betrayal. While keeping this breadth in mind it is necessary to narrow down the fields with which I will be working to those that have direct implications for the topic.

Finally, it should not be forgotten that Kant's demand for a precise definition was not based on a purely empirical understanding of reality, but on his Copernican revolution that reality is a construct of the observer; that for exactly that reason, definitions must be painstakingly formulated, not because they represent external facts reflected in the senses, but because the facts themselves are defined by the observer. I will begin by discussing a few aesthetic and social concepts prevalent in the eighteenth century which are relevant to the translational conceptions I will be developing.

2.2 Translation as a Genre

The "genre" of translation is the one that has provided more prefaces and defences of method and indeed (foreign) original text than probably any other genre or form. This alone should have made discourse on translation play a central role in literary criticism, for a major part of the "originals" in Western Europe written prior to printing have been translated, rewritten and discussed in a context of translation or of a non-native language. Indeed, a large number of the experts who dealt with texts from antiquity, whether Hebrew, Greek or even Latin, have been translators of the selfsame texts, particularly when the texts have been "new".

This has not resulted in much discussion on translation in literary critical discourse, despite, for example, the immense attention given to the concept of imitation. Not only have translators themselves been invisible (Venuti) for a long time, but also the discourse on the genre as such.[14]

---

[14] For Andreas Huyssen in *Die frühromantische Konzeption von Übersetzung und Aneignung* translation as a genre is one of his points of departure; as *the* genre of the German *Frühromantiker*.

Of course translation is not a "genre" in the narrow definition of that concept, but rather, like "original", a hyperterm that encompasses all genres. There is, however, a fundamental discursive difference between the concepts of "translation" and "original". Perhaps since Edward Young's *Conjectures on Original Composition* in 1759 the concept of an "original" has been taken for granted and therefore not been much discussed. The concept of translation, both as an act and as a term defining an action precisely, has, on the other hand, been under constant scrutiny, often resulting in polemics. From Luther (or even St. Jerome), onward such polemics have often been in the form of defences – defences whose sole purpose has been to state that the text in question is a translation and nothing else. Original works often need a diametrically opposite mode of verification. In order to discard the mimetic stamp, authors have reverted to strategies of removal, such as, for example, calling an original text a translation:[15] Walpole's *Castle of Otranto* was published as a translation and the author "translated" his own mansion not only into a castle, but to a town he randomly picked from a map of Italy.[16] To write what became the first example of the genre of the "Gothic" novel, Walpole, in the middle of the Ossianic controversies, reverted to forgery in order to be original. That this novel, by any standard, is not considered to be a forgery shows at once a fundamental moral difference, for both a translation that pretends to be one but is not and a translation that pretends not to be one and is, are, by most standards, morally reprehensible. They are simply "pseudotranslations" and/or thefts.[17]

It would therefore be worthwhile, particularly in light of the endless debate on the definition of what translation encompasses – a debate that constitutes almost half of the theory of translation – to talk of "genres" of translation, to simply see that translation produces genres, in imitation and of its own; translation produces forms through imitation and in a struggle with the target language. Instead of fighting the hopeless battle for an all-encompassing definition of translation, scholars could enrich the debate by focusing on the productive aspects of translation, on its capabilities and how creative solutions emerge in practice, and theorising on their implications and ideological positions: in short, by arguing about the genres of translation instead of translation itself.[18]

---

15 See also Bassnett's and Lefevere's *Constructing Cultures* esp. chapters 2 and 3.

16 See Toury's chapter on pseudotranslations in his *Descriptive Translation Studies and Beyond* and the discussion below.

17 There are of course examples aplenty, but the most famous one is probably *Don Quixote*. See Melberg on the role of the translator in the narrative structure of *Don Quixote* (58 & 74-75).

18 This does not apply to the original but the translation. The idea is not original, literary critics rarely bother about the deeply philosophical question of "what is literature", but rather come to their conclusions through the genres and a criticism of the texts themselves.

2.3   Translation of Form

Definitions of translation, by layman and specialist alike, most often revolve around the content of the text in question. By implication it is taken for granted that everything that is said or written can be translated. The most direct expression of this view is to be found in Roman Jakobson's essay "On the Linguistic Aspects of Translation", which states that "No lack of grammatical device in the language translated into makes impossible a literal translation of the entire conceptual information contained in the original" (235). Leaving the question of ambiguity aside, which of course has implications for what is meant by "conceptual information", I only want to consider the way in which form, as poetic form, a sonnet for example, is part and parcel of a text's "conceptual information". The question needs to be examined, for if grammar cannot stop "literal translation", form certainly can.

Forms have meanings. They often indicate fixed meanings: An epic contains certain structures which form the content according to particular rules, and the same applies to the lyric, drama, etc. The form itself produces expectations that are reflected in the content. Certain forms demand content of certain kinds and exclude others. Changes in these demands are possible, and are indeed most often epochal, because conventions in literary forms reflect the symbolic and social order of their time.

Different forms have different values. A limerick, for example, is not considered to be as serious as an ode. A ballad was trivial literature until Thomas Percy redefined the formal heritage of balladry. Even the old opposition of poetry and prose was a question of formality, poetry being bound by forms conceptualised into the social hierarchies.

Forms can be translated. First, with the foreign content, for example when an epic such as the *Iliad* is translated. It is at that point where we come to a dividing line between genre and form; the former is a more general concept taking into account the narrative structure and the characters, whereas the latter includes the verse form. The form of the *Iliad* can then be translated if the metre and the content are simultaneously translated, an almost impossible task. Johann Heinrich Voss' rigourously formal translations of Homer are an example of translations where content and form are put higher in the translational hierarchy than the native language.

Jakobson, despite his bold thesis of translatability in the essay quoted above, admits at the end that "poetry by definition is untranslatable" (238). Jakobson's parameter for this conclusion is paronomasia, a problem of phonemic similarity, but it is a common conclusion from the disingenuous remark by Robert Frost that "poetry is what gets lost in translation".[19]

The question of translatability has been discussed often enough to be skipped here.[20] What most often gets lost in translation of texts is the form, and if not, then the content often suffers.[21] But as already noted, form has meaning that is inseparable from expression.

Forms alone can be translated. The Renaissance solution to the translation of the hexameter form was the invention of blank verse. The Italian dramatist and philologist Gian Giorgio Trissino (1478-1550), a follower of Dante and imitator of Greek drama, wrote his *Sofonisba* (1514-15) in blank verse in an attempt to compensate for the lack of hexameter, perhaps one of the most important steps in the development of what I metaphorically call translation without an original, although the form itself is the "original".[22] *Sofonisba* has also been celebrated as a milestone in the development of classical drama, as being the first modern play to introduce the three unities, and was later imitated, in blank verse, by the Scottish dramatist and poet James Thomson, whose play with the same title was translated into German under the aegis of Gotthold Ephraim Lessing.[23]

Blank verse was introduced into England in the sixteenth century through the direct translation by Henry Howard, Earl of Surrey, of fragments of the *Ae-*

---

[19] Jakobson's example of paronomasia fits well with his idea of "equivalence in difference", another way of proclaiming translatability. It is also one of the examples he takes in his essay "Linguistics and poetics", notably linked with the concept of equivalence in a theory of poetics. For a critique of Frost's position, see Susan Bassnett in *Constructing Cultures* (57).

[20] Derrida's dictum in "Des Tours de Babel" that translation is both impossible and necessary seems to be the best approach to the dilemma (170).

[21] The most polemical condemnation of translating form must surely be found in Nabokov's essays and paratexts with his translation of Pushkin's *Eugene Onegin*. See my *Damit wir wissen, was sie geschrieben haben* and Nabokov's own essay "Onegin in English".

[22] Although Trissino's play was written in 1514-15, it was not produced until 1554 (in French), whereas his national epic with the interesting title *La Italia Liberata da Gotthi* was written from 1526 onwards and published 1547-48. It is also often named as the work that introduced blank verse into epic poetry. In any case Trissino introduced the form for both genres.

[23] Lessing names Trissino in his "Vorrede" to the translations of James Thomson's tragedies: "Der einzige Trissino, dessen >>Sophonisbe<<, als in Italien, nach langen barbarischen Jahrhunderten, die Wissenschaften wieder aufgingen, das erste Trauerspiel war, ist mit dem Engländer [*sic*] in diesem Punkte, welchen er den Griechen, den einzigen Mustern damals, abgelernt hatte, zu vergleichen" [After long barbaric centuries, when the sciences rose again, the singular Trissino, whose "Sophonisbe" is comparable to the Englishman's work, found his models in the Greeks, the only ones available at the time] (*Werke IV* 145, my translation).

neid.[24] It is not known whether Surrey invented blank verse for himself, but he was well read in the Italian Renaissance poets and is believed to have invented the English sonnet form, which is distinguished from the Italian by the rhyme scheme. The significance of this development lies in the fact that the introduction of blank verse was a) translational in its conception, and b) an attempt to achieve the sophistication of form of the ancient sources being imitated or translated. This is the method that leads to translation without an original: the systematic and ideological application of ancient forms in writing "original" content.

The method is of course more complex than that; the imitations of Pindaric odes as practised by Ronsard in sixteenth-century France and Cowley in seventeenth-century England exemplify another aspect, whereby the *spirit* of the original is translated, but neither content nor form are directly translated, because poets considered the Alexandrine and heroic couplet to be *equivalent* to the ancient hexameter. Conversely, German poets of the eighteenth century concentrated much more on translating the form, achieving a mastery, as displayed by Hölderlin. In all these cases, however, there was an attempt to increase the prestige of the poetry through the form adopted, and in many cases this was explicitly expressed as a national project, as an attempt to raise the native language and its modern literary tradition to Parnassian heights.

2.4 Translation as Forgery

One of the ways to introduce a translation without an original could be to produce a kind of forgery: what Gideon Toury has called "pseudotranslation" in his *Descriptive Translation Studies and Beyond*. Toury defines the concept thus:

> It is texts which have been presented as translations with no corresponding source texts in other languages ever having existed – hence no factual 'transfer operations' and translation relationships – that go under the name of pseudotranslations, or fictitious translations (41).

Pseudotranslation, however, is not the same as what I have referred to above as translation without an original, which is usually an "original" text that translates/imitates a major element of a foreign poetic tradition without necessarily translating or even pretending to translate a single identifiable text. The boundaries are fuzzy in many cases, but the difference from Toury's conception of pseudotranslation is distinct in the "method": pseudotranslation or fictitious translation creates a myth of an original content (and sometimes form), whereas

---

[24]   Dryden, for one, thought Shakespeare had invented blank verse; see his essay "Rhyme and Blank Verse" in *Essays* (186).

translation without an original creates a myth of being original by leaving content out and translating form.

Enlightening as it is, Toury's text presents some problems of contradiction which need to be tackled. In fact, the essay shows well how fixed the category of an *original* national literature – as opposed to a *secondary* literature in translation – is, both empirically and theoretically, in the mind of a renowned translation scholar.

Toury's premise with regard to the existence and function of pseudotranslations is that "the most significant aspect of the production and distribution of texts as if they were translations is the fact that this constitutes a convenient way of introducing novelties into a culture" (41). The question is whether this is a fact at all. Citing Even-Zohar, Toury assumes that translations have "normally been regarded as a *secondary* mode of text-generation" and "that deviations occurring in texts which are culturally acknowledged as translations often meet with much greater tolerance – which explains why so many innovations throughout the ages have disguised their own texts as translations" (41).[25] The first problem here is the time frame: have translations always been considered a "secondary mode of text-generation"? The history of Bible translation seems to indicate otherwise; moreover, it is doubtful that in times when most texts were either written or "published" in a foreign language, translation was seen as secondary in a pejorative sense. Translation is only secondary when there is a strong subjective identity working in a native language with a simultaneous awareness of foreign languages; the Romans provide the first example of this in the West, and the nations of the modern age have followed suit.

The second problem is the assertion that translations meet with "much greater tolerance" and are therefore ideal for the introduction of "novelties" into a culture. Without denying the *ability* of translation to introduce novelty into a literary culture, this is not necessarily due to greater "tolerance" on the part of the receiving culture; in ages when translation has been considered a "secondary mode of text-generation", it has also been consigned to the "servile path" of "fluency", as Venuti has so memorably demonstrated. At such times translation has, as Toury also notes, been able to offer a link to originals that are difficult to access, originals that have prestige through canonisation, while the translators have been consigned to "invisibility". Nevertheless, translators have been truly innovative with their different approaches and methods and have introduced novelties into the target culture. In fact, pseudotranslations are usually secondary to the translations they imitate. Toury himself puts it thus:

---

[25] In the revised version of his essay, Even-Zohar's analysis distinguishes between the types of polysystems that translations function in and shows, in effect, that the status of translation can be used to define the type ("Position" 192-197).

What pseudotranslators often do, towards the attainment of this last goal, is incorporate in their texts features which have come to be associated, in the (target) culture in question, with translation – more often than not with the translation of texts of a specific type and/or from a particular source language and textual tradition. By enhancing their resemblance to genuine translations they simply make it easier for their texts to pass as such (45).

I fully agree with this; so-called pseudotranslations have been made possible by the "originality" of the translations already available, so the novelties can hardly be ascribed to the texts that imitated them "to pass as such".

The examples Toury uses are also very informative and affirm my position. The first is the most famous one, James Macpherson's *Poems of Ossian*. This mixture of translation, adaptation and plain fiction was carefully reworked into an epic form, probably under the masterful guidance of Hugh Blair, whose theoretical knowledge must have been indispensable when the young Macpherson was constructing the poems.[26] Although his use of a kind of lyrical prose was revolutionary for the epic form, it was, in fact, picked up from biblical translations, the Song of Solomon and the Psalms, and some of the lyrical spirit from Thomas Gray's translations/adaptations of Welsh material into a strict Pindaric ode form. Indeed, Macpherson himself revealed his use of pre-texts, some original (Milton) and some translated (Homer), at several points in his footnotes in the editions he saw through the press, and after his death, in 1805, Malcolm Laing published a hostile edition of *Ossian* which is, in effect, a massive indictment of plagiarism, yet another bizarre turn in the Ossianic controversies.

Macpherson's *Ossian* did, nevertheless, influence writing and translation massively in the decades following its publication. The influence was wide ranging and went well beyond the aspect of translation, firstly, in the method of collecting balladry and translating it or editing it into an epic form; the Finnish *Kalevala* is a case in point;[27] secondly, in the translation of epic poetry in Britain, where the traditional forms gave in to more experimentation towards blank verse and even hexameter; and thirdly, in the spirit and style of writing in an age of sentimentality, particularly in Germany. Simultaneously, it must be remembered that the greatest forgery perpetrated in connection with the *Poems of Ossian* was committed in the paratexts that functioned as verification. The pseudotranslation of *The Poems of Ossian* (insofar as it fits that definition, for there were more sources than Toury claims) did, however, lean on the textual strategies of existing translations to achieve its objective.[28]

---

[26] After his collecting trips into the Scottish Highlands, Macpherson reworked his materials in Blair's house. See also Gaskill, "'Ossian' at Home and Abroad" (5-26).

[27] For a discussion on *Ossian* and *Kalevala*, see Lefevere in *Constructing Cultures* (77-89).

[28] The authoritative work on Macpherson's sources is Derick Thomson's *The Gaelic Sources of Macpherson's 'Ossian'*.

Two other examples in Toury's essay shed further light on my argument. One relates to the *Book of Mormon*, which is also an example of a pseudotranslation that refers to previous translations, as Toury admits in a footnote (45). The last example Toury offers is clearer; in the first place there is no question of a source text, secondly, he claims that the pseudotranslators of *Papa Hamlet*, Arno Holz and Johannes Schlaf "were quite successful in attaining their goal, and *Papa Hamlet* indeed introduced 'Scandinavian-like' novelties into the German system" (52). The reason for Toury's claim that Arno Holz and Johannes Schlaf had introduced the 'Scandinavian-like' novelties is simple. They are native speakers of German and their pseudotranslation turned out to be an original. But as Toury himself asserts, they did not take the features that comprise the so-called novelties

> *directly* from Norwegian, or from any other Scandinavian literary works, to which the two had no access anyway. Rather, they were linguistic, textual and literary features pertinent to German *translations* of impressionistic and naturalistic texts of Scandinavian origin (51, emphasis in text).

Why the translations, rather than the imitative pseudotranslations, are not given credit for the introduction of these novelties into German literature is difficult to understand. But this truly insightful essay (or Chapter) shows very clearly how translations are constantly marginalised, even by a sympathetic commentator such as Toury. What it shows best, however, is that in order to be original one must be national, and vice versa.[29]

---

[29]   The rise of the novel in eighteenth-century France is also enlightening in this context. Jürgen von Stackelberg has noted that in France the novel as a form was considered to be English and as the market expanded rapidly a large number of pseudotranslations were produced with the extant *translations* as a model (17).

2.5 Translation as a Figure

SOME TRANSTEXTUAL RELATIONS

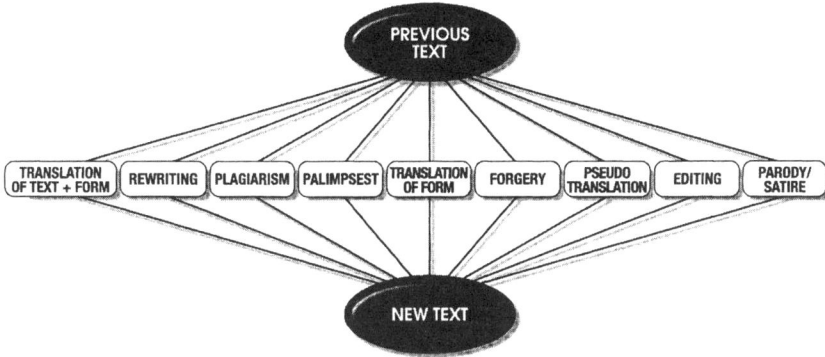

This is a simplified abstraction of the transtextual relations discussed above and below.[30] The first box on the left indicates what most people would consider to be "translation proper", the repetition of a text in the same form in another language. I am naturally alluding here to Roman Jakobson's definition of translation in "On the Linguistic Aspects of Translation" so memorably criticised by Jacques Derrida in "Des Tours de Babel": "Jakobson does not translate; he repeats the same term: 'interlingual translation or translation proper'" (173). It is a necessary illusion, or at any rate, an illusion accepted, if grudgingly at times.

Rewriting, plagiarism and palimpsest overlap to an extent, but these ideas of transtextuality have flanks not covered by each of them.

Translation of form is ambiguous and can be understood to connote the Benjaminian idea of form (or "mode" in Harry Zohn's translation), and/or the one discussed above: the concrete form or genre extant in a foreign language and/or culture. In fact, the process can also be intralingual, as the example of the *Lyrical Ballads* shows; it can even be both, as in the example of *Der Erlkönig*: Herder translated, Goethe rewrote, the form was a ballad. The forms in the concrete and Benjaminian senses probably overlap briefly in Hölderlin's poetry.

Pseudotranslation has been discussed above, and it gets its own category despite the fact that it could be defined as forgery. For some, translation is always a forgery, but the reason why forgery is included here is the fact that there is always a middleman, a forger, who makes an original, someone like Thomas

---

[30]   See also Gérard Genette's *Palimpsests* where he defines five types of transtextuality (1-30).

Chatterton who translates something out of nothing. But then again, many of his texts resemble what Macpherson and Percy had already published; there was simply no pretence of translation. It was one form of translation without an original text.

Editing includes not only scholarly editing of older texts, but also the collation of manuscripts and other interventions into previous texts, be they minor corrections of typos or active selection of text material and all kinds of euphemising.

Parody and satire are put into the same box, although the concepts are distinct in degree as Genette has shown very well in *Palimpsests* (19-30).

2.6   Translation and Native Language

The two major events that marked the beginning of the modern age, the Renaissance and the Reformation, were set in motion and in effect defined through translation. The first printing presses of Europe almost invariably printed translations into the native languages before anything else.[31] Native textuality beyond the manuscript was thus marked by translation before it ever produced original works "of its own" and even then such works had to compete in the marketplace with translations of canonised texts of great authority (the Bible, Homer, Virgil, etc.).

The Renaissance is rarely spoken of in a translational context, although in itself it was a massive translational movement.[32] The Bible translations as individual acts (Wycliffe, Luther etc.) may have been more visible than the translations of the Renaissance, but in its ideology and in many manifestations, the Renaissance was about translation. Rather than being a rebirth, it was a *re-newal* of the ancient heritage in the *native* language. This is the major point, for the renewal consisted not only in the discovery of the ancient heritage, as the standard interpretation goes, but in a re-writing in a new language. The impulses of the Renaissance and their effects on national literatures have often been mentioned, but it is the translational aspect which I want to emphasise, for it represents the method of what I refer to as a translation without an original text. The self-

---

[31]   Bibles, classics and in the case of Caxton, Thomas Malory's "pseudotranslation". Despite the use of Latin in the Middle Ages translation was a major occupation among the scribes of any "Western-European" area and it may even be argued that some of the ancient texts firmly canonised survived through translation no less than rewriting; Aristotle's *Poetics* is a case in point. Hence Louis G. Kelly's opening dictum in *The True Interpreter*: "Western Europe owes its civilization to translators".

[32]   With the exception of histories, Matthiessen's *Translation: An Elizabethan Art,* Cheyfitz's *The Poetics of Imperialism* and some parts of Lefevere's work. Cheyfitz's work concentrates on the metaphor of translation in a context of colonial politics and the power of eloquence, rather than on the act of textual translation.

fashioning, to quote Stephen Greenblatt's title, began and continued through adopting a "foreign" or ancient model, and that not only in literature.

The focus on native language for Renaissance literature, most obviously expressed in Dante's (Latin) treatise *De vulgari eloquentia*, had wide implications for the usage of the native languages.[33] Manuscript culture had naturally provided many European vernaculars with a Latin character system and of course the Renaissance did not initiate writing in the vernacular. What made the Renaissance different from the previous periods and indeed, as schoolchildren are taught, presents a decisive cut in European history, was among other things the change in attitude towards the ancient heritage and its *systematic* application as an aesthetic model, through theoretical, translational or both kinds of approaches.

The beginning of native language ideology can, then, probably be ascribed to two cultural events. The first would be Dante's work and especially the tract *De vulgari eloquentia*, the first manifesto, so to speak, of native language ideology. In this text Dante Alighieri makes his claim for writing poetry in the native language, although this does not mean leaving the classical paradigms; no, it is exactly a way of retaining them and at the same time be able to use the vernacular. It is a major step in re-evaluating the native language and, in effect, sets it up as an equal, or at least as a potential equal, of the classical languages. This in itself became a paradigm in Europe as a whole, and one of the major effects of the Renaissance was that writing in the vernacular exploded.

The other event is of course the Reformation with its evangelical focus on the word of god. Perhaps the analogous manifesto to the one of Dante can be seen in Luther's *Sendbrief vom Dolmetschen*, an essay in the form of a letter that justifies Luther's translation and his use of German. The next centuries are the success story of the native languages and there are many milestones to be seen for that movement. I will mention only a few:

1. Translations. The market for books in the vernacular grew steadily in print capitalism as Benedict Anderson has pointed out and the demand shows simultaneously the increasing importance of native languages. Another aspect of that development is the broadening base of texts being translated, either from the Latin or even other languages. Key literary texts such as Homer and Virgil etc. were also translated again and again, in addition to the translation of form which became one of major cultural feats of every new and

---

[33] Although Dante is pre-Renaissance according to many histories, he certainly inspired that historical construct and the fact that he, Petrarch, even Chaucer, do not strictly count as Renaissance poets has perhaps more to do with epochal interpretation than anything else. Whatever the label of their epoch, they certainly provided renewal in their native language on such a scale that they have themselves become classics.

native language. A language that could not master the poets and forms of antiquity remained parochial.

2.   Increasing number of tracts in Dante's vein defending or simply instructing in the use of native language to write poetry. These could take the form of a defence of poetry of which there were numerous, or instructions for poets, such as the one by the German Martin Opitz who wrote *Buch von der Deutschen Poeterey*, a kind of handbook for young poets in 1627, advising them amongst other things to translate poetry in order to learn to write it. Opitz also wrote a defence for the writing of poetry in the native language, in Latin like Dante. Another famous defender of the native language amongst others was, curiously, the German philopsopher Leibniz, curiously because he himself wrote mostly in French. In his *Unvorgreifliche Gedanken, betreffend die Ausübung und Verbesserung der deutschen Sprache*, Leibniz was actually one of the first to note that Icelandic had retained much of the ancient German language.

3.   The seventeenth century was eventful for the native language movement: the *Académie française* was established by Cardinal Richelieu, and in the German speaking area of Europe some secret language societes were established to further the cause of the German language. At the end of the seventeenth century some members of the French élite were so confident about the cultural progress of their country and language that one of them, Charles Perrault, proclaimed they had overtaken the Ancients, and so one of the greatest cultural controversies of modern time was born, that between the Ancients and the Moderns.

It would be possible to list many other events in this vein such as the beginning of writing native language grammars and dictionaries, but I will only mention one more, and that is the establishment of chairs in the native language and literature at the universities, a relatively recent phenomenon. It was only in the nineteenth century that professors of languages such as English and German started teaching at universities, thus marking the true victory of the Moderns and native language ideology.

2.7   Translation as "Imitation"

The two paradigms of a pagan Roman and a Christian *translatio,* translated later into either a universal civil or moral notion of society that yet retains its particularity or difference through concepts of time and place on the one hand and a claim to an absolute truth on the other, were perhaps most memorably expressed in Erich Auerbach's *Mimesis, Dargestellte Wirklichkeit in der abendländischen Literatur*.[34] The first Chapter of that work compares the narrative approaches of Homer and the Old Testament authors and discovers a dialectic on at least three levels. The first consists of the temporal and psychological levels of narration. Homer simply describes events as they happen, and even when he suddenly moves back in time the narration continues on that level of presence, whereas "es den jüdischen Schriftstellern gelingt, die gleichzeitig übereinander gelagerten Schichten des Bewußtseins und den Konflikt derselben zum Ausdruck zu bringen", an almost polyphonic approach in the Bakhtinian sense (15).[35]

The second level deals with the difference in claims to truth. Auerbach points out that the old (Platonic) accusation that Homer is a liar is irrelevant for its worth as an imitation, whereas the Biblical text does not pretend to be a successful imitation (i.e., a forgery of reality) but makes a claim to truth itself, even in its notions of the beginning and end of history. One consequence of this is a dire need for an exegesis if the reader is to accept the text as a living truth for him or herself, which becomes more difficult the farther away the reader is from the original in space and time:

> Dies wird immer schwerer, je weiter unsere Lebenswelt sich von der der biblischen Schriften entfernt, und wenn diese trotzdem ihren Herrschaftsanspruch aufrecht erhält, so ist es unabweislich, daß sie selbst sich, durch ausdeutende Umformung, anpassen muß; das ist lange vergleichsweise leicht gewesen; noch im europäischen Mittelalter war es möglich, das biblische Geschehen als alltägliche Vorgänge der damaligen Gegenwart darzustellen, wozu die Methode des Deutens die Grundlage lieferte (18).[36]

This method of interpretative transformation was to an extent invented by the New Testament authors. The most graphic instance of this (which Auerbach does not mention) can be seen in the structural parallels of the two biblical stories of multilingual miracles. The first narrative, the negative one of the tower of Babel, is a constant in translational discourse. The latter, the positive New Testament narrative of the miracle when the disciples "were all filled with the Holy

---

[34] Not the concept of *translatio imperii et studii,* and at the same time a deliberate echo.

[35] "...whereas the Jewish writers are able to express the simultaneous existence of various layers of consciousness and the conflict between them" (Trask 13).

[36] "This becomes increasingly difficult the further our historical environment is removed from that of the Biblical books; and if these nevertheless maintain their claim to absolute authority, it is inevitable that they themselves be adapted through interpretative transformation. This was for a long time comparatively easy; as late as the European Middle Ages it was possible to represent Biblical events as ordinary phenomena of contemporary life, the methods of interpretation themselves forming the basis for such a treatment" (Trask 15).

Ghost, and began to speak with other tongues, as the Spirit gave them utterance", is remarkably rare in that context (Acts 2,4). Both appear in their respective books right after the Divinity's own work on earth, and the latter is a conscious inversion of the former. On the political level, and in order to take the Old Testament beyond the Jewish tradition, this translation by inversion defines the invention of difference between Jews and Christians, for the evangelical assignment of Christianity, as opposed to the retentive one of Judaism, demanded a cultural translation for different cultural areas:

> Aber fast immer wirkt dies auf den Rahmen zurück, der der Erweiterung und Modifizierung bedarf; die eindrucksvollste Deutungsarbeit dieser Art geschah in den ersten Jahrhunderten des Christentums, infolge der Heidenmission, durch Paulus und die Kirchenväter; sie deuteten die gesamte jüdische Überlieferung um in eine Reihe von vorbeugenden Figuren des Erscheinens Christi, und wiesen dem Römischen Reich seinen Platz an innerhalb des göttlichen Heilsplanes (19).[38]

So the *translatio* was partly initiated through a re-interpretation (very much through translation) of the Jewish tradition and given an evangelical mission with a claim to absolute truth.[39] In its beginnings, Christianity seems to have been able to claim universality through multilingualism, an idea the Reformers could easily make use of through translation.

The third level Auerbach refers to is the stylistic relation of the sublime and class, i.e. the fact that the sublime in Homer (and most of the Ancients) is connected with the ruling class, whereas in the Bible it often represented through much more humble characters and settings. This stylistic difference, which Auerbach sees as crucial through the "konstitutive Wirkung" [determining influence] of both classes of literature "auf die europäische Wirklichkeitsdarstellung" [upon the representation of reality in European literature], enables him to represent the main strands of mimetic operation in western thought, one might think, had he not – as most do – left out the fourth, translation (27/[23]).

Yet in a way he does not, for what is *mimesis* but a certain kind of translation? One textual reality is translated into another, the same *logos* in Platonic terms is repeated in a different *lexis,* a thoroughly mimetic operation. Antoine

---

[37] "But this process nearly always also reacts upon the frame, which requires enlarging and modifying. The most striking piece of of interpretation of this sort occurred in the first century of the Christian era, in consequence of of Paul's mission to the Gentiles: Paul and the Church Fathers reinterpreted the entire Jewish tradition as a succession of figures prognosticating the appearance of Christ, and assigned the Roman Empire its proper place in the divine plan of salvation" (Trask 16).

[38] The *Koran* has also made use of similar strategies in relation to its pre-texts or genotexts in Kristeva's term. Apparently, the Koran is seen in Islam as the completion of the biblical heritage.

Berman speaks of "translational mimesis" in his *Experiencing the Foreign,* but references to *mimesis* are rare in a translational context (8).[39] This may be due to the fact that the term was conceived in a culture that did not dream of translating from the barbarian other, but was indeed at the junction of orality and writing, as some commentators since Havelock have underlined.[40] And yet one commentator, Arne Melberg, has seen Plato's rejection of the poets, which surely must be paradigmatic for the rejection of translation through the centuries, as a "loss of self; or rather: the fear of/longing for a loss of self" (20). Such a loss is reminiscent of a famous line in Dante's *Inferno* when Virgil describes the sense of being suspended in Limbo – not a description of the translator's feelings, but one that catches them perfectly, if pessimistically.[41] The same applies to Melberg's next sentence, a sentence that is almost an intralingual translation (or, as Melberg himself would put it, a repetition) of the famous and constantly quoted verses from *An Essay on Translated Verse* (1685) by Wentworth Dillon, the Earl of Roscommon; for comparison they are presented here side by side in columns. On the left we have Roscommon, on the right Melberg's interpretation of Plato:

- chuse an *Author* as you chuse a *Friend.*	We remember that Socrates imagined Homer
United by this *Sympathetick Bond,*	as the arch-imitator at the very moment he
You grow *Familiar, Intimate and Fond*;	was imitating the words of someone else,
Your *thoughts* [*sic*], your *Words,*	talking like someone else, becoming another.
your *Stiles,* your *Souls* agree,	The imitator is from that moment doomed to
No Longer his *Interpreter,* but *He* (7).	be someone else or something other than his self (20).

Melberg's sentences are of course neither on translation nor a translation, not repetition, it is not even remotely likely that he had Roscommon's lines in mind when writing his own. The coincidental fact that Roscommon also seems to lean a little towards Platonic moralism in his semi-rejection of Homer in preference to Virgil and Horace in the *Essay on Translated Verse,* the fruit of his translation of Horace's *Ars Poetica* (which incidentally bears the title *Horace's Art of Poetry made English*), is also no proof of any causal link between the texts. And still they are linked, naturally, in the common result of *mimesis* and *translation,* and in the difference of premise, and/or vice versa. Translation, as

---

39   Jürgen von Stackelberg discusses imitation as translation briefly in his introduction to *Englische Literatur des 17. und 18. Jahrhunderts in französischer Übersetzung und deutscher Weiterübersetzung* (11).

40   As quoted by Melberg from his *Preface to Plato.* Melberg rejects his argument on the grounds of its being too dialectical and, citing Gadamer, hence more Platonic than Plato (40-41).

41   Ll. 40-43 in Canto IV. Robert Pinsky's translation renders it thus: "We are lost, afflicted only this one way; that having no hope, we live in longing" (ll. 31-32).

Venuti's discussion in *The Translator's Invisibility* underlines, often results in a loss of self, be it through the translator's treading the "servile path" (Denham/Nabokov) or in the reception of his or her work.[42]

What makes the parallel of *mimesis* and *translation* even more important for my purpose is the way in which Melberg delineates how the lost self finds itself in the other: "But this Self is in the same procedure doomed to seek itself in someone else, and searching can be done only mimetically, by imitation" (20). This search, I argue, could be and is as well done through translation as through *mimesis*, despite a slight difference of quality that has most often been interpreted by implication as difference in essence.

This difference is often seen not as qualitative, but as absolute. The parallel is hardly ever drawn, so the proof lies in the absence of analogy. But it is not arbitrary, or even radical, to try to shift the perspective a little without taking cover behind a metaphor. Translation is, if anything, a mimetic operation.[43]

The term *mimesis* and the translational problems it creates for all interpreters is the best indicator of this. Even prior to translation the term was a troublemaker. As many commentators have pointed out, the term is contradictory within Plato's own discourse, or at least not unambiguous; it is for example not entirely clear whether he wants to exile all imitators from his republic, or only the "bad ones" who imitate imitations.[44] The texts in question are of course dialogues with numerous characters rewritten by Plato, but usually they are discussed as his, which in itself is a fact worth noting. Why would Plato have chosen the form if not to create a distance between himself and those who are speaking?[45] Whatever the reason, scholars have dug up the ambiguities present in other Platonic texts, and Aristotle provided a different definition of *mimesis* in his *Poetics,* which shows well that terms do not mean what they mean but what we want them to say.[46]

Plato's rejection of the poets becomes particularly ambiguous in *The Symposium* when Socrates narrates in Apollodorus' second hand narration (which Plato later wrote, presumably) what Diotima told him of Love as a creative power, born after the encounter of Contrivance, son of Invention, and Poverty.

---

[42] See Plato's *Republic* (393b-c). The notion of the "servile path" can of course lead to diametrically opposed conceptions; either the route which Nabokov delineates in the article under that heading, namely a rigorous faithfulness to the original text and author, or a the "fluent" route to serve the receiving culture.

[43] Certainly after the age of originality arrived in the latter part of the eighteenth century, the shadowpainting Plato ascribed to the painters and poets became the task of translators, a notion which, as we shall see, Benjamin rejected, partly with Platonic and partly with Aristotelian instruments.

[44] See books 2, 3 and 10 in particular.

[45] Again I refer to the discussion of Melberg, who also often speaks of Plato as the author, despite his qualifications.

[46] See Melberg (44-45).

This is in opposition to the men's dialogue earlier in *The Symposium*, which had been a traditional panegyric to the god of Love. In this charming account, Diotima argues through Socrates that Love is neither a god nor a human, but halfway between the two:

"He is a great spirit, Socrates; everything that is of the nature of a spirit is half-god and half-man." "And what is the function of such a being?" "To interpret and convey messages to the gods from men and to men from the gods, prayers and sacrifices from the one, and commands and rewards from the other. Being of an intermediate nature, a spirit bridges the gap between them, and prevents the universe from falling into separate halves" (203b/81).

Behind Diotima's (and Socrates') argument is a critique of the masculine panegyrics as untrue and illogical, eloquent lies. Furthermore, Diotima explains to Socrates that the basis of love, lack of and desire for good, has a *procreative* direction, in love and offspring (204 d-205 e/84-85).[47] In a short terminological discussion, Diotima explains the way in which the term love has been appropriated for a particular kind of love, when it truly "belongs to a wider whole, while we employ different names for the other kinds of love" (84-85). Socrates asks her for another example and she gives it by drawing an analogy:

"By its original meaning poetry means simply creation, and creation, as you know, can take very various forms. Any action which is the cause of a thing emerging from non-existence into existence might be called poetry, and all the processes in all the crafts are kinds of poetry, and all those who are engaged in them poets." "Yes." "But yet they are not called poets, but have other names, and out of the whole field of poetry or creation one part, which deals with music and metre, is isolated and called by the name of the whole. This part alone is called poetry, and those whose province is this part of poetry are called poets" (85).

In contemporary terms Diotima's analogy is an attempt at deconstructing preconceived metonymic notions of both love and poetry, and she reconstructs both into an aesthetic of immortality, of a desire for immortality enabled through love whose object is not beauty, but "to procreate and bring forth in beauty" (87). This biological inversion of Plato's idealism in the *Republic*, a metaphor of love and poetry, is almost Herderian in scope and undermines the problem of poetry as stated in the *Republic,* through the intertextualities and interstructuralities both within the *Republic* and between it and the *Symposium*.[48]

---

[47]   84 ff. in the Penguin edition. In the following I will refer to the page numbers.

[48]   Within the *Republic* the parameters, both textual and structural, are of course the moral questions of poetry that are discussed both in books 3 and 10. Between the *Republic* and *The Symposium* they are also represented both textually and structurally by love, procreation and immortality; it is particularly interesting that just after Plato indeed

Aristotle's later version of *mimesis* in his *Poetics* is much more dynamic than Plato's, an answer to both the moral criticisms of the *Republic* and the Dionysian aesthetic inherent in Diotima's argument on poetry and love. Melberg summarises it into three points:

(1) Aristotle's *mimesis* is defined by *mythos* and *praxis*, which brings the concept close to areas of time and action – in contrast to Platonic *mimesis*, which is closer to image, imagination and imitation.

(2) *Mythos* is a concept of order, which makes it possible to view literary works as structured wholes.

(3) *Praxis* refers to already structured events or chains of events, which can be perceived as meaningful and answering a purpose (44-45).

The order which Aristotle imposes on the Dionysian aesthetic is temporal and linear, but what I miss in Melberg's account is the stress Aristotle puts on character, the well-known reply to Plato's critique of the morally destructive effect of poetry in the *Republic*. To be sure, Aristotle subordinates characterisation to action, but this is precisely the reply to Plato's moral reservations, added to which is the famous notion of *catharsis* to give the truly represented characters a morally acceptable role. Aristotle translates by inversion and invents catharsis in order to let immoral characters improve morals. Subordinated to plot, time and events, the moral choices which reveal characters can only be made within the moving dynamic of the "plot". The ethic is local and individual, and at the same time a reflection, an "imitation" of one of the morally universal choices possible, understandable to any viewer and thus potentially cathartic. It is a solid, simple and classical idea of *mimesis,* aware of its imitative qualities prior to the Roman translation of *mimesis* with *imitatio*; why else would Aristotle say so defensively in the ninth Chapter of the *Poetics*:

It is clear, then, from what we have said that the poet must be a "maker" not of verses but of stories, since he is a poet in virtue of his "representation", and what he represents is action. Even supposing he represents what has actually happened, he is none the less a poet, for there is nothing to prevent some actual occurrences being the sort of thing that would probably or inevitably happen, and it is in virtue of that that he is their "maker" (37, emphasis in original translation).

As Melberg notes, Aristotle's version of *mimesis* came to be the one that prevailed in the West and became the mainstay of classical literary theory, so he was never alone in the struggle against the Platonic doubts about literature's

---

leaves a little door open for poetry's return into the *Republic* he switches the subject matter to the immortality of the soul.

claim to truth and hence its moral authority – a struggle, that, incidentally, was partly decided with neoplatonic approaches.[49]

The problem of *mimesis* was redefined and repeated to an extent through its translation into the Roman cultural sphere. Here the concept became acutely a problem of translation through its actual translation as a term and the cultural translation of the Greek heritage into the Roman. The concept was given a new name through translation, *imitatio*, the source of the English (and other languages') "imitation", a concept that has a slightly different perspective from the Greek one, for a good reason. The Greek version of *mimesis* also referred to rewritings of previous work in competition, rewritings which were presented in competitions. The idea was to present a better representation of events than the former writer had done. By the Romans, it was used not only for the representation of reality, "Darstellung der Wirklichkeit" in Auerbach's terms, or the consciously competitive intralingual translations of the Greeks, but also to translate similarly *from* the Greeks, in order to create their own Roman representation of reality that could not or should not be defined as derivative.

It is exactly at that moment, however, that "imitation" gets its first pejorative stain of derivation. Not particularly for the Romans themselves, who were happy to imitate, translate and lift without bothering much about the sources, in fact preferring this. There is, however, an uneasiness present in Horace that is decisive for the ideas on translation in Western thought, and that not only in connection with the often repeated, indeed very much Horatian, dialectic of literalism versus free translation. It is necessary to follow his tracks carefully, for his influence is most often reduced to the fine Latin quote "nec verbo verbum " (or "nec verbum verbo") without much more by way of commentary. Horace deserves more attention than this, though, for the pejorative paradigm of translation as a secondary act can actually be traced to his influence. Ironically, or rather obviously, his classification had the ideological objective of upgrading his and other Roman work; that is, to apply what was later termed *translatio studii* to make the Greek original Roman.[50]

He achieves this through analytical didacticism; that is, he defines the good and the bad through example and rhetoric and selects the right methods for the imaginary pupil poet (of the *Ars Poetica*). First one might note his classical de-

---

[49] There seem to be some parallels between a Platonic/Aristotelian dialectic and Auerbach's Judeo-Christian/Classical dialectic, although it must be stressed that the oppositions are of course neutralised to an extent through their intertextual and interstructural dependencies.

[50] He was of course no pioneer in making the Greek Roman; Cicero had made similar suggestions before, but since he was more preoccupied with translating the rhetorical tradition into Roman culture, his views on imitation are not as complex as those of Horace, whose distinctions are more exact, particularly when it comes to versification. See Albrecht on Cicero and Horace (53-58).

mand for clarity. The poet should not use obscure and abstruse terms except when absolutely necessary and then very sparingly and only those of Greek origin (ll. 46-53/p. 454).[51] This demand is followed by a very modern notion of language change, where Horace compares the words with leaves that wither and are replaced in due course (ll. 54-63/p. 454). When he discusses the correct use of poetic form a little later, the tone becomes harsher and more didactic: "If I fail to keep and do not understand these well marked shifts and shades of poetic forms, why am I hailed as a poet? Why through false shame do I prefer to be ignorant rather than to learn?" (457-459).[52]

Although Horace's mimetic ideas are thoroughly derivative of the Greek ones in the sense that they represent a translation of vision into words, he seems in his treatment to opt for a greater linguistic slant based on feeling: "Nature first shapes us within to meet every change of fortune: she brings joy or impels to anger, or bows us to the ground and tortures us under a load of grief; then, with the tongue for interpreter, she proclaims the emotions of the soul" (459).[53] The tongue is the interpreter of feelings in the soul, but if these are not in accordance with the speaker's fortunes, the interpreter will be laughed at.

A little further on in the text the famous *nec verbo verbum* appears, and it is interesting to see how exactly the context has been translated by different translators (ll. 119-135). The passage begins simply: "Either follow tradition or invent what is self-consistent" (461).[54] This is straightforward; the "tradition" re-

---

[51]   Fairclough's translation slants at times towards *nec verbum verbo*: "Moreover, with a nice taste and care in weaving your words together, you will express yourself most happily, if a skilful setting makes a familiar word new. If haply one must betoken abstruse things by novel terms, you will have a chance to fashion words never heard of by the kilted Cethegi, license will be granted, if used with modesty; while words, though new and of recent make, will win acceptance, if they spring from a Greek fount and are drawn therefrom but sparingly" (455). Roscommon's translation of this passage, on the other hand, is interesting in its slant towards the imitator and its almost whispering brackets: "Words must be chosen, and be plac'd with skill/You gain your point, if your industrious Art/can make unusual words easie and plain,/But (if you write of things Abstruse or New)/Some of your own inventing may be us'd/(So be it seldom and discreetly done)/But he that hopes to have new Words allow'd,/Must derive them from the Græcian spring" (4-5). The Latin: "In verbis etiam tenuis cautusque serendis/dixeris egregie, notum si callida verbum/reddiderit iunctura novum. si forte necesse est/indiciis monstrare recentibus abdita rerum,/fingere cinctutis non exaudita Cethegis/continget, dabiturque licentia sumpta pudenter:/et nova fictaque nuper habeunt verba fidem, si/Graeco fonte cadent parce detorta" (ll. 54-63/p. 454).

[52]   "descriptas servare vices operumque colores/cur ego si nequeo ignoroque poeta salutor?/cur nescire pudens prave quam discere malo?" (ll. 86-88/456-458).

[53]   "format enim Natura prius nos intus ad omnem/fortunarum habitum; iuvat aut impellit ad iram,/aut ad humum maerore gravi deducit et angit;/post effert animi motus interprete lingua" (ll. 108-111/458).

[54]   "Aut famam sequere aut sibi convenientia finge" (460).

38

fers to following tradition on historically known characters. Similarly, or rather more elegantly, Roscommon translates: "Follow Report or feign coherent things" (9). The question of "invention" refers to imitating a hitherto untreated subject with characters untried, so to speak, and their stature as such must be kept consistent and/or coherent. Inventively conservative as he is, Horace does not recommend this method of inventing new traditions and contradicts it forcefully in the next passage, the translations of which we will examine side by side:

Fairclough:

Roscommon:

It is hard to treat in your own way what is common: and you are doing better in spinning into acts a song of Troy than if, for the first time, you were giving the world a theme unknown and unsung. In ground open to all you will win private rights, if you do not linger along the easy and open pathway, if you do not seek to render word for word as a slavish translator, and if in your copying you do not leap into the narrow well, out of which either shame or the laws of your task will keep you from stirring a step (461&463).

New Subjects are not easily explain'd,
And you had better chuse a well known
Theam [*sic*];
Than trust to an Invention of your own;
For what originally others writ,
May be so well disguis'd, and so
improv'd,
that with some Justice it may pass for
yours;
But then you must not Copy trivial things,
Nor word for word too faithfully Translate,
Nor (as some servile imitators do)
Prescribe at first such strict uneasie rules,
As they must slavishly observe,
Or all the laws of decency renounce
(10-11).[55]

The translations reveal interesting differences and stylistic values. Whereas Fairclough's translational method seems to lack a sense of the ironic, Roscommon translates as Horace himself might have done it. The two most important points are Horace's notion of private right and public, and the way in which translation (proper) is relegated to a secondary significance, not for its mimetic quality, but for the hanging on to words of the other. In both cases the mimetic operation is translational, for the sources of public domain Horace points to are Greek. The difference in the translations lies in the relaxed notion Roscommon has of imitating texts from others, and that the "private rights" Fairclough sees in the Latin original can with "some Justice pass for yours" in Roscommon's

---

[55] "Difficile est proprie communia dicere; tuque/rectius Iliacum carmen deducis in actus,/quam si proferres ignota indictaque primus. publica materies privati iuris erit, si/non circa vilem patulumque moraberis orbem,/nec verbo verbum curabis reddere fidus interpres, nec desilies imitator in artum, unde pedem proferre pudor vetet aut operis lex" (ll. 129-135/460).

version. Two hundred years of copyright make some difference. Fairclough's note is also enlightening in our context: "By *publica materies* Horace means Homer and the epic field in general. A poet may make this his own by originality in the handling" (460).

The manner in which the two translators treat the famous phrase referring to their own activity is also revealing. Fairclough, the twentieth-century translator, speaks of a "slavish translator", whereas Roscommon's elegant formulation warns of translating "too faithfully", poking then at "servile Imitators" who "slavishly" observe "strict uneasie rules". Roscommon, being a poet, is perhaps a bit more honestly subjective than the scholar and he is also much more aware of the art of translating than the latter, who indeed must be expressing the way he feels when translating, though with an accuracy that reveals an ideological stance more than perfect scholarship.[56]

Despite their differences both translators succeed in expressing the idea of legalised theft in *mimesis* when strictly interpreted, or the idea of a public domain in a relaxed interpretation. The question of property is in both cases resolved through making the public private, colonising an original to claim it as one's own. It is exactly this act which removes translation from the mimetic operation, making it simultaneously mechanical and worthless in itself. Such an approach is, in fact, necessary for the translation of other cultures in the sense of *translatio*, particularly when the operation is to provide a "new original". Horace becomes more explicit further on in the *Ars Poetica* when he criticises degenerate Roman poets and calls for a "return" to the Greek models of metre (ll. 251-274). This is not only a critique which accords with the paradigm of a pessimistic conservatism that constantly fears the world is going down the drain; it is also based on Horace's own experience of putting into practice the *translatio studii*, an idea which acknowledges the decline and fall of former states of glory, but rescues them, in the end, through translation.

In Epistle I. xix, the one in praise of drinking prior to writing, Horace explains his route to originality. Here he attacks imitators (*imitatores*) – "mimics" in Fairclough's translation – as a "slavish herd" (*servum pecus*) before proudly claiming "I was the first to plant free footsteps on a virgin soil; I walked not where others trod" (383).[57] Again the (relatively) modern translation gives an impression of colonial annexation, as does the original, which in this case is not to be understood metaphorically, but indeed as an annexation of the Greek, not

---

[56]   Will Barnstone translated the famous line in his *The Poetics of Translation* thus: "Nor should you try to render your original word for word like an obedient [faithful] *interpres* (32, italics reversed). This attempt at redefining the Latin adjective *fidus* through repeated translation gives the impression Horace was advising translators specifically, which he was not, just imitators.

[57]   "Libera per vacuum posui vestigia princeps,/non aliena meo pressi pede" (ll. 21-22/382).

through the appropriation of content this time, but of form. This is the method by which the *translatio* finally succeeds in translating while removing all notions of translating, what I refer to as a translation without an original:

> I was the first to show Latium the iambics of Paros, following the rhythms and spirit of Archilochus, not the themes or the words that hounded Lycambes. And lest you should crown me with a scantier wreath because I feared the measures and form of verse, see how manlike Sappho moulds her Muse by the rhythm of Archilochus; how Alcaeus moulds his, though in his themes and arrangement he differs, looking for no father-in-law to besmear with deadly verses, and weaving no halter for his bride with defaming rhyme. Him, never before sung by other lips, I, the lyrist of Latium, have made known. It is my joy that I bring things untold before, and am read by the eyes and held in the hands of the gently born (383).[58]

Horace boasts in these lines of his epodes and odes, which he sees as his own because he introduced the forms or was the first to master them. What he has really done is to translate the forms themselves into Latin, thereby showing the means by which the Latin could be moulded to the needs of the foreign form, could be given the sublimity of the foreign form. It is a method that provides an opportunity for "experiencing the foreign" (in Berman's phrase) without realising it. This is the kind of translation that "original" poets prefer, the literary equivalent of throwing the discus, and being able to hurl it as far in the native language as the ancient Greeks could in theirs.[59]

Horace was not the first to translate like this; his most important forerunner was probably Ennius, the Roman who introduced the hexameter and epic form into Latin. What Horace achieved, however (if not in his own day then at least in latter-day discourse) was to create a mimetic imbalance and, through the *nec verbum verbo,* a distinctive relegation of translation out of the first class of *mimesis.* Whereas he was of course translating himself – everything but words: genre, ideas, characters, traditions. The poet's construction of identity and difference was achieved through an appropriating identification with the Greek model, the faithful translation of which Horace rejected.

Thus Horace created a *problem* of translation, for although he had succeeded in expelling it from the state of legitimacy, he left it with the one contradictory justification it has retained through the ages: the claim to truth (not of

---

58 "Parios ego primus iambos/ostendi Latio, numeros animosque secutus/Archilochi, non res et agentia verba Lycamben./ac ne me foliis ideo brevioribus ornes,/quod timui mutare modos et carminis artem,/temperat Archilochi Musam pede mascula Sappho,/temperat Alcaeus, sed rebus et ordine dispar,/nec socerum quaerit, quem versibus oblinat atris,/nec sponsae laqueum famoso carmine nectit./hunc ego, non alio dictum prius ore, Latinus/volgavi fidicen" (ll. 23-33/382).

59 By no means without exception, the mimetic levels of Joyce's *Ulysses* (and indeed other texts of his) are fascinating in this light.

the original, but of the translation). If Homer and the rest of them had been "lying", it was justified through art; if a translator was lying he was sure to be condemned for art.[60] And if he was a poet, he was not translating.

Despite their success in introducing the mimetic methods that were to be applied every time a serious cultural "Renaissance" took place, Horace and his fellow Romans were not able to convince all of the scholars all of the time. For example, in the eighteenth century Homeric translations were cleansed of Roman deities and names, which were replaced with the original ones, an act not as scholarly as it may at first sight seem, for it also served the new *translatio* of nationalism in the eighteenth century, with the aim of getting rid of the middlemen, the Romans, in order to lay the true claim to the original Greeks.

One of those who noticed this was Nietzsche. In *Die fröhliche Wissenschaft* (Book II) there is the well-known Chapter (no. 83) on translation, sandwiched between Chapters on Greek taste (no. 81), the "Non-Greek" *esprit* (no. 82) and the origins of poesy (no. 84). The short Chapter on translation is worth quoting in full:

Man kann den Grad des historischen Sinns, welchen eine Zeit besitzt, daran abschätzen, wie diese Zeit Übersetzungen macht und vergangene Zeiten und Bücher sich einzuverleiben sucht. Die Franzosen Corneilles, und auch noch die der Revolution, bemächtigten sich des römischen Altertums in einer Weise, zu der wir nicht den Mut mehr hätten – dank unserem höheren historischen Sinne. Und das römische Altertum selbst: wie gewaltsam und naiv zugleich legte es seine Hand auf alles Gute und Hohe des griechischen älteren Altertums! Wie übersetzten sie in die römische Gegenwart hinein! Wie verwischten sie absichtlich und unbekümmert den Flügelstaub des Schmetterlings Augenblick! So übersetzte Horaz hier und da den Alkäus oder den Archilochus, so Properz den Kallimachus und Philetas (Dichter gleichen Ranges mit Theokrit, wenn wir urteilen dürfen): was lag ihnen daran, daß der eigentliche Schöpfer dies und jenes erlebt und die Zeichen davon in sein Gedicht hineingeschrieben hatte! – als Dichter waren sie dem antiquarischen Spürgeiste, der dem historischen Sinne voranläuft, abhold; als Dichter ließen sie diese ganz persönlichen Dinge und Namen und alles, was einer Stadt, einer Küste, einem Jahrhundert als seine Tracht und Maske zu eigen war, nicht gelten, sondern stellten flugs das Gegenwärtige und das Römische an seine Stelle. Sie scheinen uns zu fragen: "Sollen wir das alte nicht für uns neu machen und uns in ihm zurechtlegen? Sollen wir nicht unsere Seele diesem toten Leibe einblasen dürfen? Denn tot ist er nun einmal: wie häßlich ist alles Tote!" – Sie kannten den Genuß des historischen Sinns nicht; das Vergangene und Fremde war ihnen peinlich, und als Römern ein Anreiz zu einer römischen Eroberung. In der Tat, man eroberte damals, wenn man übersetzte, – nicht nur so, daß man das Historische wegließ: nein, man fügte die Anspielung auf das Gegenwärtige hinzu, man strich vor allem den Namen des Dichters hinweg und setzte den eigenen an seine Stelle – nicht im Gefühl

---

60   The true paradox of translation can be put thus: There are only two things for which translators are condemned; for translating the words wrongly and translating the words literally.

des Diebstahls, sondern mit dem allerbesten Gewissen des *imperium Romanum* (422-423).[61]

This concise description of the *translatio* may not be very original, as Douglas Robinson notes in the introduction to an English translation in his anthology *Western Translation Theory from Herodotus to Nietzsche*, but it offers an insight into ideological manipulation through translation as *mimesis* that few would have expressed before Nietzsche (262).[62] Still, it is obvious that Nietzsche's description is firmly embedded in the mainstream of Romantic and historicist thought, and fails to recognise how these had completely appropriated the soul instead of the body with their more subtle methods. This could be done through translation that took not only literalism but also formalism to new heights, as was the case with the Homeric translator Johann Heinrich Voß and his Romantic contemporaries Schleiermacher and Schlegel; it could be done through translation of form; it could be done through the large-scale theft (preservation?) of archaeological remains; in short, the age Nietzsche refers to as having the historical sense necessary to appreciate the ancient originals did not discard the *translatio* but rather added a new dimension to it, denying in the

---

[61]   "The degree of historical sense of any age may be inferred from the manner in which this age makes *translations* and tries to absorb former ages and books. In the age of Corneille and even of the Revolution, the French took possession of Roman antiquity in a way for which we would no longer have courage enough – thanks to our more highly developed historical sense. And Roman antiquity itself: how forcibly and at the same time how naively it took hold of everything good and lofty of Greek antiquity, which was more ancient! How they translated things into the Roman present! How deliberately and recklessly they brushed the dust of the wings of the butterfly that is called moment! Thus Horace now and then translated Alcaeus or Archilochus; and Propertius did the same with Callimachus and Philetas (poets of the same rank as Theocritus, if we *may* judge). What was it to them that the real creator had experienced this and that and written the signs of it into his poem? As poets, they had no sympathy for the antiquarian inquisitiveness that precedes the historical sense; as poets, they had no time for all those very personal things and names and whatever might be considered the costume and mask of a city, a coast, or a century: quickly, they replaced it with what was contemporary and Roman. They seem to ask us: "Should we not make new for ourselves what is old and find ourselves in it? Should we not have the right to breathe our own soul into this dead body? For it is dead after all; how ugly is everything dead!" They did not know the delights of the historical sense; what was past and alien was an embarrassment for them; and being Romans, they saw it as an incentive for a Roman conquest. Indeed, translation was a form of conquest. Not only did one omit what was historical; one also added allusions to the present and, above all, struck out the name of the poet and replaced it with one's own – not with any sense of theft but with the very best conscience of the *imperium Romanum*" (Kaufmann 262).

[62]   It is also noteworthy that Nietzsche's examples could just as easily refer to the translation of form Horace describes in the quote above. In fact, his example from Horace refers exactly to that passage quoted above.

process that any kind of *translatio* was necessary for "original" works of art. The aesthetic of beauty as truth, which Keats most forcefully (after Shaftesbury) lays claim to, requires the notion of an unmediated, non-mimetic relationship between the artist's creation and the original. In the words of Paul de Man in his "The Rhetoric of Temporality":

> The poetic language of genius is capable of transcending this distinction [between experience and its representation] and can thus transform all individual experience directly into general truth. The subjectivity of experience is preserved when it is translated into language; the world is then no longer seen as a configuration of entities that designate a plurality of distinct and isolated meanings, but as a configuration of symbols ultimately leading to a total, single, and universal meaning (188).

During the age of originality (of genius), *mimesis* was transformed and renamed as originality and translation was firmly consigned to the role Horace originally conceived, indeed for the same purpose. The difference between his and Nietzsche's century was simply the fact that Horace could translate directly from the Greeks, whereas *translatio* as practised in Christianity referred to the Romans and later translations of that empire. So prior to Nietzsche's age, Horace had been imitated more than anyone else.

Such an inherent contradiction is bound to lead to tensions that can be kept under control only by ideology – an ideology that fictionalises the unity of the mimetic operation by denying its translational aspects; indeed these aspects must necessarily be taken out of the equation if that imagined unity is to be paraded as a reality. It is the same sort of operation the nation requires in order to see itself as one.

The best proof of translation as a necessary negation of *mimesis* – not even an imitation of a "true" reality, but simply a linguistic reformulation of a truth manifested in the unity of experience and representation – can be seen in Heidegger's *Der Ursprung des Kunstwerks* (1935). Heidegger's work, with its two removes from "das Dinghafte des Dinges" to "das Werkhafte des Werkes", which read like a rendering of Plato's movement from the idea to the imitation in the second degree in *The Republic,* seems at times to be obsessed with the gulf created between artistic operations of representation and translation:

> [Die] Übersetzung der griechischen Namen in die lateinische Sprache ist keineswegs der folgenlose Vorgang, für den er noch heutigentags gehalten wird. Vielmehr verbirgt sich hinter der anscheinend wörtlichen und somit bewahrenden Übersetzung ein *Übersetzen* griechischer Erfahrung in eine andere Denkungsart. *Das römische Denken übernimmt die* griechischen *Wörter ohne die entsprechende gleich-ursprüngliche*

Erfahrung dessen, was sie sagen, ohne das griechische Wort. Die Bodenlosigkeit des abendländischen Denkens beginnt mit diesem Übersetzen (15, emphasis in text).[64]

Heidegger sees a translational operation in the appropriation of Greek names and words into Latin, but what is more interesting in our context is Heidegger's claim that experience must, of necessity, find a word which is able to express the truth of that experience. Translation is impossible, or has rather swept the ground away from what he terms "abendländische[s] Denken" [Western thought]. This amounts to an inversion of the *translation*, a conviction that the translation and transport of the Greek heritage functions as a verification of the falsification of all subsequent translations, all renewals and Renaissances; time, space and language have made an "authentic" life in the West impossible.[65]

Derrida's commentary on this passage in "Restitutions of the Truth in Pointing" concentrates on the loss of *speech* implied by Heidegger's assertion:

> Let's go back to before the allusion of the "famous picture" to the point where the Chapter "Thing and Work" names "the *fundamental* Greek experience of the Being of beings in general." I emphasize *fundamental* (*Grunderfahrung*). The interpretation of the thing as *hypokeimenon* and then as *subjectum* does not only produce (itself as) a slight linguistic phenomenon. The transforming translation of *hypokeimenon* as *subjectum* corresponds, according to Heidegger, to another "mode of thought" and of being-there. It translates, transports, transfers (Heidegger emphasizes the passage implied in *über*) over and beyond the *fundamental* Greek experience: "Roman thought takes over (*übernimmt*) the Greek words (*Wörter*) without the corresponding co-originary experience of what they say, without the Greek word (*Wort*). The absence-of ground (*Bodenlosigkeit*) of Western thought opens with this translation." (*Truth* 287-288, emphasis in text).[66]

---

64   "[T]his translation of Greek names into Latin is in no way the innocent process it is considered to this day. Beneath the seemingly literal and thus faithful translation there is concealed, rather, a *trans*lation of Greek experience into a different way of thinking. *Roman thought takes of the Greek words without a corresponding, equally authentic experience of what they say, without the Greek word.* The rootlessness of Western thought begins with this translation" (Hofstadter 23).

65   The absence of the Bible may seem conspicuous, but the thesis is embedded into well-known notions of *translatio*.

66   "Revenons en-deçà de l'allusion au « célèbre tableau » au moment où le chapitre *La chose et l'œuvre* nomme « l'expérience grecque *fondamentale* de l'être de l'étant en général ». Je souligne fondamentale (*Grunderfahrung*). L'interprétation de la chose en *hypokeimenon* puis en *subjectum* ne (se) produit pas seulement (comme) un léger phénomène linguistique. La traduction transformatrice de *hypokeimenon* en *subjectum* correspondrait à un autre « mode de pensée » et d'être-là. Elle traduirait, transporterait, transférerait (Heidegger souligne le passage en *über*) par-dessus et au-delà de ladite expérience grecque *fondamentale* : « La pensée romaine reprend (*übernimmt*) les mots

45

Derrida stresses Heidegger's use of originary myth and word fixation in both senses of the term, the destruction of the "co-originary experience" through translation. It amounts to a Babelian ban on speech:

> The ground (of thought) comes then to be lacking when words lose speech [*la parole*]. The "same" words (*Wörter*) deprived of the speech (*Wort*) corresponding to the originarily Greek experience of the thing, the "same" word, which are therefore no longer exactly the same, the fantomatic doubles of themselves, their light simulacra, begin to walk above the void or in the void, *bodenlos* (288).[67]

The problem of *mimesis* seems more often to be what it means than what it is, or the curious fact that it is one of those abstractions whose meaning is constitutive for itself as an experience; in other words the term is an inversion of itself, needing the meaning to be definable as an experience.

According to the American art historian Meyer Schapiro, Heidegger creates this meaning by ignoring experience, but as Derrida points out in his commentary, both Schapiro and Heidegger are essentially restituting, returning the work of art to an owner through the object represented; it matters whose shoes are painted, it may be seen as implied that the deictic act of pointing to a farmer (Heidegger) or the artist himself (Schapiro) is a parallel if not a synchronic gesture: "Without even looking elsewhere or further back, *restitution* re-establishes in rights or property by placing the subject upright again, in its stance, in its institution" (260-261). One of Derrida's American editors, Peggy Kamuf, explains it thus:

> Whose shoes are they? While Schapiro and Heidegger disagree over their attribution, the colloquy of Derrida and his interlocutors finds a secret correspondence beneath the overt disagreement: together, the two great professors attribute or restore the shoes to some owner, some subject (to Van Gogh himself or to a peasant). The gesture of restitution is essentially the same even though a great gulf divides the Heideggerian meditation on the origin of the work of art from Schapiro's historicism. From out of this gulf arise specters or ghosts of a recent German past, one that left mountains of abandoned shoes all over the European landscape (*Between* 277).

(*Wörter*) grecs sans l'expérience co-originaire correspondante de ce qu'ils disent, sans la parole (*Wort*) grecque. L'absence-de-sol (*Bodenlosigkeit*) de la pensée occidentale s'ouvre avec cette traduction »" (*La Vérite* 328). The literal version of the word "bodenlosigkeit", "absence-of-ground" instead of "rootlessness" in Hofstadter's edition is interesting, perhaps focalising the argument even more.

[67] "Le sol (de la pensée) vient donc à manquer quand des mots perdent la parole. Les « mêmes » mots (*Wörter*) privés de la parole (*Wort*) correspondant à l'experiénce originairement grecque de la chose, les « mêmes » mots, qui ne sont donc plus tout à fait les mêmes, les doubles fantômatiques d'eux-mêmes, leurs simulacres légers, se mettent à marcher au-dessus du vide ou dans le vide, *bodenlos*" (328-330).

However reminiscent his empirical mistake in the attribution of the shoes may be of "Blut und Boden" ideology, Heidegger might have protested that his restitution was to raise the monolithic subject from the grave and he certainly did not intend to return anything to the artists, rather the reverse, he saw creativity as a kind of *fetching* ("drawing-up" in Hofstadter's translation) that is diametrically opposed to the subjectivity of modernity: "Weil ein solches Holen, ist alles Schaffen ein Schöpfen (das Wasser holen aus der Quelle). Der moderne Subjektivismus mißdeutet freilich das Schöpferische sogleich im Sinne der genialen Leistung des selbstherrlichen Subjektes" (87).[67]

Wherein does creativity lie according to Heidegger? And what are the consequences? In this long essay his steps need to be carefully traced, backwards, in order to see the carefully constructed contradictions that are everything but antithetical. Close to the end Heidegger couples history with art, (i.e., art as the origin of changes in history). This happens through a *shove* which transports history into movement, not as a linear account of events but as the movement of a people from what it has left behind (forgotten?) into what it has been provided with:

> Immer wenn Kunst geschieht, d.h. wenn ein Anfang ist, kommt in die Geschichte ein Stoß, fängt Geschichte erst oder wieder an. Geschichte meint hier nicht die Abfolge irgendwelcher und sei es noch so wichtiger Begebenheiten in der Zeit. Geschichte ist die Entrückung eines Volkes in sein Aufgegebenes als Einrückung in sein Mitgegebenes (88-89).[68]

This shove (*Stoß*, "thrust" in Hofstadter's translation) is, remarkably, the result of the *translatio studii* as we have seen it many times by now. True, Heidegger does not use this terminology, but he translates into his private language. Despite this the thought is clear:

> Immer wenn das Seiende selbst die Gründung in die Offenheit verlangt, gelangt die Kunst in ihr geschichtliches Wesen als Stiftung. Sie geschah im Abendland erstmals im Griechentum. Was künftig Sein heißt, wurde maßgebend ins Werk gesetzt. Das so eröffnete Seiende im Ganzen wurde dann verwandelt zum Seienden im Sinne des von Gott Geschaffenen. Das geschah im Mittelalter. Dieses Seiende wurde wiederum verwandelt im Beginn und Verlauf der Neuzeit. Das Seiende wurde zum rechnerisch

---

[67] "All creation, because it is such a drawing-up, is a drawing, as of water from a spring. Modern subjectivisim, to be sure, immediately misinterprets creation, taking it as the self-sovereign subject's performance of a genius" (Hofstadter 76).

[68] "Whenever art happens—that is, whenever there is a beginning—a thrust enters history, history either begins or starts over again. History means here not a sequence in time of events of whatever sort, however important. History is the transporting of a people into its appointed task as entrance into that people's endowment" (77).

beherrschbaren und durchschaubaren Gegenstand. Jedesmal brach eine neue und wesentliche Welt auf (88).[69]

The transformation, the movement that has "verwandelt", is taken out of the historical context of political events and firmly embedded in art as the constructor of a new beginning. It is, however, obviously a Heideggerian translation of the *translatio*. Curiously enough, there is no question of "Bodenlosigkeit", "absence-of-ground" here, but a new world that opens up. The contradiction seems blatant, raising the question of how this is possible in the space of 70 pages.

The answer I suggest is the closing off of *mimesis* and translation, a forgetting of words while taking advantage of the process. In this Heidegger is in the mainstream of Western thought since Horace, and, furthermore, he is trying to smuggle the poets back into Plato's Republic, not as subjects but as producers of essential art. This is possible and perhaps even necessary in Heidegger's version, because poetry is the essence of art and constructs truth (86). This regression takes place through the medium of language, native language, because this is the route to the well of origins and the essence of poetry:

> Die Sprache selbst ist Dichtung im wesentlichen Sinne. Weil nun aber die Sprache jenes Geschehnis ist, in dem für den Menschen jeweils erst Seiendes als Seiendes sich erschließt, deshalb ist die Poesie, die Dichtung im engeren Sinne, die ursprünglichste Dichtung im wesentlichen Sinne. Die Sprache ist nicht deshalb Dichtung, weil sie Urpoesie ist, sondern die Poesie ereignet sich in der Sprache, weil diese das ursprüngliche Wesen der Dichtung verwahrt (85).[70]

This alone does not support my argument of *native* language, but it has to be seen in the context of Heidegger's coupling of a people's language and history. Considering that this context is partly the myth of the *translation,* it contains almost the eschatological feeling of the German thirties:

---

[69] "Always when that which is as a whole demands, as what is, itself, a grounding in openness, art attains to its historical nature as foundation. This foundation happened in the West for the first time in Greece. What was in the future to be called Being was set into work, setting the standard. The realm of beings thus opened up was then transformed into a being in the sense of God's creation. This happened in the Middle-Ages. This kind of being was again transformed at the beginning and in the course of the modern age. Beings became objects that could be controlled and seen through by calculation. At each time a new and essential world arose" (76-77).

[70] "Language itself is poetry in the essential sense. But since language is the happening in which for man beings first disclose themselves to him each time as beings, poesy—or poetry in the narrower sense—is the most original form of poetry in the essential sense. Language is not poetry because it is the primal poesy; rather, poesy takes its place in language because language preserves the original nature of poetry" (74).

48

Die jeweilige Sprache ist das Geschehnis jenes Sagens, in dem geschichtlich einem Volk seine Welt aufgeht und die Erde als das Verschlossene aufbewahrt wird. Das entwerfende Sagen ist jenes, das in der Bereitung des Sagbaren zugleich das Unsagbare als ein solches zur Welt bringt. In solchem Sagen werden einem geschichtlichem Volk die Begriffe seines Wesens, d.h. seine Zugehörigkeit zur Welt-Geschichte vorgeprägt (84).[71]

Heidegger is on the other hand working very much within a German tradition of philosophy of language here; the echo from W. v. Humboldt (and thus Herder) is not to be proven directly, due to Heidegger's individuality of style, but there are passages in, for example, Humboldt's "Nationalcharakter der Sprachen" that make such quotes feel familiar.[72]

Heidegger's definition of language feels, perhaps necessarily, even more familiar. It has to be kept in mind that he is of the opinion that language is essentially poetry (85). His division of language into two functions, banality and an almost mystical function of art, is reminiscent of two famous essays on translation. Schleiermacher's "Ueber die verschiedenen Methoden des Übersetzers" divided language – and consequently the approaches of translators – into two main categories, the commercial and artistic, and creates a difference between "Dolmetschen" and "Übersetzen" for that purpose (39-40). Schleiermacher's model of moving the reader to the author and vice versa can be interpreted as an attempt to build a connecting bridge between the subjectivity of the two subjects, author and reader. In "Methoden" this is done across languages; in *Hermeneutik und Kritik* it is an intralingual operation, with the same objective, common to all hermeneutics, of making two subjects understand each other while retaining their subjectivity, an operation doomed to fail, for the receiver is never unchanged by the text received and the text is never the same in any reception.[73] At the same time, hermeneutics represents an attempt to mediate (*Aufheben*) the difference between the subjects by creating a monolithic mean-

---

[71] "Actual language at any given moment is the happening of this saying, in which a people's world historically arises for it and the earth is preserved as that which remains closed. Projective saying is saying which, in preparing the sayable, simultaneously brings the unsayable into the world. In such saying, the concepts of an historical people's nature, i.e., of its belonging to world history, are formed for that folk, before it" (74).

[72] For example: "Insofern aber die Sprache, indem sie bezeichnet, eigentlich schafft, dem unbestimmten Denken Gestalt und Gepräge verleiht, dringt der Geist, durch das Wirken mehrerer unterstützt, auch auf neuen Wegen in das Wesen der Dinge selbst ein" (Humboldt, *Werke III* 73). [When, however, language describes, it actually creates the body and contours for unformed thought, and the spirit enters, supported by the activity of many, also in new ways into the essence of things themselves (my attempted translation)].

[73] For radical reflections on the hermeneutic project and its validity today, see John D. Caputo's *Radical Hermeneutics.*

ing for the text. Then again, it has to be said that Schleiermacher did not make such a sharp distinction; he talks of "verwaschene [...] Grenzen" [overlapping boundaries] between the two types of language he sets up, and he also, in a hermeneutic manner (or is it?), broods over whether it is necessary to translate even what people of one's own class and dialect have to say ("Methoden", 39).[74] This indeed raises the question of whether his translation theories are not in opposition to his hermeneutics and the Romantic, or rather Fichte's notion of subjectivity, which defines the subject through the non-subject.[75]

The latter essay with which Heidegger's *Der Ursprung des Kunstwerks* seems to have an elective affinity is Benjamin's "Die Aufgabe des Übersetzers", the premise of which is that "Rücksicht auf den Aufnehmenden für deren Erkenntnis" [consideration of the receiver] never proves fruitful for the work of art (156).[76] This is partly due to the fact that "[i]hr Wesentliches ist nicht Mitteilung, nicht Aussage" [Its essential quality is not statement or the imparting of information] (156/15). This is the point where we can return to Heidegger and his meditation on the "Entwerfen der Wahrheit" through poetry, one version of truth that is (83). But for this "drafting" (projection) of truth a specific definition of language is needed, aspects of which have been mentioned above:

> Um das zu sehen, bedarf es nur des rechten Begriffes von der Sprache. In der landläufigen Vorstellung gilt die Sprache als eine Art von Mitteilung. Sie dient zur Unterredung und Verabredung, allgemein zur Verständigung. Aber die Sprache ist nicht nur und nicht erstlich ein lautlicher und schriftlicher Ausdruck dessen, was mitgeteilt werden soll. Sie befördert das Offenbare und Verdeckte als so Gemeintes nicht nur erst in Wörtern und Sätzen weiter, sondern die Sprache bringt das Seiende als ein Seiendes allererst ins Offene. Wo keine Sprache west, wie im Sein vom Stein, Pflanze und Tier, da ist auch keine Offenheit des Seienden und demzufolge keine solche des Nichtseienden und des Leeren (83).[77]

The division is made by differentiating between banal understanding of "Mitteilung" and a higher, mystical mode that brings being as a being first of all

---

[74] A recent translation of Schleiermacher's essay can be found in Robinson's *Western Translation Theory from Herodotus to Nietzsche* (225-238).

[75] See for example his *Grundlage der Gesammten Wissenschaftslehre* (1794).

[76] A recent translation of Benjamin's essay can be found in Venuti's *The Translation Studies Reader* (15-25).

[77] "To see this, only the right concept of language is needed. In the current view, language is held to be a kind of communication. It serves for verbal exchange and agreement, and in general for communicating. But language is not only and not primarily an audible and written expression of what is to be communicated. It not only puts forth in words and statements what is overtly or covertly intended to be communicated; language alone brings what is, as something that is, into the Open for the first time. Where there is no language, as in the being of stone, plant, and animal, there is also no openness either of that which is not and of the empty" (73).

into the open, an originary translation of being, metaphorically speaking. The final sentence of the quote is finally reminiscent of Herder's premise in his *Abhandlung über den Ursprung der Sprache*, which will be dealt with in detail later on. Herder's premise, which is based on Aristotle's *On the Soul,* asserts that speech, what divides humans from animals, is the result of the different "Sphären" in which animals and humans live. Heidegger uses different arguments to draw this division, but nonetheless makes language, native language it must be, the essence of being human.[78]

The text that best shows Heidegger's affinity with Schleiermacher and Benjamin are his own thoughts on translation in the lectures published as *Der Satz vom Grund* (1957), where he negates his own negation of translation in *Der Ursprung des Kunstwerks. Der Satz vom Grund* accepts the translatability of experience, indeed sees it as an experience in itself: "Eine Übersetzung wird dort, wo das Sprechen der Grundworte von einer geschichtlichen Sprache in die andere *über*setzt, zur Überlieferung" (171, emphasis in text).[79] The last word can hardly be translated with "tradition" as the dictionary suggests, for it indicates "delivery" through the act of translation. It means more. According to Heidegger, this "delivery" can be a burden, when it becomes stiff, "erstarrt", but it can also liberate in the sense of its etymological origin, "liberare": "Als ein Befreien hebt die Überlieferung verborgene Schätze des Gewesenen ans Licht, sei dies Licht auch erst nur das einer zögernden Morgendämmerung" (171).[80] The traditional qualification with regard to translation comes forth in the last sentence, but Heidegger's position has opened up and he has apparently gone in a similar direction to Benjamin: "Der gedachte Zug besteht darin, daß die Übersetzung in solchen Fällen [Werk des Dichtens oder des Denkens] nicht nur Auslegung, sondern Überlieferung ist" (164).[81] From the premise in the brackets one can also see that Heidegger makes use of Schleiermacher's distinction between two kinds of translation; in fact he rewords Schleiermacher thus: "Übersetzen und Übersetzen ist nicht das Gleiche, wenn es sich hier um ein Geschäftsbrief handelt und dort um ein Gedicht" (163).[82]

The route taken by Heidegger in *Der Ursprung des Kunstwerks* to his conception of the opening up of being by drafting the truth through language as po-

---

[78]   Neither Herder nor Heidegger can have been thinking of "universal grammar"; it is exactly the nativity of language that defines its essence.

[79]   "A translation happens as delivery, where speech *trans*lates the fundamental words of one historic language into another" (my translation)

[80]   "As a liberation the delivery lifts hidden treasures into the light, even if it is only the light of the hesitant dawn" (my translation).

[81]   "The feature is based on that the translation [a work of poetry or thought] is not only interpretation but delivery" (my translation).

[82]   "Translation and translation is not the same thing, when in one case it is a translation of a business letter and a poem in the other" (my translation).

etry was not as original as one might think, but then again Heidegger's claim to "originality" lies rather in his style than in his content, the philosopher – any philosopher – always being engaged in a dialogue with his predecessors, anyway. The route is a Heideggerian way of tracing back his steps to a neo-platonic aesthetic originally introduced into European thought with a bang by Boileau's translation of Longinus' *On the Sublime*.[83] What Heidegger achieves, on the other hand, is truly brilliant; putting his finger on the moment when the first steps towards an aesthetics of subjectivity were taken in a complex synthesis of rationalist and sensationalist thought. The central point of Longinus' poetics, the ecstasy of the sublime, going out of oneself and uniting with the world in being one and at one with it, was, arguably, one of the most important elements in the progression of eighteenth-century aesthetic thought, focusing the experience of the subject into an identity with that experience – not an individual, subjective experience but a collective aesthetic and historical truth (74-77):

> Die Bewahrung des Werkes vereinzelt die Menschen nicht auf ihre Erlebnisse, sondern rückt sie ein in die Zugehörigkeit zu der im Werk geschehenden Wahrheit und gründet so das Für- und Miteinandersein als das geschichtliche Ausstehen des Da-seins aus dem Bezug zur Unverborgenheit (77).[84]

The individual *movement* establishes, then, a "Für- und Miteinandersein" through a sense of belonging to "im Werk geschehenden Wahrheit", a description that fits the "aesthetic ideology" that seems to have taken over some of the functions of religious experience in the eighteenth century.[85] This may explain why Kant's transcendental philosophy gave artists such a subjective jolt, having made them the divine originators of their own works of art. For Heidegger, art is the origin of the work of art and the artist: "Der Ursprung des Kunstwerkes und des Künstlers ist die Kunst. Der Ursprung ist die Herkunft des Wesens, worin das Sein eines Seienden west" (63).[86] This may seem not only tautological but almost circular in its logic, but that is only an appearance; the origin of the work

---

[83]   The tract was "found" in the Renaissance tradition already in the sixteenth century, but it is probably Boileau's translation that made it famous and a real contribution to aesthetic discourse.

[84]   "Preserving the work does not reduce people to their private experiences, but brings them into affiliation with the truth happening in the work. Thus it grounds being for and with one another as the historical standing-out of human existence in reference to unconcealedness" (Hofstadter 68).

[85]   See also Hegel's *Phänomenologie des Geistes,* particularly a passage in the Chapter "Die Wahrnehmung" in which he defines the individual versus the universal and the following Chapter, "Kraft und Verstand" where he discusses "die Einheit des Fürsichseyns und des Füreinanderseyns" (95 & 109).

[86]   "Art is the origin of the art work and of the artist. Origin is the source of the nature in which the being of an entity is present" (57).

of art is in the *movement* itself, nothing revolutionary for Zen-Buddhists, as Heidegger's later *Unterwegs zur Sprache* was to confirm.

Heidegger, then, sees the origin in a movement that brings truth to light in the form of works of art. The artists themselves are not the creating subjects but art itself, a kind of autonomy similarly expressed in Benjamin's "Aufgabe". He re-translates the poets into Plato's totalitarian Republic by returning the representation of art as an object – a thing, a product, a work – to the artists, and at the same time robs them of their private subjectivity, transforming it into the essence of art. This has taken art radically away from the idea of *mimesis* as we have seen it in some forms, or so at least Heidegger himself asserts:

> Oder soll gar mit dem Satz, die Kunst sei das sich-ins-Werk-Setzen der Wahrheit, jene glücklich überwundene Meinung wieder aufleben, die Kunst sei eine Nachahmung und Abschilderung des Wirklichen? Die Wiedergabe des Vorhandenen verlangt allerdings die Übereinstimmung mit dem Seienden, die Anmessung an dieses; adequatio sagt das Mittelalter; ὁμοίωσις sagt bereits Aristoteles. Übereinstimmung mit dem Seienden gilt seit langem als das Wesen der Wahrheit (33).[87]

Heidegger is at this point asking the questions he must in order to question what he claims has been said about the appreciation of works of art, and rejects here *mimesis* in the Aristotelian form; he is somewhat unfair a little earlier when he claims that "bislang hatte es die Kunst doch mit dem Schönen und der Schönheit zu tun und nicht mit der Wahrheit" (33).[88] Not only Keats but a number of poets and philosophers discussed beauty and truth almost as interchangeable; indeed it was the interface between the disciplines of aesthetics and moral philosophy, both being occupied with the perfectibility of humanity and human character. Indeed the pedagogical power of literature in the eighteenth century was seen in terms of claims to truth; in the enlightened circles it was usually enough that moral truth was beauty, to see it the other way around probably took a Romantic like Keats.[89] But in spite of Heidegger's constructing his own premises in order to reject them, one thing remains clear – his absolute rejection of *mimesis* as a reproduction or representation of reality: "Meinen wir, das

---

[87]   "But perhaps the proposition that art is truth setting itself to work intends to revive the fortunately obsolete view that art is an imitations and depiction of reality? The reproduction of what exists requires, to be sure, agreement with the actual being, adaptation to it; the Middle Ages called it *adaequatio*; Aristotle already spoke of *homoiosis*. Agreement with what *is* has long been taken to be the essence of truth (36-37).

[88]   "But until now art presumably has had to do with the beautiful and beauty, and not with truth" (36).

[89]   Although Shaftesbury had been bold enough to claim in his *Sensus communis*: "For all beauty is TRUTH" (120).

Gemälde entnehme dem Wirklichen ein Abbild und versetze die in ein Produkt der künstlerischen... Produktion? Keineswegs" (34).[90]

Heidegger is absolutely sure that the work of art, even if produced through a movement from a source (which for him is of course not the empirical object, although he needs one), is not an "Abbild" of reality and/or simply a product of the artist's production. His origin of the work of art is art that constitutes itself from its own source, which he does not name divinity but which has a mystical touch to it. His way of differentiating artistic creation from classical notions of *mimesis* is not very "original". Neither in his adaptation of the Longinian paradigm with all the philosophical discursive additions nor his simple cut between truth and beauty as if aesthetics up to that point had only been occupied with the latter. For, as Jacques Derrida states, "mimesis, all through the history of its interpretation, is always commanded by the process of truth" (179). This is taken from "The Double Session" in *Dissemination,* one of several of his texts which are occupied with the notion of *mimesis,* and indeed other referential operations among which language itself must be counted as well. What is important in this context is the way in which Derrida examines two aspects of the terms used in connection with translation (problems):

1. either, even before it can be translated as imitation, *mimēsis* signifies the presentation of the thing itself, of nature, of the physis that produces itself, engenders itself, and appears (to itself) as it really is, in the presence of its image, its visible aspect, its *mimeisthai,* reveals as much as it hides. *Mimēsis* is then the movement of the *phusis,* a movement that is somehow natural (in the nonderivative sense of this word), through which the *phusis,* having no outside, no other, must be doubled in order to make its appearance, to appear (to itself), to produce (itself), to unveil (itself); in order to emerge from the crypt where it prefers itself; in order to shine in its *alētheia.* In this sense, *mnēmē* and *mimēsis* are on a par, since *mnēmē* too is an unveiling (an unforgetting), *alētheia* (193, emphasis in text).[91]

Derrida's doubling is creative in its unveiling of the hidden, a very Heideggerian move without the same consequences, as the reiterated but parenthesised

---

[90] "Is it our opinion that the painting draws a likness from something actual and transposes it into a product of artistic—production? By no means" (37).

[91] "1. ou bien elle signifie, avant même de pouvoir être traduite par imitation, la présentation de la chose même, de la nature, de la *physis* qui se produit, s'engendre et (s') apparaît telle qu'elle est, dans la présence de son image, de son aspect visible, dans son visage : le masque théâtral, en tant que référence essentielle du *mimesthai,* révèle autant qu'il cache. La *mimesis* est alors le mouvement de la *physis,* mouvement en quelque sorte naturel (au sens non dérivé de ce mot) par lequel la *physis,* n'ayant ni autre ni dehors, doit se dédoubler pour apparaître, (s') apparaître, (se) produire, (se) dévoiler, pour sortir de la crypte où elle se préfère, pour briller dans son *aletheia.* En ce sens, *mnémè* et *mimesis* vont de pair, puis *mnémè* est aussi dévoilement (non-oubli), *aletheia*" (237).

(itself) bears witness to. First and foremost, Derrida accepts the term and its idea, whereas Heidegger rejects it explicitly, as we have seen above: the Greek (or at least the Aristotelian as well as the medieval) version is simply no good; perhaps an example of his own thesis of the "'Bodenlosigkeit des abendländischen Denkens'"?

Heidegger, interestingly, mentions both Aristotle and the medieval notions in his dismissive sentence quoted above. As I have argued, the ideological stance towards translation hinges on the (Horatian) "translation" Heidegger claims is responsible for the "Bodenlosigkeit" (absence-of-ground) of Western culture. Derrida also hinges his definition on that definitive break, the source of the *translatio* in the broadest sense:

> 2. or else, *mimēsis* sets up a relation of *homoiōsis* or *adaequatio* between the two (terms). In that case it can more readily be translated as imitation. This translation seeks to express (or rather historically produces) the thought about this relation. The two faces are separated and set face to face: the imitator and the imitated, the latter being none other than the thing or the meaning of the thing itself, its manifest presence. A good imitation will be one that is true, faithful, like or likely, adequate, in conformity with the *phusis* (essence or life) of what is imitated; it effaces itself of its own accord in the process of restoring freely, and hence in a living manner, the freedom of true presence (193, emphasis in text).[92]

Derrida stresses that in "each case *mimēsis* has to follow the process of truth" (193). The two modes he presents are very much in key with the dual notion born with the Roman "translation" of the idea of *mimesis*, which so effectively removed translation in the act of translation out of the equation. Derrida's second definition, on the other hand, could well be used as a definition for translation; certainly the vocabulary connected to such definitions old and new is there: "true, faithful, like or likely, adequate, in conformity with", etc. And yet translation is not fully there, or only implicitly as a linguistic referential operation. The part about "effacement" is indeed in key with Venuti's "invisibility", but somehow translation is not fully present, or at least only traceable through the terms usually applied to it; perhaps Derrida himself has forgotten translation.

---

[92]   "2. ou bien *mimesis* met un rapport d'*homoiosis* ou d'*adaequatio* entre deux (termes). Elle se laisse alors plus facilement traduire par imitation. Cette traduction veut dire (ou plutôt produit historiquement) la pensée de ce rapport. Les deux faces se séparent en vis-à-vis : l'imitant et l'imité, celui-ci n'étant autre que la chose ou le sens de la chose même, sa présence en manifestation. La bonne imitation sera l'imitation vraie, fidèle, ressemblante ou vraisemblable, conforme, adéquate à la *physis* (essence ou vie) de l'imité ; elle s'efface d'elle-même en restituant librement, et donc de manière vivante, la liberté de la présence vraie" (237-8).

If he has, he is certainly not alone, but it is noteworthy that the notion of *mimesis* was itself not very visible during the age of originality. Auerbach's *Mimesis* is a good example, of course. When the book was published in 1946, the author was certainly not following a "trend" in choosing its title. As Bernhard F. Scholz notes in a preface to a recent collection of essays bearing the same title, Auerbach

> konnte [...] wohl kaum erwarten, daß der von ihm gewählte alte Begriff der Mimesis, der allenfalls noch Platon- und Aristoteles-Spezialisten geläufig war, noch einmal, und zwar aufgrund des Erfolgs seines Buches, zum Ausgangspunkt für die moderne Diskussion zum Problem der Repräsentation werden sollte (7).[93]

The first thing to note is that the term was forgotten, unused except by specialists. This is undoubtedly due to the fact that the age of originality had repressed all ideas of "imitation", let alone "translation" as belonging to the arts. Auerbach's subtitle perhaps throws some light on this: "Dargestellte Wirklichkeit in der abendländischen Literatur". This subtitle, which is of course a translation of the title, the concept *mimesis* and the two millennia of discourse behind it, including Auerbach's own, is continually mentioned by scholars who refer to Auerbach's work. Their problem lies in the defining frame of a translation of a definition, the way in which the translation itself unintentionally manipulates the concept and thus creates the problem of definition – perhaps an instance of Heidegger's "Bodenlosigkeit", the lack of the exact Greek experience behind the "word" that makes its meaning. On the other hand, as we have seen, not even Plato and Aristotle agreed on that point.

Other scholars in Scholz's volume harp on the problem of definition; Gottfried Gabriel does not see the "lack of theoretical reflection on the relation between reality and literature [as] necessarily a symptom of insensibility for certain problems" but rather that Auerbach considered it "obvious [...] that we have access to reality [and] that literature makes an essential contribution to this access" (35). Gabriel, whose intention is to disqualify scepticism and postmodern criticism *per se* by leaning on the authority of Kant, uses the oft-noted subtitle to round off his essay:[94]

---

[93] "Auerbach could hardly expect that the old term he selected, Mimesis, which was mostly known only among specialists in Aristotle and Plato, would become again, due to the success of his book, the starting point for the modern discussion on the problem of representation" (my translation). The full German title is *Mimesis: Studien zur literarischen Repräsentation.*

[94] Although he says at one point that the "post-modern view is, therefore, nothing more than an exaggeration of the modern view" (38). The modern view here refers to Kant; Gabriel differentiates between Kant's notion of construction and post-modernist views of fiction (his terminology), whereby it is not easy to discern whether there is an overlap or not.

Looking at our author Auerbach, it should be mentioned here that the original subtitle of his book (*"Dargestellte Wirklichkeit"*) might be better understood as "presented reality" than "represented reality". At least the factual translation "Representation *of* Reality", which implies a possible separation of reality from its mode of representation seems to be misleading (42).

Gabriel's use of translation to get at the author's meaning is in itself not remarkable, and indeed such application is at the basis of all definition. And, as a matter of fact, it is constructed via translation. More remarkable is the idea that he seemed to be refuting earlier, that fictional representation as (part of) constructed representation (in the Kantian form), is present in this welding of "presentation" and "reality".

Margit Sutrop and Frank Zipfel also discuss the terminological problem in their essays and both are, like their colleague Gabriel, interested in rejecting the "postmodern criticism of the concept of representation in Western literature" (46). Zipfel's essay is particularly interesting in this context, as it presents an attempt at "rescuing" one of the French theorists who, rightly or wrongly, has sometimes been consigned to a (French) postmodernist "school", namely Gérard Genette. In his "Nachahmung – Darstellung – Fiktion?" Zipfel painstakingly analyses the problems of terminology and definition. Considering the fact that he is explicitly attacking postmodern criticism, both his method and results are surprising.[95] The premise is that "Genette erweist sich in diesen Schriften als ein Literaturwissenschaftler, dessen Überlegungen mit sorgfältig ausgearbeiteten Begriffsunterscheidungen verbunden sind" (165).[96] This is a premise that most scholars, modern and postmodern, would subscribe to, only from a different perspective, and it is clear that Genette is a scholar who is certainly interested in terminology; his own contribution to the conceptual reservoir of literary criticism is not only a proof of his success, but also the focus of his researches.

But Zipfel's premise misses an important part of Genette's own style, his irony and indeed the self-deprecatory humour with which he discusses his own previous definitions and results; an example is the opening of *Palimpsests,* which represents a revision of a previous definition, but even that does not seem to be stable, for he gives the exact date of this new definition, claiming to *believe* on October 13, 1981 that there are five types of transtextuality; one almost expects him to give the time of day as well (1).[97] The first of these definitions is

---

[95]   See for example page 172 and particularly note 18 where he rejects Christopher Prendergast's inclusion of Genette in the company of Barthes, Kristeva and Derrida (183). Jonathan Culler, on the other hand, claims in his "Foreword" to Genette's *Narrative Discourse* that it is "one of the central achievements of what was called 'structuralism'" (8).

[96]   "In these writings, Genette comes forth as a literary critic whose contemplations are supported by a thoroughly differentiated terminology" (my translation).

[97]   Page numbers refer to the English translation.

Kristeva's term "intertextuality", which he, however, defines in a more concrete sense than Kristeva herself would prefer.[98] The whole discussion is seriously ironic, for example the footnote on the term "paratext" refers to it as ambiguous and hypocritical, and when he speaks of "metatexts" Genette notes that "transtextuality" is a form of transcendence, an opposite of immanence, he "believe[s]" (430).

Genette's discussion on imitation in Chapter 14 concludes with an almost chatty dialogue with the reader on terminology before he says that the term "mimetism" will have to do (*Palimpsests* 81). Such moments, not to forget the joking comment on the table of contents, or the ironic postscript of the second edition, dated April 13, 1983, in which he expressly underlines mistakes other authors would have silently corrected, do not allow for an interpretation of his terminology or conclusions that is in key with German conventions in critical discourse.[99] In fact, his concluding remarks in *Palimpsests* do discuss two structuralisms, rejecting neither, and in the end he highlights the duality of the object (not the subject); the author quoted twice in these closing remarks is Borges, and the quote from "Pierre Menard, Author of the Quixote" includes not only the concept with which Genette titled his book, but also one of Derrida's key concepts perfectly expressed: "I have reflected that it is legitimate to see the "final" Quixote as a kind of palimpsest, in which the traces – faint but not indecipherable – of our friend's "previous" text must shine through" (*Fictions* 95).[100] Borges finds a similar solution to Roscommon's for the sympathetic translator: "Unfortunately, only a second Pierre Menard, reversing the labors of the first, would be able to exhume and revive those Troys..." (95).

---

[98] See Kristeva's *Revolutions in Poetic Language*, Chapter 8, where she is indeed discussing "mimesis". She shows irritation at the traditional use of the term "intertextuality", for she is referring to a process or a "*passage from one sign system to another*" (59). This is what she prefers to call transposition rather than intertextuality: "The term *inter-textuality* denotes this transposition of one (or several) sign systems into another: but since this term has often been understood in the banal sense of "study of sources," we prefer the term *transposition* because it specifies that the passage from one signifying system to another demands a new articulation of the thetic—of enunciative and denotative positionality" (59-60). Kristeva's defence of her own invention is probably a lost battle and it shows perhaps best that the passage of "intertextuality" from her own pages did not happen in the way she denoted it.

[99] The hiatus between the interpretation and original is in itself an interesting translational problem. When "translating" Genette into German literary critical discourse, Zipfel takes the native tradition for granted and does not consider the discursive differences that the German translator certainly managed to produce.

[100] Benjamin may be traced here: "Die wahre Übersetzung ist *durchscheinend*, sie verdeckt nicht das Original, steht ihm nicht im Licht, sondern läßt die reine Sprache, wie verstärkt durch ihr eigenes Medium, nur um so voller auf Original fallen (151, my emphasis).

It also appears that Zipfel's premise only served his argument in another direction, for although he praises Genette for his "sorgfältig ausgearbeitete[n] Begriffsunterscheidungen", he is forced to admit that "[l]eider wird festzustellen sein, daß in diesem Falle [his interpretation of *mimesis*] auch bei Genette die Interpretationen vielfältig und die Verwendungsweisen zum Teil uneinheitlich sind" (166).[101] Actually, as Zipfel rightly notes, the term is extremely vague after two thousand years of use and the fact that it has been used in several fields of discourse has not sharpened its contours. The question remains of whether it possesses the potential towards the simplification Zipfel desires, or rather claims, for literary criticism, and whether it is correct to embark, as he does, on a deconstruction of Genette's use of the term, to rescue him from the deconstructionist school and to undermine this school at the same time. In the end, his "deconstructive" method is a palimpsest of Genette's own irony.

Last but not least in the discussion on Auerbach's subtitle, or if you will, translation, is another German literary critic, Peter Pütz. In his *Leistung der Form. Lessings Dramen* he discusses the term "Darstellung" and relates it to Auerbach's subtitle, which he claims thus avoids the "mißverständliche Übersetzung in >>Nachahmung<<, indem er sowohl das Objekt der Darstellung als auch deren formende Tätigkeit hervorhebt und somit der irrigen Annahme bloßer Wirklichkeitsdoppelung vorbaut" (18).[102] With regards to translation, this seems to be overstated, because Auerbach does occasionally use the term "Nachahmung" synonymously with the Greek term and the subtitle, for example in Chapter VIII, "Farinata und Cavalcanti", and more importantly, in the opening words of his "Nachwort", where he formulates the research object of his work (177):

Der Gegenstand dieser Schrift, die Interpretation des Wirklichen durch literarische Darstellung oder >>Nachahmung<<, beschäftigt mich schon sehr lange; es war ursprünglich die platonische Fragestellung im 10. Buch des Staates, die Mimesis als Drittes nach der Wahrheit, in Verbindung mit Dantes Anspruch, in der Komödie wahre Wirklichkeit zu geben, von der ich ausging (515).[103]

---

[101] "Unfortunately it must be said that in this case Genette offers several interpretations and his application is partly inconsistent" (my translation).

[102] "...misleading translation of "Nachahmung" [imitation], which foregrounds both the object of representation and its forming activity and thus the erronous belief of a reconstructed reality" (my translation).

[103] "The subject of this book, the interpretation of reality through literary representation or "imitation," has occupied me for a long time. My original starting point was Plato's discussion in book 10 of the *Republic*—mimesis ranking third after truth—in conjunction with Dante's assertion that in the *Commedia* he presented true reality" (Trask 554).

This is as close as Auerbach comes to an explicit definition of the concept, a fact often noted by scholars, although one could also try and see the whole volume of over 500 pages of detailed analysis of Western literature from Homer's *Odyssey* to Virginia Woolf's *To the Lighthouse* as a discursive definition of a subject too complex to be reduced to a sentence.

Pütz underlines his argument by citing another translation of the concept in Olof Gigon's translation of Aristotle's *Poetics,* the first Chapter, where Aristotle differentiates between "künstlerischer und nichtkünstlerischer Darbietung" [artistic and non-artistic presentation] (18). Again movement comes to the fore, whereby Pütz claims that

> Das darlegende Ausführen wird von einem einzigen Zentrum aus gesteuert und orientiert sich an nichts anderem als an der verantwortlichen Instanz dessen, der ausführt. Mimesis als Darstellung hat dagegen nicht nur ein einziges Ausgangszentrum, sondern sie ist stets bezogen auf das, was dargestellt wird und was in der Übersetzung >>nachgeahmt<< überdeutlich und verzerrt zum Ausdruck kommt (18-19).[104]

This claim is also very clear and puts the whole mimetic operation into the hands of a single "centre" in an attempt that might boldly dissolve all pre-texts, forms and even historical events, were it not for the afterthought that follows: "Festzuhalten bleibt allerdings, daß dem >>Nach-<< ein Vorgegebenes zugrunde liegt, an dem die Mimesis Maß nimmt" (19).[105] Pütz's differentiation of "Darstellung" and "Darlegung" in what follows is based on Aristotle's differentiation, the novelty being a translational improvement of the concept. "Darstellung", then, is *mimesis* "proper", or representation, resulting in a work of art of which "Darlegung" is an interpretation, or rather an interpretative representation. The time factor plays a role, insofar as Pütz makes it a point of difference in order to claim that "Darlegung" fulfills the role of a secondary text and indeed is parasitically dependent on the work of art: "Ohne die zeitliche Priorität des Kunstwerks wäre die Darlegung kaum imstande, die an ihm nachzuvollziehende Erkenntnis zu gewinnen und zu artikulieren" (20).[106] It could be argued against this, that some works of art *need* interpretation (in a broad sense) if their "Erkenntnis" is to be articulated at all. The examples abound: almost everybody

---

[104] "The interpretative representation is directed from a single centre and is only accountable to the instances of the one that represents. Mimesis as representation has, on the other hand, not a single point of departure, but always refers to what is being represented and which in the translation as "imitation" comes through as overclear and distorted" (my interpretation).

[105] "The fact remains, however, that before the "Nach" [after] something given resides, which constitutes a measure for the mimesis" (my interpretation).

[106] "Without the temporal precedence of the work of art, interpretation would hardly be able to extract and articulate the knowledge that can be grasped in it" (my translation). To which I firmly agree.

needs Homer in translation, even with a knowledge of ancient Greek, which in any case is not a living nor any reader's native language (which Pütz's argumentation in essence presupposes). The cultural context of all ancient, medieval and any texts more than a few years old is different than that of the receiver, native or foreign. Even canonised texts such as Shakespeare's often carry half a page of footnotes on every page for native speakers.

On the other hand, Pütz is not trying to dismiss "Interpretation" or "Darlegung", only attempting to define it by establishing what it is not in relation to "Darstellung" which he claims deserves what he calls the "kognitive Primat" (19). "Darlegung" is only a fragment and does not claim to be more, with perhaps an interesting exception:

> Die Interpretation erhebt nicht den Anspruch, die komplexen Bedeutungen der Darstellung auf der Ebene einer einsinnigen und allzeit gültigen Darlegung zu reduzieren, was dem Erkenntnischarakter von Kunst sogar zuwiderliefe und ihren Vorsprung mißbrauchen hieße. Auf Totalität verzichtend und zu Partikularität verurteilt, kann darlegende Interpretation lediglich vereinzelte Abschattungen darstellender Erkenntnis nachvollziehen, und zwar immer nur in den Grenzen ihres vielfältig bedingten Standorts. Eine adäquate Erfassung der ganzen Darstellung ist – wenn überhaupt – nur zu leisten in der zeitlich unabsehbaren Geschichte ihrer Rezeption, d.h. in der allenfalls fiktiv zu denkenden Gesamtheit ihrer darlegenden Deutungen, wobei dieses Ziel nicht schon als Summe aller einzelner Auslegungen, sondern erst als geschlossene Gestalt erreichbar wäre. Die >>endgültige<< Darlegung müßte die Form einer Darstellung haben (21).[107]

There is no *summum bonum* of interpretation, obviously, but the relation is clear; the "original" incorporates in its totality a knowledge potential that can be partially realised through interpretation, but hardly fully, except in the "Form einer Darstellung", which is, as we have seen, also the thesis of Borges' narrator in "Pierre Menard". This raises the question of whether Pütz is referring to a hermeneutic circle that ends and begins in a repetition, a copy, or a utopian ideal of a perfect rewriting, a translation that is more than the inadequate Platonic shadow of an original. Perhaps this is to be done in translations without origi-

---

[107] "The interpretation does not claim to be able to reduce the complex meanings of the representation to the level of an unambiguous and final interpretative representation, which would even be against the character of art as knowledge and abuse its advantage. By disclaiming totality and being confined to particularity, interpretative representation is only able to grasp individual shades of representative knowledge and that always and only within the parameters of its position. An adequate grasp of the whole representation is, if at all, only possible in the temporally unforeseeable history of its reception, i.e. at best in a fictively conceived entirety of its representative interpretations, whereby this goal could not be achieved through a sum of all individual interpretations, but only as a fully closed *Gestalt*. The "authoritative" interpretative representation would have to be in the form of a representation" (my translation).

nals, in works that not only translate but add knowledge to the original, are not interpretations but take the potential further into a realm of the truly new, breaking out of the synchronic hermeneutic circle as if it were a vicious one, creating a virtuous one for the time being.

The only problem might be the denial of the original "original", the operation that denies the reference for what it is, a translation, repetition, intertextuality, transposition, transformation, but this denial of truth may be its only claim to its own truth and knowledge; without this denial it cannot be *experienced* as knowledge, as truth. So the artist is forced to lie in order to tell the truth. This seems to be the direction Pütz takes when he, perhaps consistently, leans on Peter Handke's twisting of Plato's notions of *mimesis* and truth in an Aristotelian manner. Pütz refers to the latter's conclusion that poetry is more philosophical and true than history; he presents Handke's version thus:

> Das Erzählen hat nicht nur eine kommunikative, sondern auch eine kognitive Funktion, und zwar – so paradox es scheinen mag – kraft seiner Fiktionalität. Darüber reflektierend fragt sich Handke: >>Ist nicht ohnehin jedes Formulieren, auch von etwas tatsächlich Passiertem, mehr oder weniger fiktiv? *Weniger*, wenn man sich genügt, bloß Bericht zu erstatten; *mehr*, je genauer man zu formulieren versucht?<< Diese Zuordnungen bedürfen der Erläuterung, da der Begriff des Genauen offensichtlich äquivok verwendet wird. Im naturwissenschaftlichen Sinne bedeutet er Exaktheit, die – so Handke – ein hohes Maß an Fiktionalität erfordert (30).[108]

The scholar is of course moved by Handke's use of "genauer" and renders this use equivocal, although it is probably intended by Handke to be exactly in harmony with his version of a knowledge that goes back to Aristotle, but which one can find in Oscar Wilde's "The Decay of Lying" and Milan Kundera's *The Art of the Novel*.[109] Handke's "exactness" is precisely the fictive, artistic expression that goes beyond the "Darlegung" of an event. It is the necessarily added truth that turns fact into knowledge. As Heidegger puts it in his *Plato's Lehre von der Wahrheit*:

---

[108] "Narration has not only a communicative, but a cognitive function as well, and indeed—paradoxical as it may seem—through its fictionality. Reflecting upon this, Handke asks himself: 'Is not every formulation, also of something that actually happened, more or less fictive? *Less,* when one is satisfied with mere reporting; *more,* the more exactly one tries to formulate?' This categorisation needs to be explained, since the conception of exactness is obviously equivocally applied. In the scientific sense it stands for an exactness that—according to Handke—requires a great measure of fictionality" (my translation). The quote from Handke is from his *Wunschloses Unglück* (26). (Page 24 in the first edition). The final words of Handke's "memories" of his mother contain a promise that "später werde ich über das alles Genaueres schreiben" [later I will write more exactly about all of this] (105).

[109] "Knowledge is the novel's only morality" (6). See also my *Damit wir wissen, was sie geschrieben haben* (26).

Die Erkenntnisse der Wissenschaften werden gewöhnlich in Sätzen ausgesprochen und dem Menschen als greifbare Ergebnisse zur Verwendung vorgesetzt. Die >>Lehre<< eines Denkers ist das in seinem Sagen Ungesagte, dem der Mensch ausgesetzt wird, auf daß er dafür sich verschwende.

Damit wir das Ungesagte eines Denkers, welcher Art er auch sei, erfahren und inskünftig wissen können, müssen wir sein Gesagtes bedenken. Dieser Forderung recht genügen, hieße, alle >>Gespräche<< Platons in ihrem Zusammenhang durchsprechen. Weil dies unmöglich ist, soll ein anderer Weg auf das in Platons Denken Ungesagte zuleiten (5). [110]

It is probably not overstatement to say that Heidegger includes at least poets in his concept of "Denker", but that is in itself not crucial; what is, is the simulacric constellation of the "unsaid" and "fictional", the truth as a fact beyond the facts that has to be sought for and created during that search. The renewal of reality can then follow when the facts are reinterpreted with the aid of the desire of knowing what one does not know, the desire that Diotima told Socrates in the *Symposium* (and he Agathon) was at the basis of love; as soon as it has been fulfilled there can be no desire anymore.

What makes the desire strong is the lack of transparency. The wish to know what is beyond the known has been the major drive of human epistemological desire, the mystery being the battlefield of (humanist) humanity and the divine. And now, when the limits of knowledge have almost been reached, when the divine unknown has, as Nietzsche prophesied, lost the battle, humanity stands before the frightening moral questions previously delegated to divinity, i.e., what to do with knowledge of the world from its outer limits of space to its inner core of genes.

It is not a new moment in history, but one that recurs when humans become victims of their own hubris and think they know everything, and that they are able to control nature through that knowledge. As always, they forget themselves, the cause of all instability, and forget that all transparency is imagined, the true folly of security that imagines everything can be translated into meaning and that all fictions have been interpreted. The feeling that there is an end – the end of history, first prophesied in the Bible, but also by Hegel and Fukuyama among others; the end of work (Rifkin); the end of humanism (Sloterdijk) – is prevalent, but perhaps all these endings can be translated into the end of truth as truth. That would also mean the end of imitation, beginning it anew.

---

[110] "The knowledge of science is usually expressed in sentences and presented to people as understandable results for use. The 'learning' of a thinker is the unsaid in what is said and which people are exposed to so that they can waste themselves for it.
So that we can experience and know therefrom the unsaid of a thinker, of any type, we must attend to what he says. To do this demand justice would mean to speak through all of Plato's 'dialogues' in their context. Since this is impossible, another route into Plato's unsaid needs to be taken" (my attempted translation).

2.8 Translation of Power and Dreams

Perhaps the fear of imitation represents a fear of language, the power of language being the only thing that can make one, push one, to do something, anything, for somebody else. The literary anxiety of influence (Bloom) is perhaps more an anxiety of language, natively powerful as a sublime manifestation and sublimely frightening as a foreign power. We have visual dreams in order to escape the logic of language.[111]

2.9 Translation as a *tertium comparationis*

Metaphor is the translation of a vision into words. Imitation is the translation of a reality into words. Words are the primal instrument of power. Communication is power.

Of the trio of translation, imitation and metaphor, translation is a kind of *tertium comparationis*, an operative element that makes possible the connection between a vision and its metaphor, between a reality and its imitation. Metaphors, the textual manifestations of imitations, have been translated from their non-verbal state, formed to the logic of language through the act of translation. That this method could be applied to move these objects across the hurdles of different languages is what truly made humanity godlike; for it is the ultimate rebellion against the curse of the tower of Babel and in itself a new spiritual version of that tower, a tower of translation. It is the way in which Christ the human God made his word known through his apostles, translators of words into many languages and not of visions into one language as the previous prophets had been.

In the moment of conclusion, when Umberto Eco, in effect, admits that his search for the perfect language has foundered, he comes to translation as a kind of *tertium comparationis*: "If such a *tertium* really existed, it would be a perfect language; if it did not exist, it would remain a mere postulate on which every translation ought to depend" (346). He has no alternative, however, and in a work published multilingually (in translation) in a series called "The Making of Europe" he nobly, if rather lamely, argues for "a community of peoples with an increased ability to receive the spirit, to taste or savour the aroma of different dialects" (351). These people, claims Eco, should not necessarily know many languages perfectly, but rather be able to understand each other through passive understanding of the other's language. This is like a kind of dream which imagines an Italian speaking his native language to an Englishman who understands Italian and answers in English, a language the Italian understands. This Utopia leaves out the necessity of translation, and holds desperately to the native language at the same time.

---

[111] My *mimesis*.

But it is only possible to retain the native language through translation; a dialogue in two languages can, at best, be conducted by experienced translators or through the mediation of an interpreter; dialogues always interact with the already said and thus translation would be central, even in a dialogue between the kind of Europeans Eco introduces. As long as there are different languages, translation will be the substitute, if not the perfect language. It is the human answer to the divine wrath of Babel.

2.10 Translation as a Genetic Metaphor

The modern successors to the Old Testament prophets and the New Testament apostles are the geneticists who are learning the language of God as written in the human cell.[112] As soon as they have mastered it, they will be able to control the translation of that language and that means that they will be able not only to clone human beings and thus produce an identical copy of a human being, an imitation, but what is more powerful, more dangerous, they will be able to manipulate the translation of the genetic language and truly create a new species, a new original. Through the most radical and microscopic of all acts of translation, Frankenstein, originally a pathological metaphor, has finally been translated into a real possibility.

2.11 Translation as Reproduction

Translation is an act of reproduction in two senses. It reproduces a text in another language, another culture, another world, and at the same time it begets it with the previous text. Geneticists have therefore chosen the right term, translation, to describe one of the most important operations of reproduction within the cell. But ordinary, mundane sexual reproduction is also a sort of translation in this sense, the combination of two different codes to create a third that is formed only of what the parent codes have contributed.[113]

This is how sexual nature operates and how we prefer things; it is the way we see something as "new". This is best proven when one examines the relationship between the previous and the following. If identical, the following is automatically detested; it is only a repetition and nothing new. In the antiquarian bookshop, the second edition of a book is almost always worth less than the first, and anyone knows the difference in price between an original painting and a copy, even if both are made by the same artist. But at the same time paradox

---

[112] The metaphor is Bill Clinton's, I believe. It is not coincidental in this context. The language of genetics abounds with terms like "translation", "transcription", etc. This metaphorical vocabulary refers to the procreative activity within the cell. Cf. the section "Translation and Definition" above.

[113] A possible interpretation would be to name femininity *logos* and masculinity *lexis*.

raises its head, for in the case of a painting, the copy is not only worth less than the original, but if made by the same artist it will reduce the value of the original. When someone else produces the copy, however, then the copying is an act that may even raise the price of the original, for why should one copy a second-rate work? When reproduced in a book, the copy of a painting is as good as worthless in itself and yet in that form probably raises the fame and worth of the original; it has displaced it in reality and raised its spiritual relevance.

The same can be said of books; in the end, the nth edition may be worth little more than its raw production costs and at the same time displace the original object. The reverence with which we handle, say a Manuscript of Goethe's *Faust,* as opposed to our carefree treatment of a cheap paperback edition, illustrates this very well, and yet both texts include the same words in the same order; they are identical in what we seek in them. Or are they?

Similar reasons might keep most people from reproducing themselves through the act of cloning, not the fact that they find it morally reprehensible, because it simply is not, when considered as a moral issue. The fear of the exact copy is probably stronger, for it kills the original through its likeness. The sameness dissolves individuality and makes the masses manipulable; this fear is expressed by Oscar Wilde's quip that "all women become like their mothers. That is their tragedy" (*Plays* 270) and Simone de Beauvoir's dictum in *The Second Sex* that the double assassinates the original through sameness (600).[114]

And translation in the banal sense of textual transfer? In an age of originality, it works the same way as the copy made by another artist, even more so. A translation not only raises more money for a copyrighted text, but also increases its literary or spiritual worth. This is achieved through the coeval sameness and difference as well as through greater distribution. Translation works as procreation metaphorically masqueraded as cloning with only the language gene changed.

In our current social and reproductive terms, translation produces the legitimate children of marriage, begotten within acceptable norms securing that the offspring will be formed according to the standards of bourgeois society. Art, on the other hand, begets the illegitimate children of illicit love whose formation may be impossible to manage with the instruments of bourgeois society. As Aldous Huxley foresaw in *Brave New World*, only the latter is endangered by the absolutism of information.

---

[114]   Indeed, de Beauvoir refers to Wilde's *The Picture of Dorian Gray.*

2.12　Translation as Canon

What would the three constitutive works of the "Western Canon" (Bloom), *The Iliad, The Odyssey* and the *Bible,* be without translation?[115] The answer is not nothing, but relatively unknown or, at best, retold and rewritten. Even humanistic education since the Renaissance has not produced great numbers of Greek and Hebrew scholars who could really tackle these works in the original (what originals would they have had?). Their interpretations would have been – and are, no doubt – learned and important, but only for them and their peers; the rest of the world, poets rewriting and readers reliving, would not have been influenced to a great extent. The hypothetical question above is justified because it sheds light on the reception of works that have been given universal artistic and religious (hence canonical) status and that have been read in one translation or another by most of their readers. The Bible was, furthermore, long read in a translation into a language already dead; St. Jerome's *Vulgate* was not only a translation, but read in the readers' second or third language.

The question of translation and canon is complex. Firstly, the concepts seem to be almost inseparable, which is perhaps not surprising, for it is through biblical translation that the question of canonising texts becomes relevant. Secondly, translation is also a significant criterion for the potential canonicity of a work of literature: it becomes canonical, to a great extent, through translation. Authors are eager to be translated and if they have been, the publishers are sure to mention that in a blurb on the jacket of the next edition or book. Thirdly, as has been noted, many authors have tried to authenticate an inaccessible (often literally inaccessible!) text by calling it a translation. This looks like a canonising appearance of which the famous pseudotranslations are great examples, as are fictive texts whose authors cleverly, if perversely, use the stamp of translation to create a distance from the mimetic straitjacket of plain "representation". Finally, canon is related to language from various perspectives: a) to become "canonised" or escape the margin, a minor language must translate the key canonised texts of the hegemonic cultural sphere; b) a major language uses translation to appropriate or "colonise" the foreign, often without really wanting to "experience" it (this is how the Roman ideology of translation originates as well as the related demand for fluency, a term Venuti connects with canon in *The Translator's Invisibility*). To which it might be added that when a language has gained an almost absolute hegemony translation is drastically reduced.[116]

---

[115]　Harold Bloom lists all three in his canonical list appended to the *Western Canon.* He also chooses the translations, thus canonising certain English translations of the works.

[116]　This applies to languages of empires, for example the Roman, the British, the American.

Most of the above points have become commonplaces, and only the first and the last require further discussion.

Before going any further, it is right to consider the term *canon*. There are two points worth making in this context: the first is the fact that it came into usage in this sense in the late fourth century, contemporaneously with St. Jerome's *Vulgate;* the second is that this Greek term was then taken to signify "rule" in the sense that it ruled which texts belonged to the canon of sacred texts.[117] That this rule was established through the act of translation is clear, but if we consider the term canon in the more modern sense as a collection of the most important texts of world literature, due to their, as Harold Bloom has it, "aesthetic supremacy", the role of translation becomes less clear (16). At the risk of matriculating myself into what Bloom refers to throughout *The Western Canon* as the "School of Resentment", I propose in the following to examine some of the premises he himself gives for his conception of canon in the light of translation and national literature.

Bloom's avowed objective in *The Western Canon* is to rescue literature, literary criticism and what he terms "aesthetic value" from their manipulation and watering down by "anti-canonists" of all sorts: those who have rejected the standardised canon by focusing on ideology, class, gender and race, for example (3). He himself claims explicitly that his canon is neither ideological nor metaphysical, without, however, defining the value of his aesthetic beyond a little quote of Oscar Wilde's famous dictum that "all art is perfectly useless", which becomes a little problematic when one considers his strong, essentially Borgesian, belief that we (whoever that is) have been invented by literature, particularly by Shakespeare (16-17). Although evidently polemically intended, some of his assertions go beyond the ironic in their Johnsonian moralism and reveal the age-old paradigm of old age that the world is going down the drain, once again. This anxiety of decline is indeed strange from someone so familiar with the canon, for how can one prophesy doomsday now, after three-thousand years of success?

The greatest problem with Bloom's *Western Canon* is – pardon the repetition – precisely his canon. Bloom does not of course claim that the canon is closed and that he provides the reader with the definitive one. In his main text he leaves out the ancients and medieval authors for reasons of space and begins with Shakespeare and Dante, the latter of whom is the chronological starting point of what he terms to be the "Aristocratic Age".[118] This is in itself signifi-

---

[117] Apparently, it was first used in this sense by Athanasius of Alexandria in a letter dated 367 CE. See *OCB* on canon, apochryphal books and translation.

[118] Following Giambattista Vico in his *New Science* and in the "wake" of Joyce's *Finnegan's Wake* he divides the epochs of the Western world into a Theocratic Age (from antiquity to Dante); Aristocratic Age (from Dante to Burns); Democratic Age (from Burns to Yeats); Chaotic Age (from Yeats onwards) (1-2).

cant, for it also marked the start of literary use of native languages and perhaps the point where classical languages (Greek, Latin) ceased to function as a major canonical instrument, in the sense that only works written in or translated into these languages were canonical. The linguistic particularisation ensures the instability of the canon as can best be seen when one considers Bloom's canonical choices, both in his main text and the appendicised lists at the end of book. Of the 26 authors he discusses in the main text, 13 are English speaking; of the 140 authors listed under the "Aristocratic Age" 76 are English speaking; of the 507 listed in the "canonical prophecy" under the heading of "The Chaotic Age" 282 are English speaking (80 from Great Britain and Ireland, 7 from the West Indies, 12 from Africa, 3 from India, 8 from Canada, 11 from Australia and New Zealand and 160 from the USA). Now, it is only natural that an English-speaking critic should have greater knowledge of literature in that language, and it is clear that such a list is not final, but the notion of a *Western* canon, on the other hand, and Bloom's strong language in its favour, indicates a closure of some sort, a closure based on "aesthetic values" beyond native language that includes a "roughly quantifiable aspect", as Bloom himself claims (37).

To compare, one can look at a recent essay by Andreas F. Kelletat in which he examines the German canons of World literature as published in the 1960s and 70s:

> Die "Meisterwerke der Literatur" wurden in sieben Sprachen verfaßt, die eine Hälfte jener Werke wurde auf Deutsch geschrieben, die andere Hälfte verteilte sich recht gleichmäßig auf die Sprachen Griechisch, Lateinisch, Italienisch, Französisch, Englisch und Russisch (*Jahrbuch* 367).[119]

As the quote indicates, the objective here was to examine which languages were "canonised" in collections of "world literature", but it also reveals the fact that another "Western canon" (which even includes the ancients) in another language claims about 50% of its contents for literature in the native language. At one point Bloom states directly that his defence of the canon "is in no way a defense of the West or a nationalist enterprise", but even if one accepts this, it is clear that nation and native language have a considerable influence on the content of a canon. On the other hand, even such "nationally" oriented canons are bound to have certain overlaps, but these are again dictated by linguistic knowledge and/or translation.[120]

---

[119] "The "Masterpieces of world literature" were written in seven languages, half of them in German, the other half is quite evenly distributed between Greek, Latin, Italian, French, English and Russian" (my translation).

[120] As has been noted, Bloom often names certain translations of the foreign texts he canonises, but not in all cases, even within the same language.

It is of course the overlap, where the true canon and translation are coeval if not inseparable, that is of greatest interest, for it represents versions of the platonic *logos* which seems to be at the back of many translation theories, perhaps because of the feeling one has that the linguistic "object" is at the same time pre- and postlexical, indeed almost prelingual. Benjamin calls it "Aura" in his *Das Kunstwerk im Zeitalter seiner Reproduzierbarkeit* and "Form" in "Die Aufgabe des Übersetzers" – no synonyms, but overlapping terms in the work of art, in the canonising act of translation as Benjamin describes it early on in the latter essay: "ob es seinem Wesen nach Übersetzung zulasse und demnach – der Bedeutung dieser Form gemäß – auch verlange" (157).[121] Following this, Benjamin postulates that certain works are translatable, must be translatable, only to cast doubt on it later on in the essay: "Ja [*sic*] diese Aufgabe: in der Übersetzung den Samen reiner Sprache zur Reife zu bringen, scheint niemals lösbar, in keiner Lösung bestimmbar" (164).[122] Paul de Man has noted the ironic use of "Aufgabe" in the title of Benjamin's essay and the irony of translational canonisation, comparing translation and literary criticism:

> Both criticism and translation are caught in the gesture which Benjamin calls ironic, a gesture which undoes the stability of the original by giving it a definitive, canonical form in the translation or in the theorization. In a curious way, translation canonizes its own version more than the original was canonical (*Resistance* 82).

The ironic gesture includes, therefore, the canonical act of translation or critical discussion which at the same time "de-canonizes" it by putting the original "into motion" without reproducing or imitating it (83). De Man refers here to the original text itself; one must assume that an imitation of the *logos* is another thing, as was discussed above. The question is whether the translator translates the original text or the original *logos*.

The uneasiness of this point has often been addressed, for example in George Steiner's *After Babel*. Steiner thinks that "[g]enuine translation will [...] seek to equalize", although he is of the opinion that it is in fact impossible; a position that seems to stick to a perfectly stable original with a perfectly secondary translation. But after introducing a notion of "fidelity" that is neither "literalism" nor "any technical device for rendering 'spirit'", Steiner's hermeneutic approach also allows for a "dialogue" between original and translation:

> The translator, the exegetist, the reader is *faithful to* his text, makes his response responsible, only when he endeavours to restore the balance of forces, of integral presence, which his appropriative comprehension has disrupted. Fidelity is ethical, but also, in the

---

[121] "Does its nature lend itself to translation and, therefore, in view of the significance of the mode, call for it?" (Zohn 16).

[122] "Indeed, the problem of ripening the seed of pure language in a translation seems to be insoluble, determinable in no solution" (Zohn 20).

full sense, economic. By virtue of tact, and tact intensified is moral vision, the translator-interpreter creates a condition of significant exchange. [...] There is ideally, exchange without loss (302).

The "integral presence" is another way of expressing the inexpressible of what makes a *logos* an "aura", "Form", even "spirit" (despite Steiner's protest), or what Marilyn Gaddis Rose suggests, "interliminality" (7-8). As already noted, the terms are no synonyms and yet they all refer to the intangible, if not metaphysical, aspect of literary art and indeed all art, irrespective of its form of representation. I say metaphysical, for although that term often represents what authors want to avoid when using the former terms, perhaps fearing accusations of superstition or theological ideology, it is what in the end makes literature able to be sublime, to go beyond the body in time and space, to be worthy of canonisation. Bloom certainly stresses more than once in *The Western Canon* that his position is not metaphysical, and yet he is certain that some authors, strong authors, create a *logos* (not his term) that survives translation, which is, admittedly, no metaphysics, but hardly a strictly empirical observation.[123] When discussing Shakespeare as the "center of the canon" he claims: "Clearly the phenomenon of surpassing literary excellence, of such power of thought, characterisation and metaphor that it triumphantly survives translation and transposition and compels attention in virtually every culture, does exist" (52).

This expression of universality based on individuality in what is basically a rewording of the Longinian sublime appears to have its feet on the ground, but the notions of "literary excellence" and "power of thought" are rather subjective, as any logical positivist might tartly observe. What is more important in this sentence and indeed throughout Bloom's *Western Canon* is this Benjaminian idea of translatability, of "surviving" translation, coupled with the thesis that is most often connected to Bloom's name, namely that of *anxiety of influence.*[124] There are two main strands in Bloom's theory as presented in the *Western Canon.*[125] The first is that strong authors are necessarily influenced by each other and that they react to the anxiety of being influenced by competing with their predecessors in an ongoing Olympiad where the world records of the previous laureates provide the measure. What constitutes the tension in Bloom's theory is the strong stress on originality, which he claims is counterintuitively

---

[123] Bloom's ambivalence may be detected in phrases such as: "This reduces the aesthetic to ideology, or *at best* to metaphysics" (18, my emphasis); and: "Ambivalence between the divine and the human is one of J's [first author of the Hebrew Bible] grand inventions, another mark of an originality so perpetual that we can scarcely recognize it, because the stories Bathsheba told have absorbed us" (6).

[124] As Huyssen has noted, Benjamin was not necessarily the first; the early Romantics had similar notions (150).

[125] He simplifies it, assuming knowledge of *A Map of Misreading* and *The Anxiety of Influence.*

achieved through tackling the canonical predecessors, a kind of originality through defensive imitation. As he says: "There can be no strong, canonical writing without the process of literary influence, a process vexing to undergo and difficult to understand" (8).

There are perhaps two points that are indeed difficult to understand in Bloom's theorisation here; a) how he can discuss his subject without much reference to translation, and b) the many strong authors he claims are actually not significantly influenced.[126] The two points are in fact related and before I deal with them specifically, I will quote a few of Bloom's theses to which these points refer; this is necessary for the contrast. The factor of language, particularly foreign language, should constantly be kept in mind, for it is the translingual element, so conveniently ignored and exploited, which disturbs Bloom's argument. "Poems, stories, novels, plays come into being as a response to prior poems, stories, novels, and plays, and that response depends upon acts of reading and interpretation by later writers, acts that are identical with the new works" (9). This thesis is convincing, and I am reminded of Steiner's responsible "response" above, which referred specifically to the translator, whose rewriting is of course of another nature, more controlled by an anxiety of inaccuracy. Bloom notes that the authorial influence is necessarily defensive, but when he, however, turns to language in the following, problems arise:

> The issue is not Oedipal rivalry but the very nature of strong, original literary imaginings: figurative language and its vicissitudes. Fresh metaphor, or inventive troping, always involves a departure from previous metaphor, and that departure depends upon at least partial turning away or rejection of prior figuration (9)

Bloom brings up only intralingual examples in what follows, but this surely would have deserved an interlingual examination, as metaphors and tropes borrowed from a foreign language can most certainly have the same result; indeed in standardised languages direct translation of metaphors is avoided (banned?), to keep translation in the service of fluency, as Venuti might say. This means in practice that an original metaphor might in translation be replaced by an idiomised one, when in fact this idiomised metaphor may itself have been introduced through unacknowledged translation.

One is reminded of Heidegger's "Bodenlosigkeit" when Bloom quotes the Australian poet-critic Kevin Hart (the difference being that Hart is much more optimistic than Heidegger): "Western culture takes its lexicon of intelligibility

---

[126] To be sure, Bloom does not entirely disregard translation, and he also canonises the English translations he prefers. His remarks on translations in the Chapters on Dante and Ibsen are particularly interesting, but this awareness on the part of the author of the *Map of Misreading,* who has asserted that "'interpretation' once meant 'translation' and still does" (85) and claimed in *Poetry and Repression* that "all poetry is translation", makes his blindness all the more visible (quoted in Barnstone 7 & 19).

from Greek philosophy, and all our talk of life and death, of form and design, is marked by relations with that tradition" (10). It could naturally be maintained that Hart is ambiguous in using the term "relations", but it is also clear that a "lexicon of intelligibility" implies translatability, as becomes clear from Bloom's comments, which push the point further: "Yet intelligibility pragmatically transcends its lexicon, and we must remind ourselves that Shakespeare, who scarcely relies upon philosophy, is more central to Western culture than are Plato and Aristotle, Kant and Hegel, Heidegger and Wittgenstein" (10). Of the two Shakespeare could have read – only in translation, if Ben Jonson is to be believed – it might be argued that they had and have comparable influence upon Western culture; the hyperbole shows perhaps more than anything else that Bloom's anxiety about the aesthetic as personified in Shakespeare borders on the metaphysical, if not hysterical. Moreover, the whole motivation for his book is based on an anxiety of degeneracy (his term) and a worry on behalf of what he calls the "now-threatened Western Canon" (8). He says indeed a little later on that "[t]o quarrel on its behalf is always a blunder", a statement with which I totally agree, for how can anybody really believe that Dante, Shakespeare, Goethe and Joyce are under serious institutional threat due to new-fangled theorisation? (17) Even the feminists, post-colonialists, etc., work with canonised authors, and if they deserve to be canonised, no deconstruction should be able to drive them out of their Pantheon. Bloom's defence seems to be a constructed argument to enable him to write a book about the most prominent authors of Western culture, something he is perfectly entitled to do, but it is not necessary to pretend that they are being replaced by Alice Walker or an "unknown" author like William Heinesen, even if some of them deserved it.[127]

The two points above most difficult to understand are perhaps best seen in Bloom's discussion on Shakespeare and Goethe. First it should be recorded that he claims that "[a]esthetic value is by definition engendered by an interaction between artists, an influencing that is always an interpretation" (24). As much as I agree with this, difficulty arises when it is juxtaposed with Bloom's notion of originality, which at times seems purely hierarchical, particularly when he discusses Shakespeare and dismisses the "School of Resentment": "Clearly this line of inquiry begins to border on the fantastic; how much simpler to admit that there is a *qualitative* difference, a difference in kind, between Shakespeare and every other writer, even Chaucer, even Tolstoy, or whoever" (24, emphasis in text). What this difference boils down to is indeed very simple, but somehow a problem in Bloom's whole discourse: "Originality is the great scandal that resentment cannot accommodate, and Shakespeare remains the most original writer we will ever know" (24). It must be said in this context that as a critic,

---

[127]   Although more than a worthy contender, the Faroese author Heinesen is not included in Bloom's canonical prophecy.

Bloom himself has undermined the worn-out concept of "originality" through his famous "anxiety of influence"; to be sure, he does not rule it out, but he certainly adds a new perspective and a very useful one too; influence and intertextuality are not terms of dishonour, but simply recognition of the fact of life that authors read and use what they read, and in some cases, such as Goethe's, absorb (subsume is Bloom's term) so completely that everything they lift, borrow or steal is attached to their names with reverence.

In the case of Shakespeare, his lack of originality is not necessarily the invention of the "School of Resentment"; indeed, it has not even always been seen as a lack, but rather a question of where he borrowed and how. Byron, for one, claims in a letter in 1814 to the Scottish poet and novelist James Hogg that "Shakespeare's name, you may depend on it, stands absurdly too high and will go down. He had no invention as to stories, none whatever" (84). There is of course a touch of irony there, particularly from the future author of *Don Juan* and *Cain,* and Bloom and many others would of course dismiss this as an irreverent joke, not addressing the point of true originality as sublimity, "power of thought" and so on. But Shakespeare's lack of originality has by no means been the greatest problem of Shakespeare scholarship; this position has been reserved for his "lack of learning", or the remark in Ben Jonson's memorial poem that Shakespeare had had "small Latin, and less Greek", a great problem for the Augustan "nationalists" of the eighteenth century. Many commentators and editors, therefore, busied themselves in proving the opposite, that Shakespeare had had great learning and uncovered the ancient sources which unfortunately had been corrupted by others.

These scholars did not understand Jonson's praise, perhaps because it was so ahead of its time. If we look briefly at the context in which Jonson's "accusation" is made, it is indeed a rhetorical concession prior to an hyperbolic comparison, which again has "national" implications:

> And though thou hadst small Latin, and less Greek,
> From thence to honour thee, I would not seek
> For names; but call forth thund'ring Æschylus,
> Euripides, and Sophocles, to us,
> Pacuvius, Accius, him of Cordoua dead,
> To life again, to hear thy buskin tread
> And shake a stage; or when thy socks were on,
> Leave thee alone; for the comparison
> Of all that insolent Greece, or haughty Rome,
> Sent forth, or since did from their ashes come.
> Triumph, my Britain! thou hast one to show,
> To whom all scenes of Europe homage owe.

This certainly was a canonical prophecy at the time, but one that rightly came true. The first scholar to truly understand Jonson's damning praise, which is aimed at Shakespeare's natural ability in the Aristotelian sense, was the eighteenth-century Cambridge don Richard Farmer.[128] *An Essay on the Learning of Shakespeare* light-heartedly demolishes all Augustan desire for a Shakespeare speaking in ancient tongues while writing the plays and poems; on the contrary, with an academic professionalism of the first order, Farmer effectively shows that Shakespeare's sources from the Ancients were simply available to him as translations, translations containing the corruptions the Augustan scholars had been painstakingly trying to weed out by reverting to the originals, thus of course corrupting Shakespeare's "original" text.[129] Farmer was by no means a prototype follower of the "School of Resentment"; he was rather one of the greatest canonisers of Shakespeare, not because he had uncovered the Bard's real sources, but because he stressed the most important point that due to his ignorance, Shakespeare had absorbed his sources in his native (translated) language. His own writing was hence *original*:[130]

> I hope, my good friend, you have by this time acquitted our great poet of all piratical depredations on the ancients, and are ready to receive my conclusion.[131] – He remembered perhaps enough of his *school-boy* learning to put the *Hig, hag, hog,* into the mouth of Sir Hugh Evans; and might pick up in the writers of the time, or the course of his conversation, a familiar phrase or two of French or Italian: but his *studies* were most demonstratively confined to *nature* and *his own language* (85, emphasis in text).

In the last sentence Farmer moves effortlessly between the universal and the particular, whereby the aesthetic and humanistic conception of "nature" as human nature is modified by a particular such as native language; other authors would use customs, manners or taste. Voltaire, for example, came to such a conclusion in his *Essay on Epic Poetry,* and it seems that an interaction of this kind, or rather dialectic, has been instrumental in the development of Western literature. On the stylistic level, Auerbach has presented a mass of examples that show the tension between the classical (universal) sublime and what he in his Chapter on Shakespeare calls "[das] Realistisch-Alltägliche" (297). Bloom has a different way of putting it, but he is certainly in good eighteenth-century com-

---

[128]   Lessing is an early candidate as well; in his famous "17. Literaturbrief" he claims: "Auch nach den Mustern der Alten zu entscheiden, ist Shakespeare ein weit größerer Dichter als Corneille; obgleich dieser die Alten sehr wohl, und jener fast nicht gekannt hat" [Shakespeare is also according the pattern of the ancients, a much greater poet than Corneille, although the latter knew them very well and the former hardly at all] (*Werke V* 72).

[129]   Nabokov discusses the editorial practices available in his "The Servile Path", where he has to choose between corrupt French versions of English authors in Pushkin's poetry. Nabokov chooses Pushkin's version, i.e. the "corrupt" French translation.

[130]   See also *Shakespeare's Lives* by Schoenbaum, who is not fully convinced of Farmer's method (101-104).

[131]   The *Essay* was addressed to Joseph Cradock.

pany when he asks the existential question for not only the canon itself, but the course of literary study *per se*:

> What is the Shakespearean difference that demands Dante, Cervantes, Tolstoy, and only a few others as aesthetic companions? To ask the question is to undertake the quest that is the final aim of literary study, the search for a kind of value that transcends the particular prejudices and needs of societies at fixed points in time (62).

This is the universalist doctrine, and reminds one perhaps more of Voltaire's aesthetic values than Samuel Johnson's, who personifies this crossing between the particular and universal perhaps more than any other critic. Although Johnson is almost immaterial as a critic for readers of literatures other than the English, Bloom sets him up as the "canonical critic" and claims he is "unmatched by any critic in any nation before or after him" (183). Comparing him to figures like Goethe, Emerson and Montaigne, he also calls Johnson a "national sage", which seems to be close to what Johnson aspired to be. The problem is that Johnson's aesthetic, not unlike Bloom's, may well have aspired to be universal, but was in the end more often particular in the extreme, a fact that may explain why he could occasionally forget his Augustan principles for an English national author like Shakespeare.[132]

Bloom is aware of this danger and he responds to it in his own way, yet he comes to a conclusion that is familiar and indeed a powerful attempt to revive the "author" Shakespeare. Having asked the question quoted above, Bloom denies that Shakespeare's command of language makes him different from all other authors; what makes Shakespeare really great (and thus the author at the "center of the canon") is his "power of representation of human character and personality and their mutabilities" (63). Through this claim he naturally comes to Johnson's preface to Shakespeare, which Bloom claims inaugurated the "canonical praise of this magnificence", which, on the other hand is "both revelatory and misleading" (63). He continues with a well-known quote from Johnson, which indeed was a standard in the aesthetic (and philosophical) discourses of that time, a quote intertextually linked to a passage in *Hamlet*, which in turn is discursively linked to standard discourses of representation (Aristotle) and behaviour (cf the medieval genre of *Speculum*, intended to improve princely manners):[133] ""Shakespeare is above all writers, at least above all modern writers,

---

[132]   As Bloom notes, Johnson was not wholly comfortable with Shakespeare's deviation from classical standards. He has, however, gone far enough from those standards to leave Shakespeare more or less as he found him, something which a century and a half of rewriting and dubious editing had not done. See Jean I. Marsden's *The Re-Imagined Text. Shakespeare, Adaptation, & Eighteenth-Century Literary Theory.*

[133]   The genre dissolved into bourgeois discourse concentrating on manners, but Wieland's *Fürstenspiegel* may be one of the latest explicit entrants to it. The bourgeoisie translated

the poet of nature, the poet that holds up to his readers a faithful mirrour of manners and of life'" (63).

Note the qualification in which Johnson's classicism still lingers, as it indeed does throughout the famous preface, which thrives from the oppositional perspective, as most students of literature know. While adopting the canonical part of Johnson's dictum and indeed taking it beyond the moderns, Bloom on the other hand rejects the part on representation and reverts to an idea of opposition of characters, which has an Aristotelian flavour to it: "Shakespeare, wiser than both of these genuinely wise critics [i.e., Johnson and Wilde], saw "nature" through clashing perspectives, those of Lear and Edmund in the most sublime of the tragedies, of Hamlet and Claudius in another, of Othello and Iago in yet another" (63). The universal "nature" is represented through a clash of characters that themselves represent "perspectives", but what makes Shakespeare the canonical genius he is, is, according to Bloom, the fact that you "cannot hold a mirror up to any of these natures, or persuade yourself convincingly that your sense of reality is more comprehensive than that of Shakespearean tragedy" (63). The genre in the last sentence is a metonym for the *Übermensch* and author Shakespeare. The clash of the universal and particular has not been synthesised in Bloom's argument, because he clings to the author and creator as opposed to an idea of a text processed by a number of factors (author, his patronage, pre-texts and influence, subsequent rewriting and bowdlerisation, critical reception and canonisation, translation and, finally, the accursed political and social significance).

That Bloom's own idea of "influence" is also included in this list may come as a surprise, but it is exactly on that point, coupled with the problem of translation, that his canonisation of the "strong author" founders. His Chapter on Goethe in the *Western Canon* shows this even better than the one on Shakespeare. What arouses suspicion when reading Bloom's version of Goethe is the claim that "[i]t is difficult to overestimate the continued effect of Shakespeare on the Germans, even on Goethe, who was so wary of being influenced" (73). Coming from the author of *The Anxiety of Influence* this is strange in itself, more so when one considers Goethe. Of course, this might be supposed to indicate that Goethe, like other strong authors, simply "subsumed" all influence, but it is still unconvincing, for if any author absorbed, rewrote, translated, lifted, adapted and borrowed freely whenever he felt like it, it was Goethe. He was not wary of influence; he welcomed it for his own purposes. Of course he created something utterly new and "original", but his creative processes seem to have been influenced more by – pardon the tautology – influence than anything else.

---

the genre into the genre *Bildungsroman*, of which authors like Richardson and Rousseau were forerunners, particularly the latter's *Emile*.

Even a quick look at Goethe's work, which will be discussed in more detail later on, shows that Goethe actively and consciously absorbed from other writers and traditions, material and forms. Indeed, the case may be made that precisely this method was behind his development of national literature towards *Weltiteratur*, the term so insistently affixed to his name in German criticism.[134] Without the pre-texts or genotexts in Kristeva's terminology, foreign and native, without the translational movements that are obvious in the ballads rewritten or adapted, in the classical poetry and drama, in his heavy borrowing from Shakespeare in *Götz von Berlichingen*, his direct translation of *Ossian* at the climactic point of *Werther*, in his large scale appropriation of oriental poetry in the *Divan* and the gigantic medley of influences in *Faust*, Goethe would never have given birth to works that simultaneously can be considered national literature and world literature.

Perhaps I "misread" Bloom here, but in his Chapter on Goethe he makes translation, or rather foreign language, the neutralising factor that enables Goethe to deny that he had been influenced. This thesis is not entirely to be agreed with, not because it is wrong (on the contrary, it chimes partially with my thesis of a translation without an original), but because of the problem that the focus is on Shakespeare alone and the implied lack of subtlety in Goethe's method. At one point Bloom says of Shakespeare that he was "the only [precursor Goethe] could accept, because he wrote in a different modern language" (205). A little further on Bloom claims it "was fortunate for Goethe that Shakespeare was English, because the linguistic distance allowed him to absorb and imitate Shakespeare without crippling anxieties" (209). This is as clear as it can get, and may also be interpreted as an explanation of Goethe's incentive to use foreign sources for his own work. The translational movement, be it ever so slight or amounting to translation proper, is, then, an attempt to deny influence and seem to be original, a transtextual movement that is a palimpsest, in Genette's terminology.

Bloom's misreading of Goethe is most revealing in a very selective reading of *Faust. II. Teil,* the remarks in *Wilhelm Meisters Lehrjahre,* and the latter of two Shakespeare essays, "Schäkespear [sic] und kein Ende!"[135] It is, however, the absence of the first essay or speech, "Zum Schäckspears [sic] Tag" (1771), that makes such a misreading possible, in the first place because the first essay was written over forty years prior to the latter, which must be relevant in the case of an author who was a major part of the *Sturm und Drang* as well as of

---

134 See for example Albrecht (167).
135 Bloom writes "Schäckespear" in the title; according to Erich Trunz, editor of the so-called Hamburger Ausgabe of Goethe's works, Goethe spelled Shakespeare both Schäckespear and Schäkspear in his first essay "Zum Schäckspears Tag" (*Werke 12* 693). He does not refer to the spelling in his notes to the second one. I have not seen the originals.

what is called the *Weimarer Klassik*. The essays reflect the development of the author Goethe, and indeed the massive duality of his authorial character, present in many of his major works, from the sane and insane Werther, to the strange quartet of *Die Wahlverwandschaften*; from the poet and the politician in *Torquato Tasso* to the inseparable duo in *Faust*.[136] It should also be noted that the essays are written with totally different purposes; the first is the work of an enthusiastic youth, a statement of adoration and declaration that Goethe had made Shakespeare his own from the first page (*Werke 12* 224-225). The first essay is written under the heavy influence of Herder, who had not yet published his Shakespeare essay in *Von deutscher Art und Kunst*, but Goethe and Herder had met in Strasbourg the year before. It is also under the influence of Lessing's epoch-making "17. Literaturbrief", in which he explicitly breaks with imitating the French in favour of the English. This in itself was not new, but he coupled it with the idea which made this essay one of his most quoted:[137] "Denn ein *Genie* kann nur von einem *Genie* entzündet werden; und am leichtesten von so einem, das alles bloß der Natur zu danken haben scheinet, und durch die mühsamen Vollkommenheiten der Kunst nicht abschrecket" (*Werke V* 72).[138] This is, in essence, Bloom's thesis of the "strong author" as he describes him in the *Western Canon*, particularly perhaps, when one considers Lessing's subtle use of "scheinet", which could be translated with "appears" (i.e., it is the author who *appears* to have everything from nature who can jumpstart the other genius through influence).[139] But Lessing provides the young Goethe not only with an author to admire instead of the French contemporary canon and a profound vision of how to become a genius of equal proportions, but also with the concrete example of a piece that he could write. Lessing points out that "unsre alten Stücke wirklich sehr viel Englisches gehabt haben" [our old plays really had a

---

[136] I do not wish to equal the fictive figures of the works with the author. The duality in the works may well be due to the simple dramatic principle of creating a conflict, but on the other hand, its complementary subtlety indicates that the duality functions on several levels, one of which may be the conflicting tendencies in the author's psyche. If there is anything to this, Goethe was certainly not alone; we see this dual dialectic in most of the authors discussed in these volumes, very obviously in Rousseau, in Herder, in Adam Smith and many others. Schiller observed of Goethe in his essay "Ueber naive und sentimentalische Dichtung" that the oppositions between the character of Werther and his environment are exemplary for the "sentimental " and that such oppositions recur in characters in *Torquato Tasso* and in *Faust* (*Werke* 20 459-60).

[137] See Karl S. Guthke in "Lessing, Shakespeare und die deutsche Verspätung" where he traces Lessing's approach as far back as to Dryden.

[138] "Because *genius* can only be fired by *genius*; and the most easily by one who seems to have everything from nature and is not intimidated by the perfection of art" (my translation).

[139] Jochen Schmidt discusses Lessing's fine-tuning of language in this case in his seminal *Die Geschichte des Genie-Gedankens*, vol. I (69-73).

lot of Englishness in them] and names only one, "Doctor Faust", which he then promptly ascribes to Shakespeare, as such a work could only have been written by a genius like him. Lessing then presents a fragment, apparently translated from Shakespeare's "Doctor Faust", whereby, according to his editor, Lessing is simply fictionalising himself, by performing a pseudotranslation of a play by Marlowe under Shakespeare's name.[140]

Since nothing came of Lessing's plans of writing a *Faust* Goethe certainly had more space for his own, and the idea to do it must surely have come from this source, which he followed in both its major demands; to imitate, or at least compete with, Shakespeare and to write a play on Faust.[141] The early work, *Götz von Berlichingen,* was so marked by Shakespeare's influence that the Shakespeare admirer Herder drily remarked, "Shakespeare hat Euch ganz verdorben" (quoted by Trunz in Goethe, *Werke 12* 692).[142]

If Goethe's first essay on Shakespeare shows no trace of the author's wariness of its object, Bloom is right when he claims Goethe is wary of it in the latter, written in 1813 (parts I and II) and 1816 (part III).[143] Already in the title Goethe shows an ambivalence towards his previous idol, "Shakespeare und kein Ende" implies impatience with an ongoing and seemingly never-ending discussion. But this is more an impression, for the essay is rather an attempt to analyse why Shakespeare has taken up so much space in critical discourse and to find his place in the still-living dialectic of ancients and moderns. Added to that is an aesthetic discussion, which shows a different use of Lessing's insights, this time including the *Laokoon* and its differentiation of poetry and painting, language and vision. These points need to be examined in conjunction with Bloom's canonical discussion on Shakespeare and Goethe.

Goethe's latter essay can also be seen as a kind of answer to the naiveties of his first, which was not published, nor necessarily present in his mind forty years after he gave it as a speech on Shakespeare's birthday. There are, however, parallels, which show a development of thought, if nothing else. The first

---

[140] The mix-up of authors is probably unintentional. The myth of Marlowe really being Shakespeare was only conceived of in the latter part of the nineteenth century (Schoenbaum 446).

[141] Although Marlowe used an English translation of the first *Faustbuch* (1587) as a basis for his play, Goethe's work is of course not a rewriting of Marlowe's work. At first he may have thought he was "translating" Shakespeare's method. Goethe himself claims in *Dichtung und Wahrheit* that the "bedeutende Puppenspiel des [Faust] klang und summte gar vieltönig wider" [wonderful Faust legend of the old puppet-shows struck many and responsive chords within me] during the early 1770s (*Werke 9* 413; Smith 370).

[142] Herbert Schöffler has painstakingly picked out the intertextualities and translations from Shakespeare in his essay "Shakespeare und der junge Goethe" in *Deutscher Geist im 18. Jahrhundert* (113-135).

[143] Bloom only refers to parts I and II it appears (212). Parts I and II were published in 1815 and part III in 1826.

is in the conception of Shakespeare as a poet of "nature", something that Trunz notes developed both in *Wilhelm Meisters Lehrjahre* and in "Shakespeare und kein Ende": "Es regten sich Zweifel, ob Shakespeares Menschen wirklich so ganz *Natur* seien [...] und die Einsicht in Shakespeares bauenden Kunstverstand vertiefte sich" (*Werke 12* 703).[144] This "insight" was more Lessing's than Goethe's, as can be seen from the words of Wilhelm Meister which Trunz refers to: "[Shakespeares] Menschen *scheinen* natürliche Menschen zu sein, und sie sind es doch nicht" (*Werke 7* 192, my emphasis).[145] This kind of borrowing is typical for Goethe, and he develops it further in his "Shakespeare und kein Ende" where he distinguishes strictly between Shakespeare's ability to write for the eyes and for the mind: "Fragen wir aber nach diesen Mitteln, so scheint es, als arbeite er für unsre Augen; aber wir sind getäuscht: Shakespeares Werke sind nicht für die Augen des Leibes" (*Werke 12* 288).[146] Goethe explains himself, as he puts it, by claiming that the word is the highest and fastest way to Shakespeare's inner sense, which in turn mobilises the visual world of the imagination (288). This looks very familiar to any reader of *Laokoon*.[147]

Goethe applies not only Lessing's insights but also Schiller's opposition of the naive and sentimental, and his distinction of genre has an almost Hegelian touch to it well before the publication of Hegel's lectures on aesthetics.[148] The most important point, however, is that Shakespeare "gehört [...] notwendig in die Geschichte der Poesie; in der Geschichte des Theaters tritt nur zufällig auf" (*Werke 12* 296).[149] Goethe's line of argument is classical in the sense that he adopts the premise that many of the supernatural and sensational elements Shakespeare uses in his plays cannot be represented on the stage and thus that the plays are really not meant for the stage but for the mind:

> Er läßt geschehen, was sich leicht imaginieren läßt, ja was besser imaginiert als gesehen wird. Hamlets Geist, Macbeths Hexen, manche Grausamkeiten erhalten ihren Wert erst

---

144 "Some doubts came up, whether Shakespeare's people were wholly from nature [...] and the insights into Shakespeare's knowledge on artistic structuring became deeper" (my translation).

145 "His men appear like natural men, and yet they are not" (Carlyle, Vol. I, 167)

146 "But if we ask about his means, it seems as if he works for our eyes; but we are deceived: Shakespeare's works are not for the eyes of the body" (my translation).

147 Goethe wrote indeed twice about the same subject; only one of two essays is extant. See Trunz and his notes to "Über Laokoon" (*Werke 12* 596-597).

148 The lectures were published posthumously 1835 and edited from Hegel's papers and student notes of his lectures.

149 "belongs essentially to the history of poetry, in the history of drama he appears only coincidentally" (my translation).

durch die Einbildungskraft, und die vielfältigen kleinen Zwischenszenen sind bloß auf sie berechnet" (288).[150]

Bloom is of the same opinion as concerns Goethe's *Faust,* and he contrasts it with Goethe's judgement of Shakespeare: "Goethe had the odd notion that Shakespeare did not write for the stage, and certainly the complete *Faust* is best performed in the afterlife" (*Western* 221).[151] This oddity Bloom justifies with the fact that, "[e]merging as he did from storm and stress, or the German version of the English Age of Sensibility, Goethe naturally associated an authentically sublime drama with the theater of mind" (221). It is indeed odd to see the Goethe of his latter years so easily attached to his youthful period, which he surely had left behind him in 1813-16. What is also missing in Bloom's presentation is the way in which Goethe adopts an idea of imitation in conjunction with Shakespeare's method of composing, a method I would argue perhaps describes his own better than that of Shakespeare, for if we see an ideal of a "theater of the mind" (of whatever epoch) realised in *Faust,* Goethe's analysis of Shakespeare approaches a description of his own practice:

> Shakespeares ganze Verfahrungsart findet an der eigentlichen Bühne etwas Widerstrebendes; sein großes Talent ist das eines Epitomators, und da der Dichter überhaupt als Epitomator der Natur erscheint, so müssen wir auch hier Shakespeares großes Verdienst anerkennen, nur leugnen wir dabei, und zwar zu seinen Ehren, daß die Bühne ein würdiger Raum für sein Genie gewesen (*Werke 12* 297).[152]

What Shakespeare achieves through the epitomising of nature, according to Goethe, is different from other poets, because he does not, like them, use previous materials simply as material, but rather fixes his mind on one idea and *adapts* the material to that idea: "Hier aber nicht, wie andere Dichter, wählt er sich zu einzelnen Arbeiten besondere Stoffe, sondern er legt einen Begriff in den

---

150 "He makes that happen, what is easily imagined, yes, what is even better to imagine than see. Hamlet's ghost, Macbeth's witches, some of the cruelties attain their value first and foremost through the imagination and the different minor scenes in between are only there to support them" (my translation).

151 Which is exactly what August W. Schlegel said about *Faust* in his essay "Etwas über William Shakespeare bei Gelegenheit Wilhelm Meisters": "Am Hamlet ist [der Verstand] in der Tat so hervorstechend, daß man das Ganze, wie Goethes *Faust,* ein Gedankenschauspiel nennen könnte" [In Hamlet [reason] is indeed so prominent that one might call the whole, like Goethe's Faust, an intellectual game" (*Sprache* 94, my translation).

152 "Shakespeare's approach encounters on the actual stage some sort of resistance; his great talent is the one of an epitomator and since poets in general appear as epitomators of nature, we must acknowledge Shakespeare's great accomplishment, whereby we must deny, and that to his honour, that the stage is a worthy space for his genius" (my translation).

Mittelpunkt und bezieht auf diesen die Welt und das Universum" (297).[153] This means that Shakespeare, Goethe notes, can take any story or chronicle, even use parts of it almost word for word (which he did, particularly when using translations, as Farmer showed) and apply it to his central idea of the play; the story, the text itself, is immaterial if it is adapted to this central idea. What is original, then, is neither the idea nor the material used but the way in which the materials are put together, be they borrowed or invented, translated or imitated from "life".

Goethe himself had used this method from the outset, as the clear example of *Werther* shows, with its mixture of the actual suicide of Lessing's friend Karl Wilhelm Jerusalem, his own infatuation with Charlotte Buff, the structural quote of Homer, the biblical intertextualities, and the adaptation of Ossianic sentiment culminating in the long translation just before Werther shoots himself.[154] The central idea itself of impossible but noble love worth dying for is perhaps Dantesque as in the *New Life,* or Shakespearean as in *Romeo and Juliet,* or simply medieval as in numerous romances, but whatever the sources, physical or metaphysical, Goethe made his name with *Werther.*

Before I move on to Goethe and his contemporaries in detail, their translational synthesis of the foreign into a whole of a "Kulturnation" before the background of fragmented petty states that made up the Holy Roman Empire, I will embark on a discourse on what I see as the national literary rivalry in Britain in the latter part of the eighteenth century. This rivalry was partly expressed through the hectic translational activity of the 1760s, and I argue that this rivalry, which took place on many levels of discourse, in effect led to the cultural fragmentation of the fragile construct that was Britain. The text that arguably had the greatest effect, both in Germany and in Britain, went under the title *The Poems of Ossian.*

---

[153] "In this he does not, like other poets, select specific material for his work, but rather focuses on a concept and refers the world and the universe to it" (my translation).

[154] The structural quote to Homer refers to the famous passage when Werther leaves "nice" society and goes for a walk in "nature" to read his Homer (*Werke 6* 69). The passage he read was the one of Odysseus returning home as a swineherd, the significance of which was already noted by Schiller in "Ueber naive und sentimentalische Dichtung" (*Werke 20* 431). This is also the passage Napoleon is supposed to have criticised in *Werther* when he received Goethe in 1808. See Trunz's note in *Werke 10* (787-788).

Part II
National Literary Rivalry
in Britain

3   AN EPIC FOR SCOTLAND

3.1   The Ossianic Explosion

It is hardly necessary to introduce *The Poems of Ossian,* produced by James Macpherson in the early 1760s, poems and epics that arguably caused the first mass hysteria of modernity, not unlike what we refer to as "Beatlemania" today. The poems conquered literary Europe of their time and were translated into most European languages.[155] They caused an instant controversy, or rather controversies, for one of the greatest bones of contention was not whether they were spurious, but to whom they belonged, the Irish or the Scots.

To cut a long and oft-repeated story short, Macpherson was asked by the dramatist John Home to show him a few translations of Gaelic poetry, which he reluctantly did, with the remark that this poetry could not be translated. Home was fascinated by the result and showed it to his friend Hugh Blair, who was also "transported" and organised the publication of the *Fragments,* ghost-writing the preface, which included the assertion that the translation was "extremely literal" and a promise of an epic to be found in the Highlands (Saunders 67-78 & Sher, "Scotch Imposters" 55-63). He then organised financial support among the Scottish literati for Macpherson's journey into the Highlands to collect material, and when the 24-year-old Macpherson returned to Edinburgh with his materials he settled in the same house as Blair and reconstructed the epic *Fingal* there, discussing the translation both with Blair and the Gaelic-speaking Adam Ferguson (Gaskill, "Home" 12-18). The second epic was written by Macpherson alone, after he had been attacked forcefully and accused of falsification by Irish intellectuals in a public advertisement. Whatever Macpherson did to construct a national Scottish epic (almost on order from the Scottish literati, as Richard Sher has shown) it is a fact of literary history that these poems revolutionised literary attitudes in Europe, not necessarily with their novelty in language and style, but with the possibility of constructing a national literature from the native sources.[156]

The story of literary nationalism does not begin with *The Poems of Ossian,* but they were probably the most influential publication in this direction, in Britain, in Germany and, in fact, in the Western world *per se.* One reason for this, as many commentators have noted, was the epic form, although *The Poems of Ossian* do not adhere to strict formal criteria, neither according to the ancient Greek tradition, which used hexameter, nor the English modern one, which em-

---

[155]   Even Icelandic, and that before Milton's *Paradise Lost* and Klopstock's *Messias* were translated. See Andrew Wawn's "Óðinn, Ossian and Iceland".

[156]   See Anne-Marie Thiesse's *La Creation des Identites Nationales* where she speaks of an "aesthetic revolution" (23-66).

ployed either blank verse or rhyming couplets.[157] In fact, Macpherson (and probably Blair) fused the ballad material adapted into two different traditions, the epic and the biblical, in key with what Robert Lowth had asserted in his influential *Lectures on the Sacred Poetry of the Hebrews* (1753).[158]

But the epic form alone would not have caused any controversy, had there not been the new and purportedly ancient national content. Epics were constantly being translated and written, most often using classical or biblical stories. Poets had also used historical material for epics: Ariosto in *Orlando furioso*, Tasso in *Gerusalemme liberata*, Camões in *Os Lusiadas*, Ronsard in his unfinished *Franciade* and even Voltaire in his *La Henriade*, to name a few examples (Schweikle 128). Macpherson, however, not only discovered the shreds he could stitch together into a national quilt in line with the Renaissance tradition, but in addition conjured up a verifying apparatus in different paratexts that gave the whole an authentic, historical and national frame. Macpherson's national translation of the Renaissance method was instantly understood all over Europe, and suddenly the literary sources of the native language, folk poetry and tales, became fashionable; they needed only a little translation, interlingual or intralingual, to become fitting garments for the finer classes, and Macpherson and the Scottish literati had demonstrated the method.[159] It did not matter whether the epics or the national material were diligently collected and edited, translated, written or fabricated; the paradigm was Ossianic, for it had shown how it could function. Antiquarian work on national sources had been done all over Europe since the Renaissance, of course, but until the Ossianic explosion it was mostly confined to the quarters of scholars and antiquarians.

The Poems of Ossian represent a problematic corpus of texts, due to the various controversies that surround them. The heat with which they have been

---

[157]   For thoughts on the form, see Josef Bysveen and Derick Thomson's "Ballads to Epics". See also Horst W. Drescher on epic in "Ossian – Homer of the Highlands; or, Towards a Scottish National Epic".

[158]   For Blair's probable collaboration in the actual translation of the *Fragments* and of *Fingal*, see Howard Gaskill's "Ossian at Home and Abroad" and Richard Sher's "Those Scotch Imposters and their Cabal" on the role of the Edinburgh literati.

[159]   Several examples can be named, although many of those who collected, edited, translated or discussed these "epics" go to great lengths in negating the link to Macpherson's Ossian, proof in itself that the model was in the writer's mind; the Russian *Igor-Tale* is a case in point. The oft-noted *Kalevala*, the Polish *Pan-Tadeusz*, the Latvian *Lacplesis* (The Bear Slayer), the Estonian *Kalevipoeg* and several European epics, found, forged, composed and/or translated in one way or another are to an extent inspired by the Ossianic model; even America has its representative in Longfellow's *Hiawatha*, ("Indian Edda") which sometimes has been lambasted for its leaning on the versification of the *Kalevala*. See for example the entry on Longfellow in the *Oxford Companion to American Literature* (Hart 444) and Roman Jakobson's "The Puzzles of the Igor' Tale" (380-410).

discussed – and are even still discussed – is partly due to their "national" nature, or as Dafydd Moore aptly puts it citing Katie Trumpener in his *Enlightenment and Romance in James MacPherson's* The Poems of Ossian, "the Ossian controversy is in part 'about the politics of cultural memory and the future role of national cultures in the new multicultural [sic] Britain.'" (5).[160] The moral indignation often expressed in connection with the poems is very often disguised nationalism, as is of course some of the Scottish support, which in recent years has re-emerged in the wake of Fiona Stafford's *The Sublime Savage* and Howard Gaskill's *Ossian Revisited.* Their revisionism is on the whole, however, much more balanced and better informed than much of the ill-informed encyclopædic cant that is commonly on offer in Ossianic discourse. The major problem with many Ossianic debates is that while they seem to focus on the authenticity of a text, they are in fact about the authenticity of nations.

It is, therefore, necessary to address a few of the myths surrounding these poems which, despite their massive influence (and massive is an understatement), have been removed from the canon of Western literature.[161]

A qualitative judgment might be used to justify such a "de-canonisation", and I assume the poems did belong to the canon for a while, for it can hardly be denied that a number of critics and authors, say from Blair to Arnold, had little doubt concerning the canonical place *Ossian* deserved. Few texts have so often been compared to Homer, by people who knew their Homer very well. Actually, the list of those who admired *The Poems of Ossian*, read them, used them, translated them, reads like an excerpt from the canon itself, particularly outside of Britain where the authenticity question, or rather the national property question, did not overshadow everything else. In Germany the group of admirers included not only Herder, Goethe and Klopstock, but most of the literary figures who had anything to say, well into the nineteenth century. Bürger and Schiller, Novalis, Hölderlin are merely the most famous examples.[162] The Schlegel-brothers and Schleiermacher were more reserved, but their doubts were of a translational nature; these practising experts in translation developed strict criteria for themselves, which they applied to the work of others.[163]

---

[160] The quote is from Trumpener's *Bardic Nationalism* (xv).

[161] It is, I think, no coincidence that one of the greatest figures of the discipline of comparative literature, Paul Van Tieghem, wrote a major monograph on the influence of Ossian in France, apart from his work on and coinage of "Preromanticism".

[162] See Gaskill's "Ossian at Home and Abroad" and "Ossian in Europe". Many painters were also moved to interpret *Ossian.* Eberhard Roters has collected the best known in *Jenseits von Arkadien. Die romantische Landschaft.* He names Ingres, Gérard, Abildgaard, J.A. Koch, Runge, Caspar David Friedrich, among others.

[163] I am referring here to August W. Schlegel as a translator. See, however, for example Friedrich Schlegel's comments in "Über nordische Dichtkunst", *Kritische Friedrich-Schlegel-Ausgabe 3* (229). A.W. Schlegel's "Homerischer Epos" deals a more ironically with the subject; Schlegel notes that Werther prefers Ossian to Homer when he has gone

In addition to this, one often reads or hears that *Ossian* is "unreadable", a statement that makes one wonder what the person in question generally reads.[164] To be sure, the poems are not an easy read, as Blair warned already in his "Critical Dissertation", published with the second edition of the poems, but they are certainly readable, and some, such as the *Songs of Selma*, are beautiful poetry, particularly appealing in the constant shift of metre and prose.[165]

The second myth is what has been called the manuscript myth, which has its roots, as we shall see, in the national controversy between the Irish and the Scots that arose after the publication of the *Fragments*. Both Stafford, in her *The Sublime Savage,* and Gaskill,[166] in several essays, have effectively dealt with this question. Gaskill has considered what may have been lost, and indeed the quality of both manuscripts and *transcripts*, for as Macpherson himself claimed, some of what he used was taken down from oral recitation.

Which brings us back to the structure, not specifically as a genre, but as an intentional construct. As Gaskill noted, anybody who bothered to read Blair's and Macpherson's own paratexts should be aware of the compilatory nature of the poems ("Home" 12-18).[167] It is also a myth that any critic of substance in Macpherson's age could have been completely deceived by the methods applied, either in the main text or in the paratexts. Textual criticism had been developing since the Renaissance (with the emergence of "diplomatics"), and for classical scholars and antiquarians alike one of the main problems had been the way in which corrupt transcripts could be edited to reconstruct an original that no longer existed.[168] To quote the article in the *Encyclopædia Britannica* (Vol. 20, 1986) on the subject: "[The textual critic's] concern is with the reconstruction of what no longer exists. A text is not a concrete artifact, like a pot or statue, but an abstract concept or idea" (676). This late twentieth-century opinion is formu-

---

insane and shoots himself, thus anticipating Goethe's famous retort to Henry Crabb Robinson in 1829 (*Klassische Literatur* 99). See also F.J. Lamport's "Goethe, Ossian and Werther" (97).

[164] To my surprise, a teacher of German once told me that he always skipped the Ossian passage when he taught Goethe's *Werther*. A Johnsonian quip in response to such a statement could be to ask whether the person in question always skips the climax of a novel, or anything else for that matter.

[165] It is true of the epics, particularly *Temora*, that "no one would have wished it longer" like Johnson said of *Paradise Lost*, but this applies not only to Milton and Macpherson, but most epics, for the verse epic is a form that has become "unreadable" for modern people. They are only read by students and scholars. In fact, *Ossian* seems to represent the text that starts the movement from epic poetry in verse to epics in prose, thus making the novel a viable possibility for (highbrow) literature. And one might also ask whether *Finnegan's Wake* is "readable"?

[166] In his "Introduction" to *Ossian Revisited* (6).

[167] Blair ghost-wrote the preface to the *Fragments*.

[168] This was for example Johnson's problem when working on his Shakespeare edition.

lated for the layman by an expert in textual criticism, but it was just as well known in the eighteenth century, and probably more common knowledge, as the following quote from the third Earl of Shaftesbury shows:

> And as far as *critical Truth*; or the Judgment and Determinations of what Commentators, Translators, Paraphrasts, Grammarians, and others have, on this occasion, deliver'd to us; in the midst of such Variety of Stile, such different Readings, such Interpolations and Corruptions in the Originals; such Mistakes of Copists, Transcribers, Editors, and a hundred such Accidents, to which antient Books are subject: it becomes, upon the whole, *a Matter of nice Speculation* (*Sensus Communis* 124, emphasis in text).

This is not to say that there was no deception in the Ossianic reconstruction of the materials collected; indeed this may be one of the reasons why Macpherson (under the instructions of Blair) felt rather free in the collation and reconstruction of his materials.[169] But he was certainly not alone among his contemporaries as a manipulator or forger of texts.

It should also not be forgotten that Macpherson was educated in Aberdeen, where the famous Thomas Blackwell was principal. Blackwell's theories on the emergence of epic were common knowledge in the European Enlightenment; his German translator was Johann Heinrich Voss, who published his translation in 1776, before his Homeric translations.[170] Blackwell's *Enquiry into the Life and Writings of Homer* (1735) is an early example of historical inquiry that interprets cultural phenomena from their broader context, to use the modern jargon. Environmental influences such as climate, manners, political constitution and education make up what Blackwell terms the "progression of manners" in nations, which among other factors can be decisive for the rise of epic poetry (13).[171] He was by no means the first to raise the so-called Homeric "question" about whether Homer composed his epics alone or whether they are compilations, but he provided serious philosophical or conjectural evidence, and this sort of inquiry (or experimental reasoning, as Hume called it), partly influenced by Newton, became a major method of historical research and writing in the eighteenth century under such titles as "rational", "philosophical" or "conjec-

---

[169]   Shenstone saw this instantly and encouraged Thomas Percy to do the same with his ballads (cf. below). As we shall see, Percy did not follow this advice, although he did manipulate the texts; his paratexts, however, provide an example of his conjectural and imaginative powers.

[170]   Fiona Stafford has discussed Blackwell's influence on the young Macpherson in her *Sublime Savage* (26-37).

[171]   This is naturally reminiscent of Montesquieu, who corresponded with Blackwell. See MSS. 3648 in the National Library of Scotland. The letter was printed in *Yale French Studies* 5 (154).

tural" history.[172] It is the major shift in historical thought that makes historicism possible, and one of Blackwell's readers was certainly Herder, one of the "founders" of historicism.

Blackwell's influence on the rise of *Ossian* has in the latter-day debate become a kind of conventional wisdom, a dangerously easy reference perhaps, but in his recent *The Forger's Shadow*, Nick Groom has protested on aesthetic grounds (128).[173] He claims that "Blackwell's Homer was certainly an influence on Thomas Gray's haggard creature 'The Bard' (1757)", whereas "Ossian was entirely different. He sits down on hills in the rain and bemoans his fate, rather than shrieking from lightning racked mountain tops" (128). Perhaps, but I think Groom misses the point that Macpherson (and Blair) was not trying to create a duplicate of Homer, but translating him into a bard that expressed exactly the "progression of manners" in the Highlands of Scotland: a native equivalent, not a repetition. This is the difference between Gray's bard and Macpherson's – a difference that cultural nationalists found exciting, for it gave them the possibility of producing their own equivalents, in agreement with their heritage.

It is also clear that one reason for the harsh judgement of the Ossianic poems was the fact that they were *translated*. It certainly made them more vulnerable, for the act of translation can so easily be discredited, even by the layman who does not even speak the source language, and translation is, in fact, much more often controversially criticised than the much more speculative work of the textual critic. The young Macpherson probably saw himself somewhere between the translator and the textual critic, certainly as long as he worked under the guiding hand of Hugh Blair and the inspecting eyes of Adam Ferguson (Gaskill, "Home" 12-15).[174]

Blair's role in the affair remains ambiguous, although I have noticed one aspect of it that is often turned around. Many commentators, particularly the less informed, claim that Blair's *Critical Dissertation on the Poems of Ossian* was instrumental in paving their way among the intellectuals and poets of Europe. This may be true, but the premise is often that this can be attributed to Blair's fame as a critic. Considering the fact that Blair had barely published anything before his "Critical Dissertation" apart from a sermon and perhaps a very presentable edition of Shakespeare (for the Scots, as the editor said), it seems that it was *Ossian* that made him famous, rather than the other way around.[175] Of

---

[172] Friedrich Wolf was the major German representative of the "Homeric question" in his famous *Prolegomena ad Homerum* (1795).

[173] At the same time he honestly admits in a footnote, he also was a believer.

[174] As Gaskill notes, the mostly spurious *Temora* was written in London, after Macpherson's "removal from the sphere of influence of Blair and Ferguson" (15).

[175] The Shakespeare edition was published in 1753 by an anonymous editor. It was reprinted in 1795 with an attribution to Blair as the editor of the original edition.

course the essay speaks for itself as a major document of primitivism, but Blair was hardly well known outside of Scotland prior to its publication.

Another myth that has recently been disassembled is the notion that Macpherson managed to fool some of the finest minds of the Scottish Enlightenment into swallowing his fabrications. Sher has discussed the political motivation of the Edinburgh literati and Gaskill has examined Blair's role in particular.[176] The Edinburgh literati, including Adam Ferguson, David Hume, John Home and Hugh Blair, and supported theoretically by Henry Home, Lord Kames, were of course motivated by a nationalism that found its outlet through this translation without an original – or at least with only a semi-original. What mattered was the form and the sublimity of the text in conjunction with its antiquity. That the content was known in some other form was, for them, reason enough to accept the poems, and they were of course time and again strengthened in their belief by Gaelic-speaking Scots, biased in their judgement for nationalistic reasons.

In 1763, for example, David Hume faced the fury of the Irish in London and encouraged Blair to collect testimonies for the authenticity of the poems. This Blair did, and they were subsequently published with the second edition of the Ossianic poems in 1765. Hume's role in the story has often been distorted, probably because he changed his mind and a suppressed essay against *Ossian* was found after his death.[177] As one of the initial supporters he wanted Blair to counter the attacks he faced in London. This has been interpreted rather imaginatively by Ludwig Stern, the German Celtic scholar who supposedly dealt *Ossian* its fatal blow: he claimed that the sceptical Hume had demanded an investigation! (55). Stern's views are based on the linearity of history and race: i.e., Ireland was the motherland of Scottish Gaeldom and the "Hauptsitz der celtischen Rasse bis auf den heutigen Tag" (53). The racist ideology inherent in this line of thought has found its most unpleasant modern expression in Hugh Trevor-Roper's "The Invention of Tradition: The Highland Tradition of Scotland", where one is confronted with enlightening assertions such as: "the Highlanders of Scotland did not form a distinct people. They were simply the overflow of Ireland" (15). He does not say where and when the Irish *in toto* made up a "distinct people" or on what criteria. He moves on to claim that the West of Scotland was "[r]acially and culturally [...] a colony of Ireland", something which sheds a fair amount of light on Trevor-Roper's racial views, but rather lit-

---

[176]   In "Scotch" and "Home" respectively.

[177]   David Raynor has discussed Hume's role in his "Ossian and Hume" and comes to the conclusion that Hume was an early supporter of *Ossian,* possibly due to national feelings; why he changed his mind is unclear, Raynor cites the Hume scholar Ernest Mossner who conjectured that Hume had changed his mind after reading Johnson's *Journey.* Hume also took a personal dislike to Macpherson and may have lost faith in him personally.

tle on the relations between the Gaelic-speaking peoples in the British Isles. He also reiterates the old Irish accusation that Macpherson had stolen the indigenous literature of Ireland. The logic on the whole seems to be that an inferior race of Celts had moved to the West of Scotland from Ireland and taken along without permission stories and fables which they – and later Macpherson – used to fabricate or invent a new history. These paradigms were all invented in the furious nationalist wars that engulfed the Ossianic poems from the start.

The greatest impulse to controversy was the nationalist feeling that simmered on several levels, and it must be said that every critical instrument available was employed to discredit *The Poems of Ossian*. When one considers the one "criminal" in the case, James Macpherson, it must also be admitted that his name has been subjected to a level of unfounded slander and sneering that goes beyond any desire for an "objective" view of a literary phenomenon. If, for example, one compares the treatment of Macpherson with that of a true forger, such as Thomas Chatterton, who, like so many, imitated Macpherson's style, it becomes obvious that criticism, from Johnson onward, has uncontroversially noted the fact of Chatterton's forgery but continued to discuss the texts and their emergence in a balanced manner and often with admiration.[178] The difference between the two is not only that of (pseudo)translation versus forgery, but also the nationalist discourse surrounding *Ossian*.

It is, therefore, not my concern to judge or discuss the degree of deception perpetrated by Macpherson on an innocent world, nor do I think that is a discussion worth pursuing. *The Poems of Ossian* can be seen as a text without an author, or with the many authors an epic needs, written down through the mediator Macpherson, but it is probably one of the greatest ironies of literary history that this text, whose "author" was accused of hiding behind the guise of a translator, has no one author, and that the text's fictional author-narrator is constantly present in the text, lamenting the death of his race in his own death; he is already dead, but has been summoned by his translator to speak once again.

---

[178] Ian Haywood has researched Chatterton's imitative tactics with respect to Macpherson in his *The Making of History* (132-135). Chatterton probably learned the method of interpolating archaisms from Percy's *Reliques,* and he was very much able to imitate Macpherson. An example is "Ethelgar. A Saxon Poem". Chatterton's respectable status in comparison with Macpherson can be seen in the fine OUP edition of Chatterton's works. In an act of unintended irony the editor has categorised the works into "Authentic Works" and "Works of Doubtful Authenticity"; whereby the first category includes Chatterton's own forgeries and the second one possible forgeries of the forger by imitators.

3.2 The Fragmentation of Britain

It is legitimate, on the other hand, to consider the way in which the controversies around the Ossianic texts contributed to two different developments of the European conception of nation in Britain and Germany. In the eighteenth century, Britain as a nation and a state was a rapidly developing construct; the cornerstone had been laid with the union of the crowns in 1603, but there were not enough mansions in the house, apparently, so after the wars – religious, political and national – a second attempt to cement Britain together took place with the union of parliaments in 1707. Katie Trumpener puts it aptly in her *Bardic Nationalism*:

> As formed in 1707 by the legislative union between the kingdom of Scotland and an England that had already subsumed Wales and held Ireland in its colonial thrall, the Anglo Scottish state had the fortune or misfortune to be combined before the general formation of modern national consciouslness (15).

Britain was not a new term in literary texts, but now became most often used to signify the emerging nation state that was the growing United Kingdom. Scotsmen were more interested in the union than the "Sassenachs", both pro and contra, and delivered *Tea-Table Miscellanies* with songs from both countries. James Thomson produced an *œuvre* that glorified the land and idylls of Britain. He sang of *Liberty* and her route from Greece to Rome to Britain, a common paradigm in what may perhaps be termed classical nationalism. Furthermore, Thomson followed Trissino's example and wrote a *Sophonisbe* in blank verse in an age of rhyme; he also wrote, with another Scotsman, David Mallet, a play on Alfred the Great which included the (in)famous "Rule Britannia". There were also Englishmen who desired a harmonious Britain: the Wartons, William Collins and others showed poetic interest in different and peripheral aspects of their country and culture. Along with the cult of the sublime, the cult of a British Greece was present in poems by Joseph Warton and Mark Akenside.

This nationalistic tendency in poetry was supported by intellectual optimism expressed as early as in Shaftesbury's *Sensus Communis*:

> As for us BRITONS, thank Heaven, we have a better *Sense* of Government deliver'd to us from our Ancestors. We have the Notion of a PUBLICK, and A CONSTITUTION; how *a Legislative,* and how *an Executive* is model'd. We understand Weight and Measure in this kind, and can reason justly on the *Ballance of Power* and *Property*. The Maxims we draw from hence, are as evident as those in *Mathematicks* (74, emphasis in text).

Politically, the Jacobite rebellions were the greatest source of dissonance in all this harmony, particularly the final (third) one in 1745-6. As many commentators have noted and Linda Colley has most graphically demonstrated, anti-Scottish sentiment was high in England after the '45 and mistrust rose even higher during the Seven Years War, in the middle of which a Scotsman, Lord Bute, was made prime minister by the young king. Against that background, *Fragments of Ancient Poetry* were published, followed by *Fingal* and later *Temora*. These poems, through their astronomical success and national implications, were instrumental in focusing the work of the already active literary nationalists on the *different* poetic and linguistic sources in the fragile cultural construct that was called Britain. In fact, they caused a flurry of publications from all corners of the British Isles, often translations imitative of Macpherson's style or collections that were aimed at underlining the difference between his fraudulent work and that of honest antiquarians.

The examples abound: Thomas Percy's translation, *Five Pieces of Runic Poetry,* and his *Reliques of Ancient English Poetry* with its clear reference to the *Fragments* in the title. The Welshman Evan Evans published his *Some Specimens of the Poetry of the Antient Welsh Bards* in 1764; Charles Henry Wilson published *Select Irish Poems Translated* in 1782; and Charlotte Brooke her *Reliques of Ancient Irish Poetry* in 1789 (with Thomas Percy's encouragement), to name just a few works on the poetic side, which represent only a fraction of what was published in this vein after 1760 (Leersen 422). Antiquarians and historians seemed to have much easier access to publishers than before, and the search for manuscripts and lost "authors" reached hitherto unknown proportions. It was in these years that Percy translated *Northern Antiquities*, Thomas Warton wrote the first literary history of English literature, and people like John Pinkerton and Joseph Ritson were active; in Ireland, Charles O'Conor continued to publish and found a collaborator in Thomas Leland for a history of Ireland (Leersen 389). Subjects that in the first three decades of the eighteenth century had been confined to antiquarian circles were now often being published in quarto and bound in leather. This was not all due solely to the publication of Ossianic poetry, but it is nonetheless evident that this one event shook the crumbling neo-classicist literary system so violently that it started to fall apart.

There was a side-effect, however, and that was the fragmentation of Britain. This construct had been a symbolic reality since 1603, a political reality since 1707 (and it took on even larger proportions as such on January 1, 1801 when Ireland was absorbed) but as a cultural reality it was still under construction in 1760. The focus on difference within the British Isles provided by the Ossianic controversies and the imitative publications, poetic and historical, served to draw cultural lines of demarcation so deep that two-hundred years of English hegemony, mutual interests in the most lucrative of empires, and national wars against enemies like Napoleon and Hitler were unable to wipe them out. To be sure, they had been there before, and all nationalists, English, Welsh, Irish and Scottish, would and could go far back in history to claim something "unique" for their nation, but it was in the latter part of the eighteenth century that the several identities of the British Isles were provided with their different histories, manners, languages, literatures, traditions and races: with their modern nationality. Britain is the most obvious construct of all nations, and it is not a coincidence, I think, that at a time when it is breaking up, *The Poems of Ossian* have once again become the object of intense inquiry.

The failure of Britain is, then, a failure of translation: the translation that takes the past and successfully translates it into the chosen construct of modernity, taking along all the elements of a foreign, classical past and making them its own. The mistake in the case of Britain was that due to the controversy about one translation, these translations were diverted into different national channels and all attempts by the Empire to appropriate them were doomed to fail with the Empire itself, for it is in the essence of nationalism to go back to the "original", and that had been irretrievably defined. In the following I will be examining some of the translational approaches that led to these definitions.

3.3   *Ossian*: a Case of Celtic tribalism?[179]

Macpherson's *Fingal* is one of the few literary translations whose authenticity was doubted in an advertisement before publication (Jiriczek II, xxv).[180] The controversy that was born with his adaptation of Celtic poetry into the English language was also, to a large extent, about issues that had very little to do with the craft of translating, the way original texts should be handled and translated, even though the discussion certainly influenced greatly the way Europeans think about translation and, perhaps, the handling of manuscript and oral sources in general. The sound and the fury of the debate were fuelled by forces far removed from all straightforward academic inquiry into the authenticity of the poems. The question that seemed on the surface to be of greatest importance to the camps that established themselves was whether the poems were ancient and rediscovered, in the Renaissance tradition, or absolutely spurious. In reality, however, the debate was partly something that can be termed a battle of Celtic antiquarians, which spilled over into a personal feud between James Macpherson and Samuel Johnson.

Macpherson's method has probably always been pretty clear to anyone who bothered to read his own dissertations accompanying the poems. He "collected from tradition, and some manuscripts," which points to a stronger reliance on oral sources (Gaskill, *Ossian* 51). Macpherson defended his use of oral sources in a passage in the 'Dissertation concerning the Antiquity, etc.' that also sheds light on his editing policy:

---

[179]   This section was originally published in a different version as "Ossian: a Case of Celtic Tribalism or a Translation without an Original?" in *Transfer: Übersetzen – Dolmetschen – Interkulturalität*. Ed. Horst W. Drescher. Frankfurt/Main: Peter Lang, 1997, S. 451 – 462.

[180]   The various editions of *Ossian* are referred to by their editors.

The bards who were originally the disciples of the Druids, had their minds opened, and their ideas enlarged, by being initiated in the learning of that celebrated order. They could form a perfect hero in their own mind, and ascribe that character to the prince. The inferior chiefs made this ideal character the model of their conduct, and by degrees brought their minds to that generous spirit which breathes in the poetry of all times (Gaskill, *Ossian* 48).

This perhaps slightly circular argument reminds me of the reason given by Snorri Sturluson for his use of skaldic poetry when writing *Heimskringla*, the history of the Norwegian kings from the beginning of royal power in Norway, in the thirteenth century – a work he may have written to impress the contemporary king (Kristjánsdóttir, xx).[181] Snorri felt he had to defend his sources and maintained that although the skaldic poetry was of a panegyrical nature, it could not have deviated grossly from the historical facts, as the participants of events were present when the poems were recited, and excessive praise would amount to mockery (Laing I, 213). He then went on and added fictive descriptions and dialogues to give the narrative structure an artistic filling, quoting the poetry extensively throughout to prove his points (Turville-Petre 225-7).

Colin Kidd has pointed out the ideological ramifications of the English translation of this text in the creation of a Teutonist ideology in Scotland and has made the interesting observation that the translator, Samuel Laing, was the brother of Malcolm Laing, editor and debunker of *Ossian*. If, however, we look at the translation of the *Heimskringla* into the English language, we can compare standards of translation, bearing in mind that this translation has caused no controversy at all and is still the best-known translation of *Heimskringla* in the English language.

The translator admits straight away in the preface that he does not have considerable knowledge of Icelandic, a rather unfortunate lack of qualification for a translator of this work, but notes that he had recourse to excellent Scandinavian translations of the work, translations made for the "common man", as he himself says (Laing I, iv-v). What makes one really suspicious though, are glaring errors such as his misunderstanding of the role of the law-speaker, the central figure of the oral transmission of law in an unlettered republic, and the way in which he squeezes the poetry into stale couplets that certainly have nothing to do with the original skaldic metres, in effect projecting a clichéd classical form on poems whose very form constitutes the major part of their art.[182] As to the ac-

---

[181] The two editions of *Heimskringla* are also referred to by one of their Icelandic editors and Scottish translator. According to the Icelandic editors of *Heimskringla*, some scholars are of the opinion that Snorri may have written poetry attributed to others in the Edda and even in Egil's saga (whose author is not known, although Snorri is the likeliest candidate) (Kristjánsdóttir III, xx).

[182] Laing says in a translator's footnote that "Lagmen [from the Norwegian version of "lawmen" it appears; the Icelandic term is "lögsögumaður" or "law speaker", G.K.]

tual meaning of the poetry, which constitutes, if you like, Snorri's evidence, he also admits in the preface that it was beyond him to understand it, but that he used the Scandinavian translations as "a guide to the meaning and the spirit of original" (Laing I, v). He sums up his translation with a modesty that Macpherson lacked: "All that can be said for [t]his work is, that any translation is better than none; and others may be stimulated by it to enter into the same course of study, who may do more justice to a branch of literature scarcely known among us" (Laing I, vi).

The ambiguity of the textual debate in the Ossianic controversy is perhaps better shown by an example from Irish myth. In his book on Fionn mac Cumhaill and Celtic myth in English literature, James MacKillop dismisses Macpherson's work with the usual forgery stamp and discusses the more recent rewritings of the mythical Fionn that are derived from what he regards as the true source, the Irish Fenian cycles (83). He admits, however, given the multiplicity of sources from various times and dialects, that "if a complete and totally coherent retelling of Fionn's adventures is a superhuman burden, we can rejoice that a number of earthbound scholars have given us an interim solution, a kind of scenario of events, based on the apparent life of the hero" (17). We can be grateful for the "earthbound scholars", but their method seems somehow rather familiar. MacKillop goes further and gives us examples and I think it is best to let him speak for himself:

> Within these severe limitations the most celebrated scenarist of Fenian narratives was Lady Gregory in *Gods and Fighting Men* (1904), more than half of which is given to this end. Her version is told in eleven Chapters with sixty-four numbered episodes and is based largely on manuscript narratives which had recently been translated in such scholary [sic] Celtic journals as the *Transactions of the Ossianic Society* and *Revue Celtique*, as she acknowledged in rather incomplete footnotes. Where it suited her taste, she altered or augmented manuscript narratives with materials from oral tradition collected by Jeremiah Curtin, Douglas Hyde, and others, including some variants from Gaelic Scotland. Thus her final product was something never before seen anywhere, and it contained episodes which would have sounded unfamiliar to almost any individual inheritor of Fenian tradition. Nonetheless, for her work in arranging these tales, and even more for *Cuchulain of Muirthemne* (1902), W. B. Yeats called her the Malory of the Irish Renaissance, a compliment as much indicative of the influence of her work as of its method of organization (17-18).

Macpherson was of course to an extent author of the poems he compiled and adapted. According to Derick Thomson's unsurpassed work on the textual question, *Temora* seems to be the best evidence of that, where the author

---

were district judges appointed by the Things to administer the law" (Laing I, 213), when in fact they were trained indviduals who memorized the whole corpus of law and recited it in three consecutive assemblies. On the skaldic metres, Turville-Petre offers a good overview in *Origins of Icelandic Literature* (2-47).

Macpherson reigns, having learned his craft from the translator Macpherson. As a whole one can describe *The Poems of Ossian* as a translation without an original, a text in one manuscript underpinned by the authority of time, place and property. It was not the translation itself that caused the controversy, however, but a tribal tug of war between the Scots and the Irish revolving primarily around the mystical origin of the Celtic peoples, which was being appropriated at the time into enlightened secular discourse in an attempt to construct a respectable past for the new national collective entities that were needed in the British Isles after the resolutions of religious conflicts. That these conflicts were not resolved, and only shifted onto another level of consciousness, can perhaps best be seen in the Ossianic controversy. That this real starting point of the controversy has not often been discussed is due to the fact that scholars have concentrated on the personal feud between Macpherson and Samuel Johnson, which, incidentally, also has its roots in the national conflict.

As Joep Leerssen shows in his book *Mere Irish & Fíor Ghael*, the Ossianic controversy has a long ancestry prior to the birth of the terrible beauty of *Ossian* (393).[183] In 1753, for example, the antiquarian Charles O'Conor anonymously published his *Dissertations on the Antient History of Ireland*. This work was apparently sent to Johnson in the year 1757 by George Faulkner, a well-known publisher, antiquarian and an Irish cultural nationalist.[184] Johnson acknowledged having read the work in a very courteous letter to O'Conor expressing the hope that he would "continue to cultivate this kind of learning, which has lain too long neglected [...]" (*Letters I,* Chapman, 101/Boswell, *Life* 227-228).

Three years later Macpherson and Hugh Blair published the *Fragments of Ancient Poetry*, provoking the intellectual elite in Dublin, who, upon hearing of Macpherson's work on Fingal, published the advertisement doubting its authenticity. This advertisement obviously annoyed Macpherson, to the extent that he quoted it in full in his dissertation accompanying *Temora* in 1763. In this dissertation he attacks the Irish intellectuals head on, starting off bluntly by saying that:

Nations, small in their beginnings and slow in their progress to maturity, cannot with any degree of certainty, be traced to their source. The first historians, in every country, are, therefore, obscure and unsatisfactory. Swayed by a national partiality, natural to mankind, they adopted uncertain legends and ill fancied fictions, when they served to strengthen a favourite system, or throw lustre on the antient state of their country (Jiriczek II, i).

---

[183]   That Yeats' refrain in *Easter 1916* was inspired by Macpherson was pointed out by Derick Thomson in a paper entitled 'Macpherson's Ossian: ballads to epics' (264).

[184]   It is in Faulkner's Dublin journal that the advertisement that doubted Fingal's authenticity appeared in 1761. See Jiriczek II, xxv.

Some commentators, like Heinrich Detering for instance, have interpreted Macpherson's dissertations as a calculated hint at his own forgery, but Macpherson's twofold objective in this case was to undermine O'Conor's speculation on the origin of the Celts in Ireland and focus on the partiality of historiographers old and new.[185] In doing this he was much more digging his own grave than hinting at his own authorship. Macpherson's own use of tradition, as expressed in the dissertation accompanying *Fingal*, becomes more than questionable in the one accompanying *Temora,* when he tries to tie it to a notion of racial purity, claiming that "if tradition could be depended upon, it is only among a people, from all time, free of intermixture with foreigners" (Jiriczek II, ii). This racial argument can be traced directly to O'Conor, who contended in his 1753 *Dissertations* that:

> Our Scotic, we think, hath the preference, in Point of Purity, if not Antiquity, to all other *Celtic* dialects; and as it is evident we had the use of Letters since our first Settlements in Ireland, there can be no Dispute but that it comes nearest the original Language of the Posterity of Japhet, and must be, consequently, [...] the most *Original* and UNMIXT Language yet remaining in any Part of Europe (37).

This was, ironically, the real bone of contention between the Irish and Scots in the Ossianic question of translation and/or literary theft; an argument that primarily revolves around the racial purity or 'originality' of Celtic tribes, hence almost equating the origins of a text and language with the origins of a people.[186] Macpherson's counterattacks provide the best proof of this; in his dissertation accompanying the first edition of *Temora*, he concentrates on the linguistic evidence: "As [the Highland chiefs] had little communication with strangers, the customs of their ancestors remained among them, and their language retained its original purity" (Jiriczek II, xvi).

Macpherson knew, however, that such an assertion would not stand on its own, except perhaps among the most patriotic Scots, so he decided to provide complementary evidence for it. As a classical scholar he knew where such evidence was to be found, in the written records of ancient historians. This evidence did not, however, fit his oral and written sources, so it seems that it was at this point that he embarked upon his second career – as a poet. Thomson's work

---

[185] Detering reads a subtext in the *Dissertations* in which Macpherson allegedly hints at the work being a forgery, the motive being to underline subtly his own authorship. Accepting this by no means new notion, one must also accept that Macpherson is one of the few authors who succeeds fully in his intentions with his fictional work, and even the clumsy attempt at translating his English original into Gaelic would therefore be a part of the masterful scheme.

[186] Not surprisingly, many thinkers were at the time writing tracts on the origin of language, among them Adam Smith, Rousseau, and one of the greatest admirers of Ossian, Herder.

on Macpherson's sources points strongly in this direction; *Temora* shows a much greater divergence from the Gaelic sources he found than *Fingal* does. Having created the right pattern for his fabric of history and translation, Macpherson thus says in his preface that Ossian's "accounts agree so well with what the antients have delivered, concerning the first population and inhabitants of Ireland, that every unbiassed person will confess them more probable, than the legends handed down, by tradition, in that country" (Jiriczek II, viii). One can see in these words the reshaping of balladry to fit the shape of classical history, an attempt at rewriting tradition in accordance with written records. Macpherson's sources proved but poor garment for the classics, however, and hence he took what amounts to more than acceptable translator's licence in order to hit back at the Irish.

Continuing his attack on the Irish antiquarians, the next target was obviously one that was dear to O'Conor. One of the most important elements in his 1753 *Dissertations* is the notion that there had been a monarchy and a royal line in Ireland that was "indisputably the *most antient* in the World" (182, emphasis in text). Having already transported the Irish royal line to Scotland through the Scots of Dal Ríata, noting that "in process of Time, we find this celebrated Race becoming, by Force of Arms, Masters of almost all *North-Britain*, under KINETH MacALPINE, in the ninth century; and finally, through the Daughter of MALCOLM II. giving Monarchs to these three Kingdoms in the Person of James VI. of *Scots*, whose Posterity fills the Throne of all the British Dominions, at this day, by the succession of King GEORGE II.", his motives for writing the text take on a different quality altogether (O'Conor *Diss. 1753*, xxix, emphasis in text).[187] Macpherson was well aware of this and attacked with his own Ossian in the *Temora* dissertation, saying "one important fact may be gathered from this history of Ossian, that the Irish had no king before the latter end of the first century" (Jiriczek II, viii).

Due to the strong Irish response in London, David Hume asked Blair to provide him with testimonies from Highlanders, in order to convince the English of the so-called authenticity of the poems, although the well-known letter he sent to Blair shows that he did not think they were of historical value.[188] The publication of the *Works of Ossian* in 1765 with Blair's dissertation and the testimonies gave *The Poems of Ossian* the air of an established text, something the Irish were not ready to swallow.

---

[187] The clash between the Irish and Macphersonian inventions of origins as a clash between the ideas of a "mythic past which was sophisticated politically and culturally, rather than primitive" is discussed in Clare O'Halloran's, "Irish re-creations of the Gaelic past: the challenge of Macpherson's Ossian".

[188] This letter is printed in *The Life and Letters of James Macpherson* by [Thomas] Bailey Saunders (203-206).

Macpherson met Boswell and Johnson soon after he came to London to enjoy the fame he had been catapulted into. There were small clashes right from the start; Macpherson seems to have caused the falling out of Johnson and Thomas Sheridan by quoting Johnson's remarks on Sheridan when the latter got a pension (Boswell, *Life* 274). Thomas Percy also related in a letter to Evan Evans in 1764 that Johnson had interrogated Macpherson about the poems and that Macpherson "answered each of Mr Johnson's questions with a short round assertion" (*Letters V* 97). Macpherson and Johnson were thus already at loggerheads regarding the Ossianic question in 1764, and Johnson's low opinion of the poetry may well have been public knowledge, as the phrase in the *Journey*, "I suppose my opinion of the poems of Ossian is already discovered", indicates (176). Certainly Blair was aware of Johnson's opinion, as it was he who, after asking in 1763 whether Johnson thought "any man of a modern age could have written such poems", received the famous retort, "yes, Sir, many men, many women, and many children" (Boswell, *Life* 280). It also seems that Boswell developed a personal dislike for Macpherson. He described him as someone who "rails against all established systems", and his epithet for him, "sublime savage", was not meant as a compliment (Boswell, *Life/London*, 306/265-266). One can also speculate on what Johnson, with his hard-won honours, thought of an arrogant Scot and Highlander who had become famous overnight for translating poetry of a kind that was certainly not to his taste.

Then, out of the blue, in the summer of 1765, Johnson was awarded a degree from Trinity College in Dublin, making him a Doctor of Law (Boswell, *Life* 345-346). This degree, which Boswell says was "unsolicited", is ironic in light of the fact that Earl Gower had unsuccessfully tried to procure a degree of Master of Arts for Johnson, which he needed in order to become a schoolmaster, from the same college in 1738 (Boswell, *Life* 95-96). In the end the "Oxford dropout", in John Wain's words, had had to wrest his Master's degree out of Oxford with the help of Dr. Thomas Warton and the Rev. Francis Wise before the publication of his dictionary (Wain 57/174). Ten years after the publication of Johnson's *Dictionary,* this new doctoral degree can hardly be attributed to that great achievement, as has sometimes been implied (Wharton 152). Even if the Irish intellectuals had got wind of the long-awaited Shakespeare edition being in its final stages (probably through Edmund Burke), it does not change the possibility that they saw this as a potentially useful opportunity. Certainly Burke had aired his views about the poems publicly, as the famous letter from Hume to Blair indicates: "I was told by Bourke, a very ingenious Irish gentleman, the author of a tract on the Sublime and Beautiful, that on the first publication of Macpherson's book, all the Irish cried out: 'We know these poems; we have known them from our infancy [...]'" (Saunders 205).

The Irish intellectuals had certainly not forgotten Dr. Johnson when the better-known second edition of O'Conor's work was published in 1766, this time under his name and with a new title: *Dissertations on the History of Ireland to which is joined A Dissertation on the IRISH Colonies Established in BRITAIN*. The subtitle reads: *With some Remarks on Mr. MacPherson's Translation of Fingal and Temora*. O'Conor maintains that the "first Hints [to improve his first edition] have been communicated by Dr. SAMUEL JOHNSON" and that he, despite difficulties, "rendered a Compliance with Dr. *Johnson's* Desires" (O'Conor, *Diss. 1766* iv-v, emphasis in text). It goes without saying that the greatest "improvement" was a whole new dissertation attacking Macpherson's *Ossian* in detail, and specifically for having taken "oral Tradition *alone*, for his Guide, when all historical Scripture failed" (22, emphasis in text). This should explain why Dr. Johnson thought his opinion had already been discovered, for although he had not "committed himself in print prior to the *Journey*", as Pat Rogers observes (205), he did not dismiss O'Conor's words. The argument was hence rapidly developing into a dialogical – if not dialectical – dispute between Macpherson and O'Conor about the reliability of sources, oral or written, primitive or sophisticated, Scottish or Irish.[189]

Since the argument revolved around defending and attacking a heritage that had not been established as such and referred to something unknown to the potential English-speaking reader, other referential instances had to be invoked, in the form of written classics and what O'Conor himself neatly termed a "hypercritic" (51).[190] The reference to "classics" involved a double strategy in both cases. The first was of course to use established texts as proof for an argument. This was Macpherson's method, and one may assume that it forced him to bend his oral sources considerably to make them fit the classical model. According to Fiona Stafford in *The Sublime Savage* "the similarities between the Highlanders and the ancient people described by classical authors was designed to prove Macpherson's theory that they were the direct descendants of the Celts, while the learned references had the added benefit of bolstering the impression of scholarship" (154). One can assume that this applies not only to his dissertations, but also to the poem *Temora*.

---

[189] In a way this dialectical development reflects the age-old struggle between Catholicism and Protestantism in Britain. O'Halloran's article in *Past and Present* (1989) makes clear how Catholic scholars like O'Conor dismissed Macpherson from a historical and literary point of view that was Augustan in essence, whereas the Irish Protestants later 'drifted' towards Macpherson's texts from a more nationalist angle. This is perhaps not surprising when one considers Macpherson's editing policy; he seems to have weeded out all 'superstition' and allusions to (Catholic) Christianity, which he then used as a counterargument against the Irish. See Macpherson's 'A Dissertation' with the 1765 edition of *Temora* in Gaskill's edition (222-224).

[190] This term appears in the new dissertation on *Fingal* and *Temora* which has a title page of its own and separate page numbers: *A Dissertation on the First Migrations, and Final Settlement of the Scots in North-Britain; with Occasional Observations on the Poems of Fingal and Temora*.

O'Conor's method, on the other hand, was to lend his written sources an air of classical authority by emphasizing their factual existence and so conforming to the Augustan insistence on ancient writings as the source of modern learning. This he underpinned with the oft-repeated assertion that Ireland had been the "prime Seat of Learning in all Christendom" (O'Conor, *Diss. 1766* v). Once this first strategy of "classicality" had been established, both men could proceed to the second strategy, which was to claim greater originality for their respective sources, and hence their own "tribes", which both maintained were the most unmixed, racially and linguistically, of all the peoples in the British Isles.

O'Conor's term, "hypercritic", appears in a satirical dialogue between Ossian and Macpherson where Ossian asks the forger a final question:

> And what more, Mr. *Macpherson*?
>   What more, Ossian? Why, I will prevail with our Hypercritic, Dr. *Blair*, to summon a Cloud of Witnesses from the *Highlands* and *Hebrides* to depose *upon their poetical Conscience*, that you and I are as honest Fellows, as ever played a first and second Fiddle in *a poetical Concert*! (O'Conor, *Diss. 1766* 51)[191]

Such a passage may well explain O'Conor's need to summon a critic of Dr. Johnson's stature to justify his work. The revised text of his first edition includes one of the arguments Dr. Johnson was later to use about Macpherson having picked up names of men and places for his fictional epics (O'Conor, *Diss. 1766* 22). O'Conor also mentions a number of other intellectuals in his preface, of whom three are of greatest interest in this context. The first is Thomas Leland of Trinity College in Dublin, who according to O'Conor seems to have gone to considerable lengths to procure old manuscripts for the University so he could do research on them (xiii). O'Conor's cooperation with Leland in the effort to create a national history for Ireland is well documented (Leerssen 389-390). Leland is also one of the signatories of Johnson's diploma from the University, and Johnson thanked him personally in a letter (Boswell, *Life* 345-346/Letters Hyde I, 257). The second person is indeed Edmund Burke, who according to O'Conor encouraged him (*Diss. 1766* xv) and seems also later to have been stimulated into acquiring Irish manuscripts for the College (Love 21-35). In addition, one can see in a letter to Burke from the third intellectual mentioned in O'Conor's preface, Dr. John Curry, that Burke and O'Conor were in contact in the first half of the 1760s (Burke 203).

Critical Dissertations on the origins of the Celts by John Macpherson, Minister of Sleat in Skye, were posthumously published in 1768, but they seem

---

[191] The page number refers to O'Conor's special *Dissertation* on *Fingal* and *Temora*.

to have had little impact in refuting O'Conor.[192] At any rate, James Macpherson felt a need to address the matter and did so in his *Introduction to the History of Great Britain and Ireland*, a work in which he attempted to rebut O'Conor's version of history. This work went into three editions from 1771 to 1773, the same year in which his translation from Homer was published, as well as yet another edition of *Ossian*.[193]

In this work he again rejects the Irish Bards as an authority, O'Conor having maintained that their written records in Ireland exposed Macpherson's ignorance. Leaning once again on classical authors, Macpherson attacks O'Conor's written sources directly. O'Conor maintained in his *Dissertations* that the Irish had been "lettered" before Christ and before Roman Britain and that "the Philosophy and Jurisprudence of the Nation were committed to the *Taibble Filea*, or the wooden Tables of the Learned" (O'Conor, *Diss. 1766* viii). Having seen the etymological weakness of this argument, Macpherson asserted that "the proper terms by which the Irish, in their vulgar language, express every thing concerning letters and science, being Latin words hibernized, leave no room to doubt that they were taught first to read and write by persons who spoke the Roman language" (*Introduction* 114). Macpherson followed this line of argumentation, knowing that it "deprived himself of the authority of the Poems of Ossian, which seem to strengthen the fabric which he means to rear." (*Introduction* 95-96) Leaning on Hume, he denied the authority of the Celtic orders of learning, maintaining that men of religion, Druids as well as Priests, were enemies of history (*Introduction* 6). The objective was to undermine O'Conor and his Irish manuscripts, but may also explain his editorial policy with regard to the poems, especially *Fingal*. Nevertheless, by supplanting them with vague allusions to "profane writers from antiquity" (*Introduction* 17), he destroyed not only the authority of the oral sources, which were his strength, but also the originality of *The Poems of Ossian*, which gave them the only authority an oral source could have. This gamble was to cost him dear.

Another mistake was his personal attack on Dr. Johnson. He does not name him, of course, but after O'Conor's second edition anybody could read Johnson's name into the following:

Some men of letters in England are not silent spectators of the contest. [...] They abet absurdity, on account of its antiquity; and with a determined scepticism against argu-

---

192 The closeness of this work to James Macpherson's dissertations and *An Introduction to the History of Great Britain and Ireland* is discussed by Fiona Stafford in *The Sublime Savage* (152).

193 According to one of Macpherson's biographers, T. Bailey Saunders, Hume praised the *Introduction* whereas Pinkerton attacked it; an interesting reception considering Pinkerton's role in creating a Teutonist ideology within the Scottish nationalist framework (218).

ments deduced from reason, cherish with affected credulity, fictions that disgrace common sense with their obvious folly. In a pretended, but awkward compliment to the Irish, they hope to dishonour the Scots, by fixing on them an Hibernian origin; and by an oversight, not uncommon with the prejudiced, they weaken their system by their illiberality and rage (*Introduction* 89-90).

Most commentators, beginning, interestingly, with Boswell, have tried to explain Dr. Johnson's sweeping judgments on the state of Gaelic letters in Scotland as a national prejudice, and Gaskill for example, adds that in the Ossianic argument about 'originals', he was right, even if he did not know it (67). But prejudiced as Dr. Johnson may have been, he was not simple-minded. He already knew roughly how *Ossian* had come into existence, and his adversary, Macpherson and not the Scots *per se,* had provided him with the necessary ammunition. He therefore went to the Hebrides with a distinct goal in mind, knowing full well that Macpherson's 'originals' must have partly consisted of transcripts of oral recitation, as Gaskill points out (72).[194] It is also clear from the *Journey* and his letters to Mrs. Thrale that he did try to find out whether Macpherson's oral sources were strong, and he did ask about manuscripts, despite his lack of Gaelic (Johnson, *Letters I,* Chapman 360-363). He then went to Edinburgh and met Blair, and they had an argument so monumental that word of it spread to London (Johnson, *Letters I,* Chapman 397).[195] In this argument Johnson may well have realised the nature of Macpherson's manuscripts and originals.

Johnson may have underestimated their quantity, but the argument was still won, as one can deduce from the confidence he expresses in the famous letter to Macpherson: "I thought your book an imposture; I think it an imposture still. For this I have given my reasons to the publick, which I here dare you to defy." (Boswell, *Life* 579)[196] This might also explain the remark in the letter he wrote to Boswell that "if [Macpherson] had not talked unskilfully of *manuscripts*, he could have fought with oral tradition much longer" (Boswell, *Life* 589, emphasis in text).

Oral tradition was what Dr. Johnson, diligently aided by Macpherson and O'Conor, managed to discredit most of all in his *Journey,* not because he despised it so, but because it was the only shelter Macpherson had when it came to discrepancies between manuscripts and translation. Because this tradition had

---

[194] Or as Katie Trumpener argues: "[…] the journey itself seems conceived as a repetition and refutation of Macpherson's prior collecting journey through the Highlands […]" (71).

[195] Blair even asked Boswell to tell Johnson that he had not instigated the rumour (Boswell, *Life* 562)

[196] This famous letter is most often quoted in a doctored version, as Fiona Stafford shows in her 'Dr. Johnson and the ruffian: new evidence in the dispute between Samuel Johnson and James Macpherson'.

been supported in the testimonies Blair collected from gentlemen in the Highlands, it became all-important for Dr. Johnson to say that one of them, the Rev. McQueen (whom he does not name), would not deceive him directly, despite the fact that his "testimony had been publicly produced, as of one that held Fingal to be the work of Ossian" (*Journey* 176). This he underlined with his version of the phrase borrowed from Aristotle, and it seems from Boswell's account of the controversy that this aspect was the only one that he was not quite sure of[197] – at least he needed to repeat it in the face of the strong response from Scotland. Two months after the publication of the *Journey* Boswell says that "he was also outrageous, upon his supposition that my countrymen 'loved Scotland better than truth', saying, 'All of them, – nay not all, – but *droves* of them, would come up, and attest any thing for the honour of Scotland'" (Boswell, *Life* 589).

The advertisement from Macpherson's publisher, Thomas Becket, an inversion of the Irish advertisement 14 years before, therefore posed no threat in the controversy and Macpherson was now so roundly beaten that he was reduced to compiling a Gaelic 'original' of his own adaptation, perhaps the act which finally condemned him to the forger's bench.[198] His countrymen took up the banner he left lying, but, like Donald MacNicol in his *Remarks on Dr. Johnson's Journey to the Hebrides*, they were reduced to calling on the oral tradition and the Bards, whom Macpherson and his opponents had discredited in their tribal argument over whose fantasy of origins was closer to history. For the Irish the victory was, therefore, pyrrhic, although their historical and poetic reputation may have been enhanced somewhat in the short term, as Leerssen points out (399). *Ossian's* damnation into the annals of forgery has made Celtic heritage "tawdry", in Arnold's description, and the blame lies not wholly with Macpherson.

The sturdy moralist Dr. Johnson, on the other hand, who himself, as a parliamentary writer, was guilty of deception and forgery, gained a lot from the affair; his victory has long been considered that of a good scholar who knew by instinct what was right, even if his methods may have seemed a bit excessive on the surface. He was indeed a good scholar, so he did not rely on instinct, but on the evidence he had and could use. He was also rewarded accordingly by his contemporaries. Three months after the *Journey to the Western Islands of Scotland* appeared, he was finally made Doctor of Civil Law by the University of Oxford.

---

[197] The phrase, *Plato is dear to me, but dearer still is truth*, is only ascribed to Aristotle.

[198] The wording of this advertisement is interesting: "I hereby declare that the originals of FINGAL and other poems of Ossian lay in my shop for many months in the year 1762, for the inspection of the curious" (Gaskill, "What" 67). The phrase, not including *Temora*, must stem from Macpherson. See also Gaskill's "Introduction" in *Ossian Revisited*.

3.3.1 The Subversive Loyalty of Translation[199]

Translation of key texts has been a political act at least since Luther, if not since Wycliffe. The protestant obsession with the biblical texts as an authority beyond human fallibility marked from the beginning the politicisation of Bible texts, since their interpretation was a formidable political instrument. On the other hand, such authorities were always marked by the fallibility of translation, the problem of which was dual: any *nec verbo verbum* translation was unreadable, while an evangelical one was always vulnerable. This was apparent even in Wycliffe's time, and his followers produced two versions, the latter of which was more user-friendly.[200] Luther went farther by attempting to combine the two methods and at the same time underpin his authority by going back to the Hebrew and Greek "originals".[201] Yet, when attacked for mistranslation, he appealed in his "Eyn sendbrieff Vom Dolmetzschen" both to himself as a translator and the German language itself as authorities, in effect taking the established authority of the passive source, the "originals" into the active political sphere of individuals and society (Störig 18-21). His success has also long been considered a beginning of German linguistic and literary identity.

While on his way to London from Edinburgh in 1603, another political scholar and translator, King James VI/I, quickly realised that a new translation of the Bible, "consonant as can be of the original Hebrew and Greek", might be one of the ways to cement the two kingdoms together.[202] The attempt was not successful politically if one looks at the struggles of the seventeenth century, but it did create a unified standard text that became one of the pillars of English literature, providing authors and translators with an uncontested linguistic and literary source. Moreover, through its royal "authority" it brought what may perhaps be termed the spirit of the original to the British Isles, as may be deduced from the translators' dedication:

> Great and manifold were the blessings, most dread Sovereign, which Almighty God, the Father of all mercies, bestowed upon us the people of *England*, when first he sent Your Majesty's Royal Person to rule and reign over us. For whereas it was the expectation of many, who wished not well unto our *Sion*, [...]

This translation of Zion to England became part and parcel of the protestant British nationalist ideology of the eighteenth century, as Linda Colley has ar-

---

199 This section was originally published in a slightly different version in the journal *Scotlands* 4.1 (1997): 71-85. I thank the Edinburgh University Press for the permission to use it.
200 See for example K.B. MacFarlane's *Wycliffe and English Non-Conformity* (104-105).
201 See W. Schwarz, *Principles and Problems of Biblical Translation* (205-212).
202 See A.C. Partridge, *English Biblical Translation* (105) and *The Oxford Companion to the Bible* (759).

gued in *Britons: Forging the Nation 1707-1837* (29-43), and in his *Britannia's Issue,* Howard D. Weinbrot goes so far as to maintain that "the mid-century Celtic revival depends upon Hebrew language and genealogy" (407).[203] Through the authority of the Bible, the Hebrew language and translations of Hebrew texts certainly became an ideological factor at the back of poetical discourses and controversies in the eighteenth century, as the Ossianic controversy itself shows best; the idea of languages being directly derived from the Hebrew, however, was by no means a new notion then, and it was not restricted to attempts by Celtic antiquarians to link their ancestors to the authors of the Christian world.[204] In fact, most of the fictions on the origins of barbaric peoples at the margins seem to follow this pattern: an intellectual at the centre "discovers" writings or a language at the margin of his cultural domain and tries to elevate it – and the culture of the centre along with it – by linking it to the linguistic and thus genealogical authority of the Bible. The Danish scholar Ole Worm did this in 1636 with the Icelandic heritage in the *Runir seu Danica litteratura antiqvissima,* a text which later became one of Thomas Percy's sources for his ideas on "runic" poetry. Olof Rudbeck in Sweden also theorised on a Hebrew linguistic source of the Lappish or Sami language in the late seventeenth century.[205] All of these cultures later produced "evidence" in the form of texts which perfectly fit the primitivist tenets of the mid-eighteenth century, evidence which Hugh Blair alludes to in his "Critical Dissertation on the Poems of Ossian".[206]

The Enlightenment of course eliminated many such seventeenth-century etymological fantasies, but the search and ideas survived in a more sophisticated form. They became, in fact, part of the arsenal in the antiquarian wars of the latter half of the eighteenth century, a time when a multitude of cultural authorities were being redefined and replaced. The antiquarians and translators of that age supplied the new meanings to a great extent, being the Janus-faced figures that could provide the growing nation with the dioscurian feeling of belonging to a human heaven on earth. This complex undertaking could only be realised with methods that combined the desire to retrieve a "lost" original and the intellectual

---

[203]   The difference between the two is that Colley sees this development as a subjective Protestant ideology of the elect, whereas Weinbrot develops a theory of British philosemitism.

[204]   See for example Fiona Stafford's discussion *The Sublime Savage* on the influence of Robert Lowth's *Lectures on the Sacred Poetry of the Hebrews* (1753) on Macpherson's diction (86-91).

[205]   *Íslensk Bókmenntasaga II* (493); Wilhelm Friese "Barock in Nordeuropa. Fremde Einflüsse und Eigenständigkeit" (105-117); E. Ekman, "Gothic Patriotism and Olof Rudbeck" (52-63).

[206]   In Howard Gaskill's edition of James Macpherson,*The Poems of Ossian and Related Works* (347-349, 543-548). Afterwards referred to as Gaskill.

achievement of the Enlightenment. The politics of the day finally instrumentalised these undertakings for its own ends.

John Home, tutor of the Prince of Wales and discoverer and mentor of James Macpherson, was certainly aware of the political implications of poetry, having resigned his job as a Presbyterian minister in his native country after writing the blank verse tragedy *Douglas* because the Kirk could hardly tolerate a minister writing for the theatre. This now unread tragedy, often condemned as unreadable, is in fact readable when compared to some of the drama of the time, perhaps too readable. The language requires no dictionaries, the plot is predictable and the verse goes down without any major problem. What makes the text *Douglas* interesting is its relevance to *Ossian* and the skilful mixing of genres and diverse authorities. The text has a ballad source (Childe Maurice/Gil Morrice in Percy), the drama takes place before the background of an anachronistic Danish invasion, and Home manages to weave into the plot an evil figure with a conspicuously Gaelic-sounding name, Glenalvon – a character that reminds one of Iago in his scheming – and an orphaned nobleman, Douglas himself, who as an infant was saved by a pastoral shepherd who found the child in a basket floating on a river.[207] On top of this, Home hints at Oedipus in the mother/son relationship and crowns the piece with an off-stage sword fight in which the main protagonists die, leading to Lady Randolph's rushing out and throwing herself into a river.

What seems to be missing in the tragedy is a tragic hero. Home, in effect, inverts the tragic flaw and changes it into virtue when creating his hero. The impeccably virtuous Douglas dies, his death brought about not only by Glenalvon's scheming but also by his own virtue, as can be seen from Lady Randolph's justified question: "[...] are these the fruits of virtue?" (65). Lady Randolph herself, on the other hand, might be considered a candidate for a tragic heroine, having married the man a family feud forbade her to marry, only to lose him after three weeks and having to give birth to their only child in secret before disposing of it. Whether Home named the tragedy wrongly or not, it is clear that he skilfully combined motifs from folklore, pastoral poetry, the Bible, Shakespeare and Greek classical drama. He also hoped he could increase the prestige of his native country and contribute to the reconciliation of "the sister kingdoms", as Lady Randolph underlines with her abhorrence of wars in which the "fruit of Scotch and English wars" kills the young in their prime (4).[208] In his prologue Home puts the age-old strife into a greater historical and literary frame:

---

[207] Hugh Blair uses *Douglas* as an example for a most "distinguished Anagnoris[i]s" in his *Lectures on Rhetoric and Belles Lettres III* (292).

[208] Richard Sher pointed out the political relevance of *Douglas* to the Ossianic project in "Those Scotch Imposters and the Cabal" (55-63).

> In ancient times, when *Britain's* trade was arms,
> And the lov'd music of her youth, alarms,
> A god-like race sustain'd fair *England's* fame:
> Who has not heard of gallant *Piercy's* name?
> Ay, and of *Douglas*? Such illustrious foes
> In rival *Rome* and *Carthage* never rose!
> From age to age bright shone the *British* fire,
> And every hero was a hero's sire.

Apart from the racial allusion to a "god-like race" that "sires" heroes, the analogy to Roman antiquity is a typical nod to the ancients that becomes uncomfortable when the fate of Carthage is considered. Home makes up for this in the final words of the prologue by appealing to English generosity:

> This night a *Douglas* your protection claims;
> A wife! a mother! pity's softest names:
> The story of her woes indulgent hear,
> And grant your Suppliant all she begs, a tear.
> In confidence she begs; and hopes to find
> Each *English* breast, like noble *Piercy's*, kind.

Despite David Garrick's rejection of the tragedy for the Drury Lane theatre, the English were generally kind during its successful run at Covent Garden in 1757. Thomas Gray, who studied the ballad source while he was correcting *The Bard*, said in a letter that Home seemed to him "to have retrieved the true language of the Stage, which had been lost for these hundred years" (*Letters II* 503-505, 515). Home, whose interest in the Highlands of Scotland was not new, went on with the young James Macpherson to retrieve something of greater significance in the hope of attracting further English kindness, and again his attempt became embroiled in political controversy, for the *Fragments of Ancient Poetry* and *Fingal* roused not only the wrath of Irish scholars, who considered the Scottish project an attempt at cultural theft, but also many Englishmen, who saw the poems as an upstart Scottish attempt to gain favour at court through a new literary pedigree: an ancient epic couched in biblical language with all the trappings of serious scholarship.[209]

The numerous controversies surrounding the Ossianic poems – the intra-Celtic one on property, the antiquarian and historical one on authenticity, the poetical one on form and the simple envy of those who disliked the Scottishness of the Earl of Bute – all contributed to their impact, an impact that was to be strengthened through their rapturous reception in Europe. One of the most frequently repeated critical accusations in the twentieth century has been that Macpherson was able to pull off his con by catering to contemporary primitivist

---

[209]   See above and Stafford, *Savage* (77); Sher, "Scotch Imposters" (58).

tastes in literature. Partly true, this assumption is also a metonymic falsification, for the Ossianic project catered to *and* formed these tastes in a more complex manner, which is perhaps why some of the leading lights of the Enlightenment accepted the fictional framework. *The Poems of Ossian* were, then, despite the opposite intent, seen by many as a subversive element, poetically in form and strength and politically as a living and potent symbol of a new Scottish hegemony at the court of a king who attempted right from the start to use the power he had.

The poetic controversy concerned translation from the outset. Macpherson's initial reluctance was based on the impossibility of translating the original ballads; he maintained to Home that a translation "would give a very imperfect idea of the original," a statement very true to the end.[210] Indeed, Macpherson's problem was to find a medium of expression for what he must have felt was beautiful poetry in a language which still maintained a stiff poetic hierarchy according to neoclassical standards. That he found it in the language in Gray and the Bible was no coincidence; after all, Gray was one of the first to be sent a specimen of the *Fragments* and the clergymen and scholars Home and Blair were, like Macpherson himself, certainly aware of the linguistic possibilities offered by biblical texts. In his later *Lectures on Rhetoric and Belles Lettres*, Blair discussed Hebrew poetry in the *Book of Job*, the *Psalms of David* and *Songs of Solomon*:

> There is not the least reason for doubting, that originally these were written in verse or some kind of measured numbers; [...] Taking the Old Testament in our Translation, which is extremely literal, we find plain marks of many parts of the original being written in a measured Style; and the 'disjecta membra poëtæ' often show themselves (*Lectures III* 166-167).[211]

The intertextual relationship in spirit to the preface to the *Fragments* in the words "extremely literal" on a translation that was supposedly the "disjecta membra" of an original epic gives reason to assume that Blair must have considered the style and language of Macpherson's translations similarly. Blair, Home and Macpherson went further, however, and produced an epic, the most important element of the poetical controversy; it was the epic form that gave the poems the grandeur of a national monument, something nationalists in many countries were to understand perfectly in the next century when they constructed epics like the *Kalevala* for precisely the same purpose.[212]

---

[210] Quoted in Stafford, *Savage* (78).
[211] See also Derick S. Thomson, *The Gaelic Sources of Macpherson's 'Ossian'* (13).
[212] To have an epic is apparently still considered to be a mark and justification of nationality; recently I heard a Latvian scholar forward this argument as a self-evident truth in a discussion on national identity. The epic in question, *The Bear Slayer*, is a

Although the creators of *Ossian* had been careful enough "to hear the savage youth repeat, In loose numbers wildly sweet"[213] what they wanted to produce, the result did not sound so sweet in many English ears, as the Scots' Cato, John Wilkes, expresses well in the *North Briton* in November 1762:

> Oh forbear
> To spoil with sacrilegious hand
> The glories of the classic land.
> ...Better be native in thy verse–
> What is *Fingal* but genuine Erse?
> Which, all sublime, sonorous flows
> Like Hervey's *Thoughts* in drunken Prose.[214]

With characteristic insight Wilkes hits a nerve connected with all the major aspects of the Ossianic controversies: the replacement of authority, classical Latin and English, the ambiguity of authenticity and property and last but not least the formal one. The prose of the Ossianic poems, so elementary for the translation, so authoritative in their biblical and primitivist echo, subverted a major strand in the English poetic tradition, that which leant on the Latin poets and their versification. This trend was not new, of course, but it was not a simple offshoot of the old battle of the Ancients and the Moderns, for it was more ambivalent. John MacQueen, for instance, has shown in his *Progress and Poetry* how pioneers like Ramsay rejected the ancients whereas the Scottish *literati* continued to lean on predominantly Greek models (*Enlightenment 1* 70-71). Gray's *The Progress of Poesy* describes the route of the Muses from Greece through Rome to Albion as their country of choice:

> Till the sad Nine, in Greece's evil hour,
> Left their Parnassus for the Latian plains.
> Alike they the pomp of tyrant Power,
> And coward Vice, that revels in her chains.
> When Latium had her lofty spirit lost,
> They sought, oh Albion! next thy sea-encircled coast.[215]

---

construct of the nineteenth century. See also Josef Bysveen, *Epic Tradition and Innovation in James Macpherson's "Fingal."* and Thomson, *Gaelic Sources* (3).

[213] Thomas Gray, *The Progress of Poesy*, ll. 60-61.

[214] Quoted in Saunders, *The Life and Letters of James Macpherson* (186).

[215] A similar idea appears in the *Athenæum* of the Schlegel brothers in Germany: So allgemein ist [...] der Karakter [der Elegie], so weltbürgerlich ihre Gesinnung, daß sie es ungeachtet ihrer zarten Weichheit doch nicht verschmähte, die härtere Sprache des großen Roms zu reden, ja sogar aus dem südlichen Mutterlande nach Norden zu wandern. [...] Sie ist nun nicht mehr bloß eine schöne Antiquität: sie ist hier einheimisch, und lebt unter uns (108) ["The character of the elegy is so general, its attitude so weltbürgerlich [worldly civil] that it, despite its tender softness, did not

The content is underlined by the subtle combination of alliteration, be it Bardic or Skaldic, rhyme and a strict Grecian form which suggests where the original authority lies. The alliteration is even more marked in *The Bard* and turns up again in the "Nordic" odes or imitations in 1768.[216] The same happens in William Mason's final ode in *Caractacus*, an ode in which he "retrieved" the correct language with Gray's help.[217] Answering his friend's request for criticism of the draft in a letter, Gray at first criticises Mason for merging "the Celtic religion with that of the Goths" and claims this is "the doctrine of the *Scalds*, not the Bards" (*Corr. II*, 551). He is, however, so "sorry to have so many good verses & good chimæras thrown away", that he suggests that it might "be permitted (in that scarcity of Celtic Ideas we labour under) to adopt some of these foreign whimsies, dropping however all mention of Woden, & his Valkhyrian [sic] Virgins [...]" (*Corr. II*, 551). This Mason consequently did, and the final version of the ode, which was written and published during the Seven Years War, became a remarkable mixture of the Pythagorean and/or druidic idea of metempsychosis, or the transmigration of souls, and Valhalla, the "Gothic Elysium" in Gray's phrase, where warriors spend their afterlife fighting battles after which the fallen rise to fight another day.[218] Mason achieves this by letting Death urge the Britons to go to the battlefield:

> Go then to conquest, gladly go,
> Deal forth my dole of destiny,
> With all my fury dash the trembling foe
> Down to those darksome dens, where Rome's pale spectres lie.

The warriors need not worry about death themselves, however:

> No, my Britons! battle-slain,
> Rapture gilds your parting hour:
> I, that all despotic reign,
> Claim but there a moment's power.
> Swiftly the soul of British flame
> Animates some kindred frame,
> Swiftly to life and light triumphant flies,
> Exults again in martial ecstacies
> Again for freedom fights, again for freedom dies.

---

refuse to speak the rougher language of Rome, and, yes, even travel from its southern motherland towards the north. It is not a beautiful antique anymore: it is native here and lives among us" (my translation).]

216 The image of a web of fate is common to both poems as well.

217 The title is interesting: *Caractacus, Dramatic Poem: Written on the Model of the Ancient Greek Tragedy* (68-70). See also Gray's letter to Mason in *The Correspondence III* (550-552).

218 See Weinbrot, *Britannia's Issue* (371 & 493).

It is perhaps no wonder that Macpherson and Blair wanted to separate the Celt from the Goth and create a gentler warrior.[219] In this they had classical models to refer to, directly and indirectly. This was deliberate and not done in a deceptive manner, as Fiona Stafford has pointed out (*Savage* 137-138). The function of these imitations was rather to invite comparison than to discreetly plagiarise. Others, however, have seen it as discreetly Jacobite. Murray Pittock maintains that "[j]ust as the exile of 1688 and accompanying hopes of restoration had been linked to the *Aeneid,* so the eighteenth-century experience of diaspora underlined its force as a Jacobite text" (*Poetry* 181-182). Pittock says further that "Macpherson's use of Vergil's Troy is not merely the adaptation of the Scoto-Roman ethos to the needs of Celtic patriotism, but is an analogue of the world of contemporary experience which underlies *Fingal*" ("Forging" 125). It may not come as a surprise that the poet who used phrases like "the joy of grief" and "terrible in thy beauty" could also be called a "sophisticated and latitudinarian Scottish whig"; ambivalence was Macpherson's forte on all levels.[220]

The sophisticated critic (and *Ossian's* "midwife", in Howard Gaskill's phrase) Hugh Blair also made clever use of Virgil – or rather Dryden – in his *Critical Dissertation on the Poems of Ossian* with a distinct goal in mind. Dryden's *Fables Ancient and Modern* were prefaced by one of his several texts on translation, in which he compared Homer and Virgil, having had the experience of translating both:[221]

[...] I have found, by trial, Homer a more pleasing task than Virgil, though I say not the translation will be less laborious; for the Grecian is more according to my genius than the Latin poet. In the works of the two authors we may read their manners, and natural inclinations, which are wholly different. Virgil was of a quiet, sedate temper; Homer was violent, impetuous, and full of fire. The chief talent of Virgil was propriety of thoughts, and ornament of words: Homer was rapid in his thoughts, and took all the liberties, both of numbers and of expressions, which his language and the age in which he lived allowed him. Homer's invention was more copious, Virgil's more confined; so that if Homer had not led the way, it was not in Virgil to have begun heroic poetry [...] (*Essays* 275-276).

It seems from this that one of Virgil's greatest translators is relegating him to the second division of epigones, and may possibly have cast a shadow over Virgil in the eighteenth century. Perhaps the frequency of translation can be

---

[219] See Nick Groom, "Celts, Goths and the Nature of Literary Source" (288-289).

[220] See Derick Thomson, "Macpherson's Ossian: ballads to epics." (264) and Colin Kidd, *Subverting Scotland's Past* (223).

[221] Dryden's translations also have a political background as Pittock has pointed out (*Jacobite Politics* 11), although the *Oxford Companion to English Literarture* (5th ed.) maintains that they were "politically less compromising" than his plays, yet adds that "[i]n all these translations he made frequent but subtle allusions to his Jacobite principles" (295).

used as an indicator. If the Penguin collection of Virgilian translation, *Virgil in English,* can be relied on as representative of the number of translations of quality, it appears that the book has got eight or nine examples from the sixteenth century, twenty-four from the seventeenth and only six from the eighteenth, followed by nine from the nineteenth century.[222] Admittedly, the evidence is not conclusive, but the drop from twenty-four to six examples (four of which were published before 1710) in a work that should be representative of Virgilian translation cannot be the fruit of editorial canonisation only.

Blair seems to have sensed that there was space in the classical canon when he wrote his *Critical Dissertation,* and he uses a very similar method to Dryden's when comparing Ossian with Homer:

> Homer is a more chearful and sprightly poet than Ossian. You discern in him all the Greek vivacity; whereas Ossian uniformly maintains the gravity and solemnity of a Celtic hero. This too is in a great measure to be accounted for from the different situations in which they lived, partly personal, and partly national. [...] Both poets are eminently sublime; but a difference may be remarked in the species of their sublimity. Homer's sublimity is accompanied with more impetuosity and fire; Ossian's with more of a solemn and awful grandeur (Gaskill, *Ossian* 357-358).

Blair has not forgotten Virgil completely, however, and mentions him in passing in a phrase that almost hints at incredulity: "This is indeed a surprising circumstance, that in point of humanity, magnanimity, virtuous feelings of every kind, our rude Celtic bard should be distinguished to such a degree, that not only the heroes of Homer, but even those of polite and refined Virgil, are left behind those of Ossian" (358). Indeed, Ossian has some of the Virgilian features described by Dryden, but there is one Aristotelian difference which explains why Blair hardly bothers to mention Virgil: "Aristotle studied nature in Homer. Homer and Ossian both wrote from nature. No wonder that among all the three, there should be such agreement and conformity" (358). Originality lies in the prophetic sphere of natural beginnings, where the language first took form in poetry, and this form lent it authority.

And yet it is not as simple as that. There are probably several reasons for the "marginalisation" of Virgil in the eighteenth century. The first could be that Dryden's translation had made new ones superfluous, as Gransden, the editor, suggests (*Virgil* xxvi). This is improbable, as can be seen in the case of Pope's (and his collaborators') Homeric translations, which are certainly among the standard texts in English and still did not put a stop to Homeric translation. It is actually more likely that the massive impact of Pope's translations had the effect of upstaging Virgil through their native "originality". The Jacobite influence,

---

[222] The editor explains the exclusion of four other eighteenth-century translators in the "Introduction" (xvii).

which again was Dryden's doing, may have played a role in a Whiggist age; that might also explain the "comeback" in the nineteenth century when Toryism had fully adjusted to the Hanoverians, whose nationalist propaganda became very Roman in flavour during the Napoleonic wars (Colley 232). As a matter of fact, scholars do not agree on the importance of Virgil in Britain. Klaus von See maintains that the English never forgot they were part of the Roman Empire and that Virgil still plays a greater role in England than Homer does (45). The editor of *Homer in English,* George Steiner, admitting that there is a "significant Virgilian note in English literature", sees it nevertheless as stemming from an "etymologically spurious identification of Britons with Roman descendants of Aeneas" and contends that it "pales beside the centrality of the Homeric" (xviii).

The contradictions may perhaps be resolved by looking at one of the basics of poetry, form. When Macpherson published his *Fragments* of an epic in measured prose, the response was not only enthusiasm or incredulity but also versification. The prose was both a solution to a translation problem and a creation of authority, but some of the more conservative may have missed the point. Burke's *Annual Register 1760,* for example, published a rapturous review with extracts of the *Fragments* in Macpherson's version. Two versified versions were also printed. This was also the case in the *Annual Register* for 1761 on *Fingal.* The review was more critical this time and focused on the authenticity question, which is not surprising. Macpherson's *Dissertation Concerning the Antiquity &c.* and a versification of the *Songs of Selma* are also included.[223] Other versifications followed and as the attack from Wilkes above shows, Macpherson's prose was considered to be a soft spot (Saunders 235-236).

The best indicator for the importance of form can perhaps be seen in Macpherson's reaction. For the corrected and improved octavo edition of 1773 he wrote a peculiar new preface, a preface which many have considered to give the forgery away, since he talks of himself as author. The preface is, however, interesting for other reasons. Noting with satisfaction that "[a]ll the polite nations of Europe have transferred [*The Poems of Ossian*] into their respective languages" he goes on and ascribes the hostility in England to the fact that he was born on the wrong side of the Tweed (Gaskill, *Ossian* 409). Brushing such criticism off with characteristic modesty by comparing himself to Virgil, he then turns to the more important critique of the poems:

> The following poems, it must be confessed, are more calculated to please persons of exquisite feelings of heart, than those who receive all their impressions by the ear. The novelty of cadence, in what is called a prose version, tho' not destitute of harmony, will not to common readers supply the absence of the frequent returns of rhime. This was the opinion of the Writer himself, tho' he yielded to the judgment of others, in a mode,

---

[223] *Temora* is not reviewed in 1763, whereas there is a review of Dr. Warner's *The History of Ireland.*

which presented freedom and dignity of expression, instead of fetters, which cramp the thought, whilst the harmony of language is preserved. His intention was to publish in verse (Gaskill, *Ossian* 409-410).

Macpherson, having acknowledged the help he got in devising the correct language for his translation, was by now, however, of the opinion that rhyme "could not atone for the simplicity and energy, which they would lose" (Gaskill, *Ossian* 410). Examples of a poem translated from Norse into Gaelic and again by him into English (one in his cadenced prose and one in verse) were then given to validate his claim.

Such a feeble answer to the criticism Macpherson obviously wanted to counter would have been uncharacteristic, and one can speculate on how much that criticism influenced his decision to embark upon a translation of *The Iliad* in his cadenced prose, which was published in the same year as the *Ossian* edition. Indeed, in the preface to *The Iliad* Macpherson expresses his reasons for executing the translation with arguments similar to those above:

> The fetters, which the prevailing taste of modern Europe, has imposed on poetry, may well be admitted, as an excuse, for a man of the best genius, for not succeeding in the characteristical simplicity of Homer. The same taste may likewise be permitted to seduce him into those modernised terms of language, which however pleasing they may be in themselves, are utterly inconsistent with the solemn gravity of an ancient epic poem. The best translators have not, in short, occupied the whole ground. The simplicity, the gravity, the characteristical diction, and, perhaps a great part of the dignity of Homer, are left untouched (xv-xvi).[224]

The colonial expression, "occupied the whole ground", certainly shows an attitude on the function of translation in culture, but more important is the attitude on the function of language in translation, an attitude that Macpherson tries to reinforce with his translation of *The Iliad,* the epic with which Blair compared *Fingal.*

This comparison seems to have annoyed Macpherson's best-known opponent, Dr. Johnson, especially, and may well have been one of the factors that moved him to "put Ossian out of its place".[225] The famous letter to the "ruffian" specifically says that Macpherson's "abilities, since [his] Homer, are not so formidable".[226] Literary history accepted Dr. Johnson's judgment and Macpherson's *Iliad* "lapsed into oblivion", as Steiner says in an introductory note to an extract from the text in *Homer in English*. When Steiner discusses Pope's trans-

---

224 Also quoted in Stafford, *Savage* (85).
225 See *Johnson and Boswell in Scotland. A Journey to the Hebrides*, ed. Pat Rogers (114). See also Paul Baines "Putting a Book out of Place": Johnson, Ossian and the Highland Tour" (239).
226 See Fiona Stafford, "Dr. Johnson and the ruffian" (70-77). The letter is also published in Boswell's *Life* (579) and Saunders' *Life of James Macpherson* (250).

lation in the Introduction, however, he considers the problematic "conflict between the archaic matter of the epic fable and the new criteria of Cartesian-Newtonian rationality, between the semantics of myth and a language whose ideals are those of the logic of the Enlightenment". This conflict proved difficult to resolve as Steiner concludes:

> Augustan verse will not really resolve the contradictions. But by virtue of its clarity, concision and supple flow, the heroic couplet prepares the ripening of modern prose (this interaction is already manifest in Dryden). In regard to Homeric translations, this development is, throughout the nineteenth century, shadowed, as it were, by nostalgia for a lost poetic rhetoric and for the sonority of the Authorized Version (xxv).

Steiner then quotes the well-known prose translation of Lang, Leaf and Myers, who were influenced by Macpherson in exactly this manner, as Steiner himself indicates in his introductory note to an excerpt from Macpherson's translation. Indeed, a closer examination of Steiner's volume, which is representative of Homeric translation in English, reveals a striking fact: Apart from Shakespeare's tragedy and Caxton's rewriting, every Homeric text, imitation or translation, composed prior to Macpherson's translation was rhymed; after his translation, rhyme was the exception. Blank verse, hexameter and prose were attempted, but the few rhymed texts were generally oddities or non-translations.[227] Perhaps Dr. Johnson's annoyance was based on rational fear.

Dr. Johnson was also aware of the political implication of his travel journal, a copy of which he sent to the King the minute it came from the press (Boswell, *Life* 572). The two opponents seemed to be in competition for political favour after the famous controversy, as they both wrote pamphlets against the cause of the American colonies. Johnson wrote *Taxation no Tyranny* in 1775 and Macpherson *The Rights of Great Britain asserted against the Claims of America* in 1776, which was apparently the more successful of the two (Saunders 259). Despite this, it was clear that Johnson had defeated Macpherson and seriously undermined the authority of the Ossianic poems as a contribution to the budding British nation. Since Macpherson himself had consigned the poems to their fate in his preface of 1773, it was up to others to try and regain some ground for the poems and the Scottish pride associated with them. The time was ripe to show some classical loyalty.

In the year in which Boswell managed to get two of his old friends, Dr. Johnson and Wilkes, to dine together and discuss their favourite subject, the Scots, another edition of *Fingal* was brought out. The so-called Warrington edition was published in 1776 and again in 1777 in expensive quartos in the versification of Ewen Cameron. The edition is prefaced with an attack on Dr. Johnson and a re-publication of the testimonies Blair had collected in the Highlands

---

[227]   Another interesting translation is Lydgate's merger of Homer and the Old Testament.

at the urging of David Hume in 1763. Cameron compares Ossian's language to that of the Old Testament and Homer, and, leaning on Blair, adds in a footnote that "this is the Reason why in the Notes to the Poem of *Fingal*, we have all along chosen to compare *Ossian* with *Homer*, rather than *Virgil*" (23-24). Cameron's versification, however, bears more resemblance to Augustan poetry than to the authorities he claims. For clarity, the texts are compared in columns:

Macpherson:

Cameron:

Happy are thy people, O Fingal, thine arm shall fight their battles: thou art the first in their dangers; the wisest in the days of their peace. Thou speakest and thy thousands obey; and armies tremble at the sound of thy steel. Happy are thy people, Fingal, chief of the lonely hills.[king of resounding Selma! 1773] (Gaskill 91).

Illustrious King of *Trenmor's* noble Line!
O'er all the Rulers of the North you Shine:
The Sons of *Morven* bless your happy Reign;
When Battle calls, you lead them to the Plain,
And first in Danger as the first in Sway
Your single Valour often turns the Day.
To you remotest Realms Obedience yield,
And Armies tremble when the Sword you
        Wield.
Illustrious King of *Trenmor's* noble Line!
O'er all the Rulers of the North you Shine!

The passage from the fifth book of Fingal is transformed almost beyond recognition in this intralingual translation, in an Augustan attempt to give the text current relevance in the crisis the Empire found itself in. The allusion to the obedience of remote realms echoes the American conflict and the vocabulary referring to Fingal in the text abounds with Latinate terms like "monarch" and "sovereign" instead of simply "king", as Macpherson put it. Fingal has become a reflection of George III. For Scotland and the British Empire, *The Poems of Ossian* had been translated again, this time to suit the old order. It was, however, too late.

4   RELIQUES FOR ENGLAND

4.1   Thomas Percy's Goths and their Ghosts

When Fingal rises to meet and defy the supernatural spirit of Loda in *Carric-Thura: A Poem,* the ghost of Odin says: "Dost thou force me from my place [...]? The people bend before me. I turn the battle in the field of the valiant. I look on the nations and they vanish (161)". Macpherson thinks this pagan ghost may be some sort of an opposition introduced by Ossian, as the poem, according to "tradition", is "addressed to a Culdee or one of the first Christian missionaries" (460). As Macpherson later found out, the Gothic ghosts that he himself had roused from their slumber with *Ossian* were able to oppose him with something akin to missionary zeal.

The jolt which the publication of the *Fragments of Ancient Poetry* and the epics following them sent through the British literati reveals how deeply rooted the identification of literature with nation already was. The plant needed more nurturing, however, and so it happened that many minor writers offered to produce the fertiliser necessary for further growth. For this purpose the ghost-writers of the nation – antiquarians and translators whose activity is not as self-centred as the so-called "original" author's – proved to be invaluable. Both categories of writers can be seen as 'ghost-writers': the eighteenth-century antiquarian taking the compost of history and distributing it for the good of the nation, and the translator ghost-writing the foreign text for his nation. Subsequently, authors were able to use the achievements of these 'ghost-writers' for their own work, linking it with what had become a self-evident heritage. Susan Manning, for example, has argued that [Henry] "Mackenzie learned about the value of 'ghost-writing' to Scottish literary expression as a young author in the 1760s, from Macpherson's *Fragments of Ancient Poetry,* and the subsequently recovered 'Poems of Ossian'" ("Ghost-Writing" 88). But the Scots were not alone in taking advantage of the 'spectral' success of *Ossian,* for a number of Irish, Welsh and English, and indeed continental writers jumped on the 'ghost-writing' bandwagon.[228]

One such ghost-writer was Thomas Percy, Bishop of Dromore and editor of the *Reliques of Ancient English Poetry,* a key figure in the creation of English and European national literatures. The *Reliques,* and especially their editorial paraphernalia, were instrumental in making ballads respectable and contributed to the publication of a flurry of such collections, both in the British Isles and in Europe. These collections were nothing new in Britain, but the *Reliques* were, as Nick Groom puts it, "a pivotal text, marking the precise point at which early

---

[228]   See also Groom's Chapter "Ghost" in *The Forger's Shadow* (105-139).

eighteenth-century Augustan Neo-Classicism became late eighteenth-century Gothic Romanticism" (*Reliques* 1996, 2).

As can be seen in Percy's apologetic preface to the *Reliques*, ballads were not considered to be poetically correct fare for polite society and "[t]o atone for the rudeness of the more obsolete poems, each volume concludes with a few modern attempts in the same kind of writing" (*Reliques* 1858, xxvii). This mingling of modernity with 'antiquity' is typical of Percy's method on several levels in his work. Moreover, Percy's method can seen as representative in part of the construction of a national literature, as it carefully combined a number of essential features needed for such a construct. These features are the aesthetic, the formal, the historical, the genealogical, the religious and the moral, all contributing to the effect of giving the national the status of the classical. Percy achieved this translation – or rather transformation – of one "great narrative" into another by systematically applying these features to construct a new history of the Gothic or Teutonic tribes, which differentiated them from the Celts. His method consisted of constantly comparing the classical qualities of the Goths to the barbaric elements of the Celts, even while occasionally admitting, perhaps in the rhetorical tradition of *concessio*, that the Goths themselves were "barbarians". Having conceded a similar status among the barbaric peoples, which primitivism had made respectable to some extent anyway, he then picked up the classical literary and proto-anthropological vocabulary and infused it into his discourse on the Goths, adding a religious strand for good measure. In the following his method will be examined in detail, through the prefaces, essays and notes of the *Five Pieces*, the *Reliques*, and *Northern Antiquities*, which indeed "invented and raised an amazing superstructure of fiction", to use his own words (*Northern* xvi).

4.1.1 Percy's Projects and Methods

In one sense Percy did not begin with the *Reliques*. They were more the fruit and final synthesis of several other works on which he worked simultaneously. In another sense, however, the *Reliques* were Percy's starting point. He found the basis for them, the so-called folio manuscript, while visiting a friend in 1753. Indeed, he saved the 'manuscript', which in fact was "a seventeenth-century commonplace book containing transcripts of ballads, metrical romances, and popular songs", from his friend's fireplace (Groom, *Reliques* 1996, 1). During the next few years the newly ordained cleric transcribed some passages from the 'manuscript' and showed it to "several learned and ingenious friends", the most important being William Shenstone and Samuel Johnson (*Reliques,* 1858, xxvi).

Shenstone's correspondence with Percy actually seems to have begun in November 1757, at the time when he started to consider publishing the 'folio manuscript', having been persuaded by Johnson to do so (*Letters VII*, v-vii & 1-

12). In his first letter, Percy relates to Shenstone that Johnson had even promised to write extensive notes, and solicits additional support from Shenstone. This was the beginning of a long cooperative effort between Percy and Shenstone, whereas Johnson seemed to have little time for the project, being occupied with his Shakespeare edition (Brooks, *Letters VII*, xvi-xvii).

Percy's first request for assistance illustrates in a nutshell how the two worked together. Although Percy intended to edit and publish his 'manuscript', he obviously wanted to cast his net wider, both in an aesthetic and antiquarian sense. Already in the first recorded letter, Percy asked Shenstone to send him the "Scotch Song intitled Gil Morris" because he wanted to collate it with his MS, which included a "Copy of [this] Song under the Title of *Child Maurice*" (*Letters VII*, 3). Shenstone complied and asked in the accompanying letter whether the MS version, "*Child* Morrice [sic] be not the juster title" (*Letters VII*, 5). Percy did not take up his friend's suggestion in the *Reliques;* he published the ballad under the title *Gil Morrice,* but did use Shenstone's reflection in an editor's note (*Reliques* 1858, 75).

The aesthetic intervention based on Shenstone's first letter is of more significance. As he had been asked, he sent Percy the ballad and enclosed three additional stanzas to be inserted "[i]n place of the 14th Stanza" (*Letters VII*, 7). The first of the three concludes with the following, to which a note from Shenstone is added:

> His hair was like the threeds of gold
> Shot frae the burning Sun;
> His lips like roses drapping dew;
> When as his race (the Sun's) was run*
> His breath was a perfume.
>
> * I wish you would mend this Rime.

This Percy duly did, in a manner he suggested to Shenstone in a letter in October 1758, dropping the penultimate line and replacing "Shot frae the burning Sun" not only with a suitable line to rhyme, but also with a classical reference that sticks out in a ballad that contains no other such references: "Drawne frae Minervas loome" (*Letters VII*, 14-15 & *Reliques* 1858, 79). Percy notes this change at the end of the ballad in the published version, but there is a twist to this line in the ballad, as it is also "Norse" in the sense that it includes a *kenning*, a "condensed metaphor" consisting of two (sometimes more) nouns, in a genitive construction (Crossley-Holland xxxiii). The content seems also to be of a mixed derivation, as Percy certainly had seen Old Norse poems such as *Darraðarljóð*, later to appear as *The Fatal Sisters* in Gray's adaptation, with the classical image of the loom, albeit in a rather gory context.[229] As Kevin Crossley-Holland observes in his *The Norse Myths*, "[m]any of the kennings are rooted in myths with which the poem's original audience was clearly familiar", thus linking, for instance, a god and a common noun to form a metaphor such "Freyja's tears" for gold, as this goddess wept tears of gold in one of the Norse myths (xxxiii). Percy was well aware of this poetic device and included an explanation of it in his preface to *Five Pieces of Runic Poetry Translated from the Islandic Language*, so it can be presumed that the web of wisdom "Drawne frae Minervas loome", inserted and underlined in a note, could be a trace from his occupation with the skaldic poetry, and even a conscious and doubly intertextual reference to classical authorities, one of which he himself was instrumental in constructing.

4.1.2 From Hobby to Expertise: Rehearsing for the Reliques

Before Percy published his *magnum opus*, however, he worked on several other projects, most of which were translations. He translated pieces from Ovid and Tibullus which were published in James Grainger's *Tibullus*. Again his letters to Shenstone reveal his conscious appropriation of classical sources into an English context. This is evident, for example, in his metrical observations. When describing the two translations he claims he "attempted [them] in our English elegiac Stanza" (*Letters* VII, 11). Further on in the letter, written in January 1758, he gives his reasons for this and reiterates that the metre is "ours":

> I have purposely chosen this our Elegiac Stanza both for this Elegy of Ovid, and for the first Elegy of Tibullus himself, which Dr. Granger [sic] has solicited from me; and I should adopt it always in any similar Translations: for as we have in our language a kind of METRE, peculiarly suited to the plaintive turn of Elegy, in the same Manner as the ancients had their Pentameter, (a METRE sufficiently appropriated by the successful application of it by *Hammond* in his Elegies;) on this account, it gives me, I must own, great offence whenever I see any other Measure applied to this Subject: not less than it would to see Latin Elegies attempted in the Heroic or Lyric Measures (*Letters* VII, 11).

This "English" elegiac stanza is certainly different from the classical one, and it still retains the name of elegy, not only in Percy's case but in the English tradition. The classical elegy consists of distichs in a dactylic hexameter and pentameter, and is of course unrhymed. The form Percy picks up from Hammond is in iambic pentameter quatrains, rhyming *a b a b*, the same as Gray used for his *Elegy Written in a Country Churchyard*. There is, in fact, a permanent dichotomy between the classical Greek form and English practice, not only in the case of Gray and Percy. If one looks at the definition of "elegy" in the *Oxford Companion to English Literature* (5th ed.) this becomes apparent, for under

---

[229] The loom and the Greek goddesses of fate, the so-called Moira, may also be behind the metaphor.

the heading of "elegiac" the editor gives the following definition: "(1) In prosody, the metre consisting of a dactylic *hexameter and *pentameter, as being the metre appropriate to elegies; (2) generally, of the nature of an *elegy" (310). In the definition of "elegy", however, the editor focuses on the content of elegiac poems as "reflective" and "poems of mourning", and give examples of the "great English elegies": Milton's *Lycidas* (which has a subtitle using the term "lament", not "elegy"), Shelley's *Adonais*, Tennyson's *In Memoriam*, Hopkins's *Wreck of the Deutschland* and finally Gray's *Elegy* – all examples of elegies that combine the elegiac modes of reflection and mourning (310). The prosodic element is absent here, which is not surprising when one considers that none of these elegies is in the elegiac metre. Even Johnson himself was at a loss to explain the arbitrary term "elegy" in English letters when he wrote about James Hammond in his *Lives of the Poets*:

> Why Hammond or other writers have thought the quatrain of ten syllables elegiac, it is difficult to tell. The character of the Elegy is gentleness and tenuity; but this Stanza has been pronounced by Dryden, whose knowledge of English metre was not inconsiderable, to be the most magnificent of all the measures which our language affords (63).

On the one hand this may reflect the lack in English letters of metrical revolutionaries like Klopstock and Voss in Germany, but on the other it may also be due to the different translational developments of the two national literatures, the English traditionally more often adapting and bending their sources, whereas the Germans tended to take their cue from foreign models which they then applied rigorously.

Another difference may also be partly ascribed to Percy's success in raising the Gothic spirit in English literature from what he constructed as native sources. He did this via translation, using the foreign sources as a basis, for this project could not be realised simply by publishing the 'folio manuscript'. The 'project', for want of a better word, was also not fully conceived at the outset, as his correspondence with Shenstone in the late 1750s shows. At that time Percy's occupation with the ballads was more of a purely antiquarian nature than anything else. The same can be said about his interest in Old Norse poetry, which may have been aroused through his friendship with Edward Lye, vicar of Yardley Hastings in Northamptonshire, a parish neighbouring Percy's own Easton Mauduit. Lye had edited and published Junius's *Etymologicum-Anglicanum* with supplementary material in 1743 and was an authority on Anglo-Saxon and Old Norse literature. Johnson used Lye's edition when working on his *Dictionary* and mentioned in a letter to Bennet Langton in 1766 that "Mr. Lye is printing his Saxon and Gothick Dictionary; all THE CLUB subscribes" (*Life* 363). Lye's *Dictionarium Saxonico-et Gothico-Latinum* was, however, only published posthumously in 1772.

Lye's influence on Percy was considerable and not only confined to teaching him the runic alphabet and helping him translate the Old Icelandic poetry, which they translated from the Latin versions anyway, for a very good reason (Groom *Celts* 282). Lye's knowledge of the available sources on Old Norse and Anglo-Saxon literature, in addition to his linguistic antiquarianism, provided Percy with the necessary ammunition for his constructive work on the Goths on a linguistic and religious level, both of which fields became central to his elevation of the Goths and enabled him to differentiate them from the Celts. In his translator's prefaces to the *Five Pieces of Runic Poetry* and *Northern Antiquities* he skilfully combined these with the contemporary aesthetic and proto-anthropological discourse.

Percy had been studying Old Norse material in the late 1750s and was of course aware of his friend's published and unpublished projects, but it was only after the publication of Macpherson's *Fragments* that he started sending his other friend, Shenstone, translations of what he then termed "an ancient Celtic, (or rather Runic) Poem, translated from the Icelandic" (*Letters VII*, 70). At this point, Percy still thought of the Celtic and Germanic peoples as one, having probably read Paul-Henri Mallet's *Introduction à l'histoire de Dannemarc*, (1755 & 1763) a work which he translated and published in 1770 with corrections relating to the Celtic/Germanic differences.

As Nick Groom has noted, the publication of Macpherson's *Fragments* seems to "have galvanized" Percy and Shenstone in their intent to publish the ballad collection including the 'runic' poems (*Reliques* 1996, 15). Suddenly their antiquarian 'hobby' had been provided with the possibility of real literary relevance in both popular and critical terms. The aesthetic of native antiquity had arrived, a paradigm awaiting national material dressed up in the formal elegance, moral authority and historical dignity of the ancients.

Shenstone was not very impressed by the "Celtic" poetry Percy sent him, if one compares his reaction with what he said about Macpherson's *Fragments*. The problem was the obscurity of the material. A few weeks earlier he had read satires on Gray's and Mason's poetry, *Odes to Obscurity and Oblivion* by Robert Lloyd and George Colman the Elder (published anonymously), burlesques that attacked the obscure sources of odes such as Gray's *The Bard*. These burlesques, which have now sunk into obscurity by comparison with the objects of their parody, were noticed at the time, as attested by Johnson's remark to Boswell in the *Life*, where he considers them to be Colman's best work, an opinion that is in key with his attack on Gray in *The Lives of the Poets* (*Life* 606).

Shenstone, whose focus was on the aesthetic element, was thus fearful that these poems would be burdened with notes and explanations, and he advised Percy to keep these at a minimum or even to omit poems that required notes or explanation (*Letters VII*, 74). In the event, as Nick Groom has shown, Percy, the antiquarian, did not follow this advice and produced extensive notes and dissertations with almost all his publications, translations, editions and even original texts such as *The Hermit of Warkworth* (*Reliques* 1996, 30-35). All this antiquarian paraphernalia had a very definite function, apart from making the texts accessible to the public. Groom puts it succinctly in his "Celts, Goths and the Literary Source": "Percy's response to Macpherson's *Ossian* was to invent a Gothic tradition, and in the end he invented himself" (295). He began by publishing the *Five Pieces of Runic Poetry.*

4.2 Translating Kinship

The fact that Percy clinched deals with his publisher, James Dodsley, on the publication of the translations of *Five Pieces of Runic Poetry* and *Song of Solomon* on the same day, May 21, 1761, and on his edition of the ballads the following day, is in itself not remarkable, but it is interesting in light of the fact that these three texts, in addition to *Northern Antiquities,* became the classical pillars of his new Gothic castle (Groom, *Making,* 84). The *Five Pieces* provided the aspects of antiquity and originality, *Northern Antiquities* a belated historical aspect, *Song of Solomon* the religious one and the *Reliques* a synthesis of his project in a national context.

Five Pieces of Runic Poetry Translated from the Islandic Language was published in 1763. The text had been ready for the press since 1761, but as Percy himself noted, "the publication has been delayed by an accident". This "accident" seems to have been the publication of *Fingal* and *Temora,* as Shenstone's query in a letter in December 1761 suggests: "How happens it, I beseech you, that you have suppressed the *Runick Fragments etc.,* 'till Mr M'Pherson has Published *His* Poem? Why will you suffer the Publick to be quite *cloyed* with this kind of writing, ere you avail yourself of their *Appetite?*" Shenstone then moves on to say that he had actually subscribed to *Fingal* (*Letters VII,* 124-5, emphasis in original). This shows, of course, how much *Ossian* was on Shenstone's and Percy's minds, and it also shows that they were very well aware of the way in which Macpherson had adapted his sources, as another letter from Shenstone perfectly demonstrates: "Let the Liberties taken by the Translator of the Erse-Fragments be a Precedent for *You*. Many old Pieces, *without* some alteration, will do nothing; and, *with your* amendments, will be striking" (*Letters VII,* 118, emphasis in original).

Percy only partially followed this advice. He did, however, imitate another feature of Macpherson's construct, namely the editorial paraphernalia, adding prefaces, notes and dissertations. The function of the editorial paraphernalia was identical; to construct a poetic and yet "historically" founded identity, a kind of poetic genealogy.

Percy opens his preface to the *Five Pieces* by stating the then already common belief in the difference between the northern and southern inhabitants of Europe, the northern being

> known under no other character than that of a hardy and unpolished race, who subdued all the southern nations by dint of courage and numbers. Their valour, their ferocity, their contempt of death, and passion for liberty, form the outlines of the picture we commonly draw of them: and if we sometimes revere them for that generous plan of government which they every where established, we cannot help lamenting that they raised the fabric upon the ruins of literature and the arts (A2r).

The tone of this "thesis" shows a positive view of barbarians, their only drawbacks being their "unpolished" state and the fact that they ruined "literature and the arts". Other characteristics would undoubtedly have been considered "manly" at the time, and their love of liberty is underlined by the "generous plan of government". The "antithesis" then annuls all the negative qualities in one paragraph:

> Yet there is one feature of their character of a more amiable cast; which, tho' not so generally known, no less belongs to them: and that is, an amazing fondness for poetry. It will be thought a paradox, that the same people, whose furious ravages destroyed the last poor remains of expiring genius among the Romans, should cherish it with all possible care among their own countrymen: yet so it was. At least this was the case among the ancient Danes, and from the similarity of their religion, manners and customs, is equally credible of the other nations of the Teutonic race (A2r-A2v).

The ferocious destroyers of literature become amiable poets who at any rate had only destroyed the "expiring genius among the Romans". In an effortless, analogous sweep, using key words like "religion, manners and customs" this quality of the "ancient Danes" then becomes general for the "Teutonic race" – and that before the "discovery" of *Beowulf*. This was, however, only a stepping stone in the argument, for Percy claimed that, due to their "remoteness", presumably from the Roman south, "we are better acquainted with the peculiarities of their character, and have more of their original compositions handed down to us, than any of the northern nations" ([iii]). This, of course, leads to the key argument of textual preservation, namely manuscripts, many of which, according to Percy, were still extant.[230] The existence or non-existence of manuscripts, the struggle of orality vs. textuality, became, as we have seen, the pivotal point in the Ossianic controversies; for Irish scholars like Charles O'Conor, manuscripts were the definitive proof when accusing Macpherson of literary theft, and Johnson's point on manuscripts has been noted above (O'Conor, *Diss.*1766, 26; Hudson 161-176; Baines, *Book*, 235-248; Boswell, *Life* 589).

---

[230] That was correct, but Percy had only seen these in printed books with Latin translations.

Having established his manuscript sources, Percy then elevates them by claiming that the invention of poetry had been "attributed to the gods", which is not only a correct reading of Snorri's *Edda*, but also provides a parallel to the Greek muses, an argument he underscores forcefully later in the preface. First, however, he defines the makers of the poetry, the poets, noting, "[t]hose that excelled in it, were distinguished by the first honours of state: were constant attendants on their kings" (A3r). Their social importance is then underlined by a very neat definition that includes the notion of the bard and a thoroughly neo-classical function of poetry: "These bards were called by the significant name of SCALD, a word which implies "a smoother or polisher of language"" (A3r-A3v). The Latin footnote to this quote indicates he has this from Torfæus, but he adds that "the name of BARD also [Isl. Barda] was not unknown among the Islandic poets" without giving a source, which is understandable. Perhaps he is thinking of Tacitus' *Germania*, (ch. 3) in which the word *barditus* is used for the warrior poets who sang before battles to embolden their fellow warriors (Sveinsson 73-4).

Percy then moves on to the common argument of "purity" of language and refers to the language in the title, "Islandic", which he maintains "is to this day in use" (A3v). More important for his argument, however, is the parallel he draws, referring to this language as "the mother of the modern Swedish and Danish tongues, in like manner as the Anglo-Saxon is the parent of our English" (A3v). He notes then, that

> [b]oth these mother-tongues are dialects of the ancient Gothic or Teutonic; and of so near affinity, that, in the opinion of the learned, what was spoke in one of them, was without much difficulty understood by those, who used the other. Hence it is, that such as study the originals of our own language have found it necessary to call in the assistance of this ancient sister dialect (A3v-A4r).

Percy's speculation is not without foundation, as nineteenth-century grammarians were later to show. His application of the facts is by no means a simple linguistic comparison, however, but a conscious attempt at the amalgamation of the Old-Norse and Anglo-Saxon cultures. They may well have had numerous linguistic and literary elements in common, as the example of *Beowulf* shows best, having been composed in Britain in Old English about a "Geatish" (from Sweden) hero who goes to Denmark to fight. The poetry which Percy offers in translation, on the other hand, was written in Iceland hundreds of years after the Viking age and the settlement of the country, in a language that belongs to another branch of the Germanic languages, and although Percy was of course unaware of such classifications, he certainly was aware of the linguistic difference, having tried his hand (with the aid of Lye) at translating the texts himself.

After establishing the kinship of the languages, Percy moves on to one of his most important arguments, which is that of the characters of writing. Here, as elsewhere, he was misled by his seventeenth-century sources, and he refers to Ole Worm in his discussion of the 'runes'. As can be seen from the title of the translation, the runes were a central element in the attempt to give his sources not only a written basis, but a specifically antiquated one, the texts being coded in an ancient manner, in another alphabet, just like, for example, the Greek. That Percy considered such an alphabet might have an effect cannot be proven, but why discuss it in detail and put it into the title of the book when it is only a hindrance to understanding the poetry? Percy even had examples of runes printed as epigraphs under the titles: *Egill's Ode* and *Regner's Ode* followed by a motto by Lucan, the same author Macpherson had used for the motto of *Fragments*.[231] Putting the 'runic' and classical texts in parallel invites comparison on the same level in the poetic hierarchy.

What Percy did not know was that Worm had simply been ghost-writing a fantasy for him. It is an established fact that the whole corpus of Old Icelandic texts was written in Latin characters, which should not be surprising, considering that they were all written by Christians, many of them monks (Sveinsson 59). What Worm had done was simply to transcribe the Latin characters into runes, also with the distinct motive of giving the material an air of antiquity.[232] He may have believed he was proceeding correctly, for he had some evidence in Swedish and Danish runic stones, and the famous thirteenth-century scholar Saxo Grammaticus had already propagated the myth of the runes. Worm went even farther than Percy, in trying to link the language with Hebrew, a practice that was common among scholars in the seventeenth century and well into the eighteenth century as well, as the example of Charles O'Conor in his 1753 *Dissertations on the Antient History of Ireland,* quoted in the Chapter on Celtic tribalism, shows very well (37 & Guðmundsson 493).

The significance of the runes as written sources for Percy's translation is also underlined by the fact that directly after he discussing them he takes on Macpherson's fragments, but this time in a kind of "inverted" concessive manner, first acknowledging their pioneering impulse and then attacking their 'antiquity':

A few specimens of these [i.e. the 'runic' verses] are now offered to the public. It would be as vain to deny, as it is perhaps impolitic to mention, that this attempt is owing to the success of the ERSE fragments. It is by no means for the interest of this little work, to have it brought into a comparison with those beautiful pieces, after which it must appear

---

231 See Fiona Stafford's discussion of Macpherson's choice of an epigraph in *The Sublime Savage* (100-1).

232 I thank Einar Gunnar Pétursson of *Árnastofnun* in Reykjavík for confirming this for me. It is also evident from Worm's letters to the Icelandic bishop Brynjólfur Sveinsson in the late 1640s that he is trying to get original "runic" poetry for his second edition of *Runir seu Danica antiquissiama.* In the first edition he had only been able to use Danish and Swedish examples from runic stones.

to the greatest disadvantage. And yet till the Translator of those poems thinks proper to produce his originals, it is impossible to say whether they do not owe their superiority, if not their whole existence entirely to himself. The Editor of these pieces had no such boundless field for licence (A4v).

Percy points out in the following that every poem he produces "has already been published accompanied with a Latin or Swedish version; by which every deviation would at once be detailed" (A4v-A5r). This may perhaps be seen as a slip, as he has tried to give the impression that he translated from the "runes" of the "Islandic language", but he seems to have been certain that the texts he did translate, namely the Latin and Swedish translations, were precise and accurate.

Other elements of the publication were also in the "context of Macpherson's *Fragments*" as Groom puts it: the similarity of the two volumes is striking, as is the layout, although Groom maintains that there are distinct differences in the quality of paper and ornament indicating that the *Five Pieces* "was not designed to be bound sympathetically with the *Fragments*, but to replace it" ("Celts" 284). Groom also holds that the difference can be seen in the fact that "Percy's poems were not translated in the Ossianic idiom and were prefaced with notes, clarified with footnotes, and concluded with endnotes" (284). When one, however, takes into account that Macpherson had by this time (1763) already published his epics lavished with notes and dissertations, this argument seems overstated. As to the idiom of the translations, an example from the "Incantations of Hervor [sic]" is fitting: "I must go to my seamen, Here I have no mind to stay longer, Little do I care, *O royal ancestor*, about what my sons hereafter quarrel" (19, my emphasis).[233] The parallelism at the beginning is a little forced, but justifiable in the translation and it reminds one of such devices in the Ossianic poems. There are other similarities in the structure of the dialogue. The "Incantations of Hervor"[234] is a fragment taken from the saga *Hervarar saga og Heiðreks* and presents a poetic dialogue between the warrior Angantýr, who lies buried in his burial mound, and his "Valkyrie" daughter Hervör, who wants to claim his magical sword which has been buried with him. Such dialogues between the living and the dead are not altogether unfamiliar to readers of *Ossian*,[235] and, moreover, Percy adds the names of the "characters", Hervör and her dead father, into the prose translation, using the same layout employed in the dialogues in the *Fragments*. The combination of language, content and form

---

[233] As Clunies Ross points out in her edition of *Five Pieces*, Percy partly follows Hickes' translation in this passage with the significant change that "friend" becomes "ancestor". As she understatingly says, "Percy's alteration does not really bring the translation closer to the sense of the Icelandic" (87).

[234] The modern title is *The Waking of Angantýr*.

[235] For example the second fragment in which Shilric returns to find Vinvela who has "expired from grief", and of course in the expanded version of the first fragments in *Carric-Thura*.

thus completes a structural quote that may have been intended to "replace" the *Ossian* poems, but certainly within a recognisably similar frame of reference.

Percy underlined this frame with other parallels to Macpherson's Ossianic poems. One topos in them was of course the warrior woman who was inadvertently killed by her lover. The warrior woman presents an aspect of femininity important for the "age of sentiment" and in a sense, the *Poems of Ossian* represent better than any other texts of the time a dialectic between the masculine and the feminine, the heroic and the elegiac, the epic and the lyrical, the ferocious and the magnanimous, the rational and the irrational, the Appollonian and the Dionysian. Percy has a problem with this synthesis, but he makes a feeble attempt at infusing a "feminine" element into the poetry, accusing his fellow antiquarians for its neglect in the past:

> But tho' most of the Islandic poetry, that has been printed, is of the rougher cast; we are not to suppose that the northern bards never addressed themselves to the softer passions, or that they did not leave behind them many pieces on the gentler subjects of love or friendship. The misfortune has been, that their compositions have fallen into the hands of none but professed antiquarians: and these have only selected such poems for publication as confirmed some fact in history, or served to throw light on the antiquities of their country (A6v-A7r).

As elsewhere in the preface, Percy says more about his own objectives than about the text and times he is trying to interpret. The uneasy amalgam of "roughness" and "softness" is in line with the argumentative structure throughout the preface, initially conceding the common prejudice in order to argue against it without completely giving it up, since it still functioned as a source of difference in the masculine paradigm of the hardy and vigorous northerners versus the soft and effeminate southerners. It is also worth noting that Percy refers to the "northern bards" after having introduced the term "scald" for them. Again he seems to want to differentiate and at the same time retain qualities of what he is rejecting. His slighting of his fellow antiquarians seems also to be revealing, if not self-defeating. Obviously, Percy was aware of the fact that the selection of such poems served the distinct purpose of "[confirming] some fact in history" or "[shedding] light on the antiquities of their country", something he was indeed doing himself in this and later publications, yet at the same time it was a "misfortune".

Percy was, nevertheless, ready to make use of the northern warriors' rougher qualities when he emphasized the difference between them and the Celts, relying on the sublime features of the manners and customs of his northern ancestors regarding language and religion. Here he reverted to neo-classical tenets influenced by Longinus and compared the texts with those of the ancient Greeks. In a paragraph on the language and metaphors, he maintains "that the productions of the Islandic poets, tho' quite original and underived, are far from being so easy and simple as might be expected: on the contrary, no compositions abound with more laboured metaphors, or more studied refinements. A proof that poetry had been cultivated among them for many ages" (A5r-A5v). For the time being, Percy, lets go of the primitivist argument, preparing his explanation of the *kennings*, which indeed abound in the so-called *dróttkvœði* (court-poetry)[236], being part and parcel of the court-poet's specialist knowledge and a mnemotechnical instrument in an oral culture. Percy was of course not aware of that, believing that the poetry had been written in runes, so he provides an explanation that seems to him conveniently plausible:

> It was the constant study of the northern SCALDS to lift their poetic style as much as possible above that of their prose. So that they at length formed to themselves in verse a kind of new language*, in which every idea was expressed by a peculiar term, never admitted into their ordinary converse (A5v).

Percy is of course referring here to the Longinian definition of the sublime in language, which "consists in a consummate excellence and distinction of language," a notion that was a commonplace in the eighteenth century (Longinus 125). The "new language" he is probably referring to is what Snorri calls *heiti*, a poetic word that is not commonly used, although Percy is wrong in thinking such words were not used in "ordinary converse" (Sveinsson 144-5). Again his sources may have misled him, but his argument was not so much empirical as comparative, for the note indicated by the asterisk says that the "new language" was: *"[c]alled by them, after the manner of the ancient Greeks,* (Asom-maal,) THE LANGUAGE OF THE GODS" (A5v).[237]

Percy is in his element in comparative mode, and when he discusses whether to "subjoin or suppress" the originals, again an allusion to Macpherson, he not only uses the authenticity argument to supply the "proof" of their existence, but adds:

> They have also a further use.–It has been said by some critics that the prevalence of rhyme in European poetry was derived from the Latin rhymes, invented by the monks in the fourth and fifth centuries: but from the original of EGILL's ODE, it will be seen that the ancient Gothic poets occasionally used rhime [sic] with all the variety and exactness of our nicest moderns, long before their conversion to Christianity; and therefore were not likely to adopt it from the monks; a race of men they were either unacquainted with, or held in derision (A7r-A7v).

---

[236] Old Norse poetry is usually divided into two main groups, eddukvæði or eddic-poetry and dróttkvæði or skaldic-poetry, which I have translated here directly into court-poetry which is nearer to Nordal's coinage of the word. Eddic poetry is characterised by a simpler metre and unrhymed, whereas skaldic- or court-poetry is in complex metres with many *kennings* and sometimes rhymed (Sveinsson 100-1).

[237] The "original" in the brackets seems to be an unsuccessful Danish coinage, which might indicate the level of linguistic knowledge the translator and his editor had.

Again Percy manages to pick up several discursive strands in a compact and otherwise straightforward, albeit highly speculative, statement. The "further use" displays at once that the "ancient Gothic poets" were not only metrically on a level with our "nicest moderns", but that these "originals" effectively prove that the same poets had been there before the Latin monks supposed to have invented rhyme, with the implication that rhyme may be indeed a Gothic invention. The argument for this possibility has a similar ring to Macpherson's arguments in his *Dissertation Concerning the Antiquity &c of the Poems of Ossian the son of Fingal*, wherein he maintains that Ossian's religion may be what it will, but "it is certain that he had no knowledge of Christianity, as there is not the least allusion to it, or any of its rites, in his poems; which absolutely fixes him to an æra prior to the introduction of that religion" (Gaskill *Ossian*, 46). This was, of course, one of the weighty "internal proofs" for the antiquity of *Ossian* supplied by the translator in the translations and the dissertation. The difference, and it is an important one, is that Percy does not use his argument as a proof of the antiquity of the texts, for that was already established in the printed books with their "runic" origins. His is a formal/aesthetic objective that conveniently links to Macpherson's "antiquity" argument.

Percy's ignorance is of course understandable, given the unreliable sources he had at hand before most of the extensive and more reliable research into the Norse texts had taken place, but his conclusions are ideologically motivated and move within well developed neo-classical paradigms as well as new ones drafted by the general trend in primitivism and himself. Percy did not know that Egill Skalla-Grímsson had probably picked up his knowledge of rhyme through encounters with Christians on the British Isles, and that his "ode" was indeed the first known poem with end rhyme in Norse. He simply assumes that this poem, purportedly composed by the Viking warrior-poet in the tenth century and written down by Christians a few hundred years later, proves that the Goths in general had used rhyme before they came into contact with the Latin rhymes of the monks.

Percy seems once again to be trying to synthesise the "ancients" and the "moderns", carefully selecting his specimens to include not only one of the few rhymed poems of the corpus, but also some of the more complex and ornamental court-poetry. Apart from *The Incantations of Hervor,* the *Five Pieces* he translated belong to the skaldic court-poetry tradition and not the more "primitive" eddic poetry. These poems, *Hákonarmál, Harold's Complaint, Höfuðlausn* and *Krákumal* are all courtly panegyrics, and if not the most baroque of the ones available to Percy, they are certainly not the most simple. Indeed, Hugh Blair lashed out at this element of obscurity in his *Critical Dissertation* when he himself translated directly from Ole Worm parts of *Krákumál* (Gaskill, *Ossian* 347). As Nick Groom has suggested, Blair may have been attempting to contrast the more magnanimous and elegant Ossian with the barbaric Norse battle description, but his criticism of obscurity, peculiar as it may look in a dissertation on Ossian, is justified, for Ole Worm's mistranslation has delivered one of the longest surviving topos of the Vikings, and one which Blair faithfully translates: "we shall be drinking ale out of the hollow skulls of our enemies" ("Celts" 289 & Gaskill *Ossian,* 349). The mistranslation is based on the misunderstanding of the *kenning* "bjúgviðir hausa" which is a metaphor for horns (the bent wood of heads) out of which the warriors wanted to drink their ale. That the image of bloodthirsty Vikings drinking ale out of skulls became a topos can perhaps best be seen from Boswell's teasing of Percy during the quarrel between Johnson and Percy about Pennant's book *A Tour in Scotland and Voyage to the Hebrides.* As the two friends Johnson and Boswell jokingly mocked the thin-skinned Percy, Boswell remarked: "Hang out his skull instead of a helmet, and you may drink ale out of it in your hall of Odin, as he is your enemy" (*Life* 933).

Percy rounds up his preface by acknowledging the support of Edward Lye, referring to him as the editor of "JUNIUS'S ETYMOLOGICON and the GOTHIC GOSPELS", and then sums up the final argument for his publication:

> Its aim at least is to shew, that if those kind of studies are not always employed on works of taste or classic elegance, they serve at least to unlock the treasures of native genius; they present us with frequent sallies of bold imagination, and constantly afford matter for philosophical reflection by showing the workings of the human mind in its almost original state of nature (A8r-A8v).

Once again the concession at the beginning is undermined by the far weightier arguments of "native genius" and the primitivist tenet so much in vogue after Rousseau. Most interesting is the self-evident way of presenting the Norse poems as native products, Percy having carefully appropriated this heritage for the "Gothic" or "Teutonic" nations in general, a practice that was to be followed diligently by others, especially Germans, and was one of the most important foundations of the canonisation of northern literatures, their elevated status in turn serving the new modernity and cultural hegemony of the north that was now firmly in place.

Percy's anonymous publication was, then, one of the first steps in his reinvention of the Gothic paradigm, perhaps the most important step, for it moved within two familiar frames of reference for his contemporaries, with the aid of which Percy gave the ballads a new literary pedigree. The first frame was of course the neo-classical one, and although he always concedes that it does not fit, he skilfully readjusts it through the primitivist paradigm, which presented a new way of looking not only at the "treasures of native genius" but also at the classics. Indeed, primitivism has its roots in a new aesthetic applied to the classics, marked by Longinian and neo-platonic precepts about how literature should be experienced and hence a re-canonisation of the same classics. Simply put, it increased the importance of the Greeks and reduced that of the Romans; this shift, slight as it may be in some cases, shows the new emphasis on originality overshadowing the doctrine of imitation.

Percy achieved this not only through skilful application of the available paradigms, but also through the structure of his argumentation, which made use of concession, the perfect rhetorical instrument for this type of argumentation, whereby the new paradigm is not intended to replace the former in a revolutionary manner, but rather to function as a new perspective containing important elements of the old one, which in fact provides one of the arguments for the new one. It was a kind of rejection through appropriation.[238] Percy had found the method of what was later termed "conjectural history" useful for the revision of the Gothic heritage, and he continued to use it in his edition of the old ballads.

4.3   Constructing Classics: Reliques of Ancient English Poetry

Percy's *Reliques* was one of a number of texts published in Britain in the 1760s which became all the rage in Europe. Macpherson's *Ossian*, Sterne's *Tristram Shandy* and Ferguson's *Essay on the History of Civil Society* are all examples of British texts that were avidly read and translated in Germany. All four works, which incidentally originated in three different parts of the kingdom, gave impetus to the varied intellectual movements in Germany at the time, especially *Ossian* and the *Reliques* in the case of Herder, whose work on and enthusiasm for the texts were to leave a permanent mark on his own opinions and writings. *Ossian* and the *Reliques* were very much bundled together in German reception, particularly on the part of Herder. In a way they complemented one another. This was of course not Percy's intention, but after Macpherson's publication and roaring success, the *Reliques* were inevitably absorbed into the Ossianic phenomenon. They invited comparison, and Percy was well aware of the aesthetic and editorial demands that the Ossianic poems made on his work, which originally was conceived of as simple ballad miscellany with the working title "A Collection of Old Ballads" borrowed from a similar anthology published in the 1720s (Groom, *Reliques* 7).

It would be wrong to maintain that Percy's chronic antiquarianism in his editions was due to the influence of Macpherson's epics, however, for as his indirect translation of a Chinese novel shows, by 1761 he was already active in his intercultural commission as an interpreter of what was obscure and foreign, simultaneously explaining and differentiating. It can be argued, on the other hand, that his historical, aesthetic and editorial approaches became indelibly stamped by Macpherson's *Ossian*. In this sense, his ideological aims are irrelevant; after *Ossian* the editorial and aesthetic direction for any respectable anthology was

---

[238]   Percy was by no means alone in applying this method. Both Harold Bloom and J.G.A. Pocock have formulated it in different contexts. I will discuss the method in connection with "conjectural history" in more detail further on.

pre-defined, and Percy was obliged to respond to these new demands. His response in the *Five Pieces* was obvious and he did not even try to disguise the fact, as the above has shown. In the *Reliques* he proceeded more subtly, building partly on the foundation he had established in the *Five Pieces* and also on other works, especially Richard Hurd's *Letters on Chivalry and Romance* (Groom, "Celts" 287-8).

What made the *Reliques* so fascinating to Percy's contemporaries, especially the English and Germans, was his reconstruction of a Gothic architecture that simultaneously appropriated and rejected neo-classical norms. In short, he succeeded in making the national heritage classical, by replacing the classics with, as it were, new classics. The ballads themselves were not the pillars of this construct, but rather the cement. By putting them into a suitable literary context, historically and aesthetically, Percy canonised a new corpus of literature. This he achieved through editing and refining the sources, and by supplying historical and aesthetic editorial paraphernalia that was bound to impress any scholar of the time. The painstaking notes and comments provided the solid bricks needed for the structure, but the main pillars of his work were the accompanying essays, "An Essay on the Ancient Minstrels", "Ballads that Illustrate Shakespeare", "Essay on the Metre of Pierce Plowman's Visions" and "An Essay on the Ancient Metrical Romances".

The *Reliques* open with a dedication to Lady Elizabeth, Countess of Northumberland, and Percy did not miss the opportunity to underline his distant kinship with her, making a point of saying that she was "IN HER OWN RIGHT BARONESS PERCY" (*Reliques,* 1767, vii). The objective was as Bertram H. Davis has observed to "assure his book, this parcel of old ballads that he never ceased to feel uneasy about, a ready passage into fashionable circles" (*Percy,* 78). This decision proved to be a prudent one, for originally Percy had intended to dedicate the ballads to his recently deceased partner, William Shenstone. In the end Shenstone was only mentioned in the preface, along with another supporter of more fame, Samuel Johnson.[239] The dedication was ghost-written by him in August 1764, an ironic exercise in reverse for the man who had written the famous letter to Lord Chesterfield rejecting his patronage (Davis, *Scholar-Cleric* 125). This was about the only help Johnson rendered to Percy in his project, although he did, according to Percy hold "a council of war" with him in May 1761, wherein some basic editorial strategies were laid down (*Letters VII* 96).

The extent of Johnson's ideological input can only be speculated upon, but the fact remains that he was one of the first to encourage Percy to publish the ballads and he did give him some support, especially emotionally. The dedication also shows very clearly that the two scholars thought about the work in very

---

[239]   Johnson was not amused, see Percy's letter to Farmer March 26, 1765 (*Letters II* 87).

similar terms and used similar methods for emphasising its importance despite the defect of its being merely a collection of ballads. Johnson used the same rhetorical device of concession in order to provide a powerful antithesis. His first concession is as follows: "Those writers, who solicit the protection of the noble and the great, are often exposed to censure by the impropriety of their addresses: a remark that will perhaps be too readily applied to him, who having nothing better to offer than the *rude songs of ancient minstrels*" (*Reliques* 1767, vii-viii, my emphasis). Stating the neo-classical obvious, as it were, enables Johnson to revert to more (for him) uncharacteristic primitivist arguments, for he goes on to say: "But this impropriety, it is presumed, will disappear, when it is declared that these poems are pretended to your LADYSHIP, not as labours of art, but as effusions of nature, shewing us the first efforts of ancient genius, and exhibiting the customs and opinions of remote ages" (viii). The proto-anthropological element of primitivism, combined with its aesthetic (i.e., "customs" and "effusions of nature" which add up to "ancient genius"), is characteristic of the "invention of tradition", to use Hobsbawm's phrase, that was an ongoing European project of the time, at least in Britain and Germany. In a sense, these inventions, primarily with the aid of primitivism, were not an attempt to replace the neo-classical world, but to create parallel worlds. Hence, they relied heavily on neo-classical paradigms, and as Johnson himself shows best, not with the aim of discarding them.

Johnson justifies the "attention" to the "reliques of antiquity" further on in the dedication and reverts to the common argument of inquiring into social development from barbarity to civilisation, having stated that it "is prompted by natural curiosity to survey the progress of life and manners" (ix). As usual, "manners" is a key word, implying the specificity of the "nation", justifying the "attention" to "rude songs". In his concluding paragraph, Johnson then effortlessly glides into calling the minstrels "Bards" and does not hesitate to use the arguments of Macpherson and Blair about the influence of poetry in unlettered societies: "By such Bards, MADAM, as I am now introducing to your presence, was the infancy of genius nurtured and advanced; by such were the minds of unlettered warriors softened and enlarged; by such was the memory of illustrious actions preserved and propagated" (ix). Perhaps this was what he meant when he told Boswell that Macpherson "might have fought with oral tradition much longer", but it sits uneasily with his other famous assertion in the Ossianic controversy that a "nation that cannot write, or a language that has never been written, has no manuscripts" (*Life* 589 & 578).

The dedication was of course written ten years before the famous controversy between Johnson and Macpherson. There are strong indications, however, that Macpherson's work was very much present in Percy's and Johnson's discussions during Johnson's lengthy visit to Easton Mauduit in the summer of 1764. On July 23, Percy wrote a letter to the Welsh scholar Evan Evans, who had recently published his *Some Specimens of the Poetry of the Welsh Bards* (another offshoot of Macpherson's success), which was of course discussed by Johnson and Percy in conjunction with it (*Letters V* 95-8). Percy told Evans that "Mr Johnson [...] is very much pleased with your performance" and that he hoped that Evans would "be able to rescue from oblivion, whatever remains of British genius can be recovered" (95-6). The only drawback to Evans's work in Johnson's opinion, however, is the "credit that [Evans had] given [...] to the Pretensions of McPherson and his Erse Poetry" (96). Percy then lists a number of arguments against the authenticity of *Ossian*, some of which undoubtedly stem from Johnson himself. He further relates even an earlier encounter between Macpherson and Johnson, of which *Ossian* was the subject (*Letters V*, 97). As the editor of the fifth volume of *The Percy Letters*, Aneirin Lewis notes that there is no mention of this meeting in Boswell's *Life* and it "provides the only known evidence that Johnson ever spoke to Macpherson about Ossian" (97). As evidence it can be taken at face value, as Percy was probably relating what went between him and Johnson only days, if not hours, earlier.

The dedication was, then, conceived of and written during a time in which Johnson and Percy were very much preoccupied by the Ossianic poems, and considering that it picks up some of Macpherson's and Blair's primitivist assumptions, it can certainly be seen as an attempt to answer their by-then prevalent paradigm by trying to take a place within it.

The dedication was of course signed by Percy alone and it was only in 1791 that Johnson's assistance came to light, actually through the blunder of Boswell, who at Percy's request cancelled a page of his *Life of Johnson* where he disclosed Johnson's ghost-writing of the dedication, while forgetting, however, to delete the index reference (Davis, *Percy* 79). And although, as Davis has observed, the dedication "has long been given a place in the canon of Johnson's works" it has rarely been seen in this context (79).

After the dedication, Percy himself opens the *Reliques* with a characteristically apologetic preface, conceding that he is "sensible that many of these reliques of antiquity will require great allowances to be made for them" (*Reliques*, 1858, xxvii). In fact, he made great allowances simply by his choice of title and reference to "antiquity". The title includes three key words, "reliques", "ancient" and "English" added to which is not the word "ballads" but "poetry". The title shows in a nutshell Percy's amalgamation of the religious, national and classical, and despite all concessions he carefully puts the ballads into a completely new context and manages through this method to give them more than an aura of importance.

Percy is also careful to refer to others, persons of literary authority, in the preface: Johnson and Shenstone, who importuned him to publish, have already been mentioned; and of course other collectors and critics who had discussed ballads, such as Dryden and Addison.

His references to numerous manuscripts have a double function. First, he is latching onto the above-mentioned authority of manuscripts in general *vis à vis* oral tradition, although he also used oral tradition to "legitimate [...] [his] project and allow [...] his editorial fiddling, enabling him to position the minstrels at the moment of national literacy", as Nick Groom has observed (*Reliques,* 1996, 57). In doing this, Percy subtly leans on Macpherson's method, refining it to perfection by using and simultaneously undermining the authority of manuscripts in order to edit them and thus secure the aesthetic acceptance of the ballads. As the Chapter on the Celtic tribalist clash showed, Macpherson himself later attempted to fall back on manuscripts, with fatal consequences for his work, but perhaps he was partly inspired by Percy.

4.3.1 Minstrels in the Making

Percy's opening essay on the ancient minstrels is a highly skilful work of scholarly construction, in which the concessions of the preface are systematically eradicated. The weight of historical evidence introduced in conjunction with an aesthetic elevation, not to say manipulation, is such that the eighteenth-century reader, reading this essay before a single ballad has appeared in the text, could not afterwards consider the ballads as merely trash from the streets. Indeed, so much of the material was new or originally constructed that even fellow antiquarians had difficulty divining Percy's meaning.

The first protest came from Samuel Pegge in a paper read before the Society of Antiquaries in 1766. As Davis has shown, "Pegge expressed the view that Percy in his essay had given 'a false, or at best, an ill grounded idea' of the 'rank and condition' of the minstrels in Saxon times" (*Percy* 93). [240] This argument must have disturbed Percy considerably, for it threatened to destroy the cornerstone of his Saxon structure, and he went to great lengths to address the problem. He revised his *Essay on the Ancient Minstrels in England* so greatly for the second edition that it more than doubled in length, and added thirty-eight pages of notes which had not been in the first edition (Davis *Percy* 95). As Davis has noted, Percy thereby deviated from his restrained editing policy and "abandoned his chosen role as an editor seeking to please a general audience and was now a scholar addressing other scholars" (95). The tension between the popular and scholarly editor had been there from the beginning, as Groom has demonstrated in his introductory essay to the 1996 reprint of the *Reliques,* 'The Formation of Percy's *Reliques*' (1-68). Shenstone had focused on aesthetic factors from the start with regard to selection of ballads, notes and typography, and he may have saved the *Reliques* from looking like an "explosion in a typesetter's shop", as Groom puts it (32).

---

[240] See also Percy's letter of Oct. 22, 1766 to Farmer where he discusses Pegge's "strictures" (*Letters II,* 109-114).

This tension between the scholarly and the (neo-classical) aesthetic reflects very well the originality of Percy's pivotal position. He was fusing together hitherto separate worlds and produced the synthetic artefact of art as an historical and national monument. He was not the first or most prominent representative of this project, but his systematic application of the numerous paradigms available made the *Reliques* an undeclared manifesto that reached wide beyond scholarly and literary circles in England.

That the first protests came from English antiquarians is therefore understandable. Percy's dramatic innovation went beyond standard antiquarian practices, both in his historical interpretation and indeed the editing of the sources. He was particularly sensitive to the antiquarian objections and as Davis points out, although he changed the *Essay* to silence Pegge's criticisms, the pair of them became friends (96). Percy acknowledged Pegge's objections in the third edition (1775) stating at the same time, however, that Pegge "acknowledged [his objections] to have been removed" (*Percy* 96). As Percy did not change his position in the revised version, but rather reinforced it with more material and notes, it can be said that he managed to make the initially sceptical Pegge see the new light.

Pegge had attacked the analogy of the Nordic skalds and Saxon minstrels and doubted two 'royal' anecdotes of King Alfred and the Danish King Anlaff, who were supposed to have dressed up as minstrels to gain admittance to an enemy camp. The first point is more important, as it challenges the fundamental argument in Percy's construction of the minstrel as distinct from the Celtic bard, although they are essentially the same. In the first edition, Percy simply states that "our Saxon ancestors" were the "brethren" of the "northern SCALDS" and seems to take it for granted that his readers accept this kinship, which he had indeed set up in his preface to the *Five Pieces* (*Reliques,* 1765, xv).

In the second edition of 1767 most of the changes Percy made were to the *Essay on the Ancient English Minstrels.* In the advertisement to this edition he notes that the "principal alterations will be found in the ESSAYS [...]: particularly the first" (xvii). He maintains that he does this "in consequence of some considerable information, which has lately occurred to him on this subject" (xvii).[241]

This is not entirely true, as a close reading in conjunction with his preface to the *Five Pieces* will show. Percy ultimately did away with Shenstone's advice and rewrote the text as a full-blown antiquarian piece. The essay is so encumbered with notes that Percy has a double set: in addition to ordinary footnotes, all important and/or obscure elements in the text are marked with a letter in brackets and then dealt with in detail in endnotes under the heading of "Notes and Illustrations Referred to in the Foregoing Essay". In the fourth edition these

---

[241]   He speaks of the editor in the third person.

notes go from (A) to (G g).[242] The major changes, however, are the introduction of old evidence on the "scalds" in addition to classical aesthetic features, and further anecdotal evidence from the antiquarian drawers. In the following the essay will be dealt with in its final form of the fourth edition, although most of the changes were added to the second one. It should be kept in mind that Percy did not really retract anything, or "confess to error" in Davis's words, but rather stuffed the earlier version with more evidence (94).

Percy starts by historicising his minstrels, referring to them as "an order of men in the middle ages who subsisted by the arts of poetry and music, and sang to the harp verses composed by themselves, or others" (*Reliques,* 1858, xxxii). It is obvious from this new opening sentence that Percy is not about to discuss any conveyors of trash, but an organised group of craftsmen, who not only produced original works of art, but also presented them in a most refined manner, while playing the harp. The harp, an instrument with biblical and classical origins, plays a significant role in the construction of almost all national models in the British Isles.

The classical element is not missing either, and is, in fact, neatly tied up with the religious. In the "Notes and Illustrations", he talks of the "clerical appearance" of the minstrels, and adds in a footnote that "this peculiarity had a classical origin, though it afterwards might make the Minstrels sometimes pass for Ecclesiastics" (lix).

In addition, he connects them and their popularity to the "spirit of chivalry", recently elevated by Richard Hurd's *Letters on Chivalry,* and puts them into context with what may perhaps be termed a proto-hermeneutic method after Bishop's Lowth's *De Sacra Poesi Hebræorvm,* by insisting that "their songs tended to do honour to the ruling passion of the times" (xxxii).

Despite his conscious divorce of the Celtic and Germanic heritage in the *Five Pieces* and later *Northern Antiquities,* which he had already begun working on when preparing the *Reliques* for the press, Percy makes use of the bardic paradigm of the Celts in describing his minstrels. He does not discard his distinction, of course, but modifies it enough to make use of the bards, who, contrary to his minstrels, were already, as it were, canonised:

> The Minstrels seem to have been the genuine successors of the ancient bards (C), who under different names were admired and revered, from the earliest ages, among the people of Gaul, Britain, Ireland, and the North; and indeed by almost all the first inhabitants of Europe, whether of Celtic or Gothic race;[1] but by none more than by our own Teutonic ancestors,[2] particularly the Danish tribes (xxxii-xxxiii).

---

[242] Some of the notes are even numbered as well, F.f.2 after F.f., for example. The fourth edition was "ghost-edited" by Percy; the editorship is ascribed to his nephew. See for example Davis *Thomas Percy* (1981) (100).

Note (C) refers to several sources, some of which Percy knows are not very reliable, such as Geoffrey of Monmouth. The footnotes of the quote refer in addition to Tacitus and to Percy's Nordic sources, among them Pelloutier, Bartholin, Worm, Torfæus, his own preface to the *Five Pieces* and the by-then (1794) published *Northern Antiquities*. These little notes perhaps show best how Percy wove together his tapestry for the Gothic ballads. In the following he repeats his borrowed description of the "scalds" from the preface of the *Five Pieces,* referring to them as "Smoothers and Polishers of language", a description later used by Thomas Warton in his preliminary essay "Of the Origin of Romantic Fiction in Europe" in *The History of English Poetry,* (xxxi).[243] Percy has thus given his minstrels a historical dimension by relating them to an order whose primary function was to improve language – noble ancestors for a polished age. He also reiterates ancient notions of the divinity of the skaldic poetry, "[t]heir skill was considered as something divine; their persons were deemed sacred; their attendance was solicited by kings" (xxxiii). Here, Percy is not just referring to ancient superstition, but working within a framework that was very much in vogue at the time, through Lowth's and Hurd's aforementioned works. It goes without saying that this approach of instrumentalising divinity and nobility subsequently put the ballads into a completely different perspective.

Having reinforced the basis he built on in the *Five Pieces*, Percy has to concede that after the Norman Conquest the "Poet and the Minstrel early with us became two persons" (xxxiii). As usual, Percy turns his concession into its opposite. The lack of sources on the minstrels forces him to provide an explanation in key with his historicising objective. The poets, often monks, composed verses as before, but the minstrels "continued a distinct order of men for many ages after the Norman conquest; and got their livelihood by singing verses to the harp at the houses of the great" (xxxiii). The notes (D) and (E) indicate how Percy fills out his white paper. He begins by asserting that the "word Scald comprehended both characters among the Danes" (lxii). He does, however, find a distinction among the Anglo-Saxons, maintaining that they referred to poets too with words that connote song and maker, giving the Greek word $\pi o\iota\eta\tau\acute{\eta}\varsigma$ as the origin, in key with Sidney's *In Defense of Poesy*. The minstrel on the other hand was referred to as a "gleeman" or simply harper.[244] Both terms for the minstrels are of significance. The term harper has of course its bardic/religious connotation, but later in his notes, Percy painstakingly explains the etymology of "gleeman" for a specific aesthetic purpose, skilfully bringing the term into contemporaneous context. The latter note, (E), then provides evidence from Du

---

[243] As is discussed elsewhere, this text leans heavily on Percy without agreeing with him. Percy's new "toolbox" came in handy, however.

[244] Percy uses a mixture of alphabets for Anglo-Saxon terms in his notes, including Greek characters.

Cange and others for the minstrels having "swarmed" the courts in the middle ages, lavished in financial and official rewards (lxii).

In the *Essay* itself, Percy deals with the problem of scarce records in a different (if by now familiar) manner. Again he asserts that the "profession of oral itinerant Poet was held in the utmost reverence among the Danish tribes; and therefore we might have concluded, that it was not unknown or unrepresented among their Saxon brethren in Britain, even if history had been altogether silent on this subject" (xxxiv). The paradigm of an "oral itinerant Poet" is of course Homeric, as can be seen in Blackwell's *Enquiry into the Life and Writings of Homer*.[245] In what follows, Percy establishes the kinship of the Anglo-Saxons through their origins as Angles and Jutes and notes that the Danes who invaded England during the Viking age were in fact making "war on the descendants of their own ancestors" (xxxiv). The blood relationship serves then as a basis for the much repeated proto-anthropological argumentation: "From this near affinity we might expect to discover a strong resemblance between both nations in their customs, manners, and even language" (xxxiv).

Winding up the first part of the *Essay,* Percy takes the progeny of the skalds and bards and applies to them what at first may seem to be a semi-derogatory term:

> [T]he Anglo-Saxon Minstrels continued to possess no small portion of public favour; and the arts they professed were so extremely acceptable to our ancestors, that the word 'glee', which particularly denoted their art, continues still in our own language to be of all others the most expressive of that popular mirth and jollity, that strong sensation of delight, which is felt by unpolished and simple minds (I) (xxxv).

This little linguistic excursion is far from being as modest as it seems. In the first place it is a conscious attempt at bringing the minstrelsy into contemporaneous aesthetic discourse. The historicity of the term "glee" is underlined, and even if Percy concedes its vulgarity in eighteenth-century terms, he easily defuses derogatory notions by making use of the aesthetic and primitivist vocabulary, writing of a "strong sensation of delight", which approaches a definition of the sublime. The term itself also retains a hint of the Longinian idea of ἔκστασις discussed in the Chapter on aesthetic background. That Percy is not merely rounding off the section in an elegant manner can be seen by the gigantic note he refers his readers to.

The note covers three and a half pages in small type in the 1858 edition and is the second longest of the *Notes on the Foregoing Essay,* the longest one being the last, where Percy partly answers Joseph Ritson's criticisms. In four sections, Percy painstakingly traces the etymology of the term and all similar expressions he can find in several languages, such as Anglo-Saxon, Latin and Old-Norse. He

---

[245]   Blackwell calls Homer "a blind stroling Bard" (5).

is very much inclined to link it with musician and harper, but also hints at other kinds of performing, although he rejects the connotation with "stage-playing" as "an idea too modern" (lxvi). He does not, however, completely sever the link with drama, as the *Essay on the Origin of the English Stage* shows. His primary concern, though, is to explain the reasons for the term's social decline, which he mainly blames on the clergy, particularly "those of the monastic profession" (lxvi). He then explains the clergy's antipathy through the fact – established by himself – that the "Anglo-Saxon Harpers and Gleemen were the immediate successors and imitators of the Scandinavian Scalds; who were the great promoters of Pagan superstition, and fomented that spirit of cruelty and outrage in their countrymen the Danes" (lxvii). Percy was probably unaware of the fact that those who did write and rewrite the Old Norse texts were in many cases monastic clergymen, as the "scalds" belonged to an oral culture. His exegesis is, then, an attempt to position his construct of minstrels in an aesthetic and historical frame of reference that puts them, and thus the ballads, into a completely new and much more acceptable context.

Percy's next strategy is to widen and anglicise the historical frame. By inserting legends on Alfred the Great, with the well-known folklore motif of the disguised head of state (in itself a significant semiotic switch which often can be found in national foundation mythology: James V and Peter the Great for example), he manages to give the profession of minstrels a royal touch exceeding even the usual honour of their being in the king's closest circle, for if Alfred the Great himself was a minstrel, how could they have been a base order of men? The question is naive, but it is in key with the objectives of a text that may appear extremely "scientific" and antiquarian, but whose prime function was to build an aesthetic and historical bridge to his degraded material.

4.3.2 Pillars of Dramatic Support

The success of Percy's constructive art, however, was due not only to his creation of an Anglo-Saxon antiquity through foreign sources with a living continuum to his own time, but also to his use of more recent cultural monuments and traditions, which indeed gave a national and more scholarly substance to what was then certainly an obscure heritage to most scholars, let alone readers. When Percy published his *Reliques,* the eighteenth-century construction of Shakespeare as *the* national bard was in full bloom; Johnson's edition was published in the same year, and in the previous decades several editions had been edited by Rowe, Pope, Warburton, Hanmer and, last but not least, probably Hugh Blair (1753 & 1771)[246]. Indeed, the 1760s witnessed the publication of three key texts on Shakespeare: Johnson's edition, Percy's significantly titled essay in the *Reliques,* "On the Origins of the English Stage, &c", under his heading *Ballads that*

---

[246]   At least it was attributed to him.

Illustrate Shakespeare, and Richard Farmer's *Essay on the Learning of Shakespeare* (1767).

Percy was in close contact with both Farmer and Johnson while preparing the *Reliques* and, although he was more at the receiving end, he was also a contributor to later editions of Johnson's *Shakespeare* and Farmer's *Essay* (*Letters* II, 13 & 121-129).[247] In a sense, Percy became somewhat of an expert in the field, as can perhaps best be seen by the fact that he maintained a long correspondence with one of the greatest Shakespeare scholars of the eighteenth century, Edmund Malone, who saw reason to express his "warmest acknowledgements" to Percy in the preface to his *Supplement to Shakespeare* in 1780 (Tillotson, *Letters* I, v). It may even be maintained that Percy was one of the first to apply the method of "conjectural history" to the mysterious bard, "evidence" about whom consisted mostly of anecdotal "tradition", in Schoenbaum's phrase, at the time.[248] What Percy did was to stop staring at the irresistibly empty page under the famous name and approach the subject from a completely new angle. Admittedly, this was not so much due to the inspiration of genius as to the fact that he was trying to connect his scorned balladry to the great bard. Furthermore, his intended subject was the drama itself, and not Shakespeare directly. Despite this, he may have opened up a new approach in Shakespearean scholarship by concentrating on the cultural context of Shakespeare's plays, life and age. Serious critics before him, for example Dryden and Pope, and Johnson just after him, had focused mostly on the Shakespeare of the texts and were very much preoccupied with the bard's abilities with regard to the prevailing norms of form and decorum. Percy, on the other hand, tried to reconstruct the development of the English stage both before and during Shakespeare's time.

Percy's reconstruction is mostly directed by genre. He begins by examining the mystery and morality plays of the late Middle Ages. Curiously enough, his best source for how they were performed is the German/Flemish novel, *Till Eulenspiegel,* in Copland's version from the middle of the sixteenth century. As he moves on from the mystery plays to the morality plays he detects "something of a fable or plot, and even attempt[s] to delineate characters and manners" (*Reliques* I, 1858, 103). The two, rather familiar terms at the end indicate the direction in which he is heading. One does not have to wait long, for he has in

---

[247] In Johnson's case he actually contributed notes but in Farmer's case his assistance was more of an inquiring nature, i.e. he sent Farmer a long list of questions on points which were not clear to him and Farmer made use of those queries when improving his second edition.

[248] See S. Schoenbaum's *Shakespeare's Lives* (41-96). Percy mentions in his first footnote to the essay "Warburton's Shakesp. V. p. 338.—Pref. to Dodsley's Old Plays.— Riccoboni's Acct. of Theat. of Europe, &c. &c. These were all the Author had seen when he first drew up this Essay" (*Reliques I*,1858, 102). This looks like a modest hint from Percy that he is indeed doing something original.

front of him two plays, "printed early in the reign of Henry VIII; in which I think one may plainly discover the seeds of Tragedy and Comedy" (103). The first is "*Every Man*", of which he gives a short synopsis before concluding that it

> is a grave solemn piece, not without some rude attempts to excite terror and pity, and therefore may not improperly be referred to the class of Tragedy. It is remarkable that in this old simple drama the fable is conducted upon the strictest model of Greek tragedy (104).

Percy hits his argument home by pointing out that the three unities are strictly adhered to, that the stage is never empty, even when Everyman has to leave to "receive his sacraments", during which "Knowledge descants on the excellence and power of the priesthood, somewhat after the manner of the Greek chorus" (104). For encore Percy adds that "except in the circumstance of Every-man's expiring on the stage, the Sampson [sic] Agonistes of Milton is hardly formed on a severer plan" (104). As before, Percy manages in a paragraph to allude to both old English "antiquities" and classical Greek ones, focusing on the neo-classical structural paradigm that still retained its authority. Added to that is Milton's play, which adheres strictly to the neo-classical categories and is a "national" authority in itself.

In the second instance, when discussing a prototype English comedy, *Hick Scorner,* Percy uses a similar method. While conceding that the play is deficient, he points out twice that it shows "real characters and manners" (105). He concludes that the writers of the morality plays were "upon the very threshold of real Tragedy and Comedy" and that the coming Renaissance reinforced the development (105).

Percy's constructive art has ripened, for once he has established the link, he moves back chronologically to discover the origins of the morality plays. Apparently a Norman monk had put one on shortly after the Conquest, which for Percy is significant in light of the fact that an "eminent French Writer thinks it was even the first attempt towards the revival of Dramatic Entertainments in all Europe" (105). In what follows he also says that it appears that the "Germans are obliged to the English for the invention of this sort of spectacle, unknown to them before that period" (106).[249] The English influence on European drama has certainly become dramatic by this point in Percy's account, despite the dry antiquarian tone, and his final argument in the section is a little anticlimactic, for he finishes it off by pointing out that translations of Greek and Roman classical plays were indeed put on in the mid-sixteenth century and that the morality plays "assumed the name of Masques, and with some classical improvements,

---

[249]   There may be something to this theory, but the English were more active at a later stage in Germany, namely in the seventeenth century when English itinerant troupes toured there. See Horst Oppel's *Englisch-deutsche Literaturbeziehungen.* (Vol. 1, 42-53).

became in the two following reigns the favourite entertainments of the court" (109). Nevertheless, continuity had been maintained, and the classics, in the form of translation, hint at a taste already forming.

In the final section, Percy returns to the mystery plays, which had not survived the Reformation, presumably due to their idolatrous nature. Percy, however, manages to find historical continuity for them as well, for they

> appear to have given birth to a Third Species of stage exhibition, which, though now confounded with Tragedy and Comedy, were by our first dramatic writers considered as quite distinct from them both: these were Historical Plays, or Histories, a species of dramatic writing, which resembled the old Mysteries in representing a series of historical events simply in the order of time in which they happened, without any regard to the three great unities. These pieces seem to differ from Tragedies, just as much as Historical poems do from Epic: as the Pharsalia does from the Æneid (109).

By now, Percy's method has become systematic, leading him to Shakespeare, and the little anecdote of his possibly having watched the old Coventry play of Hock-Tuesday in the presence of Queen Elizabeth herself.[250] As Schoenbaum points out, this is one of the many unfounded Shakespeare "traditions" and "[l]ater biographers would eagerly follow up on the Bishop of Dromore's intriguing speculation" (*Lives* 94). Percy's objective with the anecdote and the whole section is to underline the "Histories" as a specific genre, a specifically English genre which, although Shakespeare did not invent it,

> yet he cultivated it with such superior success, and threw upon this *simple inartificial* tissue of scenes such a *blaze of Genius*, that his Histories maintain their ground in *defiance* of Aristotle and all the critics of the Classic School, and will ever continue to interest and *instruct* an English audience (111, my emphasis).

Once again Percy manages to reject the "Classical School", primarily with primitivist arguments, and at the same time retain a moral claim of instruction. Here he leans on a "tradition", as he puts it himself, "mentioned by Gildon, that, in a conversation with Ben Jonson, our Bard vindicated his Historical Plays, by urging, that as he had found 'the nation in general very ignorant of history, he wrote them in order to instruct the people in this particular.'" (112). In a footnote Percy then excuses himself for being at variance with his friend Malone with regards to this "tradition".

What is perhaps most curious about the essay is the absence of a discussion on ballads, something which might have been expected from the heading. Percy was obviously more concerned, as many of his forerunners and contemporaries were, with finding a national costume for Shakespeare so that his works could be presented as at least rooted in classical drama, yet at the same time be seen as

---

[250]   This anecdote appeared first in the fourth edition of 1794.

uniquely English. The influence of the ballads themselves is then discussed in the introduction to each ballad. In most cases the link is simply a quote or an echo in the plays. Two ballads have the same subject as the plays (*King Lear* and *Titus Andronicus*), but in both instances Percy is unable to ascertain which came first, ballad or play.[251] What he has managed is to give Shakespeare back some of the original classical dignity which had been lost through the dogma of Augustan critics such as Rymer, and in addition to that, to link his own ballads to the national Bard, whose canonisation was already beyond any critical intervention, as the preceding century had shown.

4.3.3 Back to Basics

The essays in the second and third volumes of the *Reliques* repeat many of the arguments in previous essays and the preface to the *Five Pieces*, and they serve the same purpose. The difference lies in the subject matter, which perhaps shows best that Percy had a distinct goal in mind and that the evidence he found and used was interpreted to reinforce his previous results. The short essay on "The Alliterative Metre, without Rhyme, in Pierce Plowman's Visions" is a case in point. He opens by citing his major source on the Old Icelandic poetry, Ole Worm, on the alliterative verse of the skaldic poets. He explains the system plainly and adds that "[t]here were many other niceties observed by the Icelandic poets, who [...] retained their original language and peculiarities longer than the other nations of the Gothic race [...]" (*Reliques* 1858, 216-17). This is followed by a quick analogy to their "brethren the Anglo-Saxon poets", who "occasionally used the same kind of alliteration" (217). Before Grímur Thorkelin's "discovery" of the Old English *Beowulf*, Percy did not have much material to refer to, but his speculation pre-empts some of the research done later.

More importantly for Percy, he can show that there is a more recent poem that retains the alliterative metre, a poem with canonical qualities from a religious and aesthetic point of view. He hopes to "gratify" the reader with the information that the author is Robert Langland a "secular priest", one of whose imitators, Owen Rogers, was a "follower of Wicliff [sic]", the significant point being that a metrical continuum could be established before and after Langland. The so-called "alliterative revival" was of course a term unknown to Percy, but he certainly may have established some of the different theses which have since been discussed in connection with this "movement" in Middle English poetry, for example by Turville-Petre. Once again, Percy can be seen as a pioneer in the research of neglected material, and his speculations have remained part of the later discourse on the topic, as can be seen when one compares his observations with those of an early twentieth-century authority on the subject, W.P. Ker.

---

[251] Percy is quite sure, however, in his letter to Warton in June 1761 (*Letters III* 16).

Percy follows the thread of alliterative verse in ancient volumes of English poetry and Garrick's collection of old plays before returning to the metre of Piers Plowman and presenting his discovery: "In the folio MS. so often quoted in these volumes, are two poems written in that species of versification" (219). In an artistic touch Percy then quotes the two poems before revealing that the latter, *Scottish Feilde,* contains "a very circumstantial narrative of the battle of Flodden, fought Sept. 9, 1513. With a scholarly hand he then dates the poem by showing that a death lament in the poem refers to James Stanley of Ely a "prelate [who] died March 22, 1514-5 [sic]" (220). Having dated the poem with double certainty, he comes to his point:

> Thus we have traced the Alliterative Measure so low as the sixteenth century. It is remarkable that all such poets as used this kind of metre, retained along with it many peculiar Saxon idioms, particularly such as were appropriated [sic] to poetry: this deserves the attention of those who are desirous to recover the laws of the ancient Saxon Poesy [...]: I am of the opinion they will find what they seek in the metre of Pierce Plowman (220).

In 1912 W. P. Ker argued similarly in his Clark lecture on "Chaucer, and the Scottish Chaucerians". When discussing the "significance of Dunbar's alliterative poem", which he maintains "is nearly the last of its race in this island of Britain" he goes on to say that "[t]he very last is the poem of *Scottish Field* – a poem on the battle of Flodden in the alliterative metre of *Piers Plowman* – which is essentially the same as the metre of *Beowulf"* (*Form* 88). Ker, essentially using Percy's argumentation, has here established the link from an Anglo-Saxon epic to a Middle-English poem. It may be presumed that had Percy known of *Beowulf,* he would have used this link as well.

That he did not know of *Beowulf,* or know it well enough to use it, may be due to the fact that he did not manage to meet the Icelandic scholar Grímur Thorkelin, an acquaintance of Pinkerton who made a copy of the so-called Cotton MS with the intention of publishing it (*Letters* VIII, 84).[252] Thorkelin found the manuscript of *Beowulf* in the British Museum in 1786 and Percy was apparently unable to meet him in Dublin in 1788, although he asked Pinkerton in a letter to tell Thorkelin he would "be glad to be of Service to him in any of his literary Researches" (84).

Whether or not Percy was aware of *Beowulf* and its significance for his thesis is in itself of no importance, for he had already delivered results on the basis of his knowledge, results that were accepted and repeated long after. Besides, Percy's ignorance, if ignorance it may be termed, was partly due to his being in the vanguard of scholars researching and instrumentalising native ancient literatures. In a sense, he was a pioneer in the construction of national canon. What

---

[252]   See also George Clark's *Beowulf* (4).

Macpherson and Percy achieved was to give a new "national" movement in literature the decisive impulse and to promote on a hitherto unprecedented scale the search for "undiscovered" manuscripts and folklore of all kinds. Antiquarians had of course been thumbing through old manuscripts for a long time, but the new movement had altogether different implications and importance after the Ossian "episode", to use Smart's term for the explosion.

The complexity of Percy's arguments can be better understood in light of the contemporary British neo-classicist discourse on versification. What made Percy's little essay almost revolutionary was the fact that he discussed alliterative verse at all. Alliteration had long been considered equivalent to doggerel, and although a few well-known writers such as Gray and Mason were using alliteration by then, it remained an oddity in British verse. Percy thus slaloms, as it were, between the reigning standards and the forgotten ones he has discovered and in the end tries to tie them together in an historical and evolutionary frame. A good example of this is when he records the demise of alliterative verse:

> Yet when rhyme began to be superadded, all the niceties of Alliteration were at first retained along with it; and the song of *Little John Nobody* exhibits this union very clearly. By degrees the correspondence of final sounds engrossing the whole attention of the poet, and fully satisfying the reader, the internal embellishment of Allliteration, was no longer studied , and thus was this kind of metre swallowed up and lost in our common Burlesque Alexandrine, or Anapestic verse,[1] now never used but in ballads and pieces of light humour [...] (221).

As so often, Percy's footnote is even more interesting than the statement in the body text itself. There he explains metre and give as an example that of Robert of Gloucester (1260-1300) who apparently had developed Saxon verse before Langland by discarding alliteration for rhyme. He then inconspicuously adds that

> Robert of Gloucester wrote in the western dialect, and his language differs exceedingly from that of other contemporary Writers, who resided in the metropolis, or in the midland counties. Had the Heptarchy continued, our English language would probably have been as much distinguished for its different dialects as the Greek; or at least as that of the several independant [sic] states of Italy (221).

This peculiar note shows well the dimensions of Percy's thought, the historical continuities he was creating and, last but not least, the classicist analogies with which he time and again spiced his text. In two sentences he links a Middle-English poet with the seventh-century Heptarchy (the subject of the quote from Gloucester's poem) and at the same time brings in an historical analogy with the two source countries of classical authority.

This is not to say that Percy's scholarship should be dismissed as purely speculative or ideological; he was probably one of the experts on English prosody at the time, and certainly the one who brought to light varieties and variants that had been shoved aside with the classicist poetical ideology. This applies not only to his metrical expositions but also to his ballads, for which he created an artistic awareness through his historicisation and metrical analysis. The numerous references to Percy's ballads by the famous German philologist Andreas Heusler in his *Deutsche Versgeschichte* show the importance of the ballads themselves in the *Reliques* for prosodic development in Germany.

Percy closes his *Essay on the Alliterative Metre* in a familiar vein by conceding that

> the old alliterative and anapestic metre of the English poets being chiefly used in a barbarous age, and in a rude unpolished language, abounds with verses defective in length, proportion, and harmony; and therefore cannot enter into a comparison with the correct versification of the best modern French writers; *but* making allowances for these defects, that sort of metre runs with a cadence so exactly resembling the French heroic Alexandrine, that I believe no peculiarities of their versification can be produced, which cannot be exactly matched in the alliterative metre (222, my emphasis).

The antithetical "but" not only undermines the concession, but introduces historical analogies that simply liquidate it; the rude and unpolished language is capable of the same feats as the French heroic metre, and its defects are purely historical.

The final essay of the *Reliques* seems a bit repetitive despite covering new subject matter, for it returns to the argumentation for the skaldic origin of the ancient metrical romances.[253] Percy's objective is the same as before, to create a lineage from his Gothic skalds to the ancient English poetry and romances he is discussing. The publication of Hurd's *Letters on Chivalry and Romance* in 1762 provided him with an important strategy for the project, because "Hurd redefined the Gothic by paralleling the cultural and artistic fecundity of ancient Greece with medieval Europe, re-evaluating the medieval by redefining the Hellenic" (Groom, "Celts" 288). Hurd's *Letters* were a serious attempt at elevating the Gothic, not at the expense of the classical, but through a social analogy of manners, a method which Percy mastered in the essays.

Percy manages, however, to criticise his fellow scholar a little by pointing out at the beginning that the metrical romances are "a subject the more worthy [sic] attention, as such as have written on the nature and origin of Books of Chivalry, seem not to have known that the first compositions of this kind were in Verse, and usually sung to the Harp" (*Reliques III*, 1765, i-ii). He may be gently insinuating that Hurd had not really read any of the romances, but his references to "Verse" and "Harp" are really intended to reinforce Hurd's argu-

---

[253] The order of the essays in the *Reliques* is not chronological. The last essay Percy wrote for them is in fact the first one on the minstrels, the "counterattack against Macpherson" as Groom puts it ("Celts" 292).

ment.[254] He then moves on in a primitivist vein, claiming that the "first attempts at composition among all barbarous nations are ever found in Poetry and Song" (ii).

In the first two editions of the *Reliques* this essay has the primary objective of relating how the mostly historical poetry of the skalds slowly developed into fiction, albeit with historical foundation. In contrast to Hurd, who explains the prevalence of fairies and supernatural matter in Gothic romance through comparison with Greek epic poetry, Percy ascribes it more to the development of writing; that is, with the introduction of writing the historical nature of skaldic poetry became less important, as history was now preserved in annals and other monastic manuscripts. Hence the role of the skald became that of entertainer rather than historian. This theory, which may not sound far-fetched, makes perhaps too much of the historical quality of medieval oral poetry and indeed written annals. On the other hand, it is also in key with Percy's theory of the minstrels and their degradation in English society and letters. Despite his attempts at differentiation, Percy has so united the figures of the skald, the bard and the minstrel as historians in his head that they easily intermingle. An example of this can be seen in two paragraphs where he says first that "with marvellous embellishment of this kind the Scalds early began to decorate their narratives" and continues by asserting that "of the great multitude of romantic tales still preserved in the libraries of the North, most of them are supposed to have had some foundation in truth, and the more ancient they are the more they are believed to be connected with true history" (*Reliques III* 1765, v). Again one can see how Percy is attempting to give his Gothic construct a respectable and solid base in "libraries" and "true history". In the next sentence he then says that "it was not probably till after the historian and the bard had long been disunited, that the latter ventured at pure fiction" (v). The skald becomes bard, but this is not the point Percy is making, bard obviously being just a synonym for skald, because he makes this development responsible for the "fabulous and romantic songs which for a long time prevailed in France and England" (v). The knowledgeable reader might gasp at the effortless hybridity of Percy's argument, but this is not all, for he concludes with the icing on the cake:

> Yet in both these countries the minstrels still retained so much of their original institution, as frequently to make true events the subject of their songs; and indeed, as during the barbarous ages, the regular histories were almost all writ in Latin by the Monks, the memory of events was preserved and propagated among the ignorant laity by scarce any other means than the popular Songs of the Minstrels (v).

There are two footnotes to these sentences: one referring to Mallet's *Northern Antiquities,* which Percy had already begun to translate by then, and the

---

[254]   See Groom ("Celts" 288).

other to his famous (or infamous) manuscripts. Along with these paragraphs they show the extent of Percy's construction.

Such a manipulation of the terminology may also be indicative of Percy's confidence, despite the numerous rhetorical detractions in his essays. He was, after all, treading new ground and he was well aware of that. It was not until his friend and correspondent, Thomas Warton, published his *History of English Poetry* in 1774 that he had to react to a real threat to his "system", as he and his contemporaries were wont to call their constructive creations. This publication added a twist to the already complex and obscure discourse that was growing on the origins and development of British national literatures, and which will be discussed in a section of its own.

4.4 Translating Difference[255]

4.4.1 *Difference in Antiquities*

Percy's second translation concerning the Norse heritage of the "Goths" had already been advertised in the preface to the *Five Pieces*, almost with a sense of urgency, as he claims it is "in great forwardness, and will speedily be published" (A6r-A6v). *Northern Antiquities: or a Description of the Manners, Customs, Religion and Laws of the Ancient Danes and other Northern Nations; including those of Our own Saxon Ancestors* was, however, only published in 1770, although it is apparent from the second edition of the *Reliques* that it was already in the press by 1767.[256]

The original was a work in French by Paul-Henri Mallet of Geneva (1730-1807), who from 1752-1760 was a professor of French in Copenhagen. The two volumes Percy translated, *Introduction à l'histoire de Dannemarc, où l'on traite de la religion, des loix, des mœurs et des usages des anciens Danois* (1755) and *Monumens de la mythologie et de la poësie des Celtes et particulièrement des anciens Scandinaves [...]* (1756), were a kind of prehistory of Denmark, commissioned partly through the agency of a high-ranking Danish official, A.P. Bernstorff. This commission was a nationalistic enterprise in the tradition of Worm appropriating the Old Icelandic and/or Old Norse texts for the Danish state.[257] Slowly but surely, the pedigrees of kings were being replaced by pedi-

---

[255] Parts of the following were published in the book *Norden och Europa 1700 – 1830*, ed. Svavar Sigmundsson. Reykjavík: Háskólaútgáfan, 2003.

[256] Percy cites the unpublished translation by page numbers in the 1767 edition and they are the same in the 1775 edition. See also Margaret Clunies Ross, "Percy and Mallet. The Genesis of Northern Antiquities" where she argues on evidence from Percy's diary that he had in fact finished work on the translation by 1767.

[257] This argument is in itself in key with Icelandic nationalism since the 19th century and reflects some of the nationalistic tendencies in the Nordic countries. The term Old Norse is now mainly used in English for the language and texts spoken and written in

grees of nations, buttressed by national histories, national languages (which themselves were provided with pedigrees) and national literatures. In most cases, if not all, they were constructed with the help of the classics, antiquarian enterprise, scholarly literary, historical and linguistic research and, last but not least, translation in the widest sense of the word.

Percy himself provides a prime example of this process, having been active in all the above fields. His literary historical scholarship and antiquarianism was spiced with analogies to the classics, and his linguistic work, though hardly recognised in the discipline of comparative-historical linguistics, was of some pioneering substance. His preface to the translation of Mallet's work bears witness to this.

Despite being anonymously published, Percy's translation is far from being the work of a humble "invisible" translator, to use Venuti's term. It is much more what might be termed a critical translation, in which the translator decisively intervenes and reconstructs not only the text, but also its substantial axioms and conclusions. That this is the case is obvious from the translator's preface, which deviates markedly from other such texts of that self-deprecating genre. This is of course due to Percy's knowledge of the sources Mallet had used, and indeed what he considered to be his superior knowledge of the subject. The question then arises why he bothered to translate such a text in the first place. Why not write a new one, a better one?

My speculative answer is that this text was precisely the one best suited to Percy's purpose, namely to achieve a decisive split between the Celtic and the Gothic. The reasons for this are several. In the first place, Mallet's work was already well known in Europe and was even making waves in Britain. Gray was familiar with it, and Oliver Goldsmith (also an acquaintance of Percy's) had reviewed it favourably in the *Monthly Review* in April 1757 (Gray, *Corr. II* 551; Clunies Ross, "Percy and Mallet" 112-13). Secondly, translating the piece provided Percy with the opportunity to attack its flaws in their place instead of hav-

---

Iceland and Norway from ca. 1100-1350. The majority of the extant texts were, however, written in Iceland during this period and this has led some to speak of Old Icelandic, as can be seen in the *Icelandic-English Dictionary* of Cleasby and Vigfússon. Icelandic is thus the "classical" language of the Nordic countries (to use Einar Haugen's term in his *The Scandinavian Languages*. This has not prevented nationalists in Norway and Denmark from speaking of the language of the *Eddas, Sagas*, and *Heimskringla* as Old Norwegian or Old Danish (which is particularly dubious, since linguists have classified Danish as belonging to the Eastern Scandinavian languages as opposed to Western Scandinavian). This little 'tug of war' about the "property" of the old texts and their language is a result of the systematic nationalist appropriation of the old heritage by all the countries, Icelanders included. Indeed, it shows in a nutshell the ideological function of native 'ancient' literatures, languages and history for the nationalist project. What is important to note in this context, is that Percy, in effect, uses exactly the methods of Worm and Mallet for his 'Gothic ancestors'.

ing to refer to and correct the author's incorrect theses. Thirdly, this approach enabled him to deal with the sources Mallet used and show how he had misinterpreted them. Fourthly, and most importantly, his translation was intended to displace the original in the English-speaking world, an effort not unlike the attempt to replace Macpherson's *Fragments* with the *Five Pieces,* as Groom has argued ("Celts" 284). Percy's *Northern Antiquities* was a combination of translation and palimpsest.

Although the translation of *Northern Antiquities* had the same objective as the translation of the *Five Pieces* (i.e., to support the 'Gothic' origins of the English), it represents a reversal of its predecessor's method. The translation of *Five Pieces* was an attempt to translate kinship, to prove that the Anglo-Saxons and the Scandinavians had the same origins. In *Northern Antiquities,* Percy tries to translate difference, to prove that the Celts and Anglo-Saxons (Teutons, Goths) were, as he repeatedly puts it himself, *ab origine* different peoples. He had not explicitly made this point in his preface to the *Five Pieces,* but in his "Notes to the Foregoing Essay" in the *Reliques* he had been

> careful to trace the Descent of the French and English Minstrels only from the itinerant oral Poets of their Gothic ancestors the Franks and the Saxons, and from the SCALDS of their Danish brethren in the North. For though the BARDS of the ancient Gauls and Britons might seem to have a claim of being considered as their more immediate predecessors and instructors; yet these, who were Celtic nations, were *ab origine* so different a race of men from the others who were all of Gothic origin, that I think one cannot, in any degree, argue from the manners of the one to those of the other; and the conquering Franks, Saxons, and Danes, were much less likely to take up any customs from their enemies the Gauls and the Britons, whom they every where expelled, extirpated, or inslaved, than to have received and transmitted them from their own Teutonic ancestors in the North, among whom such customs were known to have prevailed from the earliest ages (*Reliques I* 1767, lxvi).

This militant note contains the thesis of Percy's translator's preface to the *Northern Antiquities.* Here his focus is on the question of 'manners' which he refers to as if the difference were self-evident.[258]

Percy dedicated his translation of *Northern Antiquities* (signing as "the editor") to the Duke of Northumberland, and this time he seems to have written the dedication himself. He is careful to put the object of his dedication into a contemporary context, with the obvious aim of setting his "national" genealogy into the same. Percy hopes that the work will amuse "the most polished Noblemen of the present age" and help them to "trace, to their source, those peculiarities of character, manners and government, which so remarkably distinguish the Teu-

---

[258] It is also interesting in the light of his correspondence with the Welsh scholar Evan Evans, which is discussed below in connection with Percy's 'controversy' with Thomas Warton.

tonic nations". Percy is also concerned with the genealogy and achievements of the duke's ancestors by the name of Percy. This may explain the anonymous publication, but may also be in key with what Groom maintains, that Percy "in the end reinvented himself" ("Celts" 295). Such personal contextualisation clearly shows the implications Percy thought his work had for the present. It is one of the central doctrines of nationalist historicism that is at work.

4.4.2 Difference in Manners

The preface to *Northern Antiquities* begins by dismissing the main body of work Mallet had written and was writing, namely the history of Denmark, which he concludes is only interesting for the natives of Denmark itself (i). This is a bit odd, since the work was written in the language of diplomacy, French, not for the natives, but for others. It also shows that Percy's interest in his 'brethren' only lies in the appropriation of the 'mutual' source of the Teutonic peoples. What is the same on the diachronic axis is completely different on the synchronic one.

Percy's attack on the author is remarkable and hardly has an equivalent in the annals of translation. He asserts that the

> author had been drawn in to adopt an opinion that has been a great source of mistake and confusion to many learned writers of the ancient history of Europe; viz that of supposing the ancient Gauls and Germans, the Britons and the Saxons, to have been originally one and the same people; thus confounding the antiquities of the Gothic and Celtic nations (ii).

Having confidently maintained that he was well acquainted with Mallet's sources, Percy points out the three culprits that 'drew' him into the error of his ways, Cluverius (1616), Keysler (1720) and Pelloutier (1750), authors widely read by antiquarians and scholars. He then concludes that "[t]his mistake the Translator thought might be easily corrected in the present work; and by weeding out this one error, he hoped he should obtain the Author's pardon, and acquire some merit with the English reader" (ii). The latter point was probably more important to him, and this is a rare example of a translator openly defying his text for his audience.

Remarkably, in light of the controversies on translation at the time – and indeed, most translation principles – this palimpsest of the original has caused no controversies in itself, probably because of Percy's point made in the name of learning, and because this point became the standard in the discourse on the Celts and Goths. As we shall see, the development of comparative-historical linguistics confirmed Percy's main thesis of difference, although it of course also neutralised it by finding a common ancestor for both languages.

Percy follows three main sources of difference in the preface. The first is the common focus on "character, manners, laws and language" (iii). Religion also plays a role, but the last point on language is then given special attention at the end of the preface. Percy harps so much on the terms of manners and customs that these obviously make up the central part of his argument. He invokes the authority of Cæsar's *De Bello Gallico*, and maintains that "Cæsar positively affirms that the nations of Gaul differed from those of Germany in their Manners" (xi). The footnoted Latin quote of the opening sentence of Cæsar's famous work is one of the most commonly invoked in the Celtic context: "Gallia est omnis divisa in partes tres: quarum unam incolunt Belgæ, aliam Aquitani, tertiam qui ipsorum lingua Celtæ, nostra Galli apellantur. Hi omnes LINGUA, IN-STITUTIS, LEGIBUS inter se differunt. *Cæsar de Bello Gall. lib.* I" (xi, Percy's emphasis).[259] Percy's footnote is dubious, however, when one considers that the differences recounted here apply to differences *within* Gaul, that is, among the 'Gauls' themselves and not between 'Celts' and 'Germans'.

Cæsar is nonetheless an important witness for all who want to draw a strict line between the Celts and the Germans, because he was the first to draw it; in effect, Cæsar created the "Germans" by providing a bunch of tribes with a common name. His construct is the more believable for being to some extent a first-hand account, and has thus been taken at face value by scholars, even recently. On the other hand, it has been effectively shown that his text and his construct had an altogether different purpose than simply providing information on the ethnography of the peoples living in the 'north'. This can be seen in works for specialists and non-specialists alike, and yet the terms 'Celtic' and 'Germanic' still continue the life they have acquired irrespective of any deconstruction.

An example of the non-specialist critique of *De Bello Gallico* can be seen in *Deutsche Geschichte im Überblick,* originally edited by Peter Rassow and published in 1953. In the third edition of 1972, Gerold Walser explains the construction of the term "German" and notes that it was created by Cæsar and was derived not so much from his knowledge as from his political purposes (5). He explains that until Cæsar, the Romans had used an old (and arbitrary) geographical distinction that divided the peoples north of them (and the Greeks) roughly into Celts and Scythians. He then says that the peoples on the banks of the Rhine, east and west, were probably not so distinct from one another as Cæsar's work suggests. The reason for this is not Cæsar's lack of orientation and accuracy, but simply his need to divide the peoples west of the Rhine (which he had conquered) from those east of it (which he had not) (6).[260] Walser also notes that many historians after Cæsar did not use this distinction and that it was more 'popular' among generals who fought the 'Germans' and acquired the

---

[259] A recent translation by Carolyn Hammond: "The whole of Gaul is divided into three parts, one of which the Belgae inhabit, the Aquitani another, and the third people who in their own language are called 'Celts', but in ours, 'Gauls'" (5).

[260] See Malcolm Chapman's *The Celts. The Construction of a Myth* (24-40).

name or title *Germanicus* as a sign of honour. In addition, he says that the Germanic tribes never used this name for themselves and that it disappeared in the 5th century (with the Western Empire) until the humanists in Germany renewed its honour (6).

Walser also 'deconstructs' the myth of Arminius, whose defeat of the Romans in the Teutoburg Forest has had a special place in German nationalist mythology since Ulrich von Hutten's *Arminius,* and not least through Klopstock's plays, the so-called *Bardiete* (8). Apparently, Arminius was not at all the German hero latter-day nationalists have made him out to be, but rather a disappointed mercenary who was suspended from Roman military service (8). Despite this straightforward empirical information, to which remarks are added on the dubious historicity of Tacitus, as his *Germania* was written more to influence Roman politics than to provide ethnographic information, Walser's Chapter is set in the framework of *"Germanentum"*. The German tribes, according to archaeological finds, simply lived farther east of the Rhine, and he opens his Chapter, which is the first Chapter of a history of Germany by saying:

> Die gegenseitigen Wirkungen des Römertums auf die Germanen und des Germanentums auf die Römer stehen am Anfang der mitteleuropäischen Geschichte. Für die römische und die germanische Welt sind diese wechselseitigen Einflüsse entscheidend geworden. Die Germanen verdanken Rom nicht nur ihren Namen, sondern die Selbsterkenntnis ihres Volkstums. Der Germanenbegriff ist eine römische Schöpfung (1).[261]

It is clear that the German historian accepts the construct of "German" as a genealogical fact, despite his well-informed knowledge of the term's genesis. The contradiction may seem obvious, but what it in itself makes clear is that constructed categories of thinking and labelling are resistant to knowledge of their own synthetic origins. The same applies to the notions of the 'Celts' which Malcolm Chapman has so effectively demolished in his seminal work *The Celts: The Construction of a Myth.* One of the modern works Chapman criticises is David Rankin's *Celts and the Classical World* (1996). To be sure, Chapman praises Rankin for his scholarship – he is, for example, well informed about the 'Celts' in classical writing – but at the same time Chapman claims Rankin is too attached to the synthetic collective term, 'Celt' (Chapman 163-5).

Rankin's detailed work on Cæsar also shows that despite being aware of the functions of Cæsar's text, he still sometimes takes it at face value. An example of this can be seen where he discusses a strange Celtic custom:

---

[261] "The mutual influences of the Romans on the Germans and vice versa are at the beginning of Middle-European history. For the Roman and Germanic worlds, these interactive influences are decisive. The Germans have not only the Romans to thank for their name, but also the knowledge of their identity. The concept of Germans is a Roman creation" (my translation).

Caesar also reports a custom which forbade children to be seen publicly in their father's presence until they were grown up. This would seem to a Roman to be a barbarous oddity [which was perhaps the intention, G.K.]. We can scarcely guess its purpose. Psychoanalytical explanations present themselves, but any ostensible advantage to society from the prohibition remains a puzzle. Nor do we know whether it was confined to some regions (132).

This final acknowledgement of uncertainty serves Rankin's following speculation, however: "The custom seems to have a certain analogy with Gaelic fosterage, which had the effect of binding families of the tribe in closer relationship, or the boys' regiment of Emain Macha, in which Cu Chulain was trained" (132). Such speculations on customs reaching through vast (barely documented) dimensions of space and time are characteristic of the functionality of categories such as the 'Celt'. The analogy of this strange custom can just as well be applied to the medieval Icelanders, as there are several examples in the sagas of children being reared by people other than their parents. Indeed, this was sometimes done to bind families in a closer relationship. For example, Snorri Sturluson, author of the younger *Edda* and *Heimskringla,* the history of the Norwegian kings, was given away to be fostered, but this still does not make him a 'Celt'.[262]

As a matter of fact, Rankin mentions something that Percy avoids underlining, or even contradicts in his argumentation: that despite Cæsar's taxonomic distinction, based on the political realities and natural boundaries of his own Roman empire, he "attributes this latter tenure [of land as property of the tribe] to Germans, whom he, like other ancient authors, seems to think of as a more primitive and ferocious species of Celt" (130). Again, in conjunction with this, Rankin draws an analogy of gigantic dimensions:

> The introduction of Anglo-Norman notions of law into Ireland and Scotland enrolled native chieftains and princes as the owners of the land. The tribesman's status changed as a result and he became a mere tenant instead of an integral member of a society in which his status was assured by ancestry and mutual duty in relation to his chief. This is to be seen in the changes which took place in Scottish Highland society as a result of the defeat of the Stuart cause in the war of 1745 AD (130).

Thus we have seen a strange custom of the Celts in Cæsar's time practised by the Icelanders in the twelfth century and a Germanic custom in Cæsar's time practised in the Scottish Highlands in the eighteenth century.

Percy's use of Cæsar can thus be compared to modern scholarly application of *De Bello Gallico*. It is this fact that best shows what Percy achieved with his

---

[262] Snorri's fosterage is mentioned in the so-called *Islendinga saga* by Snorri's contemporary Sturla Þórðarson. He grew up in one of the centres of learning in medieval Iceland, Oddi. See Guðrún Ása Grímsdóttir (xi).

fundamental severing and isolation of the 'Germanic' and the 'Celtic'. Before he published the *Reliques* and *Northern Antiquities*, these categories were much more fuzzy in the English-speaking world (and continued to be so for some time in the German-speaking one), and only starting to become an issue in themselves. This is, for instance, evident in John Macpherson's *Critical Dissertations*, in which he asserts the difference between the Germanic and Celtic 'nations', albeit in not nearly so militant a tone as Percy's. Macpherson even maintains that the Celts and the Germans were originally "Asiatick" peoples, but "the great distance of time from their separation in Asia, effected such a change in their manners, language and customs, that their common origin was totally obliterated from their memory" (22). This is a minor point for Macpherson, because his real concern was to disprove another kind of kinship, namely that of the Irish and the Scottish, or rather the Irish origins of the 'Caledonians', which was one of the main bones of contention between the Irish and Scottish antiquarians in the Ossianic wars (20-23).

4.4.3 Difference in Religion

Religion was another surgical instrument in Percy's operation. He has a field day with the Druids and their secretive religion, presumably after having read both the Macphersons on the subject. His strategy is obvious from the vocabulary, which is classical and Christian when speaking of the Teutonic nations, as opposed to plainly barbarian when referring to the Celts.[263]

The first marker of difference, according to Percy, is the Celtic notion of metempsychosis, or transmigration of the souls. Here he again leans on Cæsar, whose knowledge of the Celts is so good that "it is not in the power of any of the system-makers to argue and explain his words away" (xvi). To make out a Germanic opposition to the Celtic metempsychosis, Percy observes that "all the Gothic and Teutonic nations held [...] a fixed Elizium, and a Hell, where the valiant and the just were rewarded; and where the cowardly and wicked suffered punishment. The description of these forms a great part of the EDDA" (xvi). The allusion to the classical Elysium and Christian Hell is plain enough, whereas the subtle terminology of the "just" and the "wicked" is a rather free interpretation of the Eddic text, in which the places to which he is referring were reserved for those who died by arms as opposed to those who died of disease or old age, notions not exactly in key with the moral implications of his terms.

Once again referring to Cæsar, Percy then moves on to display Celtic barbarity:

> In innumerable other instances, the institutions of the Druids among the Celts were extremely different from those of the Gothic nations. [...] The former frequently burned a great quantity of human victims alive, in large wicker images, as an offering to their

---

[263]   See above and Groom ("Celts" 289-90).

Gods. The Gothic nations, though like all other Pagans, they occasionally defiled their altars with human blood, appear never to have had any custom like this (xvi-xvii).

Applying well-known paradigms of pagans versus Christians, Percy seems to ignore the fact that what he calls 'Celts' were Christianised well before his 'Goths'. Then again, he is not talking of Christian altars in either case, only representing the customs of the Goths in Christian terms and the customs of the Celts in pagan/barbaric terms. At the same time he is playing subtly on the north-south difference implied in the division of Europe into Protestant and Catholic portions. This becomes plain when he compares druids and skalds, who by implication seem to take on a religious function:

> But what particularly distinguishes the Celtic institutions from those of the Gothic or Teutonic nations, is that remarkable air of Secrecy and Mystery with which the Druids concealed their doctrines from the laity; forbidding that they should ever be committed to writing, and upon that account, not having so much as an alphabet of their own (xvii).

It is difficult not to think of Catholicism when reading this rewriting of Cæsar, but Percy is also following the manuscript paradigm he has been nurturing from the start, in particular in his comparisons between the Goths and the Celts. His own good fortune as a scholar, consisted, after all, in the discovery of a manuscript. If the Celts represent a kind of Catholic version of paganism, the Goths, of course, represent the Protestant one:

> In this, the institutions of Odin and the Gothic scalds was the very reverse. No barbarous people were so addicted to writing, as appears from the innumerable quantity of Runic inscriptions scattered all over the north; no barbarous people ever held Letters in higher reverence, [...] (xvii).

Percy repeats here his runic mantra, apparently oblivious of its weakness, because it is a perfect tool to differentiate the Goths from the illiterate Celts. In addition, runes have an aura of 'real' antiquity. This enables Percy to draw a predictable analogy with historical antiquity, for, as he says, the mythology of the Goths "is for ever displayed in all the Songs of their SCALDS, just as that of the Greeks and Romans in the Odes of Pindar and Horace" (xvii-xviii). By now, Percy has stopped to referring to classical models by implication and compares the skaldic poetry directly with the greatest of the good. Such hyperbole, already common in the Ossianic context, shows that the national emphasis on identifying classics of one's own was fully established. This does not mean the displacing of the ancient classics, but simply the revaluation of the 'native' ones and their insertion into the canon. It was only later that the classics were displaced, mostly because they were available to most readers only through translation. In the end, the Moderns did win the "battle of the books".

4.4.4 Difference in Language

What made Percy's intervention so decisive was his genealogical approach to language. This was carried out not in the great tradition of speculative etymology, which he explicitly rejects, but through what may be termed one of the first steps towards a comparative-historical linguistics. That such a critical step may be contained in a 'mere translator's preface may seem overstated to some, especially as the honour of fatherhood of this distinguished discipline has most often been attributed to the famous oriental scholar William Jones, who in his famous address to the Asiatick Society in 1786 noted the affinity of Sanskrit with Latin and Greek, and even 'Celtic' and 'Gothic'.

The reason for Jones' nomination as the father of comparative-historical linguistics is based primarily on the aforementioned observation, and less on his work as a grammarian, oriental scholar, translator and minor poet and aesthetician. On the subject of the 'real fatherhood' of the discipline of comparative-historical linguistics, there are various opinions as to the begetter, although Jones is mentioned in many cases as a kind of 'precursor'. This applies for example to the introduction of *Indogermanische Dichtersprache,* edited by Rüdiger Schmitt, in which he names Franz Bopp's *Über das Conjugationssystem der Sanskritsprache in Vergleichung mit jenem der griechischen, lateinischen, persischen und germanischen Sprache* (1816) as the fundamental book that first brought scientific proof ("wissenschaftlich fundierten Beweis") of the genetic kinship of the so-called Indo-Germanic languages (1). The terminology employed demonstrates the central direction this discipline had from the start; the biological metaphor of genetic kinship ("genetisch verwandt") is hardly a metaphor in this case, so interwoven are the strands of thought, and they were certainly there from the beginning, as can be seen in Jones' work, which not only refers to Linnæus and the construction of human races, but also includes a number of essays on botanical subjects.[264] Schmitt's introduction moves on to note Jones' precursory remarks, relating to the possible common source of Greek, Latin and Sanskrit.

In his recent *Einführung in die Indogermanistik,* Robert Brandt-Schmitt also mentions Jones as a precursor, claiming that the real originators were the Danish scholar Rasmus Kristian Rask and the German grammarian and lexicographer Jacob Grimm, in addition to Bopp (1-3). Other scholars frequently cited are the Schlegel brothers, especially Friedrich Schlegel, whose *Ueber die Sprache und Weisheit der Indier* of 1808 certainly stimulated the above "troika" of founding fathers with phrases such as "vergleichende Grammatik", which his

---

[264] See for instance Jones' "On the Origin and Families of Nations" in *The Works of William Jones.* Vol. I.

brother had used as early as 1803.[265] Jones' writings inspired Friedrich Schlegel's study of Sanskrit.

Whoever is credited with being the founding father of comparative-historical linguistics, it remains clear that the discipline had two focal points in this early phase, during the latter part of the eighteenth century and the first part of the nineteenth. The first is the discovery of Sanskrit as a "common source" of several European languages. This is perhaps not as dramatic a paradigmatic shift in linguistics as is sometimes implied, since scholars had long been working with another single 'source', namely Hebrew, and had delivered constructs of varying imaginative strength. So the idea was not new in itself, but it was possibly more dramatic in its unstated secularisation of linguistics, since the Bible and its version of the history of language were now fully pushed aside.

The second focal point was the systematic comparison of languages in various stages of their history, their grammatical and especially their inflectional structures. It is actually in this point that one can see the main reason for awarding the 'fatherhood' to Bopp. The novelty of Bopp's contribution was the delivery of a 'scientific proof', in the positivist sense, of the assumption that Sanskrit was the 'original' Indo-European language. He achieved this through comparison of inflectional systems based on Sanskrit as the common source language. Hence comparative-historical linguistics have been referred to as Indo-European linguistics (Indogermanistik).

Rask and Grimm, on the other hand, provided for a wider conception of the discipline of comparative-historical linguistics. Their discoveries derived from comparison of the lexicon, from which they were able to deduce the sound shifts Grimm has become famous for. They were certainly both grammarians, but their major contributions rested partly on their work on the historical changes which they discovered through research on the lexicon. It was essentially the comparison of words from different languages that enabled them to "see" the High German sound shift. What made them pioneers in linguistics was their extension of that research into changes in pronunciation.

This naturally has something to do with the state of linguistics prior to their contributions. Native-language grammars were not highly developed in Europe in the eighteenth century; the major works in this field were written in the nineteenth century, often by scholars at the forefront of comparative-historical linguistics. Movement towards writing grammars had, however, begun in the latter part of the eighteenth century, an appearance that needs to be considered in conjunction with the development of monolingual dictionaries. Johnson's *Dictionary* included a rudimentary grammar, and according to Baugh and Cable in their

---

[265] According to Koerner in his article on Friedrich Schlegel in the *Encyclopedia of Language and Linguistics*, Johann Severin Vater, professor in Halle, had actually used the phrase in 1801 and A.W. Schlegel in 1803 (3679).

History of the English Language, "[t]he decade beginning in 1760 witnessed a striking outburst of interest in English grammar" (273). Robert Lowth and Joseph Priestley were the main contributors in the 1760s, followed two decades later by the American Noah Webster, whose famous dictionary originated many of the slight differences between written American and British English.[266] Johann Christoph Adelung's German *Wörterbuch* (1774) may be ascribed to the same kind of interest, which marks an obvious shift in the attitude towards native languages.

Linguistics, or rather lexicography and native-language grammar, was, then, only beginning to develop when Percy made his contribution to comparative-historical linguistics. But there are of course decisive differences. Percy was certainly not occupied with seeking a common source for the European languages; on the contrary, he had already found the common source in his 'Gothic' forefathers and he had no need for a common source for them and the Celts. It is, therefore, in the method and not the premise that he can be seen as a contributor to comparative-historical linguistics.

In his grand finale to the preface of *Northern Antiquities,* Percy begins by asserting that

[t]he essential difference remarked above, between the Religion of the Celtic and Gothick nations in their Tenets, Institutions and Worship, affords strong proof that they were two races of men *ab origine* distinct: The same truth is proved still more strongly, if possible, by their difference in LANGUAGE; this is an argument of fact, that amounts in questions of this nature almost to demonstration (xix, emphasis in text).

Percy's demonstration then takes the form of what he terms a "GENEALOGICAL TABLE, showing what languages are descended from those two great Mother Tongues, by what immediate Branches they derive their descent, and what degree of affinity they severally bear to each other" (xxiv-

---

[266] Baugh and Cable have described Webster's deliberate attempts to differentiate the American variety of English from the British (357-365). The fact that Webster started his career as a linguist in the 1780s is rather significant. That the American variety of English was created by a process of what may be "termed [...] a conscious effort toward establishing language identity", as Braj Kachru notes in his article "American English and other Englishes", should be beyond dispute, but the notion of an American *language* as opposed to a *variety* seems to be overstated (23). The reason for speaking of American as a language rather than a variety seems to stem from a confusion between language and culture. Language is of course one of the greatest carriers of culture, but the differences between American and British cultures are not manifested through different languages, but merely reflected in the English language. See, for example, Trudgill and Hannah whose *International English* claims there are two main standard varieties of English; a rather questionable view considering that the rest of them become "sub-standard" (1-3). Then again it reflects the status of the two English-speaking empires, the bygone British one and the contemporary American.

xxv, emphasis in text). He admits that this is copied from the preface of Hickes' Anglo-Saxon grammar of 1689, and he must also have studied the prefatory "History of the English Language" in Johnson's *Dictionary*. Johnson's comparison of the several stages of the English language breathes the same "spirit" as Percy's with regard to the continuation of the Anglo-Saxon language from its origins, and Percy may well have been advised by the famous lexicographer on certain points in his essays in the *Reliques*, a publication in which it had been intended that Johnson should have a larger part than he eventually did. It should not be forgotten in this context that William Jones was a personal acquaintance of Percy and Johnson, indeed a member of the famous Club, though even if he had not been a member he would have been familiar with work that came so close to his interests, namely Johnson's *Dictionary* and Percy's works generally.

Percy's demonstration proceeds with the presentation for comparison of examples of the Lord's Prayer in various languages, of which his greatest trump is the version from the fourth-century Gothic translation of Ulfilas, *Codex Argenteus*, which he then juxtaposes with the following remark: "I am not able to produce any speciman of CELTIC, at least any version of the Lord's Prayer, which can be opposed in point of antiquity to the GOTHIC specimen from ULPHILAC, who flourished A.D. 365" (xxxvii, emphasis in text).

Percy undoubtedly leans on his fellow antiquarian and scholar Edward Lye in this case, but he is also using or abusing information from the Welsh scholar Evan Evans, whom he had explicitly asked about Celtic versions of the Lord's Prayer in May 1765, when the first volume of *Northern Antiquities* was already in the press (*Letters V* 110). Percy in fact sent Evans this volume soon after, but without the preface, which Evans inquired about twice, in January 1766 and again in July 1767. Why Percy did not oblige his helper and fellow scholar can only be speculated upon. The preface was of course the most interesting part of the publication for Evans, who had continually been supplying Percy with information on the Celts, in connection with *Northern Antiquities* and the difference between the Celts and Goths, since 1761. He may well have hoped that his contributions would be inserted and acknowledged. Some of his assertions on alliteration in ancient Welsh poetry were indeed printed verbatim from his letters, but subordinated in the form of a footnote to Percy's conviction that the "Welsh BARDS might possibly have been excited to cultivate the alliterative versification more strictly, from the example of the Icelandic SCALDS, and their imitators the Anglo-Saxon Poets" (197-98).[267]

Such was the use which Percy made of the information from Evans, who had informed him in September 1765 that there was no Welsh translation of the

---

[267]   This is shown in the *Percy Letters* V (55, 64-65). See also the discussion on Evan Evans in the section on the Percy-Warton "Controversy".

Lord's Prayer "near so old as the fifth or sixth century" (*Letters V* 115). Percy consequently noted in *Northern Antiquities*::

> As the CELTS were settled in these countries long before the GOTHS, and were exposed to various revolutions before their arrival, their Language has, undergone greater and earlier changes than the GOTHIC; so that no Specimen of the old original CELTIC is, I believe, now to be found" (xxvii).

Percy's use of the Lord's Prayer is interesting in the light of this discussion, as his examples are of course all translations. In using the Lord's Prayer as an example, he reverts to a tradition of language comparison that had existed since the fifteenth century, if the most renowned user of this method, Adelung, is to be believed. Adelung's *Mithridates, oder allgemeine Sprachkunde,* of which the first volume was published in 1806, uses the Lord's Prayer as a comparative example for over five hundred languages and also recounts a large number of forerunners of the method in an appendix.[268] Adelung's position in the genesis of comparative-historical linguistics is, despite this massive work of historical, phonological and morphological comparison, less than clear; he is rarely, if ever, mentioned in any encyclopaedia in connection with this discipline. This is due to his rejection of the "common source" language and his more synchronic approach compared with that of the later diachronic reconstructors of the nineteenth century. His thesis of language development, speculative as it may be, and indebted to eighteenth century theories of human evolution, may nevertheless be considered as comparative-historical. However, he casts his net much wider than the IE linguists, taking non-IE languages into account, and thus does not conform to the genealogical mould of Indo-European linguistics, which seems to be a more proper term for the discipline than is comparative-historical linguistics.

Percy was of course not a linguist in the sense of the aforementioned scholars, and his objective was not to analyse language as such, but to prove a difference between two "races". He did, however, follow up his preface with a morphological discussion under the heading "Remarks on the Foregoing Version and First of the Gothic Specimens". Here Percy compares not only the Germanic languages but also includes other points of reference, such as the Lappish (Sami) language and Basque.

That this can be interpreted as a kind of proto-comparative-historical linguistics is best seen in an examination of the second edition of *Northern Antiquities*, which was published under the editorship of I. A. Blackwell in 1847, when the discipline was speedily developing under names such as glossology, according to the editor. This edition was reprinted in 1909. It is lightly bowdlerised by the editor, who indicates that he has "necessarily been obliged to revise

---

[268]   The subsequent volumes were edited and written by J.S. Vater.

the work throughout". He also adds an English translation of the *Prose Edda* "from the original" instead of Göran[s]son's Latin version, in addition to an abstract of *Eyrbyggja Saga* by Walter Scott, which is Scott's translation of a Latin translation, which he executed in the watershed year of his career, 1814.

Blackwell modifies the subtitle slightly, and speaks of the ancient Scandinavians instead of the Danes and "incidental notices respecting our Saxon ancestors", signalling that distinction between the "Northern Nations", as Percy called them, was also developing with the discipline. Instead of Percy's "Remarks", Blackwell then inserts his own "Remarks on Bishop Percy's Preface". He begins by citing one of the 'founding fathers' of comparative-historical linguistics: "

> Professor Rask, in the Introduction to his Icelandic Grammar, observes that, "after Bishop Percy's most excellent Preface to Mallet's Northern Antiquities, the Teutonic and Celtic languages can no longer be confounded, nor comprised under the vague and unmeaning appellation of Scythian, Sarmatian &tc" (*Northern* 1909, 22).

The work Blackwell is referring to is Rask's first major work *Vejledning til det Islandske eller gamle Nordiske sprog* (1811), the text in which what later was called by Jacob Grimm "Umlaut", or vowel mutation, in the Germanic languages is first mentioned.[269]

Rask was born in 1787 and became interested in languages at an early age; his first publications came out when he was only 21 years of age and he had probably finished his *Vejledning* a year later although it was only published in 1811. His other groundbreaking work was the *Undersøgelse om Det gamle Nordiske eller Islandske Sprogs Oprindelse,* a prize essay of 1814 (published 1818) in which, among other things, he formulates the so-called High German sound shift for the first time, later also developed by Grimm and hence called Grimm's Law (Rask, *Abhandlungen I* 84). As a student in 1809 he published a nationalist polemic in German against Adelung's *Mithridates* because he felt that the Northern languages and literatures had been condescendingly treated in the book.[270] This shows that Adelung had moved him to look at language from a

---

[269] Grimm was not convinced at first as his remark in his review in 1812 shows, where he maintains that Rask's note is "mehr scharfsinnig als wahr". See Holger Pedersen. "Einleitung" in *Rasmus Rask. Ausgewählte Abhandlungen I* (xxxviii). The review was published in *Allgem. Literatur-Zeitung* (1812).

[270] "Bemerkungen über die skandinavischen Sprachen veranlaßt durch den zweiten Teil des Adelungschen Mithridates". *Zeitung für Litteratur und Kunst in den königl. Dänischen Staaten* (1809). The essay is also in *Ausgewählte Abhandlungen II.* (103-123). The text which Rask criticises was not actually written by Adelung, but by his successor J.S. Vater, who used Adelung's notes. Rask mentions this, but his critique refers to the sources which Adelung had used (107). Rask's critique is primarily aimed, however, at the uniform treatment of the Germanic languages. He wants to differentiate between

comparative (and nationalist) point of view, which he developed in his later work, although he did not see the common source in Sanskrit until later in his career.

One of the reasons for this may be the fact that Percy still seems to have been haunting Rask's mind when he wrote the *Undersøgelse*. Later IE linguists have described his negative attitude towards the Celts and the Celtic languages as one of the drawbacks of this work. According to Collinge, Rask "havered over Celtic and did not adduce Indian evidence" (3441).

In his introduction to Louis Hjelmslev's edition of Rask's works, Holger Pedersen argues: "Die Ablehnung der Verwandschaft [des gotischen und des keltischen] ist aber ein entschiedener Irrtum, der nur aus der gänzlichen Unzulänglichkeit des damals zur Verfügung stehenden Materials erklärbar ist" (*Abhandlungen I* xxiii).[271] It is more likely that Rask's error is explicable through Percy, for Rask's remarks on the Celts sound almost as if they were ghost-written by Percy. He begins his passage on the Celtic languages by discussing the "systems" that have been invented and the nationalist controversies that are attached to them, likening them to the Ossianic controversy (93). He then joins the fray himself by attacking Pelloutier, whom Percy had criticised, after which he turns to the recently founded *Académie Celtique,* which had published its first volume of transactions in 1807 with a kind of manifesto that in essence claimed the Celtic was the original European language. Rask quotes at length and adds his own remarks into the quotation, deconstucting it from within:

> Le but de l'Académie est donc 1) de reproduire l'histoire des Celtes, de rechercher leurs monuments, de les examiner, de les discuter, de les expliquer; 2) d'étudier et de publier l'étymologie de toutes les langues de l'Europe (hvorfor ikke de asiatiske med?) à l'aide du Celto-Breton ([...] Armorisk), du Gallois ([...] Kymrisk), et de la langue Erse ([...] Irsk og Skotsk) (*Abhandlungen I* 95, italics reversed).

The insertions are mainly terminological corrections "Armorisk" for "Celto-Breton" "Kymrisk" for "du Gallois", etc. Rask seems indeed to have a hunch that there is possibly a common source when he asks in the brackets "why not the Asiatic too?" [(hvorfor ikke de asiatiske med?)], but he seems to be so blinded by Percy's argument of difference that he does not follow this up. In a true nationalist manner he accuses the others of nationalism and prejudice before referring to his authority:

Nordic (Scandinavian) and "Deutsch" (Germanic) and he seems to want to set up a kind of hierarchy, referring, interestingly to the "Ursitze in Asien" (112). He may not have been so averse to the idea of a common source language at the time.

[271] "The rejection of the relation [of Gothic and Celtic] is a fundamental error which is only explicable with the inadequacy of the material at hand at the time" (my translation).

Ingen har med mere Grundighed og Sindighed angreben Pelloutiers og Eftersnakkers Paastande end den engelske Oversætter af Mallets Introduction à histoire de Dannemarc. Hans vigtigste Modgrunde ere: at de Ligheder som anføres imellem de gotiske og keltiske Folkeslags Sprog bestaa for de meste i blotte Udledelser af Navne paa Stæder og Egne, men disse ere dels usikre, dels kunne tilstrækkelig forklares af Vandringer eller Nybygder ell. desl., hvorimod Sprogene selv meget mere synes aldeles forskjellige (96).[272]

Rask repeats Percy's arguments about the difference between the Gothic and Celtic languages, and that all likeness between them is merely based on place names which may have been retained despite migration. All similarity in manners is coincidental, due to the similarity of barbarous peoples in general, and Percy's reference to Cæsar is not missing. Rask remarks regarding the social structure that "[h]os Gallerne vare egentlig blot Druiderne og Høvedsmændene fri, og Almuen næsten Slaver; hos Germanerne tværtimod vare alle lige fri, hvilket gjælder om Nordboerne og synes at være en Hovedforskjellighed in den borgerlige Indretning" (97).[273] The familiar paradigm of the democratic Germans versus the Celtic slaves is presented here and alluded to as a main distinction (that applies to northern Germanic peoples), which is at the basis of bourgeois or civil society. Subsequently, Rask rewrites Percy on religion and literature and finishes the paragraph by alluding to his former adversary, Adelung, whose *Mithridates* held up the same opinion as Percy on the difference of the languages. It appears though, Rask claims, that Adelung did not know of Percy's work (97).[274] Oddly enough, shortly after this excursion into nationalist polemics, Rask begins analysing the Celtic languages grammatically and lexically, and even comes to the conclusion that "Kymrisk" and Gothic have some

---

[272] "Nobody has attacked Pelloutier and his imitators more thoroughly and sedately than the English translator of Mallet's Introduction à histoire de Dannemarc. His most important counterarguments are: that the similiarities in language between Gothic and Celtic folk songs are simple deductions of placenames, but that these are always unreliable and may well be explained through migration or settlement, whereas the languages themselves still are completely different" (my translation).

[273] "Among the Gauls only the Druids and Chieftains were really free and the people were almost reduced to slavery, whereas among the Germans almost everbody was free. This applies to the Northern peoples and seems to be the main difference in the civil social structure" (my translation).

[274] It is correct that Adelung does not refer to Percy's *Northern Antiquities,* not even in the long list of scholars who have used the comparison of the Lord's Prayer, but he, or rather J.S. Vater who actually wrote the text, does refer to a glossary of Scotticisms in the *Reliques* (*Mithridates II* 322) It might also be added here that Adelung wrote an essay on the authenticity of Ossian in 1806 where he gathered the arguments of the 1805 Report and comes to a similar conclusion as Scott, for example. He had this essay reprinted in *Mithridates II* (104-141). See also the abovementioned essay against Adelung's *Mithridates.*

lexical items in common. He ascribes this blending to the ancient "mixed" Belgians and the influence of the Anglo-Saxons and English on the Welsh (103). Grammatically, however, Gothic is decidedly different from "Kymrisk" (102).

From the above it is evident that Percy's preface and translation stoked a nationalist fire in the young Danish linguist, even to the extent of leading his judgement astray on his own subject. On the other hand, his nationalism did not necessarily depend on Percy, as can be seen in his first reaction against Adelung. My argument in this section does not focus on Percy's nationalism, but on the way it contributed to a linguistic discipline that played a fundamental role in the national constructs of the nineteenth century. I would suggest that the supposed origins of comparative-historical linguistics have been too narrowly defined, focusing on the discovery of an "Ursprache" combined with a comparison of grammatical phenomena. This method had its origins in the diachronic and synchronic comparison of languages, as can perhaps best be seen in the words of one of the founding fathers of comparative-historical lingustics, Jacob Grimm:

> Ohne zweifel wurde durch das von der kaiserin Katharina in den jahren 1787-90 veranstaltete Petersburger wörterbuch, wenn es auch noch auf sehr ungenügenden grundlagen aufgerichtet war, sprachvergleichung überhaupt wirksam angeregt und gefördert. Allein weit größern einfluß auf sie hatte die in allen weltteilen, hauptsächlich in Indien befestigste herrschaft der Briten, durch welche das genaue verständnis einer der reinsten und ehrwürdigen sprachen der ganzen welt, die man früher beinahe gar nicht gekannt hatte, erweckt, gesichert und verbreitet wurde (9).[275]

In his *Über den Ursprung der Sprache* (1851), Grimm not only emphasises the influence of the discovery of Sanskrit in a colonial framework, but also the importance of lexical comparison, a method he applied in his own grammatical and lexicographical work. That the British conquest of India made a huge difference to the development of the discipline is undoubtedly correct, but it is probably just as correct that the national literary rivalry within the British Isles had a marked influence on the budding discipline of comparative-historical linguistics.[276]

---

[275] "It was, without doubt, the Petersburg dictionary, which empress Katherine had made in the years 1787-90, which initiated and promoted language comparison, even if the basis was insufficient. The greatest influence [on language comparison] came, however, through the presence of the British in all parts of the world, first and foremost in India, that an exact understanding of the most pure and honourable languages of the world, previously almost unknown, was aroused, saved and diffused" (my rough translation).

[276] For a detailed discussion of Willam Jones' translational activity in the colonial context, see Tejaswini Niranjana's *Siting Translation.*

4.5 The Percy-Warton "Controversy"

Thomas Warton the younger was one of Percy's greatest helpers in the preparation of the *Reliques*. During the spring days of 1761, when he was contracting with Dodsley on the publication of his translations *Five Pieces, The Song of Solomon, The Matrons,* and *Miscellaneous Pieces from the Chinese,* as well as the *Reliques* themselves, Percy wrote to Warton to seek assistance (Robinson & Dennis, *Letters III*, xix). This was no coincidence of course: Warton had been Professor for Poetry at Oxford for four years and had published his *Observations on the Faerie Queene of Spenser* in 1754, one of the pivotal works in the awakening interest in English poetry as a subject in itself.

Despite their mutual interest and assistance, Percy and Warton differed in one important point, on the Matter of Britain. This was the question about the origins of "Romantic" literature in Britain, a question which both men attempted to answer with anthropological speculation, that is, building a system of wandering peoples and languages that in the end find their promised land and culture in Britain. Warton's thesis came from William Warburton, Bishop of Gloucester and editor of Shakespeare, and Warton briefly touched upon it in his *Observations*.[277] This thesis explains the aesthetic irregularities in "Romantic" literature in the neo-classical sense by assigning its source to the medieval Arabic world. When the *Reliques* were in preparation this idea had not yet been discussed in detail by Warton and Warburton, let alone built into a "system", as Percy was doing with the Norse skalds in his essays. He was nevertheless well aware of this thesis, which of course did not easily fit into his system. Percy was even so bold as to correct it in his third letter to Warton, who was then putting the second edition of the *Observations* through to press. The point Percy makes is that "had the learned Author [Warburton] here quoted been conversant with the Ancient Writings of the Northern Nations, he would have found that the Notions, so current in books of Chivalry, of Inchantments &c, were established in Europe long before the time of the Crusades" (*Letters III* 12). Percy's argument is strong, as Warburton's hypothesis is based on the idea that the oriental influence started through the crusades. Percy, having studied the Northern skalds with his friend Lye, sees it differently and draws a linear progression from the skaldic literature to the romances of chivalry. Warburton and Warton, on the other hand, see a linear progression from the originators in the Orient to the romances of chivalry in Spain, France and Britain. Interestingly, both theses have the premise that this un-neo-classical element has migrated from abroad, and yet have no problem with making it into an almost native art, peculiar to the manners of their

---

[277] Warburton mentions this in his "Supplement to the Translator's Preface" which appeared in the second edition of Jervas' translation of *Don Quixote*, published 1749 (*Letters III* 12).

nation. What they need is an originating culture that moves into Britain, mixes with the existing population and through mutual influence creates something truly indigenous. The method for achieving this is the same in both cases.

As Robinson and Dennis, the editors of the Warton volume of *The Percy Letters*, point out, Warton did not accept Percy's "correction", but introduced Percy's information in the second edition of the *Observations* (12). Percy was not impressed, as his letters to the Welsh scholar Evan Evans show. Evans became one of Macpherson's epigones in gathering and translating "Celtic" poetry, publishing his *Some Specimens of the Poetry of the Antient Welsh Bards* in 1764, and he was one of the scholars Percy contacted in the hectic summer of 1761.[278]

Percy's introductory letter to Evans quickly arrives at the question of national literary rivalry in Britain. His inquiry into Welsh literary antiquities is directly linked to the current popularity of Scottish antiquities after Macpherson's success. He complains about not having been able to get a "satisfactory account of the literary productions" of the Welsh, following with a paragraph which shows very well the national motivation behind his own projects:

> Not so the Scotch, they are everywhere recommending the antiquities of their country to public notice, vindicating it's history, setting off it's poetry, and by constant attention to their grand national concern have prevailed so far as to have the [over "broken jargon" deleted] Dialect they speak to be considered as the most proper language for our pastoral poetry. Our most polite Ladies warble Scottish Airs, and in the Senate itself whatever relates to the Scottish Nation is always mentioned with peculiar respect (*Letters V*, 2).

The mixture of envy and admiration for the successful setting up of a "grand national concern" is spiced with irritation at "our most polite Ladies" and it can be assumed that Percy thought the books needed to be balanced somewhat, for he continues as follows:

> Far from blaming this attention in the Scotch, I think it much to their credit, and am sorry that a large class of our fellow subjects, with whom we were united in the most intimate Union for many ages before Scotland ceased to be our inveterate enemy, have not shewn the same respect to the peculiarities of their own Country, but by their supineness and neglect, have suffered a foolish and inveterate prejudice to root itself in the minds of their *com-patriotes* the English. A Prejudice, which might have been in a good measure prevented had they occasionally given us specimens of the treasures con-

---

[278] Evans had started collecting and translating Welsh poetry into Latin before Macpherson's publications. Before the success of Ossian, this can, however, be seen more as a scholarly and antiquarian project. Evans was not as "creative" in his translation work, but Macpherson's style certainly impressed him as it did Charlotte Brooke. See *The Percy Letters V* (35-36) and Leersen (428).

tained in their native language: and which may even yet be in part removed by the same means (*Letters V, 2*).

This challenge from Percy, who had already started his own project to balance the books on the English side, may well have encouraged Evans to publish his *Specimens* later on. He certainly used the word "specimens" in the title of his book, a rather duller variation on "Fragments" than "Reliques" is. Charlotte Brooke, who translated Irish antiquities for the same reasons later on, chose "Reliques" for her title. What is more remarkable, however, is the fact that all are translating their own antiquity into a new and national modernity: Macpherson from Scottish Gaelic, Percy from Old Icelandic/Norse, Evans from Welsh, and Brooke from Irish Gaelic. Britishness seems to be based on several translations, and this may be the reason for the difficulty of retaining it in a single homogenous entity, for the idea of a nation is partly rooted in a myth of the nativeness of literature. In Britain, texts in foreign languages had to be translated and appropriated, which focused the attention on the sources much more sharply than in other countries.

Perhaps this is also one of the reasons why Percy's *Reliques* were a greater success than those of the other Macphersonian epigones. He only needed to translate a few old skaldic odes and write speculative essays on the linkage between the Norse skalds and the presumed Saxon ones. His decisive material consisted of the ballads, for which he had to take some considerable flak for aforementioned reasons, but not as hefty as that encountered by Macpherson.

He had problems, however, with his Saxon skalds and the languages of romances. Warton stuck to Warburton's thesis despite acknowledgement of Percy's information. This seems to have irritated Percy somewhat, for he wrote to Evans in August 1762 just after he received the second edition of Warton's *Observations*:

> I have lately been employed in a small literary controversy with a learned friend, about the original source and antiquity of the popular notion concerning *Fairies and Goblins:* My friend is for fetching these whimsical opinions from the east so late as the time of the Croisades; and derives the words *Elf and Goblin* from the *Guelfes and Gibbeline* factions in Italy. But I think it would be impossible for Notions so arbitrary to have obtained so universally, so uniformly, and so early (see Chaucer's *Wife of Bath's Tale*) if they had not got possession of the minds of men many ages before: Nay I make no doubt but Fairies are derived from the *Duergar* or Dwarfs, whose existence was so generally believed among the northern nations (*Letters V* 33-34).

Percy overstates a little in this letter, because this "controversy" seems not to have been the subject of his correspondence with Warton at the time. In a letter written late in August 1762, just after he had read the second edition of the *Observations,* Percy expresses his admiration and then goes on to correct the minor flaws in Warton's work. As a part of the letter is missing, it is impossible to say whether Percy touched upon this "controversial" point, but Warton's answer in September does not refer to it, although the opening sentence, "I am very happy to find that you think I have revised my Observations with *some* Accuracy" may reflect a little impatience towards Percy's exactness, if not pedantry (*Letters III* 45, my emphasis).

Remarkably, this "controversy" about a fundamental difference in the views of the two scholars was not at all the subject of their frequent correspondence of the 1760s, nor later on, when, as it were, their differences came to a head. Percy was nevertheless very much occupied with the problem, as it presented the most formidable obstacle to the structure of his "system" with the "native" Gothic skalds as the forerunners of chivalric romance and indeed his balladry. His correspondence with Evans seems even to be partly geared to collect evidence for his own thesis, for some of his queries to the Welsh scholar have the obvious aim of disproving Warburton's argument. Percy's and Evans's letters of December 1763 and early 1764 demonstrate this well.

Percy wrote to Evans on New Year's Eve 1763 after a few months pause, enclosing his essay "On the Metre of Pierce Plowman's Visions". He encourages Evans in his translation work and inquires in a postscript about the "very peculiar Versification, which I am told bears a great resemblance to the alliterative metre of the old Cambrian bards" (*Letters V* 53). Considering his firm belief that the Celts and Goths were distinctly separate cultural entities, this inquiry is peculiar.

The response from Evans did not disappoint him, however. Not only does Evans confirm that the Welsh bards did use alliteration in a complex manner (he maintains that it is comparable to the laws of quantity in ancient Greece and Rome), but he points out that the English had also long ago used such measures, as could be seen by examples from Giraldus Cambrensis (*Letters V* 57-59). Percy was so pleased as to speak of an "obliging Letter" which gave him "that pleasure, which your curious researches always do" (60). He had a good reason to be pleased, for now he felt he had the analogous evidence he needed. Bearing in mind his separation of the Celtic and Gothic his argumentation is almost amusingly twisted:

> You tell me that the earlier Welsh Bards were more lax in their alliteration than their successors: and that it was not till after the Conquest that they ran into all the exact refinements of alliteration, this makes me suspect that your old poets formed their prosody after the Model of Scandrian Scalds; men, who if we may believe the Northern Histories were sought for and caressed by the *British* as well as the *Saxon* Princes of this Island. See Torfæi Orcades fol. Praefat. According to this writer Islandic was a kind of court language, as French is now, and was understood in all the northern courts of Europe and in this Island (60-61).

As the editor of Percy's letters to Evans, Aneirin Lewis, points out, Percy has here in mind a passage from Torfæus which he felt it necessary to quote in his later notes to his "Essay on the Ancient Minstrels". Torfæus had rewritten a passage from Egill's Saga which relates the adventures of the mercenary poet Egill Skalla-Grímsson in England in the first half of the tenth century. According to the saga (written in the thirteenth century), however, his abilities as a soldier were more important to the Saxon king Athelstan than his poetry (although he is supposed to have composed an "ode" to him). There is no mention of the poetic admiration of Athelstan's Welsh allies in the battle with the Scottish "king" Ólaf (Danish king Aulaff in Percy). There is also no mention of king Aulaff's dressing up as a poet and singing for Athelstan and his men prior to the battle. More significantly, the "ode" more famous in this passage is the so-called *Höfuðlausn* which Egill composed for the Norse king Eiríkur blóðöx (bloodaxe), considered to be the first Norse poem with end-rhyme.[279]

Percy's strategy is obvious. By a rather far-fetched analogy to French as a court language he wants to give the impression that Saxon and Welsh kings could be amused with skaldic poetry either in key with or influencing the native tradition. His evidence in the letter to Evans is metrical: "If you will look into *Olai Wormij Literatura Runica*, 4^0 1636, you will find that the Scalds had carried Alliteration to the highest pitch of refinement long before the era of our Willm the Conqueror" (62).

Alliteration is not the only link, however. Percy is primarily thinking of his "controversy" with Warton and moves directly on to the Welsh sources:

> What you say of your old British Romances greatly piques my curiosity and will help to decide a dispute between our Poetry Professor Mr Warton and myself. I have got in my possession a large collection of old English Romances in short metre. Mr Warton thinks they are translations from the French; I am of opinion they are rather imitations from the Welsh: the subject of most of them being adventures of K. Arthur and his Knights of the Round Table (62-63).

Percy's twist is, to use a common term of his own, ingenious. He manifests the skaldic origin of alliterative poetry for the whole of the British Isles and then the Welsh origin of the old English Romances he is working on. Warburton's hypothesis is thus linguistically and chronologically disproved. Percy went on to maintain his theory of the skaldic origins of alliteration, avoiding, however, as-

---

[279] Egill Skalla-Grímsson is an interesting figure in other respects. The anonymous (Christian) author of Egill's Saga seems to give him a kind of bridge-building role between the pagan and Christian worlds. King Athelstan manages, for example, to convince Egill and his brother Þórólfur to take a kind of first Christian sacrament before he hires them as mercenaries. Percy refers specifically to the "Ode of Egil" in his opening passage of the "On the Alliterative Metre, without Rhyme, in Pierce Plowman's Visions" (*Reliques II* 1858, 216).

signing this to the Welsh or Celtic bards directly, possibly because Evans disagreed with him on this point while agreeing with him that the old English romances were translations from the Welsh (66). Evans turns the argument around and proposes that the "Scalds borrowed this poetic ornament from their [i.e., Celtic] Bards, and even the very word Bard itself, as you acknowledge in your Runic poetry" (67). In the "Essay on the Ancient Minstrels", however, Percy notes that the bards "whether of Celtic or Gothic race" were revered and admired, "but by none more than by our own Teutonic ancestors, particularly by all the Danish tribes", saying nothing directly about the origins but implying a great deal. (*Reliques I* 1858, xxxiii).

Despite the slight ambiguity regarding the relation between the Celts and the Goths, probably due to this question of metre, Percy and Evans agreed fully on the distinct origins of the two "races". The criteria for the distinction were history, language and customs and manners. Their letters of 1764 go into detail on the matter and both men refer to their authorities at length. The most significant element of this correspondence is perhaps the fact that Percy admits to not having read the latter part of Snorri's *Edda* (i.e., the part that deals with skaldic metre in detail); his knowledge of the skaldic metre is thus from secondary sources and presumably his friend, Edward Lye.

4.5.1 The Matter of Britain

Percy's problem in the "controversy" with Warton was not the distinction between the Celts and the Goths, but whether the source texts for the old English romances were French or Welsh. In this we may see an early manifestation of the ongoing discussion on the origins of the so-called "Matter of Britain".[280] Modern scholarship has indeed confirmed that Warton was right in thinking that the romances Percy referred to in his letter to Evans were translations from French. Modern scholarship is, as we shall see, still speculating on whether the French texts themselves originated in Wales or Brittany. Percy may have convinced himself of the Welsh origins of the texts, but he also made use of the French in another way, as has been shown in the section on the "Essay on the Alliterative Metre of Pierce Plowman's Visions". In this he had the Norman influence in mind, that is, the Scandinavian origins of the Normans. Again he may appear a little ambiguous, for this essay is not only indebted to Warton's *Observations*, but also refers to the French, with whom a later development of the alliterative measure, "still retains [...] its ancient dignity; their grand Heroic Verse of twelve syllables is the same genuine offspring of the old alliterative metre of the ancient Gothic and Francic poets, stript like our Anapestic of its alliteration,

---

[280]   "The Matter of Britain" refers to Jean Bodel's (12th-13th century) division of the subject matter of the romances into "the Matter of Britain", "the Matter of France" and "the Matter of Rome". The first is Arthurian romance, the second concerns Charlemagne and his paladins, the third is classical.

and ornamented with rhyme" (*Reliques II* 1858, 221).[281] When one considers Percy's reference to the "Gothic and Francic poets", it becomes obvious that he is in fact underscoring his theory of the "Gothic" origins of his sources.

In view of his general argument and strategies this is, of course, not surprising. The argument is nevertheless interesting for its complexity, because Percy makes at least two points in one sentence. The first has already been mentioned; the second functions to show what might have developed instead of the current "doggrel", as his historicisation of one of the most important "classical" metres in French since Ronsard, who, incidentally, also introduced the sonnet form and the Pindaric ode imitation into French verse.[282] In addition, one might argue that Percy retains the French in the historical development while at the same time attempting to get rid of the Warburtonian thesis.

This is also evident from one of the "Notes on the Foregoing Essay" published in the second edition of the *Reliques* 1767, after Samuel Pegge's criticism. In this instance, Percy comes as close to Warton's point of view as possible, while taking care at the same time to retain his own:

(V) "That remarkable intercommunity, &c. between the French and English Minstrels," &c.] This might, even in a great measure, be referred back to the Norman conquest itself, when along with their French language and manners, the victors doubtless brought with them all their native prejudices, opinions, and fables; which would not fail to be adopted by the English Minstrels, who solicited their favour. This interchange &c. between the Minstrels of the two nations, would afterwards be kept up by the great intercourse that was produced among all the nations of Christendom in the middle ages, by their uniting in the general Crusades; and by that spirit of Chivalry, which led the knights and their attendants, the heralds, and Minstrels, &c. to ramble about continually from one court to another, in order to be present at solemn tournaments, and other feats of arms (lxvii).

Closely read, the note reveals, however, that Percy is simply turning Warton's argument around. He sticks to his chronological argument by attributing a native tradition to the Normans, who, of course, had roots in a Scandinavian conquest of Normandy. The reference to the influence of the crusades does not admit of any Arabian influence, but rather sets the development of minstrelsy and chivalry in an intra-European context as opposed to an inter-cultural one, as it were. As the note above shows, some cultures in Percy's world, such as the Norman and Anglo-Saxon, do manage to participate in cultural interchange. The same applies to the Christian cultures of the crusades, due to the spirit of chiv-

---

[281] See Warton's *Observations* (1754) pp. 89-90.

[282] See for instance Breuer, *Deutsche Metrik und Versgeschichte* (162-3). Breuer describes Ronsard's method as "characteristic of the adjustable attitude while appropriating ancient verse forms" "[Sie ist bezeichnend für die Kompromißhaltung bei der Aneignung antiker Formen]" (162).

alry. The interchange is not possible, however, between the Saracens and the Christians, and neither, as we shall see, between the ancient Germans and the Celts.

Percy may have thought he had settled the matter for good, for there is no mention of the "controversy" in Warton's letters after the publication of the *Reliques* in 1765, nor in any other extant letter, in fact.[283] This "controversy" between two collaborating scholars was a decidedly public and very elegant one.

The elegance is notable in Warton's *History of English Poetry*, published in three volumes (1774, 1778 and 1781), the first major work of its kind in the English language. The history itself is preceded by two dissertations, whose titles express Warton's straddling position as a discoverer of the "Romantic" and an upholder of the "Classical". The first is "On the Origin of Romantic Fiction in Europe", with the terminology of origins and the romantic in place, and the second is "On the Introduction of Learning into England" with its terminology of knowledge acquired from abroad in its place. Warton's theory of the origins of Romantic fiction is in itself as ambiguous as his uneasy position between the forming and formed moulds of thought he represents, and this is reflected in his reaction to Percy's thesis on the origins of romance in the British Isles.

Diplomatically, Warton tries to find a *via media* between the diametrically opposed theses of his scholarly friends, and to appropriate Percy's considerable contribution without compromising his own previous stance. Instead of rejecting Percy's proposition of Gothic origins or abandoning Warburton's idea of Arabic origins, he simply tries to amalgamate them. Warton's "system" seems to accept and reject both Percy's "system" and Warburton's thesis. A closer reading of his "On the Origin of Romantic Fiction in Europe" reveals, however, that Warton, in effect, deals a crushing blow to Percy's system from within, so to speak.

4.5.2 Warton's "De- and Reconstruction" of Percy's System

The opening essay of Warton's *History* is a serious and scholarly attempt to come to terms with Percy's radical renewal of British literary history. He had certainly done his homework on the sources, but although he modified his position, he did not give up his previous conviction. It must have been particularly troubling for Percy to see his system taken apart, not by a little-known antiquarian like Pegge, but by a famous scholar and helpful collaborator. Worst of all, perhaps, was the fact that Warton leant heavily on Percy's work in order to undermine it.

Warton begins by stating firmly that "it is an established maxim of modern criticism, that the fictions of Arabian imagination were communicated to the

---

[283]   The major part of their correspondence took place during Percy's preparation of the *Reliques*, from 1761 to 1765. After that the letters are few and far between, extending to the year 1783, according to the editors of *The Percy Letters*.

western world by means of the crusades" (i-ii). Having understood the force of Percy's "chronological" argument that such fabling was extant long before the crusades, he moves back in time, to the Arab conquest of Spain. The important point for Warton, and one which he discusses at length in his second preliminary essay, "On the Introduction of Learning into England", is that the Arabs "revived the sciences of Greece in Europe", on the one hand, and on the other, "disseminated those extravagant inventions which were so peculiar to their romantic and creative genius" (ii). In France, the inhabitants of Brittany or Armorica, according to Warton, gave "these fictions of the Arabians a more welcome or a more early reception" than any other "province, or district" in that country (iii). The link with the Welsh language is established, as "the Armoric now spoken in Britany is a dialect of the Welsh" (iii). In what follows he labours to provide a migratory link between Brittany and Cornwall and to maintain the purity of the Celtic inhabitants by separating them from contaminating contact with the Romans or the Saxons:

> And this intercourse will appear more natural, if we consider, that not only Armorica, [...] was still in a measure a Celtic nation; but that also the inhabitants of Cornwall, together with those of Devonshire and of the adjoining parts of Somersetshire, intermixing in very slight degree with the Romans, and having suffered fewer important alterations in their original constitution and customs from the imperial laws and police than any other province of this island, *long preserved their genuine manners and British character* [...] (v, my emphasis).

He then maintains "that a strict intercourse was upheld between Cornwall and Wales", and thus establishes Brittany, Cornwall and Wales as one cultural zone of origin, where the Arabic fabling bore fruit in the Arthurian romances. His major piece of evidence is an "antient chronicle written in the British or Armorican language", procured by "Gualter, archdeacon of Oxford", who in turn asked Geoffrey of Monmouth to translate it into Latin.[284] Geoffrey of Monmouth's *Historia Regum Britanniæ* is usually ascribed to himself, which is perhaps not surprising if Warton's depiction of translation method is to be believed (vii). Warton says that he executed the "translation with a tolerable degree of purity and great fidelity, yet not without some interpolations" (vii-viii). Warton adds in a footnote that Geoffrey confesses, "that he took some part of his account of king Arthur's atchievements [*sic*] from the mouth of his friend Gualter; who probably related to the translator some of the traditions on this

---

[284] Walter 'Calenius' is, in key with the tradition of dubious or pseudotranslations, a very mysterious figure. According to the *DNB*, "the most important fact which is known respecting Walter 'Calenius' is that he brought over from Brittany the 'British' (i.e. either Breton or Welsh) book of which Geoffrey of Monmouth professed that his 'History of the Kings of Britain' was a translation." As so often in such cases, there is an element of circular verification.

subject which he had heard in Armorica, or which at that time might have been popular in Wales" (viii). The construction of the text is taking a familiar form in this context, and Warton asserts, despite his previous judgement of "tolerable degree of purity and great fidelity" that the "speeches and letters were forged by Geoffrey; and in the description of battles, our translator has not scrupled frequent variations and additions" (viii).

Such a lax or contradictory view of the textual purity of what would be classified as a pseudotranslation in Toury's terms, may be explained by Warton's hypothesis of the genesis of the text and the fact that he is more concerned about his "oriental" thesis than the translation itself.[285] He speculates that "the work consists of fables thrown out by different rhapsodists at different times, which afterwards were collected and digested into an entire history, and perhaps with new decorations of fancy added by the compiler [...]" (ix). His description of medieval and, indeed, contemporary textual practices is matched by a shrewd understanding of the Pan-European myth of the Trojans as the founding fathers of nations.[286] He ascribes this "improbable notion" to the revival of Virgil's *Aeneid* in the sixth or seventh century and assumes that other European nations simply wanted to emulate the Romans in "claiming an alliance to the same respectable original" (x).

Warton's deconstruction of Geoffrey's text and the Trojan foundation myth serves a distinct purpose, however, and he more or less short-circuits his argumentation towards his preferred conclusion, without considering the consequences of his previous analysis. He maintains that even if Geoffrey had been author of the *Historiæ,* this would rather "confirm and establish [his] system" (xiii). Without arguing along these lines any further he simply asserts that Geoffrey's chronicle "supposed to contain the ideas of the Welsh bards, entirely consists of Arabian inventions" (xiii).

Warton seems to want to have his cake and eat it, for it does not matter when or how the text comes into existence, before or after the crusades, whether it is a rhapsodist collection or Geoffrey's forgery; the only goal is to assert its Arabic origins. He underpins the textual 'deconstruction' with a few examples of Arabic elements, crowning it by referring to the so-called prophecy of Merlin "forged perhaps by the translator Geoffrey", in which we have the "Arabians named, and their situations in Spain and Africa" (xv).[287]

It is interesting in this context to examine briefly how modern scholars have dealt with the problem of the "Matter of Britain". Roger Sherman Loomis

---

285 Malcolm Chapman calls Geoffrey's *History* "a synthetic account" in his *The Celts. The Construction of a Myth* (63).
286 Even the prologue of Snorri's *Edda* has this notion.
287 The Prophecies of Merlin or *Vita Merlin* is probably by Geoffrey of Monmouth, and an offshoot of his *Historia*, but published separately. Cf. the entry on him in the *OCEL* (386-387).

has written extensively on Arthurian romance with the objective of weeding historical truth out of a large corpus of medieval material that has gone through translations and rewritings with interpolations and mythical interpretations of all kinds. In his *The Development of Arthurian Romance*, Loomis tries to answer the question of what

> powerful forces had been at work between the eleventh and the thirteenth centuries to transform Arthur from an insular into an international figure, from the subject of a purely Welsh and Cornish legend into a king whose literary fame rivalled that of Charlemagne, even in France itself (32).

Loomis provides two answers, one of which seems to be more speculative than the other. The first agent, as he terms it, were Breton story-tellers, *conteurs,* descended from the thousands of Britons who fled during the Anglo-Saxon invasions to Brittany where they "flourished and multiplied" (32). This was of course hundreds of years before the surge of Arthurian legends, and even long before Charlemagne himself, so he provides the explanation that "[t]hey still kept in touch, though, with their cousins, the Welsh and Cornish, across the Channel, and as the Arthurian legends developed and expanded in Wales [...] so the Bretons took them up" (32-3). This almost touching description of cultural kinship across the centuries is not verifiable (except in Warton) but of course not impossible. The explanation, that the French audiences had got "somewhat bored by a monotonous diet of epics dealing with the quarrels and wars of Charlemagne and the Paladins" seems to me rather far-fetched, however (33).

The second agent is verifiable, for it is Geoffrey of Monmouth's *Historia,* first in Latin and then in a French translation (33).[288] This "second great intermediary" between the Celts and non-Celts does not rank high in the estimation of Loomis, for Geoffrey claimed to have translated it from an ancient text and this amounts to one of the "world's most brazen and successful frauds" (35). Monmouth is of course in Macphersonian company here, but it is a strange reaction from a medieval scholar who knows very well that authors at that time and long after had completely different conceptions of historical "truths" than do twentieth-century scholars. Histories were not necessarily written to ascertain empirical facts, but belonged more to a kind of panegyric, or simply served the authors hopes of promotion.

The reason for such ambivalence lies partly in the problem of translation, especially when it is done to verify historical fantasy. The two most frequently scolded perpetrators of fraud in Celtic studies are without doubt Geoffrey of Monmouth and James Macpherson. In both cases, translation is at the back of the verification process of historical fantasies. These are translations from lan-

---

[288]   The French translation or rewriting her refers to is probably the one by Wace, *Roman de Brut* (*OCEL* 1037)

guages hardly anybody understands from sources very few have direct access to, and yet at the same time the material is known.

The difference is marked when one considers, for example, the judgement on another translation, Thomas Malory's *Le Morte D'Arthur*. This translation is received more like an original text or an adaptation, without any of the criticisms dealt out to the two great frauds. Indeed, the fact that it is primarily a translation is hardly discussed. Scholars readily admit that Malory manipulated his sources but they take a primarily aesthetic view in his case. They even go to great lengths to play down what appears to be Malory's criminal career, as if it is important that he was not what the documentary sources claim him to have been. And when they report of William Caxton's bowdlerisation of the text, which consisted in making it appear as if it were meant to be a continuing narrative and leaving out Malory's colophons at the end of each Chapter or individual romance, they still hold their moral indignation in check.[289]

The same applies to texts by authors like Gerald of Wales (*Giraldus Cambrensis*); one does not see the same moral indignation as when authors such as Monmouth and Macpherson are expelled from all domains of decency.[290] Translation seems to have an exceptionally high value on the scale of morals, and when an author is successful with a purported translation, he is indeed the proverbial traitor to his craft and everybody else. This is not an attempt at sophistry to justify their methods, just a reminder that Macpherson and certainly Monmouth lived and wrote in ages when many of their contemporaries fantasised while rewriting other fantasies without ever being convicted by the grand jury reserved for purported translations. Gerald of Wales is still quoted by serious historians, and Chatterton is a romantic figure. The moral fury is reserved for fake translations outside the hegemonic canon.

In addition, there are the questions of property and origins. Both these works, Monmouth's and Macpherson's, have marked pivotal points in controversies of literary property. Macpherson's battle with the Irish has already been alluded to, and in the case of Monmouth it is the Matter of Britain, or the matter of whether the sources of Arthurian romance are to be found in Brittany or Wales, that lies behind the moral indignation of his fraud. At the same time, condemning scholars are ready to admit that "there seems to be a residue which is traditional" in Monmouth's text (Parry et al, 76). The other great problem of origins lies in the origin of the Matter of Britain itself, and this can actually be seen in the Percy-Warton controversy, namely, the problem that most of the

---

[289] See for this Eugène Vinaver's "Sir Thomas Malory" (541-552) and Roger Sherman Loomis' *The Development of Arthurian Romance* (166-185). Even the title of Malory's work is Caxton's "forgery", a mistaken one at that, but is now considered to be "tradition". See the above.

[290] I personally like Gerald's remark about the Icelanders, where he says that they are unable to tell a lie. I know this to be untrue, but it is a nice remark anyway.

original literary Arthurian romance is, in fact, written in French, most famously by Chrétien de Troyes. The material in English consists mainly of translations and later imitations. This may explain the speculative attempts by modern scholars to fix the origins of the Matter of Britain in a Celtic context, be it Breton, Welsh or even Irish. The question that arises is whether this matters, but perhaps it is an example of the metaphysical link between origins and property.

Before we lose track of Loomis' theories, it should be noted that he is of the opinion that the Arthurian legends were imported into Anglo-Saxon territory by the Normans and that they did not arrive through contact between the Welsh and the Anglo-Saxons. It seems to me that Geoffrey of Monmouth's famous *Historia* should also be mentioned in this context, because it certainly did make waves in England, too, as Warton had rightly asserted.

After dealing with Geoffrey of Monmouth's *Historia* in detail Warton turns to the Matter of France and discusses another pseudo-translation or rather pseudo-original briefly: a history of Charlemagne (in fact a version of the legend of Roland) falsely ascribed to Archbishop Turpin. According to Warton, who seems to view the text as authentic, Michel de Harnes made the translation from the Latin in the year 1207. Apart from restating the "Arabic" argument when assessing this text, he criticises his anonymous scholar friend, and aims at the foundation of Percy's "Gothic" system.

As was shown above, Percy, by way of the analogy that characterised his method, constructed a common Gothic ancestry for the French heroic verse (alexandrine) and the late medieval English alliterative metre in his essay "On the Alliterative Metre [...]". As Warton is primarily occupied with tracing the origin of the fantastic notions in "romantic" literature, the dragons and dwarfs, he does not bother much with Percy's metrical niceties, except in a sentence which of course serves the purpose of solidifying his argument. In closing his discussion of de Harnes' translation, he mentions, as if in passing: "And by the way, from the translator's declaration, that there was a great impropriety in translating Latin prose into verse, we may conclude, that at the commencement of the thirteenth century the French generally made their translations into verse" (xx). Unremarkable the phrase may seem, but this generalisation implies that the French "chivalric poetry" produced in the thirteenth century could just as well have imported the fantastic elements from the Arabs through translation, thus making Percy's analogy insignificant, if not untrue.[291]

---

[291] This remark by the thirteenth-century translator may actually reflect the changes taking place in French historical writing at the time, the ushering in of an age of prose. Verse was then considered unsuitable for "historical" writing by some authors. The translator of *Historia Karoli Magni* asserts that "Nus contes rimés n'est verais" [no rhymed account is truthful]. Indeed, some of the works by Chrétien de Troyes, the first author of Arthurian romances, were intralingually translated into prose at the time. (Tulinius, "Kynjasögur" 214-15).

Having made his two "fabulous chronicles", Geoffrey's *Historiæ* and de Harne's translation of Pseudo-Turpin, nothing less than the "foundations of romance", Warton then tackles Percy head on and makes the private "controversy" public. He begins by quoting Percy's essay "On the Ancient Metrical Romances", in which Percy states that "[o]ur old romances of chivalry may be derived in a LINEAL DESCENT from the antient historical songs of the Gothic bards and scalds" (xxii, Warton's emphasis and spelling). Warton's way of quoting is significant in itself. He drops Percy's conjunction "that" at the beginning of the sentence, making a subclause into a main clause, and also omits the main clause of the sentence, "will be shown below", emphasising the verb "may" and thus the speculative nature of Percy's thesis. The emphasis on "lineal descent" is a further attempt at undermining Percy by quoting him. That Warton cites the second edition is in itself significant in this context, not only because Percy had sent Warton the first edition upon its publication, but also because of the minor revision he had made in exactly this sentence. Instead of "will be shown below", the first edition simply said "is incontestible" (*Reliques III,* 1765, iii).

Instead of proceeding to attacking the text itself, Warton tackles Percy's sources and reinterprets them to suit his own thesis. This piece of imaginative scholarship indeed takes some unexpected twists that must have disturbed Percy considerably. Warton begins with Mallet's hypothesis (translated by Percy), that the sources of the "marvellous with which our ancestors filled their romances" could be found in the Gothic "religious opinions" (xxiii). After more than a full page of quoting he states that he does not "mean entirely to reject this hypothesis, but will endeavour to shew how far I think it is true, and in what manner or degree it may be reconciled with the system delivered above" (xxiv).

His proceeding pages present the reader with an amazing piece of constructive work, though well within the parameters of what antiquarians such as Percy, O'Conor, the Macphersons, Pinkerton and others, who were working on medieval and ancient history, offered at the time. Strangely enough, Warton seems to fall back on a similar paradigm of tribes moving from the east to a new abode in the north, a notion which he at least implicitly criticised when discussing the common European notion of tracing the origins of a people to the Trojans. Leaning on several of the sources Percy had used and some he had not, Warton gives the Scandinavians, Percy's source of written proof, an oriental ancestry, destined by his discourse to be the same as that of the Arabs. Warton puts his thesis thus:

> A few years before the birth of Christ, soon after Mithridates had been overthrown by Pompey, a nation of Asiatic Goths, who possessed that region of Asia which is now called Georgia, and is connected on the south with Persia, alarmed at the progressive encroachment of the Roman armies, retired in vast multitudes under the conduct of Odin, or Woden, into the northern parts of Europe, not subject to the Roman government, and settled in Denmark, Norway, Sweden, and other districts of Scandinavian territory (xxiv).

This thesis is a rewriting, if not a rough translation, from *Crymogæa* [Greek for Iceland], written in Latin and published in 1609 by the Icelandic humanist patriot Arngrímur Jónsson Vídalín to counter fabulous accounts about Iceland that had been circulating since the twelfth century.[292] Warton gives the Latin original in a footnote and refers to seventeenth-century authorities such as Bartholin, Worm, and Rudbeck. The paradigm of migrating peoples includes common speculations on the Scythian and Thracian origins of the Goths, added to which is an analogy of the Norse theology with the Islamic one.

Warton then presents what may seem to be a far-fetched comparison of the Gothic and Islamic hell and heaven – without providing any examples, however. This is a direct answer to Percy's preface in *Northern Antiquities,* another ingenious example of how Warton uses of Percy's arguments against him. In light of Warton's own argumentation, his assertion that in some of the "Islandic chronicles, the Turks are mentioned as belonging to the jurisdictions of the Scandinavians" looks even more strange (xxvii). This is, nevertheless, correct, for Snorri's *Edda* does indeed name Turkey as the country where Odin originates, albeit in what is almost a standard version of the migratory narrative of the Trojans being the origin of the author's people. The Turks and the Trojans are the same people in the *Edda,* and this migration, which Warton uses here as partial proof of his theory, is thus perfectly in key with the myth of the Trojan origins of nations which he had so easily dismissed himself a few pages before. It is difficult to say where exactly he has gathered the information that Odin was a Turk (which would doubtless come as an unpleasant surprise to some of the modern German neo-nazis in their "Odin-" or "Wotan-societies"), but the fact remains that he refers frequently to the *Edda,* and if he had read a translation or the numerous rewritings cited in his sources, he must have been aware of the parallels he was drawing.

His theological argumentation includes an interestingly twisted analogy, which some contemporary Celticists might see as an attempt at appropriating the Druids for the Goths. By asserting that there is "a remarkable correspondence, in numberless important and fundamental points, between the Druidical and Persian superstitions", he is able to claim that "Odin's followers imported this establishment into Scandinavia, from the confines of Persia" (xxvi). He even adds insult to injury by claiming "[t]hat Druidical rites existed among Scandinavians we are informed from many antient Erse poems, which say that the British Druids, in the extremity of their affairs, sollicited and obtained aid from Scandina-

---

[292]   Arngrímur the learned (1568-1648), as he was and is called, wrote a number of tracts to correct the myths on the Icelanders, coming partly from well-known "authorities" such as Adam of Bremen and Saxo Grammaticus. His works include *Brevis Commentarius de Islandia* (Copenhagen, 1593) translated into English 1599, *Anatome Blefkiana* (Hólar 1612, Hamburg 1613) and *Epistola pro patria defensoria* (Hamburg, 1618) (Böðvar Guðmundsson *Íslensk bókmenntasaga II*, 490-494).

via" (xxvi). This must have been hard for Percy to swallow. He had, after all, gone to great lengths in his preface to *Northern Antiquities* to prove that Scandinavian and Druidical rites were completely different.

Warton's speculations on migration and theology are matched with the information from Worm that Odin is supposed to have invented letters. As was noted above, Worm is probably the originator and populariser of the myth that the runes were used for writing the texts, poetry and sagas, which in fact were only written in Latin characters. Ironically, Warton actually makes use of the runes in the way in which they were really used, namely as short inscriptions on rocks, for this serves his "oriental" purpose. He asserts that "[t]his art or custom of writing on rocks is Asiatic. Modern travellers report, that there are Runic inscriptions now existing in the deserts of Tartary. The WRITTEN MOUNTAINS of the Jews are an instance that this fashion was oriental" (xxv, emphasis in text). Facing such a paradigm of primordial and, indeed, religious origins, Percy's manuscripts and other sources seem slightly torn at the leaves.

This was only the beginning of Warton's purposefully structured text. When he seems to be retracting, he is simply strengthening his argument. This is evident when he suddenly changes tack in his discussion on migration and admits that "many traces of oriental usages are found amongst all the European nations during their pagan state; and this phenomenon is rationally resolved on the supposition that all Europe was peopled from the east" (xxviii).[293] He is simply preparing a rift between Scandinavians, or "Odin's Goths", and "those innumerable armies of barbarous adventurers, who some centuries afterwards, distinguished by the same name, at different periods overwhelmed Europe, and at length extinguished the Roman empire" (xxviii). The difference lies in the "manners, monuments, opinions, and practices" which all point to an earlier migration of "Odins Goth's" (his phrase) than of the "barbarous adventurers", Percy's "our ancestors". The previous reference to the Scythians now becomes clear, for their name serves as a kind of a generic term for the nations conducted not only "by Odin, but by Attila, Theodoric, and Genseric", to which Warton adds "Genghizcan" and "Tamerlane" for good measure (xviii). What fascinates Warton and at the same time differentiates these "Scythian" warriors from the rest of the Gothic rabble is their "science and genius" in war (xxix). He does not labour the point, however, because he now thinks it is time to "proceed to more particular proofs" (xxix).

Here Warton comes to the heart of the matter and the point where he turns Percy's "system" around using its own elements. Having given Odin the honour of inventing letters, he now grants his noble branch of "Odin's Goths" the honour of having "planted in Scandinavia, their skill in poetry, to which they were

---

[293]   Warton's theory is interesting in the light of William Jones' hypothesis on Sanskrit being the common source of European languages (cf. below).

addicted in a peculiar manner, and which they cultivated with a wonderful enthusiasm [...]" (xxix). Warton's phrasing and terminology remain close to Percy's, especially his preface to *Northern Antiquities*, and he reinterprets and historicises the mythical sources here along the lines Percy had previously. The progress from the invention of letters by the individual Odin to the practice of poetry by the Scandinavians and their skalds is interesting in light of the sources. The *Edda* includes mythical accounts of Odin's "invention" and the way in which he and mankind acquired the gift of poetry. According to these sources Odin acquired wisdom and the knowledge of runes through his ritual self sacrifice of one eye and through hanging nine days upside down from a branch of the Ash of Yggdrasill. He acquired his gift for poetry by the slightly more down-to-earth method of theft through magical intrigue and the seduction of Gunnlöð, the daughter of the giant Suttungur, keeper of the mead of poetry.[294] Of the two scholars, Percy is a little closer to the original versions of the myths in the prefaces of his *Five Pieces*, where he, as we have seen, simply refers to the language as "(Asom-maal,) THE LANGUAGE OF THE GODS". His dubious analogy with the Greeks has also been discussed above, but the *Edda* does present the language of poetry as a language of the gods. Warton, on the other hand, latches on to the term "asamal" with a more-than-dubious etymology that makes it a synonym with "ASIATIC speech" (xxxix).

Warton leans on Percy's works on the subject to the extent of quoting without direct acknowledgement his assertion that the Gothic bards were "called SCALDS OR POLISHERS OF LANGUAGE", presumably with the same neoclassical hint in mind.[295] Warton is also in agreement with Percy on the supposition that the Scandinavians exported their bards (as he continually refers to them, perhaps because Percy had also claimed the word for the Scandinavian languages) "and by that means [...] communicated their fictions to various parts of Europe" (xxxii). Here Warton goes even further in the "Scandinavisation" of the British Isles. He concedes, almost reluctantly, that Britain was "originally peopled from Gaul, a nation of the Celts", but counters this with the suggestion of Scandinavians having colonised Britain from an early age (i.e., long before the Danelaw).[296] The contemporary Celtic antiquarians, Irish and Scottish alike, must have bristled when he maintained "that the Scutes, who conquered both

---

294   Modern rewritings of the above myths can be found in Kevin Crossley-Holland's *The Norse Myths* (15-17, 26-30). This myth has indeed interesting parallels in Celtic myth sometimes denominated "the Giant's daughter theme" in which the protagonist (e.g. Arthur) achieves his goal with similar methods. See Idris Llewelyn Foster's "*Culwch and Olwen* and *Rhonabwy's Dream*" (31-43, esp. 38).

295   They were simultaneously very 'romantic' as well, often "breaking forth into spontaneous songs and verses" (xxxi).

296   If he is thinking of the Jutes of Jutland, he is of course assigning them to a Scandinavian construct of a later date, i.e. the Vikings.

those countries, and possessed them under the names of Albin Scutes and Irin Scutes, were a people of Norway" (xxxiii). Perhaps this could have been a solution for the quarrelling antiquarians, and indeed later scholars, of the irrelevant question of whether the Scots of "Dal-Riata" were "Irish" or "Scottish". After such an argument it is unproblematic to claim the Picts as Scandinavians, a theory which became one of the central arguments in John Pinkerton's anti-Celtic campaign, along with the Scythian fantasy of origins.[297]

It should be stressed that these speculations all refer to a Scandinavian "colonisation" of Britain long before the Viking raids and the Danelaw, which Warton mentions only in passing (after an etymological excursion), as evidence that "the fictions of Odin and of his Scandinavians, must have taken still deeper roots in the British islands, at least in England, from the Saxon and Danish invasions" (xxxvi). At this point, Percy's and Warton's positions are partly reconcilable as regards the influence in Britain, although Warton has drawn a clear line between the Scandinavians and the Saxons. His deconstruction of Percy's system inverts the comparison which the latter had set up to bridge the unwritten gap between the two groups of "Goths". Admittedly, Warton had already in essence dismissed the Saxon 'line' as a "barbarous rabble", but his final blow aims at the foundation of Percy's structure, namely the written runes. Warton points out that the Saxons converted to Christianity before the seventh century and that this "entirely banished the common use of those characters" (xxxvii). This, according to Warton, led to the decline of the bardic profession among the Saxons, although he follows Percy faithfully in his depiction of the progression of the "scalders" to gleemen and finally minstrels (xl). Oddly enough, Warton compares a Saxon ode metrically to the "skaldic dialogue at the tomb of Angantyr, which has been beautifully translated into English, by Gray" (xl). Poor Percy must have been irritated at seeing his own translation ascribed to Gray by a scholar who knew both of them personally.

With hindsight, Warton's argument is, it should be stressed, very problematic. He argues that because the Scandinavians remained pagans much longer "they retained their original manners, much longer than any of their Gothic kindred" (xli). This enabled them to

produce, not only more genuine, but more numerous, compositions. True religion would have checked the impetuosity of their passions, suppressed their wild exertions of fancy, and banished that striking train of imagery, which their poetry derived from a barbarous theology (xli-ii).

In Warton's system, then, pagan poetry and manners are the key to the retention of "romantic" imagery. Having manifested this in its purest form with

---

[297]   See Colin Kidd "Teutonist Ethnology and Scottish Nationalist Inhibition 1780-1880" in *Scottish Historical Review* 197 (1995): 45-68.

the Scandinavians, he tries to deal with their later influence in the British Isles, albeit within the parameters Percy has set, for this is the argument he needs to tackle. In an approach that must have been even more devastating to Percy, this time he applies the controversial Ossianic poems in his chain of argumentation.

First, he concedes that the Danish invasions produced "a considerable alteration in the manners of our Anglo-Saxon ancestors", first with the negative influence of excessive drinking, but he draws the remarkable conclusion from this that "[h]ence it seems likely, that so popular an entertainment as their poetry gained ground" (xlii). This strange conclusion actually implies subtly that the Anglo-Saxons either did not have such poetry from the start, or that it was completely revived by the Scandinavians with their 'second' arrival. In any case, Percy's continuity from the Gothic ancestors is broken. Once again, Warton follows Percy's texts closely, relating the same anecdote from *Egill's Saga* about the ode presented to the Saxon king Athelstan. He then moves on to the Irish, Welsh and Scottish bards. He reports that "some" consider the Irish bards "to be strongly marked with the traces of skaldic imagination" (xlvi). Nor does he find it "improbable that the Welsh bards might have been acquainted with the Scandinavian scalds" and that "before their communications with Armorica, mentioned at large above" (xlvii-viii). The proof of this is a bit amusing, for he maintains that the

> Islandic poets are said to have carried alliteration to the highest pitch of exactness in their earliest periods; whereas the Welsh bards of the sixth century used it but sparingly, and in a very imperfect degree. In this circumstance a proof of imitation, at least of emulation, is implied (xlviii).

The problem here is of course the fact that Iceland had not been discovered, let alone settled, in the sixth century, besides which the earliest literary texts, written exclusively in Latin characters by Christians, very often monks, were not written until the eleventh or twelfth century. Warton has been completely deceived by his own historical dimensions, and he dates texts according to nothing more than the 'primitive' impression they give from their internal proofs of imagery and manner, or so it seems.

It is, therefore, not surprising that Macpherson's *Ossian* provides the next exhibit of evidence. Of all the argumentative somersaults Warton undertakes in this essay, this one is perhaps the most graceful – terribly graceful, to use his own terminology on *Ossian*. He does not dispute the poems' authenticity, which in 1774 must have been a bold decision for an English scholar of his standing. This choice had its reasons, of course. One might be due to Warton's fascination with primitivism, borne out in his work on Spenser and the *History*. For Warton, as many of his contemporaries, primitivism was not a foolish and naive literary fashion, but a serious moral alternative to the worn out didactics of neoclassicism. In addition, primitivism offered a national scope of origin to literature and an approach to researching the development of national literatures through the origins and development of manners.

Another reason was the "controversy" at hand, in which Warton relentlessly picked up every possible piece of evidence and interpreted it to suit his purpose. This is plain in the passage on *Ossian*, which seems to begin by expressing doubts:

> It is indeed very remarkable that in these poems, the terrible graces, which so naturally characterise, and so generally constitute, the early poetry of a barbarous people should so frequently give place to a gentler set of manners, to the social sensibilities of polished life, and a more civilised and elegant species of imagination. Nor is this circumstance, which disarranges all our established ideas concerning the savage stages of society, easily to be accounted for, [...] (liii).

It is not, unless one's name is Blair – or Warton, for that matter, for he finishes this sublimely long sentence thus:

> unless we suppose, that the Celtic tribes, who were so strongly addicted to poetical composition, and who made it so much their study from the earliest times, might by degrees have attained a higher vein of poetical refinement, than could at first sight or on common principles be expected among nations, whom we are accustomed to call barbarous; that some few instances of an elevated strain of friendship, of love, and other sentimental feelings, existing in such nations, might lay the foundations for introducing a set of manners among the bards, more refined and exalted than the real manners of the country; and that panegyrics on those virtues, transmitted with improvements from bard to bard, must at length have formed *characters* of *ideal excellence*, which might propagate among the people *real manners bordering on the poetical* (liii, my emphasis).

This passage, surely one of the more purple in the essay, reads like a minor manifesto of primitivism. It is also very reminiscent of Macpherson's own circular reasoning as quoted in the section on Celtic tribalism, though with the difference that in Macpherson's case the bards' panegyrics created "ideal characters" which the "inferior chiefs [...] made the model of their conduct, and by degrees brought their minds to that generous spirit which breathes in the poetry of all times" (Gaskill, *Ossian* 48). I deliberately quote the last sentence again, because Warton seems to have read it, and he uses it, again with the single-minded purpose that drives the text to a sole conclusion. For the Ossianic poems

> notwithstanding the difference between the Gothic and Celtic rituals, contain many visible vestiges of Scandinavian superstition. The allusions in the songs of Ossian to spirits, who preside over the different parts and direct the various operations of nature, who send storms over the deep, and rejoice in the shrieks of the shipwrecked mariner [...], entirely correspond with the Runic system, and breathe the spirit of its poetry (liii).

He then latches on to the spectral appearance of Odin under the name of Loda as a concrete example of "an essential article of Runic belief" (liii). Warton is so absorbed in his Scandinavian theory that he goes so far as to regret that *Ossian* did not introduce religion into his poems, because that would not only have opened a new source to the sublime, but also "many stronger and more characteristical evidences would have appeared of his knowledge of the Scandinavian poets" (liv).

Again, Warton seems to be overbidding Percy in his theory of the Scandinavian influence, reminding the reader that they "had conquered many countries bordering upon France in the fourth [sic] century" and mentions in passing that "Charlemagne is said to have delighted in repeating the most antient and barbarous odes", admitting, however, that "we are not informed whether these were Scandinavian, Celtic or Teutonic poems" (liv-v). His conclusion from his own "system" is thus that the "skaldic inventions had taken deep root in Europe"; this is his major concession to Percy, which he then defuses by noting that they only "prepared the way for the more easy admission of the Arabian fabling [...], by which they were, however, superseded" (lvi).[298]

Having finally returned to the point he wants to make with the essay, Warton is quick to note that the "inchantments of the Runic poetry are very different from those in our romances of chivalry" (lx). At issue is the amount and nature of superstitious elements in the poetry; Warton is certain that the quality and quantity of Arab influence make the real difference. This he underlines, incredibly (or perhaps not), by referring again to *Ossian* and the Irish "tale-tellers" whom he had previously asserted were under the strong influence of the Scandinavian skalds. According to Warton, the lack of fabulous ideas in the earlier skaldic odes and other compositions which preceded the Arabian fabling demonstrates that the "Irish tale-teller mentioned above could not be a lineal descendant of the elder Irish bards" (lx). Concerning *Ossian,* his thesis means a confirmation of the poems' authenticity: "The absence of giants and dragons, and let me add, of many other traces of that fantastic and brilliant imagery which composes the system of Arabian imagination, from the poems of Ossian, are a striking proof of their antiquity" (lx). The same applies to Welsh antiquities; the lack of "fancies" proves his own thesis.

Concluding the essay, Warton confesses "that the ideas of chivalry, the appendage and the subject of romance, subsisted among the Goths" (lxv). He has, however, argued the elements of fantasy and superstition out of the 'primitive' Norse sources, in fact giving them neo-classical cleanliness. What he allows them to retain is the "degree of attention and respect with which those nations

---

[298] This contradicts Margaret Clunies Ross' claim that "we find several influential writers, including Percy and Warton, presenting an argument for early Scandinavian poetry as the *fons et origo* of European literary culture [...]" (*Norse Muse,* 42). This may very well apply to Percy, but Warton's stance was much more ambivalent.

treated the fair sex", a characteristic which not only differentiated them from the Greeks and Romans (and by implication the Arabs), but also made them the originators of a "new state of manners", namely that of "gallantry in Europe" (lxv). The last sentence constitutes in essence what Warton is prepared to accept of Percy's system.

4.5.3 Percy's Response

Percy responded promptly. The third edition of the *Reliques* was published in 1775, the year after the first volume of Warton's *History*, and he used the opportunity to counter Warton's essay by extending his footnotes and adding a few paragraphs to his essay "On the Ancient Metrical Romances". The private "controversy" was by now public, (although Percy does not name Warton) and even if it has mostly been consigned to factual footnotes, if mentioned at all, in the secondary literature, it should not be forgotten. After all, the participants were two of the most important scholars of their day, and both contributed considerably to new streams of literature at the time, despite the historical nature of their work. The histories they told were new to contemporary readers and their influence on later poets and scholars requires no comment.[299]

In his response, Percy tackles Warton in the same field of discourse, namely that of manners coupled to what may be termed a critique of contents. He could finally cite his *Northern Antiquities*, which was published in 1770, but as Warton had already struck at precisely this source Percy had to find a new argument that reinforced his version of the influence of Gothic manners and customs. After reiterating his chronological argument, he makes the mistake of going after the content of the romances, which he maintains do not contain any "Moorish, or at least Spanish subjects". Instead, he points out, the romances all tell of "Charlemagne, and the Paladins; or of our British Arthur, and his Knights of the Round Table" (*Reliques III* 1775, viii). This argument is wrong in the sense that the adversaries of Charlemagne in the literature were the Moors of Spain (although not necessarily always historically), and they play a role in Monmouth's text as well. But this can also be reversed. Percy had, up to then, argued that the existence of skalds, manners, the Gothic origin and versification constituted verification of the "lineal descent" of "our old Romances of Chivalry" to the "ancient historical songs of the SCALDS", but now he goes for the content, apparently oblivious to the fact that the same applies to the skaldic sources.

This feeble defence draws further on an analogy of the Greeks and Romans, in which the latter through their imitation of the former also "immediately naturalized all the Grecian fables, histories, and religious stories" whereas the

---

[299]   For Percy's influence on Coleridge and Wordsworth, see for instance W.P. Ker's *Form and Style in Poetry* (98-99 & 230).

Romance writers did not know the Arabic fables (ix-x). Percy also picks up Warton's migratory argument for his own purposes, and his final defence is that of enmity between the Spaniards and the Moors, so great that there could not have been any communication between the two peoples, an argument he reiterates when discussing the Celtic and Germanic tribes. As so many writers did and do, Percy presupposes some kind of "ethnic cleansing" in the wake of a conquest. This was probably rarely the case before the onset of modern colonialism and later nationalism.[300]

The major implications of the debate between Percy and Warton in the current context lie in their groundbreaking constructive work in an example of national literary rivalry within the British Isles. Their treatment of the Matter of Britain is the first scholarly controversy over an issue that was to occupy the minds of literary historians for the next two-hundred years, and it represents a milestone in the revival of medieval studies, literary and historical. Moreover, they marked the route for coming generations in the search for origins and in the historical evaluation of medieval literature, as can be seen in numerous modern treatments of the question of whether or not King Arthur actually existed. Their method of putting the historicity of the literature they were discussing into the foreground, with the explicit objective of assigning it to certain nations or races, became paradigmatic in literary, historical and anthropological research. This does not mean that their little controversy was the major factor in this outcome; it was rather the works themselves, which moved within a dialectical frame. The failed synthesis that was borne out in this discussion naturally had major implications for the construction of a national literature in Britain and may possibly have given an important incentive for the hegemony of English literature within Britain, especially for Percy's Gothic and thus racial interpretation of the history of English literature.

The objective in the above has been to present a critique of Percy's and Warton's textual practices, how they juggle their sources in a scholarly manner and do not hesitate to draw wide-ranging conclusions from sometimes dubious premises. In many cases they simply did not – and could not – know better. Had they known, for example, that Geoffrey of Monmouth had already been translated into Icelandic in the thirteenth century, along with several romances, their approach would certainly have been different. Both are also misled by Worm on the question of runes, as indeed even some modern scholars seem to be. Their motivations are also of interest, for apart from ambition or vanity, nationalistic tendencies must constitute a major factor, especially in Percy's case.

The second major objective of the sections above is in key with the overall objective of these volumes, namely to show the role of translation in the com-

---

[300] Even James Macpherson was aware of this. In his *Introduction* he argued "that the extirpation of the people did, by no means, attend the conquest of Pictavia" (82).

plex constructive work of those pioneers of English national literature. Both scholars refer to foreign sources for their own literature and have no difficulty appropriating them as original indigenous literature in the process of delineating its history.

Their elegant and courteous "controversy" bears, then, all the marks of the constructive art many contemporary antiquarians and historians applied to a rapidly changing world. It is a prime example of the scholarly ideological interpretation or manipulation that was practised at the time, and shows particularly well the changing paradigms of historical writing, both literary and political. An anthropological focus on the customs, manners and characters of peoples enabled historians to read vast movements and migrations of history into and out of literary texts, with the aid of classical and humanist authorities. More importantly, it enabled them to infuse their material with causal explanations and to fill centuries of gaps through analogy and conjecture, creating in essence a linear continuity up to the classical age.[301] Most important, however, was that this approach was instrumental in creating national literatures with truly national moral implications, bound to the origin and fate of the nation. In a sense these scholars were creating a cultural pedigree for the nation, which enabled – and enables – it to understand itself as a distinctive entity, a causal result of hundreds of years of glorious history in a literature that concretely expresses the characteristics and manners of a people's ancestors living within them.

4.6 The Strange Case of Thomas Warton

National literary rivalry in Britain redefined existing national entities by establishing demarcation lines of a new order, delineated through language and race. Moreover, literary rivalry may well have marked the dissolution of a post-union experiment of constructing a British literature. Robert Crawford's seminal *Devolving English Literature* followed by the collection of essays edited by him, *The Scottish Invention of English Literature,* have examined the role of the Scottish literati in the institutionalisation of English literature. Simply put, Crawford's main thesis is based on two interwoven strands: first, that following the Union Scottish writers changed their viewpoint and started writing "British" literature in response to political developments (*Devolving* 45); and second, that the Union "had very little effect on the literature written in England. That simply went on being English literature" (45). The result was that Scottish intellectuals adapted to the more powerful culture, started weeding Scotticisms out of their language and teaching English literature, most notably by introducing a chair of Rhetoric and Belles Lettres in Edinburgh, first occupied by Hugh Blair.

---

[301] And later, with the development of comparative-historical or Indo-European linguistics this continuity was moved even further back and scientifically 'proven'.

The problem with this thesis is its dialectical nature, which in itself must be interpreted as a part of a nationalist agenda. It has not been swallowed without protest. Alastair Fowler points out in an article in the *TLS* (August 14, 1998) that "the most striking feature of Blair's *Lectures* is their international range" (3). He goes on, however, to show that Blair also discussed Scottish authors:

> That does not entail ignoring Scottish literature. Among prose writers Blair mentions or discusses Sir George MacKenzie, Lord Kames, Lord Monboddo, William Robertson and (less favourably) Smollett and George Buchanan. Among poets, he promotes Thomson, Ramsay and Macpherson's debated Ossian. He passes over the Renaissance poets; but that only shows the usual historical limitation of Enlightenment rationality. (Even Johnson effectually ignores literature earlier than Spenser.) (3-4)[302]

Crawford, incidentally, says as much himself in *Devolving English Literature,* but seizes upon Blair's "awkwardness" when discussing Scottish authors such as Ramsay, an awkwardness he ascribes to the use of the Scots dialect (34-5). The matter of weeding out Scotticisms is central to this debate, and yet Crawford, and to some extent his co-authors in *The Scottish Invention of Literature,* disregard the wider questions of language in this context, even though the subject is rhetoric and eloquence. This is particularly evident in the case of Adam Smith, who provided not only the idea of a university course on "Rhetoric and Belles Lettres" (and apparently some of the content), but also gave a lecture on the origins and development of language, published with the second edition of his *Theory of Moral Sentiments* in 1761 under the title "A Dissertation on the Origin of Languages or Considerations Concerning the First Formation of Languages and the Different Genius of Original and Compounded Languages".

Another problem in the discussion on the Scottish invention of English literature is the dismissal or disregard of English scholars who certainly were interested in Scottish subjects and even promoted the idea of Britishness with the same conviction as Scottish writers such as James Thomson, David Mallet and Tobias Smollett. Thomas Warton was one of them, and his contribution to the subject of English literature cannot be dismissed as negligible. This section will thus be dedicated to Warton's interest in the literary union of Scotland and England.

Thomas Warton, professor of poetry at Oxford, poet laureate and author of the first major work on the history of English literature, was an important figure in English literary life in the latter part of the eighteenth century. He has often been described as one of the pre-romantic figures standing at the crossroads of Neo-Classicism and Romanticism, and considering his ambivalence regarding things classical and Gothic, this seems accurate. Warton can be seen, along with Richard Hurd, Horace Walpole and Thomas Percy, as a pioneer in the re-

---

[302] His *Lives of the Poets* begins notoriously not with Shakespeare but Cowley.

evaluation of what carries the vague label of "Gothic" in English literature. This applies to his academic work, primarily his *Observations* and the *History*, though even his now-forgotten poetry has its moments of romantic "originality" well ahead of its time.[303]

What makes Warton, and indeed his brother Joseph, even more appropriately cross-road figures is their literary nationalism, with its links, as it were, both to the neo-classical, Johnsonian kind of nationalism, and to the new mostly primitivist or so-called pre-romantic nationalism. The two are of course related, but the former is closer to the French Moderns in the sense that it expresses its confidence and "Englishness" using or invoking classical models, thereby achieving classical excellence and even mastering the models better than the 'originals'. Johnson's classicism was in essence nationalistic, both in his anglicised imitations and in his critical standards. His own writings, too, as Ian Duncan points out, his *Dictionary*, his Shakespeare edition (with its critical ambivalence), his *Lives of the English Poets*, even his moralism, I think, bear witness to this (*Scottish Invention* 39). According to Duncan, "Johnson definitively erects the institutional superstructure of 'English Literature', a national vernacular language regulated by a native canon of classical authors" (39).

As the section on the Percy-Warton 'controversy' indicates, Warton was a different kind of nationalist, one step further than Johnson, so to speak, a cosmopolitan British patriot in the primarily Scottish tradition of the eighteenth century. It may also be speculated whether Warton did not through his publications give the study of English literature a decisive shove forward, even though his teaching consisted mainly of classical material.

Crawford's premise for the invention of the subject of English literature by the Scots as an attempt to assimilate ignores the general European context of such ideas. Whatever the Moderns achieved, the subject of native literature was still far from becoming a reality in the way modern philology, literary and linguistic, had developed. It is correct that figures such as Blair in the footsteps of Adam Smith and indeed their precursors back into the seventeenth century (if not all the way back to Dante) had a role in the creation of the subject, but the focus on Blair is based on formalities more than anything else. In this Crawford seems to fall into the same trap as those who would maintain that the invention of English literature coincided with the first chairs in Oxford and Cambridge. In this field as in others, innovative research comes before anything can be taught, and Crawford and several other scholars delineate part of this development in *The Scottish Invention of English Literature*. Most interesting in this context is how much of the invention is actually influenced by translation, as Crawford's

---

[303] He is sometimes said to have revived the sonnet form in English poetry, but there were others such as William Lisle Bowles and Thomas Edwards, the critic of Warburton's Shakespeare edition. His criticisms were published in *The Canons of Criticism,* which went into six editions from 1748 until 1758 and the sixth edition included 45 sonnets.

"Introduction" and Neil Rhodes' "From Rhetoric to Criticism" bear witness to. In his description of the failed attempt to set up a chair in eloquence at St. Andrews in the 1720s, Crawford refers to Rollin's *De la manière d'enseigner et d'étudier les belles-lettres,* translated into English 1734, which apparently was one of the most borrowed books of the library. Rhodes, on the other hand, identifies the first translation (into English) of the work of the sixteenth-century rhetorician Pierre de la Ramée, or Petrus Ramus, by the Scot Roland MacIlmaine under the title *The Logike of the Moste Excellent Philosopher P. Ramus, Martyr* in 1574, and discusses its influence on the development of rhetoric. Both essays also reveal how complex the background of such an "invention" can be and that it can hardly be fixed to the date of institutionalisation of a subject, be it named "belles lettres" or English literature.

Nevertheless, Crawford's thesis remains valid up to a point, in the sense that the more English-oriented variant of literary practice and studies was asserted, especially in the nineteenth and twentieth century. Johnson's version of English literature thus became hegemonic; this is not to say that Smith, Blair and the other Scots, and indeed Englishmen like Warton, were necessarily guilty of sweeping away the marginal versions of British literature, but rather that the project of constructing British literature failed, partly due to the national rivalry that exploded in the 1760s following the publication of *Ossian.*

A quick look at the development of German literature in the same period possibly throws more light on this thesis. Despite the fact that in the eighteenth century the German-speaking part of Europe was divided into hundreds of minor "states" and that the national "union" did not take place until 1870 under Bismarck, the intellectual elite in Germany managed to create a thoroughly German literature, so unified that even authors in German-speaking countries that remain outside of the German state consider themselves as belonging to the tradition of German literature. Students in Vienna and Zurich study "Germanistik" and get their dose of Goethe and Schiller without having any problems of marginalisation. This is probably due to the historical fact that the cultural unification of Germany took place before the political one and not vice-versa, as in Britain.

Germany's lack of a centrifugal metropolitan culture, then, enabled German intellectuals to develop the literary language through the republic of letters, irrespective of their geographical position or – perhaps more important – their native dialect. Standard German was not developed through the subordination of regional dialects to a metropolitan one as was the case in Britain. That Scots themselves – Hume, Smith, Blair – were instrumental in the Anglicisation of the Scottish language is a commonplace since Crawford's work, but his thesis has a nationalist tang to it that betrays the old paradigm of Scottish betrayal.

Crawford's assertion that English literature just went on being English literature is more convincing if one looks at the canonisation of English literature that followed. However, the question which must be asked in this context is whether the conception of English literature was so fully developed at the time. Crawford's own work casts the greatest doubt on this; there were no chairs of English literature in England until the nineteenth century, and the first chair in Scotland, Blair's of Rhetoric and Belles Lettres, was not exclusively dedicated to British or English literature, as Fowler has shown. So in a sense there was no English literature at the time, and Crawford maintains that the Scots invented it in order to integrate into the empire, whereas the English simply went on discussing English literature informally.

Thomas Warton provides perhaps the best evidence that this is not entirely correct. If one looks, for example, at his publication *The Union or Select Scots and English Poems*, a manifesto-like poetic miscellany, the assertion that English literature simply remained English literature cannot be taken at face value. Admittedly, this was not a major publication, but it did go into three editions from 1753 to 1765. And, although anonymously published, it was a miscellany from the hand of an Oxford fellow, influential enough to secure Johnson his A.M. degree from the university.[304]

The short preface is well worth an examination. Characteristically, it contains a justification for the publication and it is by no means overly modest. In fact, it recounts a number of seventeenth-century miscellanies, some of which "were not always sufficiently scrupulous and cautious in their choice, as several pieces are admitted, [...] which would otherwise have perished, and which had no other recommendation, than that they served to swell the volume" (A1). The later Professor of Poetry is engaged in a minor act of canonisation based on aesthetic criteria, but it is not primarily based on neo-classical standards, but rather his own taste. He continues by saying that "[s]ince this, many miscellanies have been published both in Scotland and England" and that it would be "sufficient to remark, that through want of care or judgment in their respective editors, they are all forgotten or neglected" (A1-A2). The only eighteenth-century miscellanies he is prepared to accept are the one ascribed to Pope, which he dismisses as being a collection mostly of Pope's own poems, and the one "lately published by R. Dodsley, which boasts the greatest names of the present age among its contributors" (A2).

Warton does not try to emulate or supersede the latter with a miscellany of canonised authors, however, for when he describes his own selection method, he is more interested in poetry that is not so well known: "It will be necessary to take notice, that our chief care has been to furnish out the following miscellany with those pieces, regard being first had to real merit, which have laid unknown and unobserved from their MANNER of publication" (A3, emphasis in text). Warton is confidently expanding the canon with his own selection and has no

---

[304]   As it says on the title page of his *Dictionary*.

doubts about his own judgement in the matter. In addition, he seems to have strong affinities for Scottish identity himself:

> that in order to render our volume still more compleat, we have had the favour of some original poems, written by a late member of the university of Aberdeen, whose modesty would not permit us to prefix his name; one of which in this edition is printed with many improvements, from a corrected copy. And from these ingenious essays, the public may be enabled to form some judgement beforehand of a poem of a nobler and more important nature, which he is now preparing (A3).

Warton is even adding new work to the canon, although there seems to be some ambiguity in the stress on the "improvements"; one might speculate as to whether they were of a linguistic or aesthetic nature. In fact, they serve an authentication purpose, for the poems are by himself (although one might be tempted to think of Beattie, who had just finished his studies in Aberdeen and who later published his *Minstrel* in the Spenserian stanza after reading Percy). This passage is also noteworthy as an introduction to a larger work, rather in the manner Blair later introduced Fingal in the preface to Macpherson's *Fragments*. What it reveals most obviously though, is that Warton certainly had no problem identifying with Scottish literature, even to the extent of using a Scottish identity as a pseudo-identity.

He opens by comparing single poems to the units of vision that make up the greater picture in a unified whole:

> As the mind of man is ever fond of variety, nothing seems better calculated to entertain, than a judicious collection of the smaller, though not on that account less laboured, productions of eminent poets: an entertainment, not unlike that which we receive from surveying a finished landscape [*sic*], or well disposed piece of shellwork: where each particular object, tho' singly beautiful, and sufficiently striking by itself, receives an additional charm, thus, as Milton expresses it, SWEETLY INTERCHANGED (A1, emphasis in text).

Warton is not only thinking of an aesthetic interchange, however, for, as the title suggests, he is also thinking of the union of Scottish and English literatures by presenting examples from both. Moreover, he obviously feels a need to present older Scottish poems:

> It is hoped that the ancient Scottish poems (amongst which THE THISTLE AND THE ROSE, and HARDYKNUTE are more particularly distinguished) will make no disagreeable figure amongst those of modern date; and that they will produce the same effect here, as Mr. Pope observes a moderate use of old words may have in a poem; which, adds he, is like working old abbey stones into a modern building, and which I have sometimes seen practised with good success (A3-A4).

Warton's reference to Pope's metaphor shows in a nutshell his own application of the primitivist project of collecting fragments to support a modern structure. Warton's fascination with ancient Gothic buildings was clearly not only a nostalgic and antiquarian hobby, but also an attempt to reconstruct an historical link with the British past, a link that included Scotland. Furthermore, it exemplifies the primitivist method as applied, for example, by Percy, even to the extent that he manipulated the orthography of his sources to make them "look" more ancient.

The *Union* includes not only Dunbar and Ramsay's version of Wardlaw's pseudo-ballad, but poems by David Mallet, Tobias Smollett and David Lyndsay, in addition to an elegy by Collins on James Thomson. The English contributors include Gray, Joseph Warton and Mark Akenside. In general, it can be claimed that the contemporary poetry in the *Union*, although formally mostly neo-classical, is advancing into the direction of the pre-romantic. The natural imagery, the appeals to fancy and imagination, the nationalistic tendency in the poetry with its rivalry with the original Greek classics, even the inclusion of ballad material, is significant for Warton's anticipation of the coming paradigms of the latter part of the eighteenth century. In short, Warton's miscellany is, as he confidently claims, a break with previous poetical traditions, and he sets it up within the new political frame of the Union.

The aesthetic tendency of the poetry reveals not only the Longinian sublime but also more romantic notions of the solitary poet transported to inspiration through communication with divine nature; so for example David Mallet's *Fragment*, which also manages at the same time to express Whiggish politics in its ending, where "Freedom's GENIUS good" appears to the solitary poet, convincing him of the "High privilege of human race,/Beyond a mortal monarch's grace:/Who could not give, who cannot claim,/What but from God immediate came!" (27). Joseph Warton's *Ode to Fancy* is also strongly coloured by the sublime and at the same time fully anticipates some of Burke's psychological interpretation, incorporating a definitive nationalistic aesthetic:

> O queen of numbers, once again
> Animate some chosen swain,
> Who filled with unexhausted fire,
> May boldly smite the sounding lyre,
> Who with some new, unequall'd song
> May rise above the rhyming throng:
> O'er all our listning passions reign,
> O'erwhelm our souls with joy and pain;
> With terror shake, and pity move,
> Rouze with revenge, or melt with love.
> O deign t' attend his evening walk,
> With him in groves and grottos talk;
> Teach him to scorn with frigid art,

Feebly to touch th' enraptured heart;
Like lightning, let his mighty verse
The bosom's inmost foldings pierce;
With native beauties win applause,
Beyond the cold critic's studied laws;
O let each Muse's same encrease,
O bid Britannia rival Greece! (35-6).

In German eighteenth-century terms this would almost amount to *Sturm und Drang*; in the rejection of "frigid art" and "the cold critic's studied laws", in the enthusiastic cultural nationalism that regards only the Greek model as a rival. Mark Akenside's *Ode on Lyric Poetry* also expresses similar feelings infused with the same poetic nationalism that wishes to replace the models he expressly admires. Akenside opens this early-modern praise of lyric poetry by beseeching: "O parent of the Grecian lyre/Admit me to thy secret strain" (179). What appears to be an homage to Greek poets – Anacreon, Alcæus, Sappho and Pindar (Akenside's spelling) – comes, however, to a conclusion more subjective and virtuous than that of the classical imitator. Akenside introduces his first hint of an antithesis in the middle of the poem, after recounting the ancient figures above as the prime examples of lyric poets:

But oft amid the Græcian throng,
The loose-rob'd form of wild desire
With lawless notes intun'd they song
To shameful steps dissolved thy quire.
O fair, O chaste, be still with me
From such profaner discord free:
While I frequent thy tuneful shade,
No frantic shouts of Thracian dames,
No satyrs fierce with savage flames
Thy pleasing accents shall invade (182).

This critique, in the spirit of the Moderns, is not as enthusiastic as Warton's *Ode to Fancy*, but in the final analysis it does lead to a similarly subjective and nationalistic notion of originality. As so often, patriotism finds its expression through the fear of an enemy:

But when from envy and from death to claim
A hero bleeding for his native land;
Or when to nourish freedom's vestal flame,
I hear my genius utter his command
    Nor Theban voice, nor Lesbian lyre
    From thee, O muse, do I require,
      While my prophetic mind,
Conscious of pow'rs he never knew,

Astonish'd grasps at things beyond her view,
Nor by another's fate hat felt her own confin'd (184).

What makes these two poems remarkable, particularly in the context of their publication in the *Union*, is the fact that they represent in content and ideology the two diametrically opposed factions of the Ancients and the Moderns, and yet their primary ideological message is the same, the replacement of the ancient models with new British or native ones. Admittedly, Warton's poem is coloured with the Gothicism his brother, along with other scholars and writers, was to propagate so effectively; but he is in effect applying the doctrines that appeared so forcefully on the European scene through Boileau's translation of Longinus. Conversely, Akenside's poem may be in a more neo-classical, Modern, vein, and yet his ode on "lyric" poetry, along with the antithetical conclusion, signifies a break with that tradition.

Thomas Warton, then, attempted to unify several opposite strands of thought in his miscellany; his own Toryism with Mallet's Whiggism; the major aesthetic oppositional positions of his age, the Ancients and the Moderns; added to which must be the prevalent classical canon with the new upcoming national one, be it expressed through Gothicism or balladry; and last but not least Scottish and English traditions in poetry. Warton seems to have been a pioneer, particularly when it comes to setting up the native tradition within a new aesthetic and historical frame. His cue seems to have been taken up by Percy, whose *Reliques* included Scottish ballads, and who even toyed with the idea of publishing a fourth volume consisting exclusively of Scottish ballads.[305] Percy's nationalist initiative was, however, much more English-oriented in the Johnsonian fashion than Warton's ever was.[306] Crawford mentions Warton only briefly in *Devolving English Literature,* where he says that

> [t]he Scottish pedagogical development was quite different from the scope and design of the Oxford Professorship of Poetry founded in 1708, whose early incumbents, such as Joseph Trapp, Robert Lowth, and Thomas Warton the Younger, lectured in Latin on Classical and Hebrew subjects, though some of their lectures were later published in translation for a wider audience (19).

Correct as that may be with regards to the institutionalisation of English literature in the universities, there are other aspects that have to be taken into consideration. Warton's research and publications in the *Observations* and certainly the *History of English Literature* can be seen as important milestones in the development of an emerging discipline, and he does not disregard Scots such as

---

[305] The ballad revival in the late eighteenth century was very much preoccupied with Scottish balladry; Ritson published *Ancient Scotish Songs* and Scott's *Minstrelsy* is another example.

[306] It was Percy who questioned the authenticity of *Hardyknute* in the *Reliques.*

Dunbar, Douglas and Lindsay in the latter. On the contrary, Warton gives all three a serious critical examination, in addition to brief discussions on Blind Harry's *Wallace* and poets like Alexander Montgomerie, Robert Henryson, Alexander Scott and William Stewart. Indeed, the main difference in his conception of the origins of English literature has been shown above to have been a definitely cosmopolitan flavour, in comparison to Percy's attempt to translate the origins of skaldic literature into the Anglo-Saxon one. Warton's own reasons for including the Scots provide the best example of his attitude:

> It is not the plan of this work to comprehend the Scotish poetry. But when I consider the close and national connection between England and Scotland in the progress of manners and literature, I am sensible I should be guilty of a partial and defective representation of the poetry of the former, were I to omit in my series a few Scotish writers, who have adorned the present period with a degree of sentiment and spirit, a command of phraseology, and a fertility of imagination, not to be found in any English poet since Chaucer and Lydgate (*History III* 1871, 204).

Warton's work on Dunbar, although of course coloured by his aesthetic ideology, to borrow Eagleton's phrase, is by no means superficial, and indeed borders on the panegyrical at times; he simply likes Dunbar's poetry. The section on Gavin Douglas is even more interesting in the context of this book, for here he analyses the Scottish poet's translation of Virgil, the first metrical version of the epic in Britain. Warton seems to want to make it a little English when he claims that "[t]his translation is executed with equal spirit and fidelity, and is a proof that the Lowland Scotish and English languages were now nearly the same" (220). This seems to be contradicted by his translation of Douglas later in the section, but then again he is not speaking directly of the languages, but of the aesthetic competence (and a new and native affectation) achieved by poets in the language: "I mean the style of composition; more especially the glaring affectation of anglicising Latin words" (220).

Warton is, however, of the opinion that Douglas's "proper walk was original poetry", and quotes one of his prologues inserted between books in his translation of the *Aeneid* as proof of this (220). His argument for the translation of the Scottish verse into English prose is remarkable, for it breathes a spirit, if not an ideology, of subjective originality which he claims transcends language and form:

> But the verses of Douglas will have another merit with those critics who love to contemplate the progress of composition, and to mark the original workings of genuine nature; as they are the effusion of a mind not overlaid by the descriptions of other poets, but operating by its own force and bias in the delineation of a vernal landscape, on such objects as really occurred. On this account, they deserve to be better understood: and I have therefore translated them into plain modern English prose. In the meantime, this experiment will serve to prove their native excellence. Divested of poetic numbers and

expression, they still retain their poetry; and (to use the comparison of an elegant writer on a like occasion) appear like Ullysses still a king and conqueror, although disguised like a peasant, and lodged in the cottage of the herdsman Eumaeus (225).

It should perhaps be stressed that the poetry Warton refers to and then translates is Douglas's prologues within a translation of Virgil. Poesy, it seems, resides in the poet's "original workings of genuine nature" and even a translation from Scots into English shows their "native excellence". The measured prose which follows on several pages is not exactly Ossianic, but it would hardly have been expected from a classical scholar's hand in Britain prior to the early 1760s.[307] In fact, this is one of the explanations for why the Ossianic texts appealed to Warton and other renowned scholars of the time: the possibility of preserving a poesy that is beyond mere language and form in a prose translation, a lyrical confirmation of the subject, even within an epic frame. The larger frame simply serves as a wider, collective or national context for the same subject.

And yet Warton's practice translation may appear to contradict some of his own views on translation in general. In her critical biography, published in 1916, Clarissa Rinaker positions Warton firmly at a crossroads of what she repeatedly terms "pseudo-classicism" and an uneasy version of romanticism which now generally goes under the term of pre-romanticism. One of her criteria is Warton's opinion about translation: "With characteristic soundness of scholarship he condemned the prevalence of translations because they encouraged 'indolence and illiteracy', displaced the originals and thus gradually vitiated public taste" (51).[308] Rinaker refers here to Warton's *Observations,* where he discusses Chaucer, also dealt with in his *History.* As Rinaker makes clear in a footnote, Warton's "condemnation" is mainly directed at translations from Middle English into modern English, but she adds: "Warton extended his criticism to translations of classical authors as well. Of course the greatest classicists, Dryden and Johnson, realized the limits of translation, that it was only a makeshift" (51).

---

[307] Of course the "Homeric wars" in Weinbrot's phrase had raged much earlier in France, partly due to the controversy about Anne Dacier's translation *vis à vis* that of la Motte. Dacier defended Homer from the "Ancient's" point of view and translated the *Iliad* from Greek, as opposed to the "Modern" la Motte who used a Latin translation and translated into verse; a constellation reminiscent of Boileau and Perrault with a view to their linguistic competence. But although Dacier explicitly propagated prose for such a translation, again as opposed to la Motte (until he changed his mind), it should not be forgotten that this seems to have had little effect in Britain, for Pope, according to Weinbrot, profited very much from her annotated translation, but did of course not translate into prose himself (*Britannia* 193-212).

[308] For a detailed discussion on Warton's contribution to the eighteenth-century discourse on taste, see Joan Pittock's *The Ascendancy of Taste.*

Rinaker expresses here the still-prevalent view of translation as a second-rate makeshift of an original that can only be enjoyed to the full in its original version. This view may be fitting for those who possess the linguistic competence to read an original, but for the rest a translation is not a makeshift, but the only way to read the text at all.[309] Even with a partial competence of ancient Greek, for example, it is to be doubted whether it is possible for a modern reader to get through the *Iliad* in the original without an understanding that is in reality "makeshift".[310] In addition, she forgets that the reception of classical texts, the Bible – in fact most of the pre-modern canon – was through translation; and even if Latin did become the universal language of European elites, it remains to be studied what kind of an understanding was achieved through the non-native reading, writing and indeed translation of that language.

Rinaker's one-sided presentation of Dryden, Johnson and Warton also betrays her own ideological (romantic) views on translation; such views certainly may be found in texts of the above authors, but all of them presented a much more complex picture than is suggested here. Dryden was one of the most important translators and translation theoreticians of the English language; Johnson may have spoken pejoratively of translation, according to Boswell in the *Life,* but his own remarks in the *Idler* nos. 68 and 69 and in his *Life of Pope* present an altogether different and scholarly understanding of the matter.

Rinaker's misrepresentation is, however, even more blatant in the case of her biographical object, Thomas Warton. He may have had some doubts about the translation of Chaucer into modern English, but his views on the influence of interlingual translation in his *History* show that he was very well aware of the role of translation in the creation of a national literature. Indeed, his *History of English Poetry* is just as much, if not more, a history of translation as it is a history of an indigenous, native literature. Time and again he refers to translations as sources; he asserts their positive influence on the genesis of genres and new modes of literary expression. In short, he shows how translations make up the foundation of what is now called English literature.

Warton notes, for example, that Chaucer used Italian and French authors as "models" and that "the *Knight's Tale,* and the *Romaunt of the Rose* [...] are imitations or translations" (*History II* 298).[311] He also maintains that French transla-

---

[309] Again one might refer to Anne Dacier's arguments in the preface to her translation of the *Iliad,* an excerpt of which can be found in Douglas Robinson's *Western Translation Theory from Herodotus to Nietzsche* (186-190).

[310] Johnson certainly was pleased enough with Pope's "makeshift" of the *Iliad.*

[311] W.C. Hazlitt's 1871 edition of Warton's *History* has an addition in brackets where Warton's assertion is refuted to an extent: "Chaucer, out of the 2250 lines of his *Knight's Tale,* has translated 270 (less than one eighth) from the 9054 lines of Boccaccio's original: 374 more bear a general likeness to the Italian poets, and 132, a slight likeness" (*History II* 298-9). This editorial insertion shows how important it is to

tions of the classics were, in fact, one of the major routes of earlier writers to them: "By means of these French translations, our countrymen, who understood French much better than Latin, became acquainted with many useful books they would not otherwise have known" (*History III* 113). Warton provides many other examples of the use of translation in the creation of an English-speaking literature and certainly does not condemn them as "makeshift", but rather sees them (more than do many of his critics and latter-day scholars) as an inevitable part of the development of a native literature.

Rinaker's interpretation should also be considered in light of Warton's own translation of Theocritus, "for which", as she herself says, "he laid aside all other literary work" (75). This translation, which was made from manuscripts recently collected in Italy by John St. Amand and bequeathed to the Bodleian library, was, according to Rinaker, "highly praised", but the only remark she makes on this work is that "foreign scholars immediately discovered its defects in precision, and it has now been entirely superseded", something that could as easily be said about his *History* (76-77). The difference is that when discussing the translation this is an argument to dismiss it from any further discussion, erase it from Warton's literary work, whereas for the *History* or any other original work, lack of precision and the fact that the work in question has been superseded would not automatically disqualify it from further discussion in a "biographical and critical study", as the subtitle of her work indicates.

Warton's ambivalence towards translation as expressed in his texts and in his practice as a writer underlines his uneasy dual or "pre-romantic" position; later, as a poet laureate, he attempted to straddle the cleft partly of his own making, by leaning perhaps a little more on the neo-classical in his always politically correct British odes on the King's birthdays and for the new year. These odes combine two objectives always present in his work: firstly, the comparison and competition with the classical models, particularly the Greek, and, secondly, the historical element is already present. In his odes for the king written in the 1780s he always combines the two subjects, although strangely enough he seems, at times, almost to reject his own primitivism and literary re-evaluation of the Gothic.

There is a development to be discerned, however, and recurring themes that are handled differently as time goes by. The first "Ode on his Majesty's Birthday" (June 4, 1785), seems to recoil from all primitivist sins of the past as he praises the "patron king" for fettering the arts: "Tis his to judgment's steady line/Their flights to confine,/ And yet expand their wing;/The fleeting forms of fashion to restrain,/ And bind capricious Taste in Truth's eternal chain" (*Works*

---

reduce the translatory element out of important "native" works. At the same time it serves as an excellent example of the step-by-step method of using translation to write an "original" work.

245). There is a Shaftesburian qualification there, but what is perhaps more interesting is Warton's use of the metaphoric "chain", a prop which is present in numerous of these laureate odes written either on the king's birthday or for the new year.

Warton's chain is not negative in the Rousseauan social sense or Macpherson's notion of the poetic fetters of form, but positive, standing for the intermediary and bourgeois constraints of taste, the controlling instance of a native literature emancipating itself from the classical models by finding a subjective standard based on precisely those models and yet at the same time abandoning them. That Warton himself was not fully conscious of this development might be deduced from the next lines in his first birthday ode for George III:

> Sculpture, licentious now no more,
> From Greece her great example takes,
> With Nature's warmth the marble wakes,
> And spurns the toys of modern lore:
> In native beauty simply plann'd,
> Corinth, thy tufted shafts ascend;
> The Graces guide the painter's hand,
> His magic mimicry to blend (246).

These almost Winckelmannian lines are typical for Warton and his presence in both major camps of eighteenth-century aesthetics, the synthesis of which was to become Romanticism. To be sure, the Greek model provides the "great example", but this example "spurns the toys of modern lore" that are planned in "native beauty". Even more significant are the lines that claim the "Graces guide the painter's hand,/His Magic mimicry to blend". They may guide him, but his "mimicry" is not pure, it is "magic" and a "blend". Warton has understood perfectly how to translate foreign antiquity into native modernity, losing what is redundant, namely the concrete original, and retaining what is necessary, its spirit and form.

In his first "Ode to the New Year, 1786" Warton becomes a little bolder; although he relies on standard neo-classical instruments, he moves the poetry subtly from Greek antiquity towards British modernity. He opens the ode with a rhetorical device, purportedly quoting Greek "bards" who maintained that "a genial isle/Crowns the broad Atlantic wave" (247). The common motif of high culture sailing towards Britain is combined with the naval power of the kingdom (and George III of course).[312] The patriotic poem underlines this naval power with another positive reference to a metaphorical chain, this time the "golden chain of commerce". There is, however, an interesting shift in the next stanza.

---

[312]   Gray's *The Progress of Poesy* is perhaps the best example of this motif, which was also picked up in a different version by German Romantics such as the Schlegels.

As might be expected, Warton not only praises British seamanship but also refers to the farmers and weavers and characteristically he carries on thus:

> Her cities, throng'd with many an Attic dome,
> Ask not the banner'd bastion , massy proof;
> Firm as the castle's feudal roof,
> Stands the Briton's social home (249).

This mixture, supported by British commerce, "Right, Order, Law" and liberty is indestructible and will in future be able to break "Opinion's speculative gloom", become an "Interpreter of ages yet unborn" and finally succeed as the "source of every splendid art,/Of old, of future worlds the universal mart" (249-50). Warton's prophetic powers are with hindsight considerable indeed, but then again his prophecy is based on a method all successful capitalistic Western societies have adopted: the successful mixture of ancient heritage with native culture, an enlightened approach towards existing ideologies in general, which he personifies as "Opinion", a capitalistic market society based on individual liberty and "Right, Order, Law", as he puts it himself.

The following years Warton wrote his odes in a similar vein, seemingly becoming more "modern" and patriotic annually. There is, however, one element worth examining in the odes between 1787 and 1790, having to do with Warton's beloved metaphoric "chains". The opening of the ode on the king's birthday in 1787, dedicated to the three poets Warton seems to consider to be his greatest predecessors, Chaucer, Spenser and Dryden, slants more in the neo-classical direction than might be expected:[313]

> The noblest Bards of Albion's choir
> Have struck of old this festal lyre.
> Ere science, struggling oft in vain,
> Had dared to break her Gothic chain (254).

These lines, coming from the author of the *Observations* and admirer of Gothic buildings and romances, seem a little odd if not opportunistic. In light of his controversy with Percy and his essay on romantic fiction in the *History* they even acquire an ironic patina when one reads the following four lines:

> Victorious Edward gave the vernal bough
> Of Britain's bay to bloom on Chaucer's brow:
> Fired with the gift, he changed to sounds sublime
> His Norman minstrelsy's discordant chime (254-55).

---

[313] This would perhaps explain the choice of poets, for although the first two would not have been considered "correct", according to neo-classical tastes that saw Waller as the first refined English poet, they were innovators and importers in form. Of the three, only Dryden held the office of Poet Laureate.

As noted in the *OED* in an entry on alliteration, Warton is actually attacking alliteration in these lines, but he is of course doing more; he is plainly canonising the poets he believes replaced the garbage of Norman minstrelsy under the yoke of French-speaking rulers with the classical tradition in the native language. This is strong stuff coming from the author of a history of English literature who had delved into the medieval and early modern literature in Britain (and had hardly surfaced thereafter) in three massive quarto volumes. But if Warton is opportunistic in these lines he adds insult to injury a year later:

> What native Genius taught the Britons bold
> To guard their sea-girt cliffs of old?
> 'Twas Liberty: she taught disdain
> Of death, of Rome's imperial chain.

The obvious element here is the chain which now has become Roman, and a metaphor for the slavery the Roman empire brought upon Britain. Incredibly, Warton suddenly uses alliteration, something he seemed to be attacking in his ode of the previous year, with considerable skill. He also invokes Norse mythology for good measure later on, and although he still nudges the Norman conquest a little for having brought "slavery from a softer clime", he now has to admit that it also gave "New grace to Britain's naked plain,/With Arts and Manners in his train" (261). Finally, he even manages, almost Whiggishly, to interpret the foreign "tyrant-king['s]" assumption of office as an epiphanic moment, turning the conqueror into a British patriot lending "lustre [...] to native laws" (261).

To conclude, it might be observed that Warton's ambivalence is perhaps not so opportunistic as the last examples suggest. It is rather a further example of his eclectic and uneasy patriotism or fledgling British nationalism in the Scottish tradition. His methods are certainly in key with what literary nationalists in other European countries did, and yet the complexity of the British situation made him aware of the difficulties inherent in the construction of a truly national culture. Hence, he may have tried to be all things to all people and failed in the venture. What his work shows most certainly is that he was very much aware of the native literature of Britain; he published major works on it, and so should be counted among the Scots who, according to Crawford, invented English literature. As a medieval and Renaissance scholar, he was also more aware than most of the use of translation in the construction of a vernacular and native literature, and this knowledge he applied both in his theoretical and scholarly work, as well as in his practical and poetical production.[314]

---

[314] Pardon the alliteration.

Part III
The German Synthesis

5   THESIS

5.1   German Imitative Nature

The German national character is rather unoriginal and imitative, Immanuel Kant claims in his pre-critical *Beobachtungen Über das Gefühl des Schönen und Erhabenen* (1764) and the "post-critical" *Anthropologie in pragmatischer Hinsicht* (1798) (*Vorkritische 2*, 875 & *Anthropologie 2*, 667). These two works, both of which make use of British authors, particularly David Hume's "Of National Characters" and Edmund Burke's *Enquiry*, might be seen as confirmation of this view through application. On the other hand, Kant himself showed in his major works that such an approach may be fruitful, that it may even be at the basis of the invention of autonomy, as Schneewind titles his history of moral philosophy. One of the best-known authors in the study of nationalism, Elie Kedourie, also honours Kant with the invention of nationalism's premise, the autonomy of the self through the *a priori* transformation of experience to a concept of the world.

If one considers German literary history, however, translation certainly plays a major role, a greater role than in the British example it seems. This may naturally be due to more openness in German letters, both in the reception of foreign literature and in the admission of this reception. It is open to question, however, whether English literature is much more "original". The difference is perhaps more in the method than in the act. The "Big Bang" of German literary language, the first unifying act of that language, must surely be Luther's translation of the Bible; even Catholics of the Counter-Reformation had to adapt their discourse and translations to that fact. Luther's own quarrel in "Sendbrief vom Dolmetschen" illustrates this very well; dogmatic points of religion are settled through translational argumentation.[315] The new construction of meaning takes place through translation.

Although German was thus the first European language to acquire a Bible translation that became the basis of the major shift in religion – the first *successful* Bible translation – German literature lagged somewhat behind in the European development. There may be different reasons behind this: the lack of a political union with a corresponding metropolitan centre, for example, and hence a weak and diffuse patronage, plus the fact that German humanism was Latin-oriented (i.e., scholars and poets continued to use Latin after the Renaissance and Reformation); even Ulrich von Hutten's nationalistic *Arminius* dialogues were in Latin.[316] Others even profited from the use of Latin by German scholars, either by translating their original Latin texts or by their translations from the German into Latin, which were subsequently translated into English. The six-

---

[315]   And a little polemics, which also belongs to translational discourse.
[316]   See Blitz for a discussion on von Hutten's nationalism (42-58).

teenth century was one of the greatest translational periods in Britain, and it provided the Elizabethans with an abundance of materials and forms which they put into use in the native language.[317]

But this did not happen in the German-speaking regions, and although the sixteenth century can boast of several works of interest in German, a native-language Renaissance did not really take place. This was not only because many scholars used Latin, for the native medieval traditions were developed further (*Minnesang, Meistergesang,* folk song, etc.)[318] Nor did translation into the native language take place, at least not on the same scale as in Britain, and what is more important, hardly any translation of forms; the poetic experiments were confined to the Latinists. The first renewal, although hardly a re-birth, was around 1600, according to Andreas Heusler, and most of the praise (and blame) has been awarded to the poet and translator Martin Opitz and his epoch-making *Buch der deutschen Poeterey* (1624).

This little tract, purportedly thrown together in three days, had wide-ranging influence on German native poetics and is often referred to as a "reform" of German metrics. Since the mid-eighteenth century, this reform has often been slighted, particularly on nationalistic grounds, as the model it adopted was predominantly French. Indeed, the Klopstockian reform of this reform may be interpreted as both a nationalistic and an aesthetic act; the crossover has rarely been as obvious as in this instance. But whatever German prosodic nationalists thought of Opitz in the latter part of the eighteenth century, he did reform German prosody enough to enable serious poets to write in the native language. In fact, earlier he had already "done a Dante" in his *Aristarchus sive de contemptu linguae Teutonicae* (1617), a speech in Latin wherein he claims Latin has outlived its usefulness and that German is the language of the future.[319] To be sure, it is no *De vulgari eloquentia,* but the direction is the same. Further-

---

[317]   Horst Oppel discusses these exchanges in his *Englisch-deutsche Literaturbeziehungen I* and names of course the *Volksbuch vom Doktor Faust,* works by Paracelsus and others, and, most interestingly, *Pammachius* by Thomas Kirchmayer, one of whose translators, John Bale, later wrote *Kynge Johan,* "das erste vollgültige Belegstücke für die tragische Spielart der Historie, die später in Marlowe's *Edward II* und Shakespeares *Richard II* ihre Vollendung fanden" (31).[the first fully valid pieces of evidence for the tragic way of playing the history as was later fully developed by Marlowe's *Edward II* and Shakespeare's *Richard II.* My translation]

[318]   Andreas Heusler describes the period in detail in his *Deutsche Versgeschichte III* (1-60). See also Winfred Sdun, *Probleme und Theorien des Übersetzens in Deutschland vom 18. bis zum 20. Jahrhundert* (esp. 19-36); Thomas Huber, *Studien zum Theorie des Übersetzens im Zeitalter der deutschen Aufklärung* and Anneliese Senger *Deutsche Übersetzungstheorie im 18. Jahrhundert.*

[319]   I am indebted here and in the following to Gunter E. Grimm's "Martin Opitz" in *Deutsche Dichter* as well as Cornelius Sommer's "Nachwort" in the Reclam-edition of *Buch der deutschen Poeterey.*

more, he translated the Renaissance model into German letters in explicit terms, and even if many of the post-Klopstockians disagreed with him in the use of a *French* model, they were happy to use his *method*.[320]

It is a standard in translational discourse to quote Opitz on the topic:[321]

> Eine guete art der vbung aber ist / das wir vns zuweilen auß den Griechischen vnd Lateinischen Poeten etwas zue vbersetzen vornemen: dadurch denn die eigenschafft vnd glantz der w[oe]rter / die menge der figuren / vnd das verm[oe]gen dergleichen zue erfinden zue wege gebracht wird (68).[322]

As a statement on translation, scholars usually note that this says little, that it is a repetition of Cicero and Horace, and "simply advising it as a means to the end of improving one's style" (Louth 10). This may be true, but such views are blind to the translation of a *system* and see only translation of texts and content. Opitz was not translating a text, an original, but rather a system of poetics, and his translation worked so well that it has been called a "reform", and indeed constituted the ruling system in German poetics for over a century.

There are several elements that support this argument. First, the context of the oft-quoted lines. They are set in the traditional paradigm of competition through imitation and show no hesitation about borrowing where one needs it. Opitz continues above excerpt thus:

> Auff diese weise sind die R[oe]mer mit den Griechen / vnd die newen scribenten mit den alten verfahren: so das sich Virgilius selber nicht gesch[ae]met / gantze pl[ae]tze auß andern zue entlehnen; wie sonderlich Macrobius im f[ue]nfften und sechsten buche beweiset (68).[323]

He goes on to draw an analogy with public competition, as in sports, which again relates to the general frame or rather ideological motivation of the work, which is patriotism. Beginning with the title, *Buch von der* Deutschen *Poeterey,* one might think this is a poetics of extant practice, but it is not, it is a translation of a translation of a method that proposes certain practices. The dedication to the mayors of "Buntzlaw" is not as enthusiastic as Rousseau's dedication to the city fathers of Geneva in the second *Discourse,* but it is thoroughly patriotic and states the desire to do some good for the "Vaterland".

---

[320] Gunter E. Grimm even refers to Opitz as a German Renaissance poet: "Wenn es einen deutschsprachigen Renaissance-Dichter gegeben hat – dann Martin Opitz" (79).

[321] See for example Albrecht (150) and Louth (10).

[322] "It is, however, a good exercise to translate occasionally from the Greek and Latin poets: so that the quality and glory of the words, the number of tropes may be of use in the invention of the same" (my translation).

[323] "This is the way the Romans treated the Greeks and the new writers do the same with old: even Virgil himself was not ashamed of borrowing whole passages from others, as Macrobius has shown in his fifth and sixth books" (my translation).

The Latin motto is taken from Horace's *Ars Poetica,* the lines quoted in part I: "If I fail to keep and do not understand these well marked shifts and shades of poetic forms, why am I hailed as a poet? Why through false shame do I prefer to be ignorant rather than to learn?" (Fairclough 458-459).[324] This refers to the didactic element of the book, but there is also a dedication to the author by Augustinus Iskra Silesius, an imitation (*Parodia*) of Horace (Carm. II Lib. II.) which in the editor's translation opens thus: "Es gibt keine Zierde des Geistes, des geschmacklos auf unbrauchbarem Papier hingekleckleksten Herzens, Martin Opitz, wenn sie sich nicht zu Formen verjüngt, die für das Vaterland schicklich sind" (74).[325]

This strain of patriotism, coupled with a desire to reform and renew German poetic language and forms, runs through the whole essay. Opitz also uses strategies that are familiar. One is to assert that poetry is universal, and that all nations can produce it (20-21). Another is to reference classical sources on the "Germans". When defining his discursive object, which he calls "Deutsche Poeterey", Opitz refers to Tacitus and what he had said of the Germans:

> von den Deutschen in dem buche das er von jhnen geschrieben / das ob vol weder Mann noch Weib vnter jhnen zue seiner zeit den freyen k[ue]nsten ob zue liegen pflegeten / faßeten sie doch alles was sie im ged[ae]chtnis behalten wolten in gewisse reimen vnd getichte (21).[326]

Opitz follows up with a quote from Lucan's *Pharsalia,* three lines that refer to the bards' role in praising the deeds of heroes – the same lines which were used as a motto for Macpherson's *Fragments of Ancient Poetry.* He then refers to the heroic songs of the ancient kings of Denmark. As we have seen, these are common paradigms in eighteenth-century nationalistic discourse.

Opitz's next step is to find an old example of a bard who could sing of his king as Lucan describes. He picks Walther von der Vogelweide, "Keyser Philipses geheimen rahte", and he cites a poem that very plainly expresses the Christian version of the *translatio studii* (22-23). This quote serves to ram home his conclusion, which in turn is followed by an offer of a method of improvement:

---

[324]   descriptas servare vices operumque colores/cur ego si nequeo ignoroque poeta salutor?/cur nescire pudens prave quam discere malo? (ll. 86-88/456-458).

[325]   "INgenI nullus decor est, ineptis/Illitæ charits inimice venæ,/Martie Opiti, nisi patriæ aptos/Vernet in usus" (9). There is no decoration of the spirit, of the tastelessly ink-spotting heart on unusable paper, Martin Opitz, if it is not renewed in forms that are apt for the fatherland.

[326]   "In the book, he has written of the Germans, that although neither man nor woman among them at the time seemed to tend to the liberal arts, they did all the same put everything they wanted to retain in memory into certain rhymes and poems" (my translation). As Sommer, the editor of the Reclam-edition, notes, Tacitus did not refer to rhyme! (79).

Das nun von langer zeit her dergleichen zue vben in vergessen gestellt ist worden / ist leichtlicher zue beklagen / als die vrsache hiervon zue geben. Wiewol auch bey den Italienern erst Petrarcha die Poeterey in seiner Muttersprache getrieben hat / vnnd nicht sehr vnlengst Ronsardus; von deme gesaget wird / das er / damit sein Frantz[oe]sisches desto besser außw[ue]rgen k[oe]ndte / mit der Griechen schrifften gantzer zw[oe]lff jahr sich vberworffen habe; als von welchen die Poeterey jhre meiste Kunst / art vnd lieblichkeit bekommen (23)[327]

The solution to the problem, then, is to imitate the Greeks in the *native* language, a demand that appeared in Germany at the beginning of the seventeenth century. The demand on its own is not enough, however, and Opitz proposes a reform which would adopt the rhetorical conventions and forms of the ancients. The route to these lies through translation, not only of texts, but of the muses themselves, to Germany. This demand appears in a translation, or rather an adaptation, of Virgil's *Georgics*:

> [...] ich bin begierde voll
> Zue schreiben wie man sich im creutz' auch frewen soll /
> Sein Meister seiner selbst. ich wil die neun G[oe]ttinnen /
> Die nie auff vnsrer deutsch noch haben reden k[oe]nnen /
> Sampt jhrem Helicon mit dieser meiner handt
> Versetzen allhieher in vnser Vaterlandt (26, italics reversed).[328]

The desire is plain, as is the method.

Opitz' "reform" contained not only this ideological component, but also very precise rules on the handling of language and verse. The most important of these are his "puristic" tendency (the demand that foreign words be left out of texts) and the true reform of metre, wherein he set the rule that German should only use alternating rhythms of stress (iambics or trochees) in line with the natural stress of the native language, instead of using a quantitative measure relying on the length of syllables. This translation of the ancient quantitative measure into a syllabic stress-metre had possibly been suggested to Opitz by Philip Sidney's *Apologie for Poetrie,* Heusler suggests (*Versgeschichte III* 79).[329] Opitz'

---

[327] "That it has been forgotten for a long time to exercise such poetry, is easier to complain about than to explain here the cause of it. Although also among the Italians Petrarch was the first to bring poetry in the mother tongue and lately Ronsard, of whom it is said that he could squeeze out his French better, since he delved into the Greeks for the whole of twelve years, from whom the poetry became most of its art, style and politeness" (my translation). Dante's absence is somehow significant in this context.

[328] "I am full of desire to write so that one can enjoy fully the master of himself. I want to bring the nine godesses who have never been able to speak in our German along with their Helicon in my hand and plant them all here in our fatherland" (my translation with a glance toward Fairclough's translation of Virgil's *Georgics*) (155).

[329] Apparently, Opitz "improved" the verse of a translation of Sidney's *Arcadia,* if the title page of the fourth edition (1643) is to be believed: "*Arcadia. Der Gräffin von*

reform subsequently set the standards for German poetry for over a century. But although it may have been suggested by Sidney, most of Opitz' examples are translations from the ancients and very often the French poet Ronsard.

There is one enlightening mistake in *Buch der Deutschen Poeterey*. At one point Opitz claims that an Italian poet had invented Alexandrines to translate the heroic hexameter verse of the ancients (50). The editor corrects this in an end-note and simply explains the origins of the Alexandrine (90). But the mistake shows that Opitz can only be referring to Trissino's invention of blank verse. What is important to note in this context is the fact that Opitz sees the (French) metre which he proposes to adopt as the metre for German (national) poetry as a translation of the ancients.[330]

German critics have tended to view Opitz' work a little differently and thus to expose their blindness towards translation by making this work of translation a native (original) construct and merely part of German literary history, when it is, in fact, part of the pan-European poetic development.[331] Gunter E. Grimm claims, for example, that one should agree with Alewyn "der das große Verdienst Opitz' in der Durchsetzung seiner einzigen Idee erblickt, der >>Nationalisierung der humanistischen Poesie durch Erfindung einer deutschen Kunstdichtung<<" (79) ["who sees that the great service of Opitz lies in the realisation of his single idea of nationalising the humanist poetry by inventing German poetic art]. If "Nationalisierung" is correct, "Erfindung" is the wrong word here, as is "Idee", for both were developed as translation, the construction of German metre as well as the method, which was principally the Renaissance method of appropriation. Grimm hence comes to the wrong conclusion and builds up a dialectic between folk poetry and what he calls "Kunstpoesie":

Die soziale Zielrichtung der neuen Kunstpoesie ist eindeutig: indem Opitz die antike Dichtung als absolute Norm propagiert und an ihr alle neueren Produkte mißt, öffnet

---

Pembrock. Herrn Philippsen von Sydney. In Englischer Sprach geschrieben / aus derselbigen Französich und aus beyden erstlich Teutsch gegeben durch VALENTINUM THEOCRITUM von Hirschberg: Jezo allenthalben auffs neuw ubersehen und gebessert: die Gedichte aber und Reymen ganz anderst gemacht und vbersezt von dem Edlen und Besten Martin Opiz von Boberfeldt."

[330] Curiously, there is a parallel development in Britain in the early seventeenth century; although rhyming couplets had been known since Chaucer (cf. above), it is only with the poet Waller in 1625 that the heroic couplet comes of age as the heroic metre of English literature; since Surrey, blank verse had been predominant, in drama and epic translation. The qualification "heroic" shows very well, as do translations such as Pope's *Iliad*, that the heroic couplet was considered the equivalent of the ancient heroic hexameter verse.

[331] Opitz himself names not only Ronsard as a model, but also the Dutchman Daniel Heinsius, who had performed a similar "reform" in Dutch poetics.

sich eine Kluft zwischen gelehrtem und nichtgelehrtem Publikum, die weit bis ins 18. Jahrhundert bestehen bleibt (79).[332]

Grimm simply forgets here that there was a Latin tradition which must have counted as "gelehrt" when Opitz published his essay; if anything, Opitz opened the "highbrow" poetry to the non-Latin-speaking native Germans. His numerous translations can be seen in the same light. When Grimm claims that it was not before the *Sturm und Drang* that people like Bürger and Herder re-evaluated folk poetry, he may well be right; whether this was in opposition to Opitz' work is another question, and it is worth noting in this connection that their appropriation of folk poetry was also within the paradigm of a translation without an original. In the theoretical discussions of the *Sturm und Drang*, it was precisely the nearness to the ancients in spirit that was accentuated; the new narrative, as it were, was that folk poetry was equal to that of the ancients. This represented the ideological thrust of what has been called primitivism (critics often forget that at least Homer and the Greek dramatists are in the group as comparable foreigners), so the same criterion can be applied to both native and foreign ancient poetry. Most of the products that go under the name of "folk poetry" were translationally rewritten according to theoretical aesthetic criteria based on more extensive knowledge of the ancients, and particularly the Greeks, than the seventeenth-century Opitz could ever have had. But he had provided the method in part, and the German eighteenth century perfected it to the extent that it could boast of poets like Goethe and Hölderlin and translators like Johann Heinrich Voss and A.W. Schlegel.

The reaction against Opitz resulted in a different revolution from the concentration on folk poetry proclaimed by Grimm. To be sure, folk poetry, "Volkslieder" in Herder's term, was part of the movement that replaced Opitz' poetics in German literature, but that was a part of the neo-classical disintegration that took place in Europe after mid-century, particularly in Britain and Germany and, in addition, the result of the national Renaissances that took place at that time. These were partly expressed in the rejection of the French hegemony in neo-classicist poetics, but also in a reappraisal of native language and its aesthetic and moral dynamics. This lead to an extensive search for origins in language and literary sources, and when both failed to fulfil the aesthetic expectations that had been constructed since the Renaissance, translation became the solution: translation of classics, translation of other recently "discovered" and "native" antiquities, translation without an original, the last of which includes not only the translation of distinguished classical forms, but also the rewriting of native

---

[332] "The social direction of the new artistic poetry is obvious: when Opitz claims that ancient poetry is the absolute norm, against which all new productions are to be measured, a gap is created between the learned and the uneducated audiences, a gap that continues to exist well into the 18th century" (my translation).

heritage into a classical form (an act that was often supported by reappraising the native forms), in short a transformation into a national literature.

Although German poets and intellectuals applied many of the same instruments and indeed texts (Ossian, Shakespeare) as the British to construct their national literature, the development in Germany, despite the country's literally fragmented state, went in a diametrically opposite direction to that of Britain. It is one of the great ironies of history that Germany managed to unite culturally long before it became a nation state, whereas Britain fragmented culturally shortly after it became a nation state.[333] In the following I will examine a few aspects of the German cultural synthesis, which was marked by a greater awareness of translation than there was in Britain. Perhaps, due to the fragmentation of their state, Germans were more open to foreign influence and therefore translated much more than the British did, indeed becoming the theoretical and practical masters of that craft on the continent. Their desire to unite politically may have been important, but their achievement of uniting culturally was decisive, and this cultural achievement was to a great extent based on translation.

---

[333] One can argue about dates, but I would argue that Britain is one of the first European nation states; in fact after the execution of Charles I, the interests of the state ruled and the Union of 1707 was a foundational moment for the British state.

6 ANTITHESIS

6.1 German Originality in Translation

The second "reform" of German poetic language is usually linked to the name of Friedrich Gottlieb Klopstock. Reforms would be more correct, because he introduced, or at least made permanent, several metrical innovations in the German language: the (formal) ode, the hexameter, and what has, for want of a better term, been referred to as "free rhythms".[334] To this it may be added that through the application of these metres and the theoretical discourse that developed – both his own and the critics' – Klopstock created an awareness of poetic language that was decisive for the development of German as a literary language and in effect gave it the cultural independence that enabled it to produce canonical works, world literature.

Klopstock's achievements have to be seen in context. Although Heusler has little desire to discuss his forerunners, Klopstock certainly had a few, both formally and discursively. Klopstock's reform was part of the aesthetic renewal in Germany that produced the term aesthetics and a number of new genres and movements.[335] This renewal was based on translation, a different kind from that which had been practised since Opitz, but no less nationalistic than that of Opitz himself; the roles were simply reversed, and Opitz's imitation of the French model as developed by his followers down to the great authority, Gottsched, were now interpreted as foreign and unoriginal, indeed not aesthetic.

The Swiss critics and translators Bodmer and Breitinger delivered the foundation on which Klopstock was able to build his monument. They started their journal *Discourse der Mahlern* in 1721 as a kind of translation of the English *Spectator*. Bodmer is perhaps best known for his translation of Milton's *Paradise Lost*, but theoretically the pair derived their theories from the Longinian aesthetic of the sublime filtered through ideas of foreign aestheticians, as Schmidt notes: "[E]s sind Ideen, wie sie in England Addison, in Frankreich Du Bos, in Italien Muratori und Calepio vertraten" (*Genie I* 48).[336] Bodmer's and

---

[334] See Heusler's *Deutsche Versgeschichte III* for a detailed analysis (211-254). Karl Ludwig Schneider's *Klopstock und die Erneuerung der deutschen Dichtersprache im 18. Jahrhundert* offers a good overview as well, to which I am also indebted in the following.

[335] According to Jochen Schmidt in his *Geschichte des Genie-Gedankens I*, Baumgarten not only wrote the first tract on aesthetics, *Aesthetica,* but invented the term as it is now used, for the science of beauty (8). Paul Oskar Kristeller has also discussed the significance of the concept in his essay "The Modern System of the Arts. A Study in the History of Aesthetics" (Part II, 33-42).

[336] "These are ideas that were represented by Addison in England, Du Bos in France, Muratori and Calepio in Italy. (My translation)." As Thomas Huber has shown, the disagreements between Gottsched and Bodmer, in particular, began with a dispute about

Breitinger's reliance on this new aesthetic, a current that arguably undermined neo-classicist aesthetics, led to their break with the critical sage of the first part of the eighteenth century in Germany, Johann Christoph Gottsched.[337]

Gottsched was the neo-classical authority in Germany in the first part of the eighteenth century. He is commonly described as the last true follower of Opitz and his reform, in the sense that Gottsched advocated the French Alexandrine metre with rhyme and had a puristic opinion of language that demanded, for example, fluent translation and clarity of expression. He and the Swiss were not much at variance in the twenties and thirties and both used the same model for their journals. In a way, Gottsched became the German Boileau, through his numerous publications on language and poetics, even more so when one considers that he was the conservative party in a German *querelle* between himself and the Swiss, who later were joined by Klopstock and poets and translators like Pyra, Haller and Lange.

The argument in Germany was of course different from the French *querelle*, if related. It was also initiated by translation and to a great extent about the translation of form. Gottsched's preferences on form have been stated, although he did publish hexameter verses as example in his *Critische Dichtkunst* (1729), hexameters that, according to Heusler, were better than what Klopstock published later (*Versgeschichte III* 247).[338] Bodmer and Breitinger, on the other hand, detested rhyme and had, as early as 1721, pointed out how harmful rhyme could be in poetry translation (Fränzel 22).

What began as a difference over aesthetic attitudes in poetics soon expanded into a full-blown controversy which became highly polemic and personal. The difference between the two camps was simple; Gottsched and his followers demanded rhyme, prosaic clarity and restraint, whereas the Swiss and their followers stood for unrhymed verse, sublimity and a poetic language that differed from prose. This argument, in fact, shows concretely how Boileau's standard translation of Longinus could lead to opinions diametrically opposed to those of neo-classicism.

---

[337] the latter's Milton translation (36-45). See also Anneliese Senger's version of the argument in *Deutsche Übersetzungstheorie im 18. Jahrhundert* (59-75).

It is an irony worth noting that the French neo-classical aesthetic, despite all references to reason (which Hume was also fond of), is in itself quite sensationalist and empirical, in key with Aristotle's philosophy. The new aesthetic of the sublime, translated into being by Boileau, which competed with traditional neo-classicism in the eighteenth century was, in turn, taken up by neo-platonists such as Shaftesbury, from there to its greatest heights by empiricists like Burke in Britain and finally driven by the rationalist elements of innate ideas in Herder's and Kant's thought in Germany.

[338] *Critische Dichtkunst* was Gottsched's most important publication and it went into four editions in his lifetime. He was not amused when Breitinger published a tract in two volumes with the same title in 1740, an obvious claim to having superseded Gottsched's work.

Gottsched, who, in his lifetime, was a critic of Johnsonian proportions (and opinions), lost the battle against the new, partly due to his formidable opponents and partly due to his absolutely inflexible stance (even Johnson was more flexible, as his Shakespeare edition and grudging acceptance of Milton show).

The aesthetic argument revolved partly around the question of who was the better patriot. Although the Swiss Bodmer and Breitinger were not so preoccupied with being "Deutsch" at the beginning of their careers in the twenties and early thirties of the eighteenth century, and were not that much at variance with Gottsched at the time, they too started playing nationalist cards in the polemics that ensued between them and the Gottsched camp.[339] Walter Fränzel has described the debate in his *Geschichte des Übersetzens im 18. Jahrhundert* (1914) and a few of his points are worth noting. The first is the difference in attitude towards both original texts and *native* language. Gottsched's perspective was the standard Ciceronian view that one should concentrate on producing an elegant and fluent translation which adhered to established norms within the language, rhyme and pure German included. Bodmer and Breitinger went for the original text and a special poetic language, without rhyme like the classics, in effect anticipating the early Romantics in their translational purism.

Both Gottsched and the Swiss appealed to their nation in their arguments, which is no contradiction, but confirms the closeness of translation and national literature, particularly when there is a need to develop a national literature. Gottsched's appeals are more didactic and rational, with the clarity and fluency of the translation in view, whereas Bodmer and Breitinger rely on the Longinian tradition of achieving excellence through language, with the original in view. In both cases there is a feeling of competition with the original, and the solutions lead to different kinds of mimesis, whereby the mimetic moment is always defined by a view towards language. It is a question of how language and form can be applied to transport a foreign original into the native language and at the same time achieve the same level of excellence achieved by the original text. The traditional method of fluency relies on established forms and tropes in the native language, which must be elegantly put together to achieve this goal of making foreign content native. The method that seeks the original relies on using the forms and tropes of the foreign language to achieve the same excellence as the foreign author, to make the foreign genre native. Both methods have an element of competition, and the differences – between the original and the translation and between the different methods of translation – are defined through language.

---

[339]   Bodmer was professor of "Vaterländische Geschichte" in Zürich from 1731-1775. Despite being Swiss, Bodmer obviously sees himself as a citizen in a German republic of letters.

The second point I want to develop from Fränzel's work is the way in which Bodmer and Breitinger come to their views on translation. The work that shows the national implications of their attitude is Bodmer's history of German literature, the writing of which in the 1730s was not only an original but also a highly patriotic act. He opens *Charakter der Teutschen Gedichte* with the claim: "Auch Deutsche können sich auf den Parnassus schwingen" (quoted in Fränzel 17). He also discusses translations in the history of German literature, which at the time was nothing extraordinary. But as Fränzel emphasizes, it is most important to remember that the Swiss also saw translation as an art that had a particular goal: "Wer recht übersetzen will, muß vornehmlich den Geist dessen haben, den er übersetzt," claims Bodmer. Fränzel interprets this as a new moment in the ideal of faithfulness, taking account of the individuality of the author (52). He is of the opinion that this idea might have come from Dryden's preface to the *Sylvæ,* where he says "there yet remains a harder task; and 'tis a secret of which few translators have sufficiently thought [...] that is maintaining the Character of an Author" (Dryden, *Essays* 163).

It was, however, the national character and its maintenance that proved decisive in the battle between Gottsched and the Swiss critics. When the French lecturer Mauvillon, stationed in Braunschweig, published his *Lettres Françoises et Germaniques* in 1740, German literature was awakened from its provincialism. This critique can be seen in comparison with two other famous works in French, those of the Prussian king Friedrich II and Mme de Staël, the latter of which denotes the new paradigm of German literature in the early nineteenth century. Mauvillon's critique was twofold: first, no German author had ever been translated into other languages, so Germans had not contributed to learning and taste; and second – and worse – German poets hardly wrote anything original, translating most of their material.[340]

According to Fränzel, Gottsched, who himself had complained of the lack of an original German author, reacted with his *Deutsche Schaubühne,* because Mauvillon had attacked German theatre particularly (64). But he was implicitly blamed for the dire situation, because he had been the leading critic during the past decade or two. Bodmer and Breitinger felt justified in their translational aesthetic and claimed in true Enlightenment spirit that they would continue to publish all authors, translated or not. But they stopped translating themselves and started publishing the German "Minnesinger" and other things medieval. Gottsched also published a translation of *Reineke Fuchs* in 1752, so he seems to have remembered the formerly despised Middle Ages, too.

---

[340] There is of course an inherent contradiction in Mauvillon's thought, which may be based on the fact that the French themselves translated little apart from the classics; in the seventeenth century the total of English books translated into French was five! (von Stackelberg 17).

But what was missing was an original author, an author the "others" would translate! The appearance of Klopstock ensured the Swiss their ideological victory over Gottsched, whose criticisms of the *Messias*, justified though they may have been technically, simply sounded reactionary.[341] With Klopstock, the craft of translation also became less important, and he and his contemporaries in all camps started criticising translators and translation.

This was in essence a national aesthetical debate after the shock of Mauvillon's essay. Gottsched for example complained about "Übersetzungssucht" in 1741, but Fränzel thinks he was only attacking the Shakespeare translations of the Prussian diplomat von Borck, who had just published his translation of *Julius Caesar* (72). Although it was in Alexandrines in line with Gottsched's preference he of course rejected the aesthetic model, and this marked the beginning of the long German discussion and polemics on Shakespeare, which went so far that the act of translating Shakespeare became a literary event of national importance and Shakespeare the literary paradigm that German national literature followed. As we shall see, Shakespeare in effect ghost-wrote the spirit of German national literature. The well-known German critic Friedrich Gundolf puts it thus:

> Schon jetzt war Shakespeare – und dies ist das wichtigste bei der an die Borcksche Übersetzung sich anknüpfenden Polemik – kein einzelner Autor mehr, den man begrüßen oder ablehnen konnte: er ward allmählich immer deutlicher das Feldgeschrei für verschiedene ästhetische Parteien der deutschen Literatur, der Kampf um ihn ward zu einer Prinzipienfrage betreffend Form und Gesetze der Schaubühne (*Shakespeare* 105).[342]

The Shakespearean controversies that ensued were, however, not the only debate of principle in poetics, translation and nationality; Klopstock's reform also meant a new paradigm in German poetics, and, in addition, the German language itself. This debate revolved around the questions of rhyme and rhythm of course, but also problems like word order, lexical innovation and borrowing. It was essentially a translational debate as well, in the problems dealt with and in

---

[341] Indeed, Heusler seems to have some problems with Klopstock, whose achievement he certainly acknowledges, but with an aftertaste of doubt. He does not define Klopstock's "reform" as a break with the past, as he does in Opitz's case; he is not convinced by Klopstock's theory of "verse feet", and he is certainly not impressed by the free verses, whose definition as *verses* he is inclined to doubt. Heusler was of course a metrical "purist" with a preference for "Germanic" metres.

[342] "Shakespeare was alredy by then – and this is important in view of the polemical debate about Borck's translation – not simply an author one could welcome or reject: he became slowly but clearly the war cry of several aesthetical camps of German literature, the battle around him became a question of the principles of the forms and rules of the stage."

the introduction of the foreign forms. The best evidence for the translational movement in Klopstock's adoption of hexameter is the fact that he attempted first to write his *Messias* in prose, not so much in an attempt to get away from the hegemonic Alexandrine metre, but rather to find a usable version of the Greek metre for the German language.[343] As Klopstock put it himself in his essay "Von der Sprache der Poesie" (1758):

> Es scheint mir, daß eine von ihren guten Eigenschaften eine gewisse Biegsamkeit sei, etwas von dem Tone andrer Sprachen anzunehmen. Derjenige würde mich falsch erklären, der glaubte, daß ich ihrem Originalcharakter hierdurch etwas vergeben wollte. Sie könnte vielleicht mehr geben, als sie nimmt. Sie ist, wie die Nation, die sie spricht. Sie denkt selbst, und bringt die Gedanken andrer zur Reife. Man wird mir also die Gerechtigkeit widerfahren lassen, und von mir glauben, daß sie einige angenehme, oder stark gezeichnete Züge der Alten und Ausländer entlehnen möge, um sich vollends zu bilden, daß ich weit entfernt bin, mich dadurch für diejenige sklavische Nachahmung zu erklären, welche die Hälfte Deutschlands angesteckt zu haben scheint, und die es noch dahin bringen kann, daß die Ausländer glauben werden, die Deutschen am richtigsten von andern Nationen zu unterscheiden, wenn sie dieselben Nachahmer nennen (*Werke* 1026).[344]

The compromises Klopstock made between the demands of the language and the metre also show a typical translational transformation, and, in fact, made it possible for him to go in the direction of free verse; such a move would have been unthinkable from the traditional Alexandrines, or indeed the alternating blank verse. What is most important, however, is that Klopstock managed to produce an original in the German language formed by an aesthetic that could not be refuted by neo-classicism, because it used precisely the same foundational construct, the authority of the ancients. The difference was really a question of translational method.

Despite the harsh criticisms from the Gottsched camp, Klopstock's reform had wide-ranging consequences that went well beyond the metrical question; the

---

[343] Heusler says Klopstock's initial hesitation was due to the warnings of his (and Lessing's) teacher in Leipzig, Professor Christ (*Versgeschichte III* 248).

[344] "It appears to me that one of the better qualities of a language is a certain flexibility, the ability to pick up some of the tone of other languages. Anyone, who would think that by saying this, I would be prepared to sacrifice some of its original character, would interpret my words wrongly. It could even give more than it takes. It is like the nation that speaks it. It thinks for itself and matures the thoughts of others. One should also do me the justice of believing my opinion that it is able to adopt certain agreeable, or clearly marked features of the ancients and foreigners to become fully educated, without thinking that I subscribe to the slavish imitation with which half of Germany seems to have infected itself, and even goes so far as to think that foreigners will correctly distinguish Germans from other nations when they refer to them as imitators" (my attempted translation).

language had been released from its standardised fetters and could go into many directions. One could even speculate as to whether this release of language may have been decisive for the use of blank verse in German theatre. On the other hand, Klopstock's hexameters did not become the A and Ω for the young enthusiasts who followed him. They were more nationally oriented, as Klopstock himself became, and in the wake of the debate on Shakespeare they rather followed the "North-South" paradigm, which was developed in aesthetic discourse and which proved to be decisive in the conception of the national and the original in the West.

In the following sections I want to follow the development of Klopstock's reform as it forked into two paradigms: first, the construction of northern antiquity and hence roots for Germanic history and literature; and second, the primary element of a classicism that developed into what has been termed metrical rigourism in poetic translation and original production, examples of which are best seen in Voss' Homeric translation, Goethe's hexameter poetry and Hölderlin's *Vollendung* of the process.

6.1.1 Klopstock the Bard

The name of "Klopstock" needed only to be mentioned in Goethe's *Werther* and the tears started streaming (*Werke 6* 27). Since this happened at the ball at which Lotte told Werther of her Albert, the tears may have had less to do with the poet than the sublime unity of feeling in the face of the impossible.[345] But although the influence of Klopstock on the age of sensibility in Germany is a subject well worth researching, Klopstock's influence on German poetics and nationalism is more important in our context. I use the terms poetics and nationalism, because throughout the eighteenth century in Germany, aesthetics and poetics were the channels of national and bourgeois feeling and thought.

As we have seen, Klopstock's poetry landed on fertile ground when he published the first books of his *Messias* in 1748. But Klopstock wrote not only the *Messias,* but a number of other texts as well. He wrote three biblical dramas (*Der Tod Adams,* 1757; *Salomo,* 1764; *David,* 1772) and three "Bardiete" on the national mythical hero Hermann (Arminius) (*Hermanns Schlacht,* 1769; *Hermann und die Fürsten,* 1784; *Hermanns Tod,* 1787). The so-called *Geistliche Lieder* were published in 1757 and 1769, and the first author's edition of his odes was published in 1771.

The titles themselves show very well that religion and nation went hand in hand in Klopstock's poetry, and it is clear from his odes as well that the "Lehrling der Griechen" was a man with a mission in a dual sense. His artistry also developed considerably, and it might be claimed that the religious had to make way for the national, particularly after he came into contact with Mallet's

---

[345]   It is the ode "Frühlingsfeier" according to Trunz (*Werke 6* 574).

work and all the more after the publication of *Ossian*. It was in the 1760s that Klopstock changed the mythological content of his odes from the ancient Greek to the Nordic, an act that since Goethe's judgement in *Dichtung und Wahrheit* has generally been seen as a mistake in German criticism (a demonstration of Goethe's infallibility).

The fact that scholars rarely challenge this assertion is perhaps evidence of their fallibility and inability to move beyond the classical aesthetic that accepts only what has been canonised through use and education. It is the classical demand for clarity that forbids all obscurity. Klopstock's changes to his own poetry must be seen as legitimate, however. After all, they appeared in the first authorised edition of his odes and can hardly be seen as a kind of eccentricity. Furthermore, Klopstock did not make the changes simply for ideological reasons, but grounded them firmly in his aesthetic of movement in language.

Klopstock began "translating" the Greek mythological figures in his odes after reading Mallet, Ossian and Percy, but this act was not at all as simple as it might at first seem, because Klopstock did not change the poems much. He sought and found equivalences in two different religious systems and simultaneously raised the unknown system to the level of the known one. For comparison I will quote the first three stanzas from "Auf meine Freunde" (1748) and "Wingolf" (1767) in columns:

Auf meine Freunde	Wingolf
Wie *Hebe*, kühn und jugendlich ungestüm,	Wie *Gna* im Fluge, jugendlich ungestüm,
Wie mit dem *goldnen Köcher Latonens Sohn*,	Und stolz, als reichten mir aus *Iduna's Gold*
Unsterblich, sing ich meine Freunde	*Die Götter*, sing' ich meine Freunde
Feyrend in *mächtigen Dithyramben*.	Feyrend in *kühnerem Bardenliebe*.
Wilst du zu Strophen werden, o *Lied*? oder	Willst du zu Strophen werden, o *Haingesang*?
Unterwürfig Pindars Gesängen gleich,	Willst du *gesezlos, Ossians Schwunge* gleich,
Gleich *Zeus* erhabnem trucknem Sohne,	gleich *Ullers* Tanz auf Meerkrystalle,
Frey aus der schaffenden Sel enttaumeln?	Frey aus der Seele des Dichters schweben?
Die Waßer Hebrus wälzten sich adlerschnell	Die Wasser Hebrus wälzten mit Adlereil
Mit *Orpheus Leyer*, welche die Hayne zwang	Des *Celten Leyer*, welche die Wälder zwang,
Daß sie ihr folgten, die die Felsen	Daß sie ihr folgten, die den Felsen
Taumeln, und himmelab wandeln lehrte;	Taumeln, und wandeln aus Wolken lehrte.
(*Oden* 8, my emphasis).	(*Oden* 9, my emphasis).

The title is not exactly translated; instead of the simple greeting it has become "Wingolf", a place of gods and afterlife described in the *Edda*, which Klopstock uses as an equivalent for Elysium later on in the ode. The other equivalences are plain to see: "Gna" for "Hebe", "Iduna's Gold" for "Latonens Sohn" and so on. Ossian is equivalent with Pindar and Ullus (Odin) with Zeus and the whole ode, along with others in the same style, makes the translational movement more than evident.[346]

This does not mean that Klopstock simply exchanged words. Very much like a translator he seeks an adequate relation between the concepts. Lines two and three in the first stanza provide a good example. Latone is the Roman name of Leto, a Titan who was the mother of Apollo, the god of music and harmony, the leader of the muses. As a figure he commonly stands for poetry. Idun, on the other hand, is the wife of Bragi, a god of poetry in the *Edda* (ch. 25). But this is not all, for her "Gold" refers to her apples which kept the Gods forever young. That, in turn, enables Klopstock to eliminate "unsterblich" in the third line and make the mythological reference a true metaphor instead of a simile. Klopstock's critics may find this kind of translation unacceptable, but the ability to understand it is more a question of educational background, as Hegel was later to point out (cf. below).

Klopstock also wrote original odes wherein he uses Nordic mythology with both ideological and poetical intent. In "Unsre Sprache" he deliberately puts the Greek and Nordic sources (including Ossian) on the same level: "Voll Gedanken auf der Stirne höret' ihn Apoll,/Und sprach nicht! und gelehnt auf die Harfe Walhalls/Stellt sich vor Apollo Bragor hin,/Und lächelt und schweiget, und zürnet nicht auf ihn" (*Oden* 201).

The ode that perhaps best describes his desire for the movement of language in poetry is "Die Kunst Tialfs", an ode that briefly bore the working title "Eisode", a reference to one of Klopstock's favourite sports, ice skating. As a matter of fact, Klopstock was fascinated by activities such as riding, skating and dancing and used them metaphorically in his poetry as well, to express the movement of language physically. In "Die Kunst Tialfs" he alludes to a famous competition in Nordic mythology, in which the god Þór was tricked by the rascal Loki in several "sports", one of which consisted in letting two of their servants, Þjálfi (Tialf) and Hugi, run a race against each other. Fast as he can run, Þjálfi loses three times to Hugi, which is no wonder as Loki later explains, because Hugi is Loki's thought and no one can beat the speed of thought.[347]

Klopstock's use of Nordic mythology in his odes was, therefore, by no means an arbitrary replacement of names and for him personally it was more than a minor change in attitude; after all, he began his career as a "Lehrling der

---

[346] The difference in spelling comes from the 1889 edition and apparently follows Klopstock's own changes.

[347] The competition is described in ch. 46 of the *Edda*. For an English version, see Kevin Crossley-Holland (80-94). There are several German translations of the Edda, an accessible rewriting is Rainer Tetzner's conspicuously titled *Germanische Göttersagen* (120-132).

Griechen". The reason for the change has been noted. Klopstock even expressly said in his correspondence with Denis, the German translator of *Ossian*, that he loved Ossian so much that he preferred him to some of the Greeks (*Briefe* 9). It also appears that it was *Ossian* that caused Klopstock to take this step of changing the mythology in some of his odes. In a letter to Denis in September 1767 he wrote:

> Wie weit sind Sie mit Ossian? Ich habe Ihre Übersetzungen noch nicht mit Macpherson verglichen. Ossians Werke sind wahre Meisterstücke. Wenn wir einen solchen Barden fänden! Es wird mir ganz warm bey diesem Wunsche. – Ich hatte in einigen meiner ältern Oden griechische Mythologie, ich habe sie herausgeworfen, und sowohl in diese als in einige neuere die Mythologie unsrer Vorfahren gebracht (*Briefe V-I* 24).[348]

Klopstock's decision is obviously related to his reading of *Ossian* and realisation of the need for a similar epic and bard in the native language, a desire felt by literary nationalists all over Europe for decades to come.

6.1.2 From Storm and Stress to Rigourism

The young Klospstockian enthusiasts who came of age in the 1760s did not hesitate to take a kind of northern orientation in their literary studies, by following Lessing's appeal to use Shakespeare's art as a model, by studying the Norse heritage and by reading the *Poems of Ossian*. All three elements are present, for example, in Herder's essays in *Von deutscher Art und Kunst*. Earlier, Gerstenberg had taken up these themes in his journal *Briefe über Merkwürdigkeiten der Litteratur* (1766-1767), particularly Percy's *Reliques* and *Ossian,* the latter of which he did not think authentic, due to the polemical article by the Irishman John O'Brien under the pseudonym of M. de. C. in the French *Journal des Sçavans* in 1764 (Leersen 400). Gerstenberg was also aware of Warton's work on Spenser. In Germany Gerstenberg represents an early "Norse" follower in line with Percy's model, a route which neither Klopstock nor Herder took.

The younger generation was not so preoccupied with history at that stage, anyway, but much more with poetic language as the native language of humanity.[349] This notion was behind their enthusiasm for Ossian *and* Homer. When Goethe made his first attempts to translate Ossianic poetry from the Gaelic in 1771 he was not so interested in the content as the sound and word order of the

---

[348] "How is your Ossian doing? I have not yet compared your translation with Macpherson. Ossian's works are true masterpieces. If we could find such a bard! I feel quite warm from this wish. – In few of my older odes I made use of Greek mythology, I threw them out and put into these and some of the new ones the mythology of our forefathers" (my translation).

[349] These ideas were derived from Hamann and Blackwell.

poetry.[350] Using only two dictionaries (by Edward Lhuyd and John O'Brien), Goethe attempted a literal and phonetic translation, somewhat Klopstockian in places: "Überm Adler-Aug der Sonn am Himmel/Weit nach Lara dem Fluss,/Wälzen düster-Nebel so dunckl' und tief./Wie trüb-Schild starck rollt im Nebel. Gehüllet siebenmal, der Mond der Nacht".

In his dissertation, *Ossian und Goethe,* Gustav König notes that these lines have no poetical value, since they represent only a philological translation prepared for Herder, who indeed made use of them for his collection of folk songs *Stimmen der Völker in Liedern* (31-32). König may be right, but there is still the struggle with language and rhythms that may have proved fruitful for Goethe's free verse hymns, as König himself attests later by referring to original English lines from *Ossian* (38-39). As a matter of fact, König' dissertation shows well that many images, lunar and misty, recurred in Goethe's poetry into his old age.[351]

Goethe's translations also exhibit a new attitude towards translation. Ironically, *The Poems of Ossian* ushered in an era of faithful translation in Germany that reached its pinnacles in Voss' translations of Homer and Schlegel's of Shakespeare (Stackelberg 14). The translations of texts, forms and hybrids took on a new dimension, and it may be argued that the synthesis of Klopstock's reform through translation of form (hexameter, ode measures), innovation (free rhythms) and foreign influence (particularly of the paradigmatic texts of Macpherson, Percy and Shakespeare) led to three of the most important aesthetic movements of German literature: *Sturm und Drang, Weimarer Klassik* and *Frühromantik.* All three were certainly strongly influenced and, in a way, defined through translation.

In the end, the *Sturm und Drang* went too far for Klopstock himself (as indeed for Lessing), not only morally, but also aesthetically.[352] This was already apparent in Herder's judgement of Denis' translation of *Ossian.* Denis had translated the measured prose into Klopstockian hexameters and Herder corrected the translation in a letter to his fiancée, Carolina Flachsland, in October 1770, before he had set eyes on Macpherson's text! (*Briefe 1* 273-276). His version is actually closer to Macpherson's measured prose than Denis' hexameters.[353] But although he applies a version of Klopstock's free rhythms or verse in his "trans-

---

[350]   I am indebted here and in the following to Catríona Ó Dochartaigh's paper "Goethe's translations from Macpherson's Scottish Gaelic" which she gave at the James Macpherson Bicentenary conference in Oxford.

[351]   An example might be "Dem aufgehenden Vollmonde" dated by Goethe himself August 25, 1828 (*Werke 1* 391).

[352]   Klopstock's break with Goethe was due to moral indignation at the latter's purported behaviour; Klopstock scolded Goethe in a letter and Goethe answered with a rebuke.

[353]   I owe this observation to Prof. A.F. Kelletat.

lation", earlier in the letter he had engaged in a comparison which deemed Klopstock a lesser poet than Ossian (270).

All of a sudden, Klopstock had become a kind of Gottsched, although he had delivered all the metrical premises the young geniuses needed for their revolt. Klopstock remained of course a major model for young poets and he was worshipped by the "Göttinger Hain" (1772) which included members such as Johann Heinrich Voss and Ludwig Christoph Heinrich Hölty.[354] But Klopstock's reform went in two aesthetic directions. One is represented by what may be referred to as the genius movement which adopted his free rhythms and developed them, and the other by a more metrically conservative group including translators like Denis and Voss. These were of course not two hostile camps like Gottsched and the Swiss, but their bodies of work exhibit subtle metrical differences that express the competitive spirit of the time.

One example is the rise of blank verse, which Klopstock was not particularly fond of; he rejected its use for epic poetry as early as 1755, in his "Von der Nachahmung des griechischen Silbenmaßes im Deutschen" (*Werke* 1045). He was not initially averse to its use in drama and employed it himself for his biblical *Salomo* in 1764, but his reservations were reinforced later. Nonetheless, blank verse made its way into the German language and although Lessing was not the first to use it, critics often attribute its successful introduction to him (Heusler, *Versgeschichte III* 172-173). In the field of epic poetry, Bürger experimented with blank verse in his translation of the sixth book of the *Iliad* and sent it to Wieland for publication in his *Teutscher Merkur*. Wieland's positive answer shows the competing metrical attitudes in a nutshell:

Dieser Tage stritten Göthe und ich mit einem enthusiastischem Anbeter des *Griechischen* Homers über das Sylbenmaas, das Sie zu ihrer Übersetzung gewählt haben. Er bestand darauf, der Hexameter würde besser gewesen seyn; *wir*, Sie hätten Recht gehabt den Jamben vorzuziehen. [...]
Wir behaupten, Homers Versification verliehre in jeder Übersetzung nothwendig, würde aber in teutschen Hexametern noch weit mehr verliehren als im Jambischen Vers, der unsrer Meynung nach, das ächte, alte natürliche, heroische Metrum unsrer Sprache ist... (Grumach 416, emphasis in original text).[355]

---

[354]   Names which, perhaps, also stand for the two mainstreams in German letters at the time.

[355]   "Goethe and I have been arguing with an enthusiastic worshipper of the *Greek* Homer about the metre you have chosen for your translation. He insisted that the hexameter would be better; *we* claim that you were right in preferring iambs. [...] We insist Homer's versification would necessarily lose somehting in any translation, but that it would lose even more in German hexameter than iambic verse, which is, in our opinion, the old, natural and heroic metre of our language." (my translation).

The nationalistic or, if you like, patriotic strain that runs through the discourse here is based on the metrical decision; it is the question of a *German* Homer that is being decided. This is even more obvious earlier on in the same letter:

> Dies würde sogleich im Aprilmonat, der izt gedruckt wird, geschehen seyn, wenn Göthe nicht gewünscht hätte das Manuscript vorher genauer mit dem Original zu vergleichen, und (wie ich vermuthe) nach Ihrem Verlangen, hier oder da eine Kleinigkeit zu ändern; z. Ex. ein ehrliches obsoletes Wort an schiklicher Stelle anzubringen und dergl. Wir sind izt stark daran, etliche hundert dergleichen Wörter, so Gott will, wieder ins Leben zu ruffen; und wir haben große Freude darüber, daß Sie ein Gleiches in Ihrem Homer thun. Wie könnten Sie auch ohne dies einen teutschen Homer geben? (415-416).[356]

In addition to the metrical Germanisation of the *Iliad*, there is a lexical one, a conscious application of archaisms that give the poetic language a special position and a national flavour, strategies also introduced by Klopstock in his original poetry and an important part of his poetics. Furthermore, the operation described here by Wieland is comparable to Klopstock's exchange of Greek mythology for Norse; it may be executed on a different level, that of the abstract lexis, but the motivation is very much the same. This is an excellent illustration of how literary nationalism works within a translational movement; it needs translation on some level – be it of form, content, in the manipulation of the lexis, or somewhere in between all of these – so that it can refer to a model *and* change it for its own purposes at the same time.

The German hexameter survived this "onslaught", however; Bürger did not translate the whole *Iliad,* despite the encouragement he got from Wieland. The translator and poet Voss, on the other hand, translated both the *Iliad* and the *Odyssey* in hexameters, and, no less important, also wrote the idyll *Luise* in hexameter.

Voss started his career very much under the influence of Klopstock. As a member of the "Göttinger Hain" he worshipped the author of *Messias* and the recently published *Oden.* At the same time, he and his friends, particularly Hölty, were absorbing the Nordic and medieval influences that were then in fashion. The early ode by Voss, "Schwergereimte Ode", combines all these influences in two stanzas:

---

[356] "This would be printed in this month of April, if Goethe would not have asked to be able to compare the manuscript with the original and make slight changes here and there according to your desire (as I assume); e.g. putting in an honest, obsolete word at an appropriate place and so on. We are very much occupied with calling back to life, if God wills, hundreds of such words; and we are very pleased to see that you do the same in your Homer. How could you otherwise give us a German Homer?" (my translation).

Was stehst du, Spötter, da und pausbackst
Schwerreimendes Gereimel her?
Gib acht, daß man dich nicht hinausbaxt,
Mit deinen Reimen, leicht und schwer.

Unmutig blickt auf deinen Jokus
Apollons stolzer Tubaist,
Und: fort mit solchem Hokuspokus!
Brummt düster Wodans Urhornist (*Werke* 180).

The attack on rhyme is inherited from Bodmer and Breitinger, and of course from Klopstock, and the absolute levelling of Apollo and Wodan is a sign of the times.

As young poets, Voss and Hölty wrote odes and ballads, but they also started translating. Hölty worked on a translation of Shaftesbury's *Characteristics* until his early death in 1776 and his friend Voss finished it. As has been noted, Voss also translated Thomas Blackwell's *Enquiry into the Life and Writings of Homer*, a translation that must have been a decisive experience for the future translator of the Homeric epics.

As a translator of Homer, Voss took the translation of text and form to new heights; his translation of form has been called metrical rigourism.[357] This rigourism, which took on a quasi-religious quality in constant revisions that were primarily aimed at the prosody of the poems, is a sign of the importance of metre in translation, and for some reason the hexameter was one of the most important metres in German poetry during the last decade of the eighteenth century. Goethe's work during these years is a good example of this and well worth an overview.

In his *Campagne in Frankreich* Goethe describes his reasons for writing the epic poem *Reineke Fuchs*. After returning from the military campaign and before the background of the trial of Louis XVI, he felt a need to forget the world and luckily found the medieval poem which Gottsched had translated in 1752 (*Werke 10* 359). As Trunz delineates, Herder had been working on an essay on the poem and Goethe began in January 1793 to translate the work on the basis of Gottsched's version (*Werke 2* 718). In *Campagne in Frankreich,* Goethe

---

[357]   Alfred Kelletat describes the publication of Voss's translation of the Odyssey thus: "Doch Ende 1781 endlich erscheint "Homers Odüßee, übersezt von Johann Heinrich Voß, Hamburg, auf Kosten des Verfassers, 1781. Sie brach sich Bahn durch alle ihre Mitbewerber und wurde, trotz vereinzelter, alteingewurzelter, oft persönlicher Ressentiments als das anerkannt, was sie war: die deutsche Odyssee" ["However, at the end of 1781 Homer's Odyssey appeared at last, translated by Johann Heinrich Voss. It left all its competitors behind and became, despite occasional and deep seated personal resentments, what it was, the German Odyssey"] (61, my translation, emphasis in original text).

himself not only presents the reasons for his decision but provides the reader with a little metrical history at the same time; the passage is worth quoting at length:

> Um nun das köstliche Werk recht innig zu genießen, begann ich alsobald eine treue Nachbildung; solche jedoch in Hexametern zu unternehmen, war ich folgenderweise veranlaßt.
>
> Schon seit vielen Jahren schrieb man in Deutschland nach Klopstocks Einleitung sehr läßliche Hexameter; Voß, indem er sich wohl auch dergleichen bediente, ließ doch hie und da merken, daß man sie besser machen könne, ja er schonte sogar seine eigenen vom Publikum gut aufgenommenen Arbeiten und Übersetzungen nicht. Ich hätte das gar gern auch gelernt, allein es wollte mir nicht glücken. Herder und Wieland waren in diesem Punkte Latitudinarier, und man durfte der Vossischen Bemühungen, wie sie auch nach und nach strenger und für den Augenblick ungelenk erschienen, kaum Erwähnung tun. Das Publikum selbst schätzte längere Zeit die Vossischen früheren Arbeiten, als geläufiger, über die späteren; ich aber hatte zu Voß, dessen Ernst man nicht verkennen konnte, immer ein stilles Vertrauen und wäre in jüngeren Tagen oder anderen Verhältnissen, wohl einmal nach Eutin gereist, um das Geheimnis zu erfahren; denn er, aus einer zu ehrenden Pietät für Klopstock, wollte, solange der würdige, allgefeierte Dichter lebte, ihm nicht geradezu ins Gesicht sagen: daß man in der deutschen Rhythmik eine striktere Observanz einführen müsse, wenn sie irgend gegründet werden solle (*Werke 10* 360).[358]

Goethe wrote *Reineke Fuchs* in hexameter to learn how to write like Voss, and because Voss' theory was like "sibyllinische Blätter" to him, he chose the process of practice. For this purpose he took up a medieval German epic and translated it into the Greek form. This little "exercise", as Goethe describes it, was received very well indeed. Herder wrote to the patriotic poet Gleim that "Goethe hat eine Epopöe, die erste und größte Epopöe deutscher Nation, ja aller Nationen seit Homer, und sehr glücklich versifiziert. Raten sie welche?" (quoted

---

[358] To be able enjoy the exquisite work deeply, I started to make a faithful reproduction, but the reason for my doing it in hexameter, was as follows.

People had since Klopstock been writing very pardonable hexameter verses; Voss, who also used this metre, hinted, however, here and there that they could be improved, yes, he did not even spare his own very well received attempts and translations. I would have liked to learn this too, but I was unable produce it. Herder and Wieland were latitudinarians on this point, and one could hardly mention Voss' work, which became more and more strict, and, for the moment, appeared awkward. The readers had preferred Voss' earlier work to the latter; I, however, quietly kept my faith in Voss, whom I knew to be a very earnest man, and would have as a younger man travelled to Eutin to learn the secret; because he, as an almost pious follower of Klopstock, did not want, as long as the worthy and universally admired poet lived, to say it directly to him: that German rhythm needs to be observed more strictly if it is to be given any foundation" (my faithful translation).

in Goethe, *Werke 2* 712).[359] The enthusiastic comparison had up to then mostly been reserved for Ossian, but Herder's joy can hardly be ascribed to the old epic itself or Gottsched's previous translation; on the contrary, he is overjoyed primarily because of the metre. Goethe had not changed the content of the poem, as W. v. Humboldt noted, and yet he had changed everything:

> Im einzelnen hat er fast nichts abgeändert, oft dieselben Worte gelassen, aber dennoch ist das Ganze durch ihn schlechterdings etwas anderes geworden. Dasjenige nämlich, was eigentlich poetische Form daran ist, dasjenige, wodurch es zu der Phantasie des Lesers spricht und seinen ästhetischen Sinn rührt, gehört ihm ganz und ganz allein (quoted in Goethe *Werke 2* 714).[360]

Humboldt does not think much of Goethe's hexameter, so he focuses his desire for originality on the language Goethe uses, although he must have known very well how strongly the language is controlled by the metre, even if the metre is not of Vossian standards. What is clear from the reception is that what Goethe himself called "eine zwischen Übersetzung und Umarbeitung schwebende Behandlung" was interpreted as a national epic by people like Herder and a subjective work of art by Humboldt (*Werke 2* 438). The only one to express doubts was the genius who had inspired the other genius, if I may translate freely from Lessing.[361] In fact, Voss found the use of hexameter for this poem odd (714). Hans Wolf Jäger even claims Voss found the archaisation of the medieval material absurd (*Handbuch 1* 517).

Voss himself, however, had also used hexameter for his idyll *Luise,* and he decided to publish it with revisions in book form in 1795; if he was moved to do so by the positive reaction *Reineke Fuchs* had met with, *Luise* in turn moved Goethe to write an idyll, in hexameter of course. The bourgeois idyll *Hermann und Dorothea* is a good example of a translation without an original. Although Goethe merges historical material with his own experience, this is only to form the skeleton of a story which is of course his, and his alone – with the slight difference that the metre and form make it comparable to Homer. The best critique to exemplify this is A. W. Schlegel's review, "Goethes Hermann und Dorothea" which was first published in the *Allgemeine Literatur Zeitung* in December and

---

[359] "Goethe has versified, and versified very well, an epic, the first and greatest epic of the German nation, yes, of all nations since Homer. Guess which?" (my translation).

[360] "He has hardly changed anything, even left the same words, and despite this, the whole has become something absolutely different. Its actual poetic form, namely, what makes this speak to the reader's fantasy and touches his aesthetic sense, is his and his alone" (my translation).

[361] In a letter to his wife, Voss claimed that he could not read Goethe's version through (Goethe, *Werke 2* 714).

again in *Taschenbuch für 1798.*[362] To save space and time, I will cite the most important parts of the review alongside my commentary in two columns.[363]

A. W. Schlegel:	Commentary:
Obgleich dieses Gedicht seinem Inhalte nach in der uns umgebenden Welt zu Hause ist, und, unseren Sitten und Ansichten befreundet, höchst faßlich, ja vertraulich die allgemeine Teilnahme anspricht, so muß es doch, was seine dichterische Gestalt betrifft, dem Nichtkenner des Altertums als eine ganz eigene, mit nichts zu vergleichende Erscheinung auffallen, und der Freund der Griechen wird sogleich an die Erzählungsweise des alten Homerus denken (42).	This is the first sentence of the review, and it goes straight to the point; the poem is in content modern and thoroughly native, but there is a foreignness in its form that would make the poem unique to someone who does not know the ancient Greek literature. For those who do know it, Homer's narrative technique is the first parallel to draw. Trunz also quotes this sentence in his so-called Hamburger Ausgabe of Goethe's works; significantly, he does not quote the following sentence (or pages for that matter) (*Werke 2* 740).
Sollte dies nichts weiter auf sich haben als eine willkürliche Verkleidung des Sängers in eine fremde altväterliche Tracht? Sollte die Ähnlichkeit bloß in den Äußerlichkeiten des Vortrags liegen? (42).	This, the second sentence, presents a justified question given the parallel drawn in the first. Schlegel uses the opportunity to make an analysis of the production of epic form.
Die historischen Untersuchungen eines scharfsinnigen Kritikers über die Entstehung und Fortpflanzung der homerischen Gesänge, die vor kurzem die Aufmerksamkeit aller derer auf sich gezogen haben, welche Fortschritte in den Wissenschaften zu erkennen wissen, geben uns zum Glücke einen festen Punkt, wovon die künstlerische Betrachtung des Homer in einer ganz entgegengesetzten Richtung ausgehen kann (44).	This reference to the (in)famous *Prolegomena ad Homerum* by Friedrich Wolf (1795), with the thesis of a collective creation and re-creation of the Homeric epics, may go back to Thomas Blackwell (whom Voss translated), although the latter spoke of Homer as an individual. In that sense it is perhaps not a new idea, but at the same time it is a break with the ideas Hamann and Herder interpreted from the same source, which concluded that poetry is the native language of humanity.

---

362   My quotations are taken from the first volume of his critical writings and letters, *Sprache und Poetik*.
363   No translation.

Wenn die *Ilias* und *Odyssee* aus einigen großen, für sich Bestand habenden Stücken zusammengeschoben, und diese wiederum, wo Lücken blieben, durch kleinere Stellen (nicht immer zum geschicktesten) aneinandergefügt sind, so hätte man ja, indem man nur immer den wohlberechneten Bau des Ganzen anstaunte, ein fremdes Verdienst, das dem homerischen Zeitalter nicht zukommt, und nach dem Grade seiner Bildung nicht zukommen konnte, das obendrein in dem Maße gar nicht einmal vorhanden ist, für das wichtigste bei der ganzen Sache zu halten (44).

It is the often-admired structure of the epics which shows that, as a united work of art, they have been put together by a different hand than that of the composer; the significance of this is that such a structure, such a genre could not have been conceived of in primitive times, when the rhapsodies themselves were composed. Although Herder could welcome such argumentation for his ideas on Ossian, it might have devalued his primitivist ideas of poetic language. In addition, the originality of the individual poet as a creator of a genre and form had been questioned.

Auf der anderen Seite ist die epische Einheit auch teilbar; kleine Stücke der *Ilias* und *Odyssee* enthalten sie noch in sich; [...]. Weit entfernt also, daß es gewaltsamer Mittel bedurft hätte, um einzelne Rhapsodien zu größeren Ganzen zusammenzuheften, in denen Übereinstimmung und lebendiger Zusammenhang schon durch die Sage gegeben war, ist diese Leichtigkeit der Teilung und Vereinigung vielmehr eine natürliche Eigenheit der Gattung [...] (45).

Schlegel backtracks slightly with regards to the genre; what remains is the prerequisite of a high level of education for putting together an epic like the *Iliad*. His direction is obvious though: it should not be forgotten that this is a review of *Hermann und Dorothea*, even if Schlegel does not start to discuss that work until after he has stated his understanding of epic and the ways in which it can be modernised. He moves on and discusses other genres, whereby he protests that drama is simply dialogue and epic merely narrative.

Überdies ist es vergeblich, aus dem Begriff der Erzählung und des Dialogs, die höchsten Vorschriften für jene Dichtarten entwickeln

A full rejection of imitation is not surprising at this stage in time, but Schlegel's *Ersatz* is interesting. The transformative process of

---

364 This tripartite division is of course much older; putting these basic genres into systematic categories with definite *functions* is modern. Percy had already hinted at such a division in his *Reliques* with the subtitle in brackets "(Chiefly of the LYRIC kind)". J.J. Eschenburg, who translated Percy's ballads and rewrote his essays under the pseudonym Ursinus in *Balladen und Lieder altenglisher und altschottisher Dichtart* in 1777 notes this division in the second essay "Über die Liederpoesie". It is no coincidence that the "lyric" gets more attention at this point in time and by these authors; they are in the process of translating the values previously attributed to ancient lyric poetry *on* their own folk poetry. The title of Eschenburg's translation bears witness to this; the ballads and songs are ancient English and Scottish "Dichtart", with the focus on the genre.

zu wollen. Dies könnte nur in dem Fall gelingen, wenn die Kunst nichts weiter als eine leidende Nachahmung der Natur wäre, wozu man sie leider oft genug herabgewürdigt hat. Da sie aber eine selbsttätige, nach Grenzen des menschlichen Gemüts erfolgende *Umgestaltung* der Natur ist, so muß die poetische Erzählung, der poetische Dialog erst *durch das Wesen der Dichtart*, die sich beider bedient, seine Bestimmung empfangen (46, my emphasis).

reality he calls "Umgestaltung" is not a subjective moulding of that reality into a work of art, but a method that is restricted or rather defined by the essence of the genre. His detailed analysis of the genre becomes more understandable, for he is setting out the criteria with which he is going to judge *Hermann und Dorothea*. Further on, he asks whether one should compete with Homer at all and concludes that this can only be done by a reversal of common imitation (52).

Aber die Harmonie der griechischen Bildung läßt schon vermuten, daß die Poesie mit den übrigen Künsten gleichen Schritt gehalten haben wird; und die Geschichte zeigt uns, wie sie sich von leichter Fülle (epische Periode) zu energischer Einzelheit erhob (lyrische Periode) und durch innige Verschmelzung beider endlich zu harmonischer Vollständigkeit und Einheit gelangte (dramatische Periode) (53).

This tripartite division, often ascribed to Hegel, recurs in Goethe's notes to the *Divan,* but what Schlegel wants to underline here is the historical development of the major genres; for comparison he uses the common analogy of the ages of man: childhood, youth, adulthood. [364] This in turn serves to prepare considerations about the simplicity of *Hermann und Dorothea.*

In diesem Stücke wie in allem wesentlichen stimmt "Hermann und Dorothea", ungeachtet des großen Abstandes der Zeitalter, Nationalcharaktere und Sprachen erstaunens-würdig mit seinen großen Vorbildern überein.
Ein Dichter, dem es nicht darum zu tun ist, ein Studium nach der Antike zu verfertigen, sondern mit ursprünglicher Kraft national und volksmäßig zu wirken, wie es einem epischen Sänger geziemt, wird seinen Stoff nicht im klassischen Altertume suchen, noch weniger aus der Luft greifen dürfen (53).

Schlegel's judgement is by now clear. Although he goes on for pages in this vein, he has already said what Goethe's epic had achieved for him and most of their contemporaries: to bring the ancient canonised epic form into harmony with a modern national cultural concept of Germany, or as the Marxist would put it, the German bourgeoisie. This refers of course not to the nation state, which is only the utopia of national religion anyway, but to the spiritual state of the nation, which must be constructed with several ideological instruments before any dream of a nation state can be conceived of.

Even though Schlegel had judged *Hermann und Dorothea* as the perfection of a national epic, due to the brilliant combination of form and content, Goethe took his experiment to its logical conclusion and started writing his epic poem,

Achilleis.[365] In a way, this was Goethe's own third stage in the act of translation of the classics without an original. The first had been *Reineke Fuchs,* where he took an extant narrative poem and rewrote it in hexameter; the second was *Hermann und Dorothea* in which he wrote most of the narrative himself in an epic form.[366] The third stage was direct comparison with Homer himself, an epic that was to fill the gap between the *Iliad* and *Odyssey.* It is perhaps understandable that Goethe tried this, after the successes of the first two; he himself claimed in a letter to Knebel to have been thinking of the *Achilleis* since the controversy on the age of the Homeric epics, and after writing his own *Hermann und Dorothea* (*Werke 2* 760).[367] That he failed was perhaps due to the criticism of the metricians whose advice he sought, but whatever the reason, he only wrote one book of the epic before giving up. Trunz is of the opinion that this was due to his inability to master the form: "Antikisierende Verse ohne Theorie wollte er nicht schreiben, und antikisierende Verse nach der Theorie gelangen ihm nicht" (*Werke 2* 765).

There was only one German poet who was able to translate perfectly into German hexameter with or without an original, and that was Hölderlin. That he developed his ability to do this through translation has recently been demonstrated in detail in Charlie Louth's *Hölderlin and the Dynamics of Translation.* Louth comes to the conclusion regarding Hölderlin's Pindaric translation that where

---

[365] I am indebted to Prof. A.F. Kelletat's unpublished lecture on Goethe as a translator for my observations on *Achilleis.*

[366] Even to the extent of imitating Herodotus by putting the names of the nine muses above each book. Schlegel sees a modern saving of space in that act, because now long passages addressing the muses could be left out (64).

[367] That Goethe's experiments were and are understood as a way of raising the potential of German poetry and poetic language to a higher "classical" level, becomes obvious when the entries in the recent *Goethe Handbuch* (1998) are examined. Jäger says for example: "Kein Zweifel, G. hob die Reineke-Überlieferung auf ein neues ästhetisches Niveau" (514). It should also be considered that the poetry being raised to a higher level is a symbol for previously non-canonised *German* poetry. In the entry on *Hermann und Dorothea* Yahya A. Elsaghe has a section devoted to the function of the form and claims: "Das Postulat eines eh und je gegebenen >>menschlichen der Existenz<< scheint seinen Geltungsanspruch in der Synthese zu behaupten, zu der eine bürgerlich-modernes Sujet und die älteste literarische Form hier zusammenfinden, zum Zeichen aber auch einer Nähe, in der sich das deutsche Bürgertum zur altgriechischen Kultur zu sehen geneigt war. Daß die letzlich uneinholbar atavistische Form eine dennoch schon empfindliche Spannung erzeugte, lassen allerdings die Versuche vermuten,diese auf das aktuelle oder aber das archaische Moment zu reduzieren: eine Prosaauflösung des deutschen Texts (1825) respektive dessen altsprachlichen Hexameterübersetzungen, deren eine, *Arminius et Theodora* (1822), G. dem Original vorzog, weil die >>Form<< darin zu ihrem >>Ursprunge zurückgekehrt<< sei (zu Eckermann, 18.1. 1825)" (531). Goethe's own words speak volumes, if the German idiom may be translated.

there is an analogy between the Pindar translation and the ideal poem imagined in Hölderlin's poetics, the workings and movements that inform these two are not, in the end, analogous merely, but at bottom identical. They have been transferred from the poetics to the translations (127).

Or rather vice versa, I would add, for Hölderlin mastered the Greek forms not through invention but through translation.[368] At the same time he was very much aware of the need to differentiate the native, the cultural character of his nation, from that of the Greeks. One result of his Pindar translation and studies in genre may have been his conception of ultimate difference through the terms "Grundton" and "Kunstcharakter". These terms were, to be sure, used in a purely theoretical discussion on genre in a fragment entitled "Über den Unterschied der Dichtarten", but if one reads his well-known letter to Böhlendorff, written after his Pindar translation and indeed a decade of translation and theorisation on poetics, it becomes plain that Hölderlin has found his difference in equivalence, if I may invert Jakobson's central idea of translation:

> Es klingt paradox. Aber ich behaupte es noch einmal und stelle es Deiner Prüfung und Deinem Gebrauche frei: Das eigentlich Nationelle wird im Fortschritt der Bildung immer der geringere Vorzug werden. Deswegen sind die Griechen des heiligen Pathos weniger Meister, weil es ihnen angeboren war, hingegen sind sie vorzüglich in Darstellungsgabe, von Homer an, weil dieser außerordentliche Mensch seelenvoll genug war, um die abendländische *junonische Nüchternheit* für sein Apollonsreich zu erbeuten und so wahrhaft das Fremde sich anzueignen (*Werke 4* 467, emphasis in original text).[369]

It is not at all paradoxical, but original when applied to the Greeks, who so often and for so long have been seen as the originators of Western culture. But after his intense study of the Greeks and his Pindar translation, which represents yet another stage in poetic experiments with language in Germany (Klopstock and metre, Goethe and Ossian, Voss and Homer), Hölderlin comes to the conclusion that the Greeks are *not* to be imitated:

> Bei uns ist es umgekehrt. Deswegen ist's auch so gefährlich, sich die Kunstregeln einzig und allein von griechischer Vortrefflichkeit zu abstrahieren. Ich habe lange daran laboriert und weiß nun, daß außer dem, was bei den Griechen und uns das Höchste sein

---

[368] He tried Homer of course, in prose and his translation of Lucan's *Pharsalia* was apparently the first hexameter translation in German.

[369] "It sounds paradoxical. But I insist on it again and put it to your test and use: What is actually national will be less and less important with the progress of education. The Greeks are, therefore, less masters of the sacred pathos because this was innate to them, whereas, from Homer onwards, they were first rate in the art of presentation, because this unusual man was soulful enough to capture the Junoesque soberness of the Occident for his Apollonian state and truly appropriate the foreign for himself" (my translation).

muß, nämlich dem lebendigen Verhältnis und Geschick, wir nicht wohl etwas *gleich* mit ihnen haben dürfen (467, emphasis in original text).[370]

Now this is paradoxical coming from this poet, many of whose texts are within the Greek cultural sphere, with the exception of songs on the "Vaterland". But it is no arbitrary decision, nor is it a naive nationalistic assertion, but a conclusion drawn from his intense translations of the Greeks; he found the ultimate poetic difference beyond form and content and was, through that knowledge, able to synthesise the differences into his own version of poetics and poetry. Hölderlin, as Peter Szondi concludes, "überwindet den Klassizismus ohne von der Klassik sich abzuwenden" (*Hölderlin* 97) [overcame classicism without rejecting it]. This can only be done by nurturing the self with a view on the other:

> Aber das Eigene muß so gut gelernt sein wie das Fremde. Deswegen sind uns die Griechen unentbehrlich. Nur werden wir ihnen gerade in unserm Eigenen, Nationellen nicht nachkommen, weil, wie gesagt, der *freie* Gebrauch des *Eigenen* das schwerste ist (467).[371]

Goethe could have done with this advice during the late 1790s, when he made precisely this mistake by following the theory too closely and letting the burden of the foreign form stifle his creativity, he who had so often mastered, lifted, borrowed and rewritten whatever he liked. Too literal a translation of form can be just as cumbersome as *nec verbum verbo*. But then Goethe found another way out and contributed elsewhere in the German synthesis of translation and adaptation, in his highly original *West-östlicher Divan*.

And now, "so what does all of this add up to?" is the logical question. The answer was given earlier in the past century in a purple passage by one of Germany's best-known critics, Friedrich Gundolf:

> Von Lessing bis Goethe ist das Bild von Hellas mit immer dichterer Sinnlichkeit gefüllt, immer näher beschaut, betastet, umarmt worden. Hölderlin zieht es ganz in sich hinein. Symbolisch dafür ist auch die Geschichte der griechischen Versmaße in der deutschen Dichtung. Erst eine spielerische oder mechanische Nachahmung des abstrakten metrischen Hexameterschemas [...] Klopstock sucht dann dieses Schema immerhin mit einem gemäßeren pathetischen Gehalt zu füllen, aber man spürt die Lücken, bald die

---

[370] "For us the opposite is the case. It is, therefore, also very dangerous to abstract the rules of art from Greek excellence. I have laboured very long at it and now I know that, apart from that which both the Greeks and we consider most important, namely the living proportion and artistry, we should not be the *same* as they."

[371] "But one's own must be just as well studied as the foreign. The Greeks are therefore indispensable for us. We will, however, exactly in our own, national traits not be able to follow them, because, as noted, the *free* use of one's *own* is the most difficult" (my translation).

überquellenden Wülste: die griechischen Maße, unterm südlichen Himmel beim Rollen des heroischen Meeres geboren, wollten sich dem protestantisch deutschen Enthusiasmus nicht schmiegen. Goethe, dem heidnischen Wiedereroberer Roms, gehorchten sie: aber sie gehorchten doch nur. Doch die Strophen und Hexameter Hölderlins sind keine metrischen Versuche, keine erfolgreichen Nachahmungen: sie sind der völlig ursprüngliche Ausbruch der inneren Griechheit in deutscher Sprache, sie sind der angeborene Rhythmus dieser Seele, ihr unbefangener, notwendiger Ausdruck, nicht ein Zeugnis seines Könnens, sondern seines Müssens ("Archipelagus" 7-8).[372]

This is, in a nutshell, the development of the nationalistic project of raising German literature and language to the level of "Weltliteratur". It is the hard work of over half a century of translation of texts and forms, with or without each other. The poet who was able to synthesise the contradictions into a true German classical poetic language was Friedrich Hölderlin, but even if he was the only one, he certainly made use of the methods and approaches of his predecessors.

---

[372] "From Lessing to Goethe, the vision of Hellas is filled with more and more sensuality, viewed more closely, touched, embraced. Hölderlin takes it totally into himself. The history of Greek metres in German poetry symbolises this too. First a playful or mechanical imitation of the abstract metrical hexameter pattern. [...] Klopstock, at least, attempts to fill this pattern with pathos, but one can sense the gaps, sometimes the overflowing swells: the Greek metres, born under a southern sky by the rolling waves of the heroic ocean, did not want to adapt to German Protestant enthusiasm. Goethe, the pagan re-conqueror of Rome, they obeyed, but they obeyed only. But the stanzas and hexameter verses by Hölderlin are no metrical experiments, no successful imitations: they are the fully original eruption of inner Greekness in the German language, they are the innate rhythm of this soul, its uninhibited, necessary expression, not the testimony of its ability, but its destiny" (my translation).

7 SYNTHESIS

7.1 Hegel and Translation into a Canon

Hegel's synthesis of material and idea into an original work of art is essentially the same as Goethe's, and he uses Shakespeare and Goethe, as well as the Greeks, as his examples; his oppositional examples are, in the best Lessingian tradition, taken from French classicism. Jochen Schmidt has interpreted Lessing's rejection of the French as still ahistorical: "Weil Lessing noch nicht historisch denkt, reflektiert er noch nicht, daß er mit seiner Ablehnung des französischen Theaters wesentlich den Stil des 17. Jahrhunderts ablehnt, den repräsentativen Stil einer höfisch-ständischen Ordnung" (*Genie 1* 164).[373] According to Schmidt, the decisive step towards historical thought in literature is taken by Herder in his Shakespeare essay published in 1773 in *Von deutscher Art und Kunst,* the collection of essays by himself, Goethe, Frisi and Möser that is one of the most important ideological documents of the *Sturm und Drang*-period. Without denying the link between socio-historical and aesthetic disourses evident in Schmidt's phrase, it should be noted that Lessing was concentrating on the aesthetics of nation rather than class, although he never went as far as Herder, or even Goethe, in combining the two.

Before addressing the great systemiser's reformulation and, indeed, epitomisation of Lessing's, Herder's and Goethe's ideas of drama in connection with the antithetical constructs of Shakespeare and French neo-classicist drama, it is necessary to look at some of the central ideas the three developed in order to create a German national theatre,[374] worthy of inclusion in the Western canon. It has to be said that this national project certainly succeeded in the end, particularly due to the systematic application of translation without an original. For Shakespeare's texts were not the model being sought; they were not what was really to be translated. What mattered was his method of *bringing forth* national characters in national history, his way of forging national literature from native elements in a sublime native language, his sublime – "Nordic" as Herder put it – closeness to the antiquity of the Greek tragedies and at the same time the fundamental difference from the sterile French model, whose hegemony was seen in terms of nation and class, even prior to the French Revolution.

The contradiction of setting Shakespeare's originality up as a model comparable to the ancients while at the same time rejecting neo-classicist (French) models which had the same ideological thrust, not to mention the apparent con-

---

[373] "Because Lessing does not think historically yet, he does not reflect that through his rejection of French theatre, he is in essence rejecting the style of the 17th century, the representative style of courtly-class order" (my translation).

[374] I am not specifically referring to the failed experiment in Hamburg Lessing participated in. Its existence shows, however, that a project of this kind was more than conceivable.

tradiction of seeking originality through a *model,* as these German luminaries seem to be attempting to do, may be resolved if one considers their fusing of ideas of the particular and universal, which takes place primarily on the aesthetic level, whereby these ideas relate to almost all the important elements of their thought. The seeming contradiction of calling for originality by referring to Shakespeare has for example been noted by Schmidt:

> Generell enthält die Paradigmatisierung Shakespeares als „Genie" einen tiefen Widerspruch. Einerseits will man vom Nachahmungsdenken abrücken, gerade im Namen des „Genies"; andererseits aber wird ein Genie als Vorbild empfohlen: Shakespeare (*Genie 1* 166).[375]

This is to misunderstand the idea of originality as it was constructed in the eighteenth century; to put it simply, it was not about imitating Shakespeare in order to be "original", but about being original "like" Shakespeare – perhaps not very original, but something altogether different from imitation. In short, Shakespeare's approach to history, character and structure could be "translated" without losing a claim to one's own originality. This is not imitation, but translation without an original, wherein it is not the texts of the original authors that are translated, but their way of writing for their own nation.

In order to do this, the foursome of Lessing, Herder, Goethe and Hegel repeatedly deconstructed the French neo-classical constructs of the seventeenth century, particularly the interpretations of Aristotle that had made his vague notions of unity into absolute rules. French neo-classicism had developed Aristotle's and Horace's demand for probability into a notion of imitative reality and made such structural elements as the five acts into an aesthetic principle.[376] Shakespeare was the prime model for this deconstruction; he had broken all of these rules and yet he was arguably the most sublime of all. He had also used the material of English and Scottish history to an effect that could be considered equal to what the ancients had achieved, another important element that could be imitated without being imitative.

There is plenty of evidence for this theory, particularly when one follows the Shakespearean threads from Lessing through Herder and Goethe to Hegel. The first of these could be the perennial problem of the ghost in Hamlet. To represent the supernatural on stage was of course a stylistic crime in neo-classical discourse, particularly as the imitative moment had to be probable not only in itself, but also as it *appeared* on the stage. This kind of demand for visual prob-

---

[375] "The paradigm of of Shakespeare as a "genius" is, in itself, a crass contradiction. On the one hand, one wants to take leave of the idea of imitation, exactly in the name of the "genius"; on the other, a "genius" is recommended as a model: Shakespeare" (my translation).

[376] They were of course not alone in juxtaposing Shakespeare and French drama, but prominent enough to be taken as the most important representatives.

ability is comparable to mediocre film and TV-realism today, where the camera (and audiences) have problems with the fantastic, even in sci-fi genres where a pseudo-scientific explanation is often necessary to meet the demand of probability. What the four German greats did was to move this probability into the realm of the historical, traditional and spiritual. They invented a new aesthetic through the interpretation of Shakespeare (as was done in Britain), or rather through the translational synthesis of the Greeks, Shakespeare and recent British aesthetics (Shaftesbury, Blackwell, Burke, Blair), as well as recent British philosophy and historical approaches (Hume, Robertson, Warburton, Lowth, Hurd, Percy). In the process they invented nothing less than the new German nation of the nineteenth century. What became the political Frankenstein of the twentieth century may, however, have begun more modestly as a ghost, ghost-written for the German spirit desiring a body it did not have.

7.1.1 Lessing's Ghosts

Lessing uses the ghost in Hamlet brilliantly in a deconstruction of the French aesthetic, not simply by saying Shakespeare has a ghost whereas the French forbid it, but by latching on to the one recent example of a ghost in a French play, that of Ninus in Voltaire's *Semiramis*. Lessing's critique in the tenth through twelfth "Stück" (1767), as he terms them in his "Hamburgische Dramaturgie", a sort of specialised *Spectator* for drama, very deftly uses the unusual circumstance of a ghost in French drama to deconstruct the imitative preconceptions of French neo-classicism, for he begins by noting the improvement this appearence has had on a tradition that was so obsessed with *mimesis* as a kind of reality that spectators were actually on stage, a stage that was never supposed to be empty nor peopled with characters who had entered without a fully rational motivation. The irrational appearance of a ghost in Voltaire's drama, in conjunction with operatic noise and stage effects, actually managed to drive the spectators back into their seats, a development Lessing fully approves of (*Werke IV* 279-280).

This circumstance only underlines, however, his general damnation of the French neo-classical tradition, a damnation discussed in aesthetic terms that are made equivalent to a national tradition and outlook. Lessing actually uses Voltaire's ghost to satirise his Moderns' view that the French have surpassed the Ancients in drama, a view he effectively personifies in Voltaire. Having praised Voltaire's ghost for driving the spectators off the stage, Lessing uses the eleventh piece of his "Dramaturgie" to compare and contrast it with the apparitions in Shakespeare's *Hamlet*. While nominally defending Voltaire's ghost, he destroys it by applying Shakespearean categories as they were being interpreted in the primitivist version of Aristotelian/Longinian poetics (i.e., by focusing on "nature" and "sympathy" as a route to what after Coleridge would be called "suspension of disbelief").[377] Voltaire's ghost is all wrong; it steps directly out of its grave (ridiculous realism, as if the ghost lived there) during broad daylight (absurd break with tradition, as any granny could have told Voltaire) after having been introduced, so to speak, by thunder (Gothic B-movie effect). To add insult to injury, Voltaire then makes the ghost noble and just, which is not exactly in key with expectations as regards such spectres (283-284).

The problem is not one of *mimesis*, but of a different standard from that developed by the neo-classicist school through its distillation of absolute rules from Aristotle and Horace. Voltaire had thought it necessary to defend his exceptional performance with the historical argument that people in previous ages had believed in ghosts, so he claimed he was perfectly justified in presenting one in a historical play. Lessing agrees that people in previous ages believed in ghosts so ancient dramatists who use them cannot be faulted for using something that was potential reality for the contemporaneous audience. But for the modern dramatist the case is different, Lessing claims in a delightful twist, making French neo-classical aesthetics briefly his own for the argument's sake. He begins by asking whether the modern dramatist may also use ghosts:

Aber hat darum der neue, diese unsere bessere Einsichten teilende dramatische Dichter, die nämliche Befugnis? Gewiß nicht. – Aber wenn er seine Geschichte in jene leichtgläubigere Zeiten zurücklegt? Auch alsdenn nicht. Denn der dramatische Dichter ist kein Geschichtschreiber; er erzählt nicht, was man ehedem geglaubt, daß es geschehen, sondern er läßt es vor unsern Augen nochmals geschehen; und läßt es nochmals geschehen, nicht der bloßen historischen Wahrheit wegen, sondern in einer ganz andern und höhern Absicht; die historische Wahrheit ist nicht sein Zweck, sondern nur das Mittel zu seinem Zwecke; er will uns täuschen, und durch die Täuschung rühren. Wenn es also wahr ist, daß wir itzt keine Gespenster mehr glauben; wenn dieses Nichtglauben die Täuschung notwendig verhindern müßte; wenn ohne Täuschung wir unmöglich sympathisieren können: so handelt itzt der dramatische Dichter wider sich selbst, wenn er uns dem ohngeachtet solche unglaubliche Märchen ausstaffieret; all Kunst, die er dabei anwendet, ist verloren (281-282).[378]

---

[377] It is perhaps the re-interpretation of Aristotle and Longinus in the eighteenth century that gave the greatest impetus to the oft-slighted "primitivism" as an aesthetic movement; after people started understanding "nature" differently in the wake of Rousseau, Aristotle's "nature" had irrevocably changed.

[378] "But can we make the same allowance for this poet, the poet with our improved knowledge? Certainly not. – But when he sets his story back in those more superstitious times? Also not then. For the dramatic poet is no historian, he does not relate what people believed had happened in previous ages, but he lets it happen again before our eyes, and he does not let it happen to attain a plain historical truth, but serve a completely different and more noble purpose; historical truth is not his objective, only the medium to his objective; he wants to make us believe and move us through make believe. If it is true, then, that we do not believe in ghosts anymore, if this disbelief necessarily hinders belief, if we are unable to sympathise without make believe: then

This interpretation of Aristotelian and Longinian principles could easily be seen as adhering to neo-classical premises. It forbids the use of ghosts on mimetic grounds; the suspension of disbelief is based on sympathy and an illusion of reality, and the use of ghosts, even in a historical work, is unsuitable for a modern audience that does not believe in them.

There are two main strands in Lessing's twist of this conception against itself. The first is to note that the question of disbelief in ghosts is ambivalent, to say the least: even those who do not believe in them have no proof of their non-existence. This argument is not merely a sophistry, for Lessing also notes that most people have a seed of belief that enables belief in ghosts that are artistically produced. If the dramatist succeeds in producing a ghost we believe in, by motivating the reasons people might have for believing in ghosts, their application is perfectly justified. The problem is only that the ability to achieve this is not common:

> So ein Dichter ist Shakespeare, und Shakespeare fast allein. Vor seinem Gespenste im Hamlet richten sich die Haare zu Berge, sie mögen ein gläubiges oder ungläubiges Gehirn bedecken. Der Herr von Voltaire tat gar nicht wohl, sich auf dieses Gespenst zu berufen; es macht ihn und seinen Geist des Ninus – lächerlich (283).[379]

The difference is mainly psychological, and that constitutes the second strand of Lessing's twist on the neo-classical *mimesis*. What Voltaire tries to achieve with a ghost that appears at midday for all to see, Shakespeare achieves by letting his appear at a more traditional time of night and with a psychological dimension added by the fact that not all can see it; Gertrude does not, for example, when her son stares at it. And Hamlet's own doubts, so important for the play, are fed by the doubt about what he has seen, a fact noted by Goethe and Hegel, as we shall see. As Lessing put it in a paradigm that was to survive both *Sturm und Drang* and the *Weimarer Klassik*: "Das Gespenst wirket auf uns, mehr durch ihn, als durch sich selbst" (284).

As Lessing was very much preoccupied with the two possible models for a German national theatre (the "Dramaturgie" was written during the first such experiment in Germany), he harps on the ghosts of Voltaire and Shakespeare in the next "Stück", as if trying to decide which one should be written into the German spirit, but he was not so fixed on the idea of a model as Jochen Schmidt claims of the "genius-movement" in the quote above. This can best be seen by

---

the dramatic poet now acts against himself, if he dresses up for us such unbelieveable fairy tales, all the art he applies doing it is lost" (my translation, believe and make believe might be replaced by deceive and deception).

[379] "Such a poet is Shakespeare, and almost Shakespeare alone. His ghost in Hamlet raises hairs, be growing they over a believing or a disbelieving brain. Mr Voltaire did not well when he appealed to that ghost; it makes him and his spirit of Ninus – laughable" (my translation with a little help from Simon Critchley).

looking at the remainder of this "Stück", in which he discusses another play by Voltaire, *L'Ecossaise*. The discussion is notable for its remarks on intertextuality and most of all, translation. Lessing thinks it worthwhile to note that Voltaire, ironically, dubbed this play a translation from the English of John Home, whose *Douglas* had been considered scandalous enough in Presbyterian Scotland to relieve the author of his cloth and calling. Apparently, Voltaire wanted to give one of his first works in the Calvinist republic of Geneva a similarly scandalous flair through such an attribution. Lessing concentrates, however, on the construction of a play through translation. He does this by comparing the English and German translations of Voltaire's play, and although he delineates what seems to be a manipulation beyond any kind of functionalism in the English translation, he sees it as the translator's right in this case, since the subject is "English". The translator, the famous playwright, drama translator and theatre manager George Colman the Elder, calls it *The English Merchant*, which is an interesting change from the original title given the rampant Scotophobia of the early 1760s during Lord Bute's ministry in Britain, but is also a deliberate echo of Lillo's title *The London Merchant*. Lessing praises Colman's translation first and foremost for the "nationale Colorit" which was lacking in the original, making knowledge of cultural conventions of the time and place of action an aesthetic criterion for both original and translation. In this case, the original shows less competence in this field and is therefore of less value.[380] Lessing also makes a moral criticism in a very bourgeois vein; he sees Voltaire's decision to let his heroine live in a coffee house as particularly un-English, perhaps a rather odd statement from the author of the tragedy of Miss Sarah Sampson.[381] Colman repairs this flaw by letting the young woman rent a decent room with an honest landlady, and in general, Lessing finds, Colman lets the characters fit the English taste better than Voltaire, whose knowledge of English customs Lessing does not rate highly.

Lessing also considers English criticism for comparison and notes that English reviewers find the play too simple and predictable, due to an English tradition of more complex plot and subplots. This, however, Lessing thinks can-

---

[380] Which is perhaps a bit strange considering the fact that Voltaire knew England very well, having lived and written there and even published in English. According to the article on Colman in the *DNB*, Voltaire satirised the translation in a polite letter a few years later.

[381] On the other hand, staying in a public "Wirtshaus" is exactly Sara Sampson's problem, for it emphasises her fall from virtuous, bourgeois society. Lessing's model for *Miß Sara Sampson* was apparently George Lillo's play *The London Merchant, or the History of George Barnwell* (1731), a middle-class domestic tragedy, yet another example of the translation of form. Lessing used Lillo's play as an example both in his preface to the translations of Thomson's plays and in his correspondence with Moses Mendelssohn and Friedrich Nicolai on middle-class domestic tragedy (*Werke IV* 144 & 193).

not be transported to German drama (although it might be argued that he tried it):

> Es ist an dieser Kritik manches nicht ganz unbegründet; indes sind wir Deutschen es sehr wohl, zufrieden, daß die Handlung nicht reicher und verwickelter ist. Die englische Manier in diesem Punkte, zerstreuet und ermüdet uns; wir lieben einen einfältigen Plan, der sich auf einmal übersehen läßt. So wie die Engländer die französischen Stücke mit Episoden erst vollpropfen müssen, wenn sie auf ihrer Bühne gefallen sollen; so müßten wir die englischen Stücke von ihren Episoden erst entladen, wenn wir unsere Bühne glücklich damit bereichern wollten (289).[382]

Lessing seems to contradict this in the next "Stück" where he discusses his own work, *Miß Sara Sampson*. The highly ironic discussion shows that Lessing could well smile at himself, but what is his complaint? "Ob der Verfasser mit allen diesen Verkürzungen so recht zufrieden ist, daran zweifle ich fast" (293).[383] He continues in this humourous vein, joking about the textual insistence of authors (himself of course), and then pokes fun at the production itself by claiming for example that "Madame Henseln starb ungemein anständig; in der malerischsten Stellung" (294) [Madame Hensel died very decently; in the most picturesque position]. This damning praise ironically undermines another of the neo-classical "rules", which criticises death on stage as undecorous and impossible to imitate realistically. Lessing's laconic and implied reference to *Laokoon* at the end of this piece aims at underlining his theorisation on the difference between visual and lingual imitation: "Wer diese Feinheit in meiner Beschreibung nicht schön findet, der schiebe die Schuld auf meine Beschreibung: aber er sehe sie einmal!" (294).[384]

The route to the difference between poetry and painting in *Laokoon* has often been commented on and it should be enough to note here that Lessing's conslusions regarding the linear dynamic of poetry (or rather language) as opposed to the static imitative moment of painting, are in essence the opposite of the platonic *mimesis*.[385] What Lessing adds, in Derrida's terms, is a new dimension to the demand for truth; a dimension we might affix to an opposition of the visual and the imaginative. The major thesis of *Laokoon* is the claim that the

---

[382] "Some elements of this critique are not fully unfounded; however, we Germans are quite happy with a more simple and straightforward plot. The English custom in this regard diverts us and tires; we love a simple plan which can be clearly seen right away. Just like the English need to fill the French plays with episodes if they are to like them on their stage, we need to offload the episodes from the English ones before we can enrich our stage with them" (my translation).

[383] "Whether the author is content with all those cuts I am inclined to doubt!" (my translation).

[384] "He, who does not see the finesse of my description, can fault my description, but he should see it all the same!" (my translation).

[385] See above on the contrast between Aristotle and Plato as delineated by Melberg.

visual arts cannot depict/imitate reality with the same precision as the poetic ones. This is a problem of beauty, as the visual arts, which owe their first responsibility to beauty, cannot represent ugliness. The visual artist, therefore, needs to approach the work differently: "What he might not paint he left to conjecture" (McCormick 16).[386] This means, in the end, that the visual artist has to sacrifice something, perhaps the truth possible in language, in order to be able to tell the truth of beauty: "Kurz, diese Verhüllung ist ein Opfer, das der Künstler der Schönheit brachte" (*Werke VI* 23).[387]

This summary is a simplification of Lessing's thesis, which includes finer differentiations within each art form; he also frequently addresses the mixed form with which he worked so much, drama, where the visual and the lingual have to operate in tandem. Lessing also shows historical awareness in his comparison of the ancient Greeks and the moderns, noting that the Greeks had additional traditions that enabled and required them to use other aesthetic media; this argument is closely related to the argument of national character, which is another source of difference in his analysis (14-23). He also draws a strict line between the north and south by referring to different reactions to pain:

> Ich weiß es, wir feinern Europäer einer klügern Nachwelt, wissen über unsern Mund und über unsere Augen besser zu herrschen. Höflichkeit und Anstand verbieten Geschrei und Tränen. Die tätige Tapferkeit des ersten rauhen Weltalters hat sich bei uns in eine leidende verwandelt. Doch selbst unsere Urältern waren in dieser größer, als in jener. Aber unsere Urältern waren Barbaren. Alle Schmerzen *verbeißen*, dem Streiche des Todes mit unverwandtem Auge entgegen sehen, unter den Bissen der Nattern lachend sterben, weder seine Sünde noch den Verlust des besten Freundes beweinen, sind Züge des nordischen Heldenmuts (14, my emphasis).[388]

This paradigm of "Nordic" heroism, based on the myth of Valhalla, was given its European currency in a Latin tract (which Lessing refers to) by the seventeenth-century Royal Danish Antiquarian, Thomas Bartholin.[389] It is one of

---

[386] "Was er nicht malen durfte, ließ er erraten" (Lessing, *Werke VI* 23).

[387] "In short, this concealment is a sacrifice that the artist has made to beauty" (McCormick 16).

[388] I know that we more refined Europeans of a wiser, later age know better how to govern our mouths and our eyes. Courtesy and propriety force us to restrain our cries and tears. The aggressive bravery of the rough, early ages has become in our time a passive courage of endurance. Yet even our ancestors were greater in the latter than the former. But our ancestors were barbarians. To master all pain, to face death's stroke with unflinching eye, to die laughing under the adder's bite, to weep neither at the loss of one's dears friend not at one's own sins: these are the traits of old Nordic heroism (McCormick 9)

[389] "Thomas Bartholinus de causis contemptae a Danis adhuc gentilibus moris". The paradigm of the gladiator is not far away, and indeed the martyr as well. Both play a role in Lessing's theorisation. Along with Ole Worm and Resenius, versions of

the most persistent myths on the "Nordic" people that was ever constructed, and had in fact become a part of the Northern/Germanic stereotype, as we have seen in the Chapters on Thomas Percy. What is notable in this context is the way in which a myth that has already become a historical reality for the writer is applied in an aesthetic discourse, which again feeds a modern national discourse. The two most important aesthetic criteria Lessing uses are of sensualistic and emotional origin: pain and pity and/or sympathy. Lessing connects them theoretically to his aesthetic discourse through ideas of *mimesis,* an essential part of which is the notion of pity or sympathy. He connects sympathy, in turn, with the mythical notions noted above by quoting Adam Smith's *Theory of Moral Sentiments,* the work in which he tried to transform the (originally aesthetic) idea of sympathy as developed by David Hume and indeed Francis Hutcheson into a new moral category. After a long quote from Smith on the levels of sympathy with physical pain, Lessing concludes:

> Wir verachten denjenigen, sagt der Engländer, den wir unter körperlichen Schmerzen heftig schreien hören. Aber nicht immer: nicht zum erstenmale; nicht, wenn wir sehen, daß der Leidende alles mögliche anwendet, seinen Schmerz zu *verbeißen*; nicht, wenn wir ihn sonst als einen Mann von Standhaftigkeit kennen; noch weniger, wenn wir ihn selbst unter dem Leiden Proben von seiner Standhaftigkeit ablegen sehen, wenn wir sehen, daß ihn der Schmerz zwar zum Schreien, aber auch zu weiter nichts zwingen kann, daß er sich lieber der längern Fortdauer dieses Schmerzes unterwirft, als das geringste in seiner Denkungsart, in seinen Entschlüssen ändert, ob er schon in dieser Veränderung die gänzliche Endschaft seines Schmerzes hoffen darf (36-37, my emphasis).[390]

The range of Lessing's discourse becomes clear when one considers that he is considering at least three different discourses: an aesthetic one with its epistemological implications, a moral philosophic one with its behavioural implications and finally a national/cultural one with its built-in north-versus-south paradigm, which is even paradigmatically linked to the previous quote through the verb "verbeißen".[391]

Bartholin went through the hands of most of the people discussed here: Herder, Goethe, Percy, Warton, Gray, etc.

[390] "We despise a man, says the Englishman, whom we hear cry out violently under physical pain. But not always; not the first time; not when we see that the sufferer is making every attempt to suppress it; not when we know him to be a man firmness in other respects; and less when we see him offer proofs of his steadfastness even while suffering; when we see that this pain can force him to cry out but not go one single step further than that; when we see that he would rather submit to a continuation of this pain than change his way of thinking or his resolve in the slightest degree, even though he knows that such a change would end suffering altogether" (McCormick 28-29).

[391] "Master" and "suppress" are McCormick's more abstract choices.

Lessing develops his theory within these parameters of pain and death and their artistic imitation, for they provide him with the extremes that vision cannot bear artistically and language can express through its abstraction. The screams of pain are not to be expressed visually and with this, coupled with a comparison of death and sleep, Lessing succeeds in cleaving the standing interpretation of Horace's *ut pictura poesis* so convincingly that Goethe claimed in *Dichtung und Wahrheit* that the misunderstanding had been "auf einmal beseitigt" and notes that he and other young men at the time had started despising the sixteenth-century tradition that had represented death visually in the "Unform eines klappernden Gerippes" ["hideous shape of a rattling skeleton" (Smith 283)] (Goethe, *Werke 9* 316).[392] Goethe refers here to a footnote in Lessing's text, a footnote that started his polemical engagement with Christian Adolf Klotz over, among other things, the question of how the ancients represented death.

Goethe's remark reveals one of the most important aspects of *Laokoon* and indeed of the whole debate initiated by Lessing, namely that of re-interpretation through re-translation and/or translation criticism. The problem was that the famous simile *ut pictura poesis* had not been interpreted as such, but as an absolute rule to be followed. Even though the comparison of the poet and the painter at the beginning of *Ars Poetica* may support the absolutist version, it is still only a comparison, and it is this fact that Lessing makes operational in his re-interpretation. He does not, as has often been claimed, cleave Horace's rule into two, but rather the (French) interpretation of a simile that had been made into a rule.[393] He does this by re-reading Horace and not so much citing as applying his insight on behalf of his own theorisation.

---

[392] This passage from *Dichtung und Wahrheit* is quoted by Lessing's editors as an example of the influence of *Laokoon* on contemporaries (*Werke VI* 873-874) .

[393] See for example Wellek's ambivalent treatment of Lessing in his *History of Modern Criticism.* Wellek sees *Laokoon* as a rejection of Horace and thinks it "sacrifices the humanistic values of the old *ut pictura poesis* theory without replacing it by a new ideal of pure painterly values" (166). This, in itself, empty statement, reveals that Wellek takes the standard interpretation of Horace for granted and shows an irritation with the insight into a realism demanded by visual arts that had rejected the Gothic for the neoclassical and had not found a fresh *source* for its originality. Lessing was not setting any rules, merely stating matters of fact. The visual arts remained in a prison of classical form much longer than the poetic ones, and it may even be argued that the art form, be it visual or lingual or both, that manages to escape this prison is the one that represents an avant-garde until its renewals have been swallowed into the canon and thus made classical. This means that criticism can bend its repertoire of theory to include the greats plus the new ones, even if their aesthetic is a break with all the previous "rules". The canon may or may not be justified, but it certainly is not rational on its own grounds.

This is perhaps better seen in an indirect reference to Horace than in the few explicit ones.[394] In Chapter III of the *Laokoon*, for example, Lessing discusses the painter Timomachus, who had painted Medea in a way that Lessing finds perfect; he had not represented her at the moment of murdering her children, "sondern einige Augenblicke zuvor, da die mütterliche Liebe noch mit der Eifersucht kämpfet" [but a few moments before, when a mother's love was still struggling with her vengefulness (McCormick 21)] (*Werke VI* 27). Horace discusses exactly this moment in a passage on drama where he claims the children should not be butchered in front of the audience (l. 185/466 & 467). This passage in Horace's *Ars poetica* (ll. 179-188) on the difference between narrating and staging contains the seed of Lessing's differentiation of the visual and lingual, although he applied it differently and put painting in the place of drama.

Lessing came to his "new" interpretation by going to the original and translating for himself; this is not explicit in the case of Horace, but it is in many of the examples he uses in the *Laokoon* and indeed in the whole of his critical *oeuvre,* which may seem astonishing to the many anthologists who have ignored his numerous discussions and criticisms on translation. That the infantry of national literary critics and even such renowned figures as Wellek have expressed little beyond mild irritation regarding Lessing's continual preoccupation with translation, not to mention his own output in the field, is not surprising. The common notion of translation as a completely secondary text in opposition to the original with its implied myth of purity from all kinds of transtextuality is still alive, despite all theories of deconstruction and intertextuality; Horace certainly wielded the axe effectually when he translated himself into originality.

Lessing's acute awareness of the malleability of a text on its route through rewriting and language is supported by his paratextual apparatus, one part of which led to the controversy with Klotz, which generated "Briefe, antiquarischen Inhalts", "Der Meusels Apollodor" and "Wie die Alten den Tod gebildet".[395] In Chapter 4 of the *Laokoon*, Lessing discusses his major point of difference with Winckelmann, whose *Gedanken über die Nachahmung der griechischen Werke in der Malerei und Bildhauerkunst* (1755) had inspired his own work. Their divergence can be summed up as follows: Winckelmann claimed that the statue of Laokoon in the group discovered in 1506 expressed

---

[394] Lessing would hardly have thought it necessary to remind his readers of the Horatian source, given its prevalence in contemporary literary discourse.

[395] As a person and academic Klotz is attacked forcefully by Lessing's editors. Klotz's fate as a "bad boy" is common in the annals of canonisation, and editors often imply slighting epithets when describing the enemy of "their" author. Klotz is described as opportunist and plagiarist, which he well may have been, although he seems to be a model of the modern academic when one considers his career: fast learner, profusive output, knew the right people. Of course he would have perished eventually, had he not had the fortune to attack an author who became canonised.

"edle Einfalt und [eine] stille Größe" [noble simplicity and quiet grandeur], as Lessing quotes right at the start in order to differ with Winckelmann's comparison of this statue and the screams of Philoctetes in Sophocles' play of that name (*Werke VI* 12/McCormick 7)).[396] To support his argument against Winckelmann's premise, Lessing at one point analyses the mistranslations that have added to the myth of a Philoctetes who quietly suffers his pain like a classical hero should (32-34). The two-and-a-half-page footnote begins by showing the original Greek text, a passage where the pain of Philoctetes is underlined by his utter loneliness, a circumstance Lessing attributes to the fact that pity with expressed pain is not enough (shortly afterwards he quotes Adam Smith on the subject); this loneliness narrated by the chorus makes the pain suffered all the more poignant for the audience. But what has happened in the rendering of the Greek text and the subsequent Latin translations? Through incorrect punctuation in the Greek and an interpolation in the Latin, the idea crops up that Philoctetes is so lonely that he would even accept the company of an evil neighbour, a notion absent from the original. But the mistranslation lives on, as Lessing shows, in James Thomson's tragedy *Agamemnon*, and, creative as he is, Lessing even likes the idea, a tribute to his openness to the creativity of mistranslation! Finally, he shows an example of a recent English translation by Thomas Franklin in which "der böse Nachbar" has become a "fellow-mourner", a sense Lessing thinks is closer to the original, and of course to his own aesthetic notions of pity, which he had discussed with Moses Mendelssohn and Friedrich Nicolai in their letters on bourgeois tragedy.[397]

Apart from Winckelmann, Lessing criticises two other scholars particularly in the *Laokoon*. The first is Pope's friend and public defender of his translation of the *Odyssey*, Joseph Spence, who in 1747 had published *Polymetis,* in which he equated painting and poetry in a somewhat Horatian fashion by claiming that "scarce any thing can be good in a poetical description, which would appear absurd, if represented in a statue or picture" (quoted in Lessing, *Werke VI* 70).[398] The second, Comte Caylus, had published *Tableaux tirés d'Iliade* in 1757 with the argument that, according to Wellek, "the more a poem furnishes images and

---

[396] See Wellek for an overview in his *History* (158-159).

[397] This "Briefwechsel" took place in 1756 and 1757 and when the discourse on "Mitleid" is compared with Lessing's discussion on sympathy in *Laokoon* (1766), one can see how he applies Adam Smith's development of "sympathy" in his theorisation. Lessing cites the second edition of *TMS* in *Laokoon.*

[398] This rewording of Horace's opening words of the *Ars Poetica* is not commented on by Lessing (nor his editor von Schirnding or Wellek for that matter), but this may be due to the minor inversion in aspect and the complete equation of poetry and painting, which was not Horace's; otherwise one might think Lessing would simply have attacked the source. That he did not shows perhaps better than anything else that he read Horace differently.

actions which can be painted the greater it is as a poem, and he had gone through the *Iliad,* the *Odyssey,* and the *Aeneid* making suggestions for paintings" (Wellek 162).

Lessing's criticisms of these two authors are well worth examining in our context, for both focus on mistranslation in interpretation, and the latter provided Lessing's later adversary, Klotz, with the ammunition that started the aforementioned controversy, a controversy about representation and translation.

In Chapter X of the *Laokoon,* Lessing discusses and deconstructs one of Spence's problems in the comparison of poetry and painting, the fact that poets waste few words on divine figures such as the muses or moral figures such as virtue or restraint. For Spence this constitutes a deficiency in poetry, for he assumes that a worthy representation of such figures should be equally fitting in both poetry and painting. Sharply, Lessing sees a weak point in Spence's argument and turns it around: the artist *needs* physical (visual) attributes such as items held by the figures to represent abstract ideas, for example a harp for the muse or a rein for the figure of restraint, whereas the poet does not need such symbolic paraphernalia; the names themselves express what is necessary without allegorical proofs (*Werke VI* 79-80):

> Dem Künstler fehlen diese Mittel. Er muß also seinen personifierten Abstractis Sinnbilder zugeben, durch welche sie kenntlich werden. Diese Sinnbilder weil sie etwas anders sind, und etwas anders bedeuten, machen sie zu allegorischen Figuren.
>
> Eine Fraunsperson mit einem Zaum in der Hand; eine andere an eine Säule gelehnt, sind in der Kunst allegorische Wesen. Allein die Mäßigung, die Standhaftigkeit bei dem Dichter, sind keine allegorische Wesen, sondern bloß personifierte Abstracta (80).[399]

Lessing elegantly underscores his criticism in a two-page footnote in which he takes one of Horace's odes as an example – indeed, one of his weakest, wherein he has "Necessitas" carry a bag of tools in a highly visual scene (Lib. I Od. 35).[400] Lessing uses Horace himself to point out the weakness of the kind of visualisation Spence demands. He then dismembers Spence's argument in an ironic discussion on one of the key terms of translation, the one that Horace himself made famous, namely that of faithfulness, personified in the goddess

---

[399] "The artist lacks these means and must therefore add to his personified abstractions symbols by which they may be recognized. But because these symbols are something different and mean something different, they make the figures allegorical.

The female figure with a bridle in her hand; another leaning against a pillar - these are, in art, allegorical figures. For the poet, however, Moderation and Constancy are not allegorical beings but simply personified abstractions" (McCormick 60).

[400] Typically, in a German translation I consulted, "Necessitas" becomes "Ananke" to give the translation an ancient, indeed a pre-Roman, flair. See *Werke* (32).

"Fides".[401] Lessing uses the same method again; he points out an argument by Spence, who claims that the Romans had put the goddess of "honesty", or "Fides", into a transparent dress to underline the meaning of her role. Lessing is rather amused by this erotic version of "faithfulness" and spots three mistakes in the one sentence he cites; he then proceeds to take it apart by showing that the three meanings that Spence missed are all closer to the more poetic and abstract notion of faithfulness. In all three cases Spence misunderstands the meaning through incorrect interpretation of the attribution, an interpretation he himself supplements (82).

The argument of Chapter X leads directly to Comte Caylus' work, which is discussed in the following Chapter: "Auch der Graf Caylus scheinet zu verlangen, daß der Dichter seine Wesen der Einbildung mit allegorischen Attributen ausschmücken solle" (83).[402] This opening sentence is then footnoted with a critique that became one of the central points of the controversy with Klotz, and indeed the other major point Goethe picked up from the *Laokoon,* namely that of the visual versions of death.[403] The ancients, claims Lessing, represented death as the twin brother of sleep and both hence as similar figures, whereas later artists tended to represent death as a skeleton. The reason for this development seems to be mistranslation, for he cites a French translation of Pausanias where in the original the allegorical figures of death and sleep lie with crossed legs ("übereinander geschlagenen Füßen"), whereas in the translation they lie with crooked legs, "krummen Füßen, oder so wie es Gedoyn in seiner Sprache gegeben hat: les pieds contrefaits" (84). Lessing concludes that the representation of death as a skeleton, implied by the notion of "crooked" feet, is a "modern" idea and that it is unfitting for a Homeric painting.

Klotz countered with a number of examples of skeletons in ancient art, and Lessing needed a detailed defence against the scholar. In the final essay of the controversy, "Wie die Alten den Tod gebildet", he returns to the translational issue that is at the root of his interpretation. First he notes that Klotz does not differentiate between a dead human and the god of death, the personification of death. This difference is not as easily discerned as it might seem from these words, for the context of the pictures is often ambiguous. Lessing thus argues in considerable detail his reasons for choosing the translation of "crossed legs" in Pausanias, and concludes by "crossing" his arguments on the representation of death and sleep as twins and the mistranslation of "crooked" for "crossed":

---

[401]   I am of course referring to the "fidus interpres". The recent English translation of "slavish translators" would probably have raised a few of Lessing's philological hairs (pardon the visualisation).

[402]   "Count Caylus, too, seems to demand that the poet adorn the creatures of his imagination with allegorical attributes" (McCormick 62).

[403]   See above.

Was folgt aber hieraus? – Sind die krummen Füße des Todes und des Schlafes ohne alle befriedigende Bedeutung; sind die krummen Füße des letzern in keiner antiken Vorstellung desselben sichtbar: so meine ich, folgt wohl nichts natürlicher, als die Vermutung, daß es mit den krummen Füßen überhaupt eine Grille sein dürfte. Sie gründen sich auf eine einzige Stelle des Pausanias, auf ein einziges Wort in dieser Stelle: und dieses Wort ist noch dazu eines ganz andern Sinnes fähig! (420).[404]

There is more to this debate than merely the pedantry of scholarship and ambiguity of translation; there is a fundamental, even religious notion of beauty, to which Lessing contributed no less than Winckelmann. It is a new return to an ancient classical beauty, reinterpreted for a linguistic and intellectual community that was beginning to believe in the beauty of its native language, and its links to truth and god. It is a language that discovers itself in reference to ancient writings and visual works, to the (translated) Bible, to an ideal of beauty that could not allow a crude skeleton to represent even the horror of death; it required something better and nobler. At the end of his final contribution on the matter, Lessing put it thus:

Die Schrift redet selbst von einem Engel des Todes: und welcher Künstler sollte nicht lieber einen Engel, als ein Gerippe bilden wollen?
Nur die Mißverstandene Religion kann uns von dem Schönen entfernen: und es ist ein Beweis für die wahre, für die richtig verstandene Religion, wenn sie uns überall auf das Schöne zurückbringt (462).[405]

It is perhaps fitting that Lessing was so preoccupied with death and its representation, insofar as he himself represents a pivotal, liminal figure, who rejects the neo-classical by returning to it; but then, what he and many after him in Germany did was to reject the French interpretation of the ancients and translate anew, for a Germany that was culturally already in the ascendant.

7.1.2 Herder's Haunting

The collection of essays by Herder, Goethe, Möser and a translation from the Italian of Paolo Frisi, *Von deutscher Art und Kunst* (1773), is one of the most

---

[404] "What follows from this? – Are the crooked feet of Death and of Sleep without any satisfying meaning; are the crooked feet of the latter impossible to see in any ancient presentation: I think, therefore, that the natural assumption from this would be that the idea of crooked feet is nonsense. It is based on this single quote from Pausanias, on a single word in this quote, and this word can easily have another meaning!" (my translation).

[405] "The word itself speaks of an angel of death: and which artist would not rather represent an angel than a skeleton?
Only the misunderstood religion can remove us from beauty: and it is proof for the true, for the correctly understood religion if it is able to bring us back to beauty" (my translation).

important documents of the *Sturm und Drang* period and it includes two of Herder's most famous essays, the one on Ossian and the poetry of ancient peoples and the one on Shakespeare. In one respect the publication represents the entrance of the major figures of *Sturm und Drang* onto the stage, authors who had grasped Lessing's and Gerstenberg's aesthetic approaches and who, armed with additional material by Mallet, Percy and Macpherson, were to take the "Nordic" orientation suggested by Lessing to its logical conclusion. Herder's essays, by far the best material in the short volume, also represent his masterful application of translation without an original, something he had vowed to do in his travel journal of 1769. Most important for the time being is to note the nationalist orientation of the publication in both title and content. It would perhaps appear unlikely that essays on Ossian, Nordic poetry and Shakespeare could be interpreted as a German "nationalist" project, but this is exactly the point Herder is trying to make. He compares what may be termed a "Nordic" aesthetic with the ancient Greek one; not, however, by rejecting the Greek simplistically as inferior, as Charles Perrault had done eighty years before in the famous *Querelle*, but by raising the Nordic "original" to the same aesthetic level while simultaneously maintaining a distinction.[406] This is an important development, for it assumes differences in geography, customs, manners, even race, and at the same time proclaims that there is universal potential for developing an aesthetic, only from different premises. The implication is that the "northern" aesthetic is more fitting, or rather in congruence with German "nature".

The essay on Shakespeare begins, fittingly perhaps, with a visual reference that has been ascribed to both Shakespeare's *King Lear* and Mark Akenside's *Pleasures of the Imagination:* a vision of a man standing on a cliff (in a storm, of course), while below the roaring ocean metaphorises the masses who "ihn – erklären, retten, verdammen, entschuldigen, anbeten, verläumden, übersetzen und lästern" [explain, save, curse him, apologise for him, worship, translate and damn him] (*Art* 65).[407] Herder pursues a double strategy in his argumentation. Firstly, he pushes all "defenders" of Shakespeare aside as mistaken. After the late seventeenth century had attempted to rewrite Shakespeare in order to rescue

---

[406] Paul de Man noted in his essay "Literary History and Literary Modernity" that Perrault's assault was "simply against literature as such" (*Insight* 153). According to de Man, Perrault's notion of the superiority of modernity was more technical than literary.

[407] For the source of the imagery, see Irmscher's *Reclam* edition, in which the editor refers to L.M. Price (149); and Pross' edition of the works, vol. I, where he also follows the route from Akenside to Lucretius' *De Rerum Natura*. Apart from Shaftesbury's "The Moralists", another possible source for Herder might be the famous lines from the *Iliad* book 17 ll. 263-265 (310-315 in Pope's version) where in Hammond's translation the onslaught of the Trojans is described "as when the sea waves roar against the current". Both Dionysus of Halicarnassus in his *De Compositione Verborum* (XV 110) and Aristotle in his *Poetics* (22) note this metaphor, whose power was supposed to have induced writers in antiquity to give up their craft.

him from barbarity, the eighteenth had, from Rowe through Pope and Johnson, among others, tried to make excuses for his occasional barbarity by referring to his purple passages elsewhere.[408] Herder's originality lies perhaps in the explicit departure from such "defences" by asserting that this approach is wrong, based on an unfounded prejudice (*Art* 65-66). Herder simply rejects the premises of both admirers and antagonists, which he sees as based on the Greek tradition and therefore fundamentally wrong:

> In Griechenland entstand das Drama, wie es in Norden nicht entstehen konnte. In Griechenland wars, was es in Norden nicht seyn kann. In Norden ists also nicht und darf nicht seyn, was es in Griechenland gewesen. Also Sophokles Drama und Shakespears Drama sind zwei Dinge, die in gewißem Betracht kaum den Namen gemein haben (67).[409]

Here Herder draws a clear demarcation line between Greek and "Nordic" drama, for which he uses Shakespeare as a metonymical representative. Herder's assertion takes a strange twist, however, when he claims that he can prove the difference by studying Greek drama and through that Shakespeare; that the one thing breeds the other, but there is a metamorphosis that makes them different:

> Ich glaube diese Sätze aus Griechenland selbst beweisen zu können, und eben dadurch die Natur des Nordischen Drama, und des größten Dramatisten in Norden, *Shakespears* sehr zu entziffern. *Man wird die Genese Einer Sache durch die Andre, aber zugleich Verwandlung sehen, daß sie gar nicht mehr dieselbe bleibt* (67, my emphasis).[410]

Herder's intention appears straightforward, until he discusses the "*Genese*", the origin that indeed creates the "thing" and thus enables him to analyse the "other", both of which simultaneously go through such a metamorphosis that they are no longer the same, which is remarkable, since the original is changed too. The argument is this laboured due to the fact that Herder wants to have his cake and eat it too. He retains the basic comparison of Shakespeare and the

---

[408] In his *Letters on England* (1733) Voltaire had praised Shakespeare for his "brilliant monstrosities" and described his way of writing as particularly English (92-96). Voltaire translates passages from Shakespeare and stresses there that he thinks nothing of "literal" translation.

[409] "In Greece, drama came into being as it could not in the North. In Greece was what in the North cannot be. It is thus not in the North and should not be what it was in Greece. Thus the drama of Sophocles and the drama of Shakespeare are two things, which, from a certain point of view, hardly have a name in common" (my translation).

[410] "I think I can prove these theses on Greece myself, and precisely through that, decipher the nature of Northern drama and the greatest dramatist of the North. One will be able to see the Origin of One Thing through the Other, yet at the same time it goes through such a metamorphosis that they do not stay the same" (my translation).

Greeks used by Lessing in the 17th "Literaturbrief" for the same purpose, to reject the French neo-classicist canon of rules, but his argument is subtler and more powerful than simply saying that the Greeks wrote from "nature" and so did Shakespeare. To be sure, from that premise he develops an aesthetic notion of "Nordic" originality comparable to the Greek one, but it is totally different as well.

In order to follow Herder's odd but effective argumentation, it is necessary to refer back to Lessing, who certainly haunts Herder's essay in a number of places. To begin with, Herder turns one of Lessing's arguments about the Greeks around – the one where he claims that the Greeks had developed their tragedy by simplifying plot in order to retain unity of place. Herder rejects this and claims they did the opposite: "Jene *simplificirten* nicht, denke ich, sondern sie *vervielfältigten*" [They did not simplify, they multiplied] (*Art* 69, emphasis in original text). Lessing had made his argument in order to differentiate between the Greeks and what he conceived of as the French school of drama, namely the seventeenth-century classicists, Corneille and Racine, but most of all their eighteenth-century successor, Voltaire. As a matter of fact, Lessing put his ideas forth in a long and detailed analysis of Voltaire's adaptation of the Italian Maffei's *Merope*.[411] Voltaire had chosen to adapt the very successful play instead of translating it, because he did not find it suited to the French "national taste".[412] His adaptation was published in 1744 and in the following year a new edition of the Italian original, along with translations into French and English, was introduced with a dissertation in which Voltaire's adaptation was attacked in turn.[413] Voltaire, who certainly relished a literary fight, retaliated with a fictional exchange of letters between himself and a certain de la Lindelle, adding to the irony by letting the fictional figure attack the Italian play savagely while he himself gave it a lame defence – a device Lessing instantly saw through (*Werke IV* 421-422).

This would not be so remarkable, were it not for the fact that Herder explicitly uses Voltaire's argument of *difference* to establish his Nordic drama as different from the Greek, and then goes on to refer to Lessing's deconstruction of the French drama: "Ich wills gar nicht einmal untersuchen, 'ob sie auch ihren Aristoteles den Regeln nach so beobachten, wie sies vorgeben' wo Leßing gegen die lautesten Anmassungen neulich schreckliche Zweifel erregt hat" (*Art*

---

[411] Lessing's analysis revolves to a great extent around the central French classicist interpretation of Aristotle that demanded the famous "three unities". The length of the discussion gives an idea of its importance in Lessing's mind; it goes on (with digressions) from the 36th to the 50th "Stück" in the *Hamburgische Dramaturgie*.

[412] As noted above, Voltaire had already introduced his notion of "national taste" in his *Essay on Epic Poetry* written in English during his exile in the 1720s in England.

[413] For a more detailed description of the "controversy", see Karl Eibl's commentary in Lessing's *Werke IV* (882-883).

72).[414] This reference is certainly extraordinary when one considers that a few pages earlier Herder had denied Lessing's premise and adopted Voltaire's.[415]

Herder polemicises against French drama in a Lessingian fashion, ultimately denying its claim to be drama at all, on the same grounds as Lessing had done in the 17th "Literaturbrief"; the French had gone so far in interpreting Aristotle and the Greeks that their drama was far from being what it claimed. But for the Germans, this did not imply merely imitating the Greeks, as has been noted, but inventing a drama of their own: "Laßet uns also *ein Volk setzen*, das aus Umständen, die wir nicht untersuchen mögen, Lust hätte, sich statt nachzuäffen und mit der Wallnußschaale davon zu laufen, selbst lieber *sein Drama zu erfinden*" (74, my emphasis).[416] This cannot be achieved by using a chorus and dithyrambics, Herder claims, when these techniques do not reflect "Nationalnatur", but by writing "Drama nach seiner Geschichte, nach Zeitgeist, Sitten, Meinungen, Sprache, Nationalvorurtheilen, Traditionen, und Liebhabereien" [drama according to its history, Zeitgeist and desires] (74 & 75). Voltaire would have been able to sign the last both as a dramatist and as a historian. Herder, on the other hand, sees the great model in Shakespeare: not in his texts themselves, but in his *method*. The method is in fact the same as that used by the Greeks, but the results are different, because they lived in a different world.

One can speculate as to why Herder feels a need to repeat *and* change Lessing's already well-known arguments. One reason may be the resignation Lessing expresses at the end of the *Hamburgische Dramaturgie,* a collection of reviews and critical essays that constitute a kind of paratext to the first actual experimental attempt to establish a German national theatre:

> Über den gutherzigen Einfall, den Deutschen ein Nationaltheater zu verschaffen, da wir Deutsche noch keine Nation sind! Ich rede nicht von der Politischen Verfassung, sondern bloß von dem sittlichen Charakter. Fast sollte man sagen, dieser sei: keinen eignen haben zu wollen. Wir sind noch immer die geschwornen Nachahmer alles Ausländischen, besonders noch immer die untertänigen Bewunderer der nie genug bewunderten Franzosen (*Werke IV* 698).[417]

---

[414]   "I do not even want to examine, "whether they follow their Aristotle according to the rules they ascribe to him," the loud presumptions against which Lessing has recently raised awesome doubts" (my translation).

[415]   Herder describes the French neo-classicist premise as resignation before the Greek perfection that cannot be equalled (*Art* 71-72).

[416]   "Let us now set a people, which would, under circumstances we are not able to examine, like to, instead of aping others and running away with a walnut shell, invent its own drama" (my translation).

[417]   "On the good natured idea to set up a national theatre for the Germans, when the Germans are no nation! I am not speaking of the political constitution, but only of the habitual character. One should almost say that they did not want to have one. We are still sworn imitators of all things foreign, and especially admiring vassals of the always

Perhaps Herder realised that imitating the Greeks better than the French by imitating Shakespeare was a hopeless undertaking, so he adopted a strategy of inventing by tapping the local source. This invention was, however, not to be trapped in a provincialism of aesthetic irrelevance, but fully equal to all the comparative instances provided (the Greeks and Shakespeare, and even above the French), yet at the same time different from all of these by virtue of being German. That there is no imitation involved expresses the desire to claim originality and individuality.

When he comes to mention Hamlet's ghost, Herder references Lessing in order to surpass him, as before, using Lessing's comparison of Shakespeare and Voltaire in the 10th and 11th "Stück" of the *Hamburgische Dramaturgie*, mentioned above. Herder first takes Lessing's interpretation to the level of a "Lokalgeist" [local spirit] which is so convincing mimetically that anyone who sees Hamlet as simply a play, "für den hat *Shakespear* und *Sophokles*, kein wahrer Dichter der Welt gedichtet" [for whom neither Shakespeare and Sophocles, nor any true poet has written] (*Art* 83). This implies that the mimetic particularisation ("Lokalgeist") becomes powerfully universal, even metaphysical, through its claim to truth by imitating its environment in a wide sense of that term.[418] This becomes evident when he speaks of the "Weltseele" that flows through each play and discusses it in connection with the unities, coming to an open Spinozistic conclusion that nonetheless, very much in the French manner, attributes the three unities to Sophocles, but not to Shakespeare: "Sophokles blieb der Natur treu, da er Eine Handlung Eines Orts und Einer Zeit bearbeitete: *Shakespear* konnt ihr allein treu bleiben, wenn er seine Weltbegebenheit und Menschenschicksal durch alle die Örter und Zeiten wälzte" (*Art* 84).[419]

Herder, then, skilfully twisted the arguments of both Voltaire and Lessing in his search for a *method* and not a *model* for German national literature; for him, Shakespeare (and indeed Macpherson and Ossian) only provided a method for *the way* in which the national source of literature was to be tapped, and it may be argued that this was his major contribution to an understanding of originality that indeed still survives in the understanding of the weft that is called national and world literature. Herder's categorisation of a national dramatist (or rather a dramatic God) in the Shakespeare essay depends on the premise that one can only achieve this status "wenn du eine Welt hervorbringen kannst" [if you can produce a world], which is not an uncommon notion of originality, and in-

---

admirable French" (my translation). Lessing comes to a similar conclusion about the German national character as Hume about the English in his essay "Of National Characters".

[418] Environment then refers to national history and character.

[419] "Sophocles was true to nature since he worked out one action of one place and one time: Shakespeare could only be true to it by letting his world events and human destinies waltz through all places and time" (my translation).

deed one that has been used to describe Goethe's achievement as a poet, for example (*Art* 86). In his *Klopstock: Religion und Dichtung,* Gerhard Kaiser claims that "[a]uch in Klopstock's Lyrik wird eine vorgegebene Welt widerspiegelt. Erst die Lyrik seit Goethe erschafft Welt" [Klopstock's poetry also reflects a given world. It is only after Goethe that poetry creates a world] (287). It appears that the programmatic hinge between the two was provided by Herder.

7.1.3. The Ghosts of Necessity in Wieland and Goethe

Before returning briefly to Goethe's Shakespeare it is right to note the major *acteur* in eighteenth-century German Shakespearean production, namely the first German translator of the works, Christoph Martin Wieland, one of the most important figures of the Enlightenment in Germany, a translator, poet, editor of journals and essayist. His prose translations of 22 Shakespeare plays appeared in the short space of four years between 1762-1766 and provided the *Sturm und Drang* with its basis of Shakespearean texts, although some of its most prominent characters had some knowledge of English.[420] Goethe's own words about Wieland's translations, both in the eleventh book of *Dichtung und Wahrheit* and the Chapter "Übersetzungen" in the so-called "Noten und Abhandlungen" to *West-Östlicher Divan,* show that these translations were central to the enthusiastic reception of Shakespeare during the *Sturm und Drang* period. Furthermore, these passages reveal the way in which Goethe interprets the development of national literature towards what he later famously termed "Weltliteratur" through the processes of translation. But first let us focus on Wieland's paratextual interpretation of Shakespeare.

In the eighth volume of his translation of the dramatic works, Wieland included a personal version of Nicholas Rowe's imaginative life of Shakespeare, an interesting mixture of adaptation and personal commentary aimed at contemporaries. In 1773, however, he wrote an essay entitled "Der Geist Shakespears". This essay was published in Wieland's journal *Der Teutsche Merkur* in August 1773, a few months after *Von deutscher Art und Kunst* had appeared, which may of course have been a coincidence. One Wieland editor, Fritz Martini, has noted the essay's exceptional closeness to the productions of the younger generation of the *Sturm und Drang* (*Werke 3,* 975). Earlier the same year, in exactly the same journal, Wieland had taken exception to the nationalistic tendencies of the young Klopstockian enthusiasts and propagated a more universal vision of literature which Martini claims found its high point "in Goethes Idee der Weltliteratur" [Goethe's idea of world-literature] (973); perhaps we have here the paradigm for Goethe's own ambivalence toward ideas of national and world literature. What is important for the present purpose is the fact that Wieland turns to the ghost of the protagonist's dead father in *Hamlet* to encourage young

---

[420]   See for example Friedrich Gundolf's *Shakespeare und der deutsche Geist* (165-166).

German poets and dramatists. First, however, a few points from the essay, which partly served to defend Wieland's own translation, particularly after the harsh criticisms in Gerstenberg's *Briefe über Merkwürdigkeiten der Litteratur* (Gundolf, *Shakespeare* 169).

Wieland seems to take up Herder's challenge to stop excusing Shakespeare's irregularities and lack of taste and recommend him for his own sake; he also joins in with both Lessing and Herder and attacks Voltaire, who Wieland claims hardly knew any English. Cynically viewed, this could be a strategy for defending the irregularities in the translation, something Wieland does later in the essay by referring to Lessing's positive remarks in the *Hamburgische Dramaturgie* and the promise of an improved version by another translator and scholar (Eschenburg). The essay reiterates many of the standard phrases on Shakespeare and human nature and then gives a few examples of the "beauties" of Shakespeare, in line with the fashionable aphoristic tendency of the time, begun perhaps with William Dodd's *The Beauties of Shakespeare* (1752), a volume which Herbert Schöffler argues constituted Goethe's initial readings of the bard of (English) Bards (*Geist* 114).

All the examples Wieland presents are taken from *Hamlet* and serve to illustrate Shakespearean morality; the closing paragraph, on the other hand, is yet another appeal to take the author as a model in a competitive manner:

> Wann ist jemals unter allen Schriftstellern ein vollkommnerer Maler gewesen als Shakespear? Und wer muß der Dichter sein, der, wenn er eine Stunde zugebracht hat, die göttlichen Werke dieses großen Mannes anzuschauen, nicht in Versuchung kömmt, seine eignen ins Feuer zu werfen? Auf mich wenigstens hat das Lesen im Shakespear diese Wirkung sehr oft getan; und vielleicht hab' ich es dieser Empfindung zu danken, daß einige meiner Versuche das Feuer weniger verdienen (*Werke 3* 284).[421]

The comparision both humbles and encourages, but in his final appeal, Wieland transforms this rather neo-classicist approach into a flaming *Sturm und Drang* spirituality:

> O! ihr jungen und alten Söhne des Musengottes, echte und unechte, leset Shakespearn! und wenn ihr nichts vortreffliches machen könnt, o! so schwört – sein Geist ruft euch,

---

[421] "Was there ever a more perfect painter among poets than Shakespeare? And what poet would not, after spending an hour with his works, not be tempted to throw his own into the fire? This, at least, has often been for me the influence of reading Shakespeare and perhaps this sentiment may be thanked for making some of my attempts less deserving of the fire" (my translation).

wie der Geist im Hamlet, zu: schwört, schwört! – daß ihr lieber nichts machen wollt! (284).[422]

Considering the plot of Hamlet and the protagonist's fate, one might be tempted to see this pathetic appeal from a normally very level-headed "Aufklärer" as an attempt at almost tasteless irony; but that would be wrong, for the appeal is earnest. It is rather yet another example of the ambivalent links between what have been surgically separated epochs in textbooks of literary history. It is also an interesting repetition of Lessing's 17th "Literaturbrief" by the *translator* of the author who was to serve as a model for the new national dramatists, and whose next step was to go beyond the translation of material while continuing to translate the spirit.

Goethe did not need Wieland's appeal, for he had already written his *Götz* and revised it after Herder's criticisms.[423] Despite these revisions, Goethe made significant use of Shakespearean material, as Schöffler has shown in a detailed analysis (somewhat reminiscent of Farmer's *Essay on the Learning of Shakespeare* in the way Schöffler uses his results to stress Goethe's originality!), so he was probably not yet ready to forget the original and translate the spirit alone (*Geist* 113-135).

Hamlet's dilemma, set in motion by a spirit (ghost), appealed, perhaps, to the young German literati of the late eighteenth century because it embodied a set of dilemmas, both in philosophical and literary terms. Actually, the haunting by Hamlet's father's ghost of the theorisation process conducted by the major German Shakespeare commentators marks the one common factor in content among very different characters. The critic who has perhaps most vividly underlined this is Friedrich Gundolf in his *Shakespeare und der deutsche Geist,* a critical work that acknowledges the decisive differences between the commentators by assigning them to different philosophical traditions or schools of thought, while at the same time synthesising these differences as necessary contributions to a German "Geist". Lessing's discourse is rational and systematic; Wieland's translation moves towards a school of sensibility that nonetheless still retains elements of a kind of "rationalism":

[Wielands] Empfindsamkeit ist ein Rationalismus der Sinne, eine rationell gelenkte Sinnlichkeit, und von den reinen Rationalisten unterscheidet ihn, daß er sich der Venunft zwar als eines unentbehrlichen Mittels bediente, Welt und Kunst seiner

---

422   "Oh, you young and old sons of the muse, real and false, read Shakespeare! and if you are unable to do anything brilliant, oh! then swear – his ghost calls you, like the ghost in Hamlet: swear, swear! – that you rather do nothing!" (my translation)

423   Wieland did, however, review *Götz* and made a strong impression on the young rising star. See Fritz Martini's "Nachwort" in Wieland's *Werke 3.*

Sinnlichkeit zugänglich zu machen, daß er jedoch niemals seine Sinnlichkeit von ihr vergewaltigen ließ, sie nie in den Dienst bloßer Vernunftszwecke stellte (146-147).[424]

According to Gundolf, Lessing and Wieland both lean on reason in their analysis of Shakespeare, and the difference in their use of *Hamlet*'s ghost is perhaps the best evidence of this, although Gundolf does not address this point. Next on Gundolf's agenda is Herder, and as we have seen, he begins from a premise similar to that of Lessing, but with different results; both are rejecting the French hegemony and both use the ghost from *Hamlet*, although Herder only as a reference to Lessing. Gundolf's analysis and comparison of the two is worth quoting:

> Der Grundwille von Herders Abhandlung über Shakespeare ist der: zu beweisen, daß Shakespeare mit Notwendigkeit Schöpfer seiner Welt ist, wie Lessings Grundwille der war: zu zeigen, daß Shakespeare den einen moralischen Endzweck der Tragödie am besten erreicht hat (179).[425]

This insight also shows effectively what kind of "model" both thinkers saw in Shakespeare: that the purpose of such a model was not to imitate it, but to adopt a method or to create a world of one's own in the same way as Shakespeare did, a problematic undertaking in late eighteenth-century Germany, for the collective organic world, preferred by Herder, for example, was fragmented and disjointed – a nation and an empire in name only. The ghost of nationalism was already about at the time, but due to the fact that there was something "rotten" in the state of Germany (in the sense that it did not exist), Herder's followers had to content themselves with the construction of a "Kulturnation" instead of an organic "Nation".

Goethe was one of Herder's early followers, and although he later went his own way, he had a greater hand in the creation of a German national literature and nationality than is often admitted. As we have seen, Goethe made considerable use of Shakespeare in order to become original and national *like* Shakespeare. It is therefore perhaps fitting that the ghost in *Hamlet* also crops up in Goethe's work, both in *Wilhelm Meisters Lehrjahre* and the essay "Shakespeare und kein Ende". Fitting, because this ghost/spirit, (the German "Geist" is a

---

[424] "Wieland's sentimentality is a rationalism of the senses, a rationally controlled sensuality and what differenciates him from a pure rationalist is that, although he saw reason as an indispensable resource to make world and art accessible to his sensuality, he never allowed it to be raped by reason, never made it serve only the objectives of reason" (my translation).

[425] "The basic will of Herder's essay on Shakespeare is the following: to prove that Shakespeare necessarily was the creator of his world, just as Lessing's basic will was to show that Shakespeare had mastered best the ultimate moral purpose of the tragedy" (my translation).

homonym for both and Shakespeare of course uses "spirit" for "ghost") can be seen as a metaphor for the national literary project that strived to create a truly imaginary German nation. By metaphor I do not intend to speculate on the intention of Goethe or the others who use the ghost in their theories; it is a metaphor, as I see it, in the sense that this ghost plays a central role in German Shakespearean discourse from Lessing, through Wieland, Herder, Goethe and Hegel.[426] In fact, one of their contemporaries, Johann Caspar Lavater, the author of the *Physiognomik,* defined genius as a supernatural form of originality: "Der Charakter des Genies und aller Werke des Genies ist *Apparition*; wie Engelserscheinung nicht kommt, sondern dasteht, nicht weggeht, sondern weg ist, so Werk und Wirkung des Genies" (quoted in Friedell 734).[427]

The appearance of the ghost in the thirteenth Chapter of the fourth book of the *Lehrjahre* provides the key to Wilhelm's analysis of the major Shakespearean tragic hero whose duty to revenge and remember his father crushes his soul:

> Und da der Geist verschwunden ist, wen sehen wir vor uns stehen? Einen jungen Helden, der nach Rache schnaubt? Einen gebornen Fürsten, der sich glücklich fühlt, gegen den Usurpator seiner Krone aufgefordert zu werden? Nein! Staunen und Trübsinn überfällt den einsamen; er wird bitter gegen die lächelnden Bösewichter, schwört, den Abgeschiedenen nicht zu vergessen, und schließt mit dem bedeutenden Seufzer: ,Die Zeit ist aus dem Gelenke; wehe mir, daß ich geboren ward, sie wieder einzurichten.'
>
> In diesen Worten, dünkt mich, liegt der Schlüssel zu Hamlets ganzem Betragen, und mir ist deutlich, daß Shakespeare habe schildern wollen: eine große Tat auf eine Seele gelegt, die der Tat nicht gewachsen ist (*Werke 7* 245-246).[428]

According to Wilhelm's interpretation, Hamlet's tragic character is defined through the duty of action that is beyond him; the final paragraph in the Chapter

---

[426]   Not to forget the best-known German translator, A.W. Schlegel, who speaks of "Weltbegebenheiten" and of course the ghost (*Vorlesungen 2* 168-169).

[427]   "The character of genius and all the work of genius is apparition, like an appearance of an angel that does not come, but stands by, does not leave, but is gone, such is the work and influence of genius" (my translation).

[428]   "And when the ghost has vanished, who is it that stands before us? A young hero panting for vengeance? A prince by birth, rejoicing to be called to punish the usurper of his crown? No! trouble and astonishment take hold of the solitary young man; he grows bitter against smiling villains, swears that he will not forget the spirit, and concludes with the significant ejaculation: "The time is out of joint: O cursed spite,/That ever I was born to set it right!"

In these words, I imagine, will be found the key to Hamlet's whole procedure. To me it is clear that Shakespeare meant, in the present case, to represent the effects of a great action laid upon a soul unfit for the performance of it" (Carlyle, *Meister I* 216).

puts it thus: "Das Unmögliche wird von ihm gefordert, nicht das Unmögliche an sich, sondern das, was ihm Unmöglich ist" (246).[429]

Goethe returns to this idea in "Shakespeare und kein Ende" as he himself notes when he discusses the two attributes of ancient and modern characterisation: "sollen" and "wollen", the former referring to the categorical duties of tragic characters of antiquity and the latter to the "will" of freedom in such characters of modernity (*Werke 12* 294).[430] The character of Hamlet is central to this discussion, which could without much ado be translated into a discussion on the "universal" and "particular", as Goethe seems to do, in fact.[431] It is best to take a second look at the essay by considering how the father of "Weltliteratur" defines Shakespeare in terms of universal and particular, national and worldly, and how he addresses the topic of imitation of his method: "Ich werde zu entwickeln suchen, was *die Nachahmung seiner Art* auf uns gewirkt und was sie überhaupt

---

[429] Harold Bloom quotes this last paragraph in his *Western Canon* and focuses on Wilhelm's description in Carlyle's translation: "A lovely, pure, noble, and most moral nature, without the strength of nerve which forms a hero, sinks beneath a burden which it cannot bear, and must not cast away. [...] Impossibilites have been required of him: not in themselves impossiblities, but such for him" (213). Bloom claims Goethe/Wilhelm Meister has misread Shakespeare: "One hardly knows what play Goethe/Wilhelm Meister was reading; certainly not Shakespeare's tragedy in which Hamlet casually slaughters Polonius, cheerfully sends Rosencrantz and Guildenstern to their deaths, and acts towards Ophelia with a brutality so obscene as to be beyond forgiveness" (213). This seems to me to be a misreading of both *Wilhelm Meister* and *Hamlet*. Goethe simply focuses on the reasons for Hamlet's psychic breakdown and is able to see the positive sides of the character of Hamlet whose tragedy is the inability to react, and it must be said that Bloom's simplification above is hardly worthy of a Shakespearean scholar of his calibre. The murder of Polonius is anything but casual, Rosencrantz and Guildenstern were not exactly innocent lambs in the plot, and the brutality of a despairing soul towards Ophelia may well be unforgiveable, but it certainly does not exclude the possibility that Hamlet had been, prior to his meeting with the ghost, a "lovely, pure, and most moral nature". It is exactly in the contradictions of his behaviour and actions that this possibility is underlined. Mad is not equal to evil.
See also Morris Weitz's discussion on A.C. Bradley's and J. Dover Wilson's treatment of this theme in his *Hamlet and the Philosophy of Literary Criticism* (4 & 117)

[430] Randolph S. Bourne uses the concepts "Necessity and Will" in his translation (Bloom, *Canon* 212).

[431] "Aber alles sollen ist despotisch. Es gehöre der Vernunft an, wie das Sitten- und Stadtgesetz, oder der Natur, wie die Gesetze des Werdens, Wachsens und Vergehens, des Lebens und Todes. [...] Das Wollen hingegen ist frei, scheint frei und begünstigt den einzelnen" (*Werke 12* 293). But all necessity is despotic. It belongs to reason, like the laws of morals and the city, or nature, like the laws of becoming, growing and passing, of life and death. [...] The will, on the other hand, is free, seems free and advantageous for the individual (my translation).

wirken kann" (287, my emphasis).[432] This shows very well that Goethe's idea of imitating Shakespeare is in line with Herder's (i.e., not to imitate the author or his texts but his way of writing originally).

Herder's influence is indeed still very marked in this essay, especially if we recount his notions of "Weltbegebenheit" [world events/matters], "Menschengeist" [human spirit] and "Weltseele" [world soul].[433] What Shakespeare managed to do, according to Goethe, was to take the reader out of himself into the consciousness of the world ("den Leser in höhern Grade mit in das Bewußtsein der Welt versetzt" [to move the reader to a higher level of world consciousness]). This is in part an elementary Longinian idea of "ekstasis", but expressed more precisely, and with a Spinozistic touch to it (288). This leads, for Goethe, to the logical conclusion that "Shakespeare gesellt sich zum Weltgeist" [Shakespeare joins the world spirit] (289).

What might be the aesthetic source of such an achievement? Goethe's answer may seem surprising, but then perhaps only to those who cite his ideas on "Weltliteratur" as opposed to "Nationalliteratur" in his dialogues with Eckermann. These statements reported by Goethe's partner have dominated latter-day discourse on Goethe's ideas of national and world literature to the detriment of a balanced considereration of his true role in establishing German national literature, a phenomenon which even the critics who discuss "Weltliteratur" with reverence take for granted. In the process, the same critics ignore essays such as "Literarischer Sansculottismus" and straightforward statements such as the answer to the above question: "Shakespeares Dichtungen sind ein großer, belebter Jahrmarkt, und diesen Reichtum hat er seinem Vaterlande zu danken" (289).[434] This is plain enough, and when Goethe argues further that Shakespeare's Roman characters are simply Englishmen in togas, the argument is not intended to diminish the Bard's achievement but rather the reverse.

After making this clear point on the spiritual source of Shakespeare's genius, Goethe views him through abstract categories which he sets up, based in essence on the then more than one-hundred-year-old paradigm of the Ancients and the Moderns. The key words in this dialectic are the above-mentioned "sollen" and "wollen", both of which can be applied to Shakespeare's characters (particularly Hamlet, of course). Indeed this, according to Goethe, constitutes Shakespeare's uniqueness, with the consequence that he "das Alte und Neue auf

---

[432] "I will attempt to develop how imitation of his kind has influenced us and how it can influence us in general" (my translation).

[433] Goethe published a poem with the title "Weltseele" in 1803.

[434] "Shakespeare's poetry is a large, living fair and this wealth he can thank his fatherland" (my translation). A.R. Hohlfeld's essay, "Goethe's Conception of World Literature", on the other hand, discusses the interaction between national literatures in the production of world literature and refers to the role of translators as the *middlemen* Goethe discussed in his letter to Carlyle in 1827 (346).

eine überschwengliche Weise verbindet" [combines the old and new in an effusive manner] (293). This makes not only Shakespeare unique, but also his characters, for the inner conflict that arises through the struggle of "sollen" and "wollen" makes them individual (particular) and general (universal) at the same time: "Die Person, von der Seite des Charakters betrachtet, soll: sie ist beschränkt, zu einem Besondern bestimmt; als Mensch aber will sie: sie ist unbegrenzt und fördert das Allgemeine" (293).[435]

At first sight, this might seem an odd view of individuality and subjectivity, and indeed a strange conclusion in an aesthetic debate that began by using Shakespeare and the ghost in *Hamlet* to particularise and differentiate the German-Nordic genius from the French one, whose aesthetic objectives were explicitly universal, even if, as the German intellectuals realised, they were in essence identical with what was seen as French. That kind of synthesis, on the other hand, is precisely what a modern national literature had to achieve to become part of "Weltliteratur" and the philosopher who synthesised these seeming oppositions was of course Hegel.

7.1.4 Hegel and Shakespeare's "Geist"

Like many important and authoritative texts, Hegel's lectures on aesthetics are based on his and his students' notes and rewritten for publication. The editor of the *Reclam* edition, Rüdiger Bubner, compares their fate to that of Aristotle's work (some of which survived only through translation), and previously I have referred to Adam Smith's lectures on rhetoric and belles-lettres, which survive only in student notes, as does, for example, the basis of one of the most important tracts of the twentieth century, Saussure's *Cours de linguistique générale.* This said, I do not wish to imply that Hegel's lectures are not trustworthy; quite the contrary, or as Bubner puts it: "Der Text verdient also durchaus Vertrauen, wenngleich er kein Original ist" [The text quite deserves to be trusted, even if it is no original] (Hegel, *Ästhetik I/II* 31).

Let us, then, also have faith in Hegel's lectures, for they are interesting in this context for three reasons: a) they pick up the discursive strands in the German reception of Shakespeare; b) they analyse and organise these strands into a system based on Hegel's own thought, but also very much on Goethe's contribution; and finally, c) they express in the clearest terms the objectives of previously mentioned authors. Hegel is able to historicise their still-living dynamic in German aesthetics. It is, therefore, best to begin where Goethe concluded regarding the individual and the general. In a section entitled "Der allgemeine Weltzustand" [The General State of the World] in the first part of his aesthetics,

---

[435] "The person, considered as a character, is under a certain necessity; he is constrained, appointed to a certain particular line of action; but as a human being he has a will, which is unconfined and universal in its demands" (Bourne's translation quoted from Bloom's *Canon* 212)

Hegel asks the question "wie solch ein allgemeiner Zustand beschaffen sein müsse, um sich der Individualität des Ideals gemäß zu erweisen" [of what character such a general 'state' must have in order to evince itself as correspondent to the individuality of the Ideal] (*Ästhetik I/II* 264/Knox, *Aesthetics I* 179).[436]

To answer, he begins by looking at characters during what he calls the "Heroenzeit" [Heroic Age], an age which he contrasts with the modern in the sense that what he terms "das Sittliche und Gerechte" is dependent on the individual during the former, whereas during the latter, morals and justice are dependent on society and the state. Hegel, however, defines true independence of character as an ability to unify the individual and general:

> Die wahre Selbständigkeit besteht allein in der Einheit und Durchdringung der Individualität und Allgemeinheit, indem ebensosehr das Allgemeine durch das Einzelne erst konkrete Realität gewinnt, als das einzelne und besondere Subjekt in dem Allgemeinen erst die unerschütterliche Basis und den echten Gehalt seiner Wirklichkeit findet (265).[437]

Perhaps a little circular as an argument, but it chimes with Goethe's thoughts on Shakespeare above and formulates a reality of subjectivity through collectivity which has its analogue in art, particularly literature; ironically, it is exactly this reality that makes national literature a literature of one's own that is also potentially world literature. Hegel comes to this conclusion, as I interpret it, through abstraction and concrete examples which I will try to relate here briefly. His lodging of the truly individual "self", for want of a better word, in character and heart rather than reason is perhaps not so "original" (then again, this comes from unpublished lectures for students), but his expression is so precise that a quote is always better than any rewriting: "In dieser Hinsicht also muß wohl das Allgemeine im Individuum als das Eigene und Eigenste desselben wirklich sein, aber nicht als das Eigene des Subjekts, insofern es *Gedanken* hat, sondern als das Eigene seines *Charakters und Gemüts*" (266, emphasis in text).[438]

Such an individual belongs to an heroic age and to a literature produced in such an age; in the modern age such individuals and individuality are impossible, due to the fact that the general, "das Allgemeine" in civil society is represented through the state and its order, and the individuals are subordinate to the state. This has consequences for the conception and writing of literature, particu-

---

436 Here and in the following I use Knox's translation of Hegel's lectures.

437 "True independence consists solely in the unity and interpenetration of individuality and universality. The universal wins concrete reality only through the individual, just as the individual and particular subject finds only in the universal the impregnable basis and genuine content of his actual being" (180).

438 "Thus in this regard the universal must indeed be actual in the individual as his own, his very own; not his own, however, in so far as he has *thoughts,* but his own *character* and heart" (181, emphasis in text).

larly epic and tragic genres, and the mimetic quality in a moral and temporal sense. This means that the heroic individual is a part of the whole moral fabric of the society he or she lives in and represents the general with his or her individual characteristics. It also means that temporal distance loses its significance, for the deeds of the forefathers are just as valid for the sons and grandsons as they are for the fathers (275-276).

This definition of the heroic is of course highly relevant for any student of nationalism, since any nationalism that has ever been successful, whether of an ethnic or materialistic variety, has always made use of precisely this idea of history to claim the deeds of forefathers for contemporary identification; a recent example of this is course the Serbian version of the "Battle of Kosovo", the defeat of the Serbs in 1389 which serves as the mythomoteur in Serbo-Orthodox-Christian nationalistic doctrine.

Hegel clarifies the method with regard to literature through an analysis of the mimetic function of memory and myth in literature, noting the contrast between using contemporary material and material from the past. The problem with using contemporary material lies precisely in its contemporaneity:

Sind die Stoffe nämlich aus der Gegenwart genommen, deren eigentümliche Form, wie sie wirklich vorliegt, in der Vorstellung allen ihren Seiten nach festgeworden ist, so erhalten die Veränderungen, deren sich der Dichter nicht entschlagen kann, leicht den Anschein des bloß Gemachten und Absichtlichen (277)[439]

And another example of the clash of reality and its mimesis, here only based on the sense of time – or rather the sense time makes of the past, for memory is the manipulable element of a mimetic representation:

Die Vergangenheit dagegen gehört nur der Erinnerung an, und die Erinnerung vollbringt von selber schon das Einhüllen der Charaktere, Begebenheiten und Handlungen in das Gewand der Allgemeinheit, durch welches die besonderen äußerlichen und zufälligen Partikularitäten nicht hindurchscheinen (277).[440]

The manipulation of the particular lies then in the hand of the artist, whose freedom to reconstruct memory is the essence of his or her art. One of the major benefits of the heroic age for the author, says Hegel, is that "der einzelne Charakter und das Individuum überhaupt in solchen Tagen das Substantielle,

---

[439] "I mean that if the artistic subjects are drawn from the present, then their own special form, as it actually confronts us, is firmly fixed in our minds in all its aspects, and thus the changes in it, which the poet cannot renounce, easily acquire the look of something purely manufactured and premeditated" (189).

[440] "The past, on the other hand, belongs only to memory, and memory automatically succeeds in clothing characters, events, and actions in the garment of universality, whereby the particular external and accidental details are obscured" (189).

Sittliche und Rechtliche noch nicht als gesetzliche Notwendigkeit sich gegenüber findet" [the separate character and the individual as such does not yet in those days find the substantial, the moral, the right, contrasted with himself as necessitated by law] (277/190). The example he takes is that of a pivotal figure, Shakespeare, who, as he notes, used material from old novels and chronicles for his tragedies, material that provided him with the opportunity to recreate characters of the above category, whereas in his historical plays he was not as successful, being bound to historical events (278/190).

Hegel then contrasts the heroic with the idyllic in an analogy between the ancient and the modern in the sense he has defined them, that is the position of the individual with regards to the general, whether the individual embodies it (heroic/ancient) or whether the general *limits* the individual (modern/idyllic). Hegel's insertion of the idyllic into this constellation may at first seem a little problematic, but it becomes understandable when one considers that he is dealing with individual characters as represented in different genres:

> Denn die wichtigsten Motive des heroischen Charakters, Vaterland, Sittlichkeit, Familie usf., und deren Entwicklung trägt dieser Boden nicht in sich, wogegen sich etwa der ganze Kern des Inhalts darauf beschränkt, daß ein Schaf sich verloren oder ein Mädchen sich verliebt hat (278).[441]

The very familiar opposition underlines Hegel's argument and contrast, although he is not afraid of taking the one example that could be used against him, namely Goethe's *Hermann und Dorothea,* which Hegel claims retains elements of the idyllic while at the same time, "die großen Interessen der Revolution und des eigenen Vaterlandes eröffnet und den für sich beschränkten Stoff mit den weitesten, mächtigsten Weltbegebenheiten in Beziehung bringt" [reveals the great interests of the French Revolution and his own country, and brings this quite restricted material into relation with the widest and most potent world events] (279/191). References to Goethe and the Herderian term (world events) serve as a foretaste to the subsequent reconstruction of the heroic in modern times, because here and over the following pages of his aesthetics, Hegel is preoccupied with deconstructing the modern, prosaic situation in the arts, contrasting the modern with the ancient by noting its limitations; in short, he seems to find bourgeois tragedy a little flat in comparison to its ancient counterpart. The reason for this is, as we have seen, the limited scope for characterisation where characters are limited by the rules and regulations of society and the state.

The Aristotelian/Horatian demand for plausibility seems to be at the back of Hegel's argument. He even sees a parallel in the modern monarchs of his

---

[441] "For this ground lacks the most important *motifs* of the heroic character, i.e. country, morality, family, etc., and their development; instead, the whole kernel of its material is altogether confined to the loss of a sheep or a girl's falling in love" (190-191).

time, who are just as bound by law and constitution as other individuals, in contrast to their predecessors of the heroic age:

> Ebenso sind die Monarchen unserer Zeit nicht mehr, wie die Heroen der mythischen Zeitalter, eine in sich *konkrete* Spitze des Ganzen, sondern ein mehr oder weniger abstrakter Mittelpunkt innerhalb für sich bereits ausgebildeter und durch Gesetz und Verfassung feststehender Einrichtungen (282).[442]

In short, he is of the opinion that the heroic or the sublime is impossible in modernity. Or is he? Hegel's example of Goethe's *Hermann und Dorothea* is perhaps not as counterproductive as it might at first seem, for Hegel finds a way to reproduce heroic situations in modernity. In a section entitled "Die Rekonstruktion der individuellen Selbständigkeit", Hegel claims that Goethe and Schiller rediscovered individual independence in their "Jugendgeist" and managed to break out of the bourgeois limitations of their environment. How, he himself asks, and answers: "Nur durch die Empörung gegen die gesamte bürgerliche Gesellschaft selbst" [Only by a revolt against the whole of civil society itself] (284/195). This is a formulated aesthetic of an "Avant-Garde", whose first consideration is to break the prevailing rules and conventions; it is perhaps a logical conclusion to the German reception of Shakespeare after Herder and his refusal to excuse Shakespeare's breaking of rules, instead interpreting this breaking of rules as new rule of itself. Unsurprisingly, Hegel takes as examples the most "Shakespearean" works of the two authors: *Die Räuber, Kabale und Liebe,* and of course *Götz.*

What makes the aesthetic of an "Avant-Garde" interesting in this context is not only its clear formulation but also the pre-Revolutionary examples, along with the discourse that follows, which reformulates Aristotelian poetics with a particular focus on the moment of collision in drama, or what is called in introductions to literary criticism "a creation of conflict". That such a normative discourse on the subject of conflict follows is perhaps exemplary for the fate of any "Avant-Garde" when faced with the bourgeoisie: it gets appropriated and makes up the next rules to break. Hegel had already formulated and systematised this method in the early nineteenth century.

This is not to say that Hegel rejected neo-classical aesthetics and its reformulation of Aristotle and Horace; some of his renewals had been anticipated by people like Lessing and indeed Herder and Goethe, and, like them, he not only rejected but also renewed and reformulated. After a long discussion on the ancients and a number of examples from them, Hegel turns briefly to some Christian material in literature, saints' legends, which he condemns for their fantastic

---

[442] "So too, monarchs in our day, unlike the heroes of the mythical ages, are no longer the concrete heads of the whole, but a more or less abstract centre of institutions already independently developed and established by law and the constitution" (193).

components, quite in the way Voltaire would have done, marking the old neo-classical line between the sublime in classical and Christian literature, so memorably demonstrated by Auerbach. But then Hegel turns to Shakespeare and the fantastical elements in his works and comes to a similar conclusion as Lessing and Goethe – by using the examples of the witches in *Macbeth* and the ghost in *Hamlet*, naturally.

Very much like Lessing, Hegel finds the function of these fantastic elements in Shakespeare's plays to be decisive for their characterisation; indeed they enable him to give the characters the freedom and independence they need to achieve heroic stature: "Die Hexen im >>Macbeth<< z.B. erscheinen als äußere Gewalten, welche dem Macbeth sein Schicksal vorausbestimmen. Was sie jedoch verkünden, ist sein geheimster eigenster Wunsch, [...]" (329).[443] Hegel could have added that the ghost of Banquo also works in a similar manner, only in reverse, as the visual manifestation of Macbeth's conscience. All in all, this chimes with Lessing's theorisation on the ghost in *Hamlet,* but we are also reminded of Goethe's distinction of "sollen" and "wollen" and Shakespeare's pivotal position between these points. Hegel then refers to Goethe's analysis of Hamlet's character in *Lehrjahre* in the passage quoted above, "eine große Tat auf eine Seele gelegt, die der Tat nicht gewachsen ist".

Hegel thus picks up two major discursive strands from Lessing and Goethe and synthesises them for his aesthetic theory. It is unsurprising, then, that he also makes use of the distinction between the German and French traditions in the following section on pathos; he is simply applying a fixed paradigm in German aesthetic discourse. Hegel's minor pinpricking of the French is by no means a kind of *Sturm und Drang* nationalism, but a reference to the old opposition of Voltaire and Shakespeare. He even sets up a pairing of Goethe and Schiller, which he compares with the Voltaire and Shakespeare dichotomy through a reference to Matthias Claudius:

Auch Goethe und Schiller bilden in dieser Beziehung einen auffallenden Gegensatz. Goethe ist weniger pathetisch als Schiller und hat mehr eine intensive Weise in der Darstellung; besonders in der Lyrik bleibt er in sich gehaltener; seine Lieder, wie es dem Liede geziemt, lassen merken, was sie wollen, ohne sich ganz zu explizieren. Schiller dagegen liebt sein Pathos weitläufig, mit großer Klarheit und Schwung des Ausdrucks auseinanderzufalten. In der ähnlichen Weise hat Claudius im >>Wandsbecker Boten<< (Band 1, S. 153) Voltaire und Shakespeare so

---

[443] "In *Macbeth*, for instance, the witches appear as external powers determining Macbeth's fate in advance. Yet what they declare is his most secret and private wish [...]" (231).

gegenübergestellt, daß der eine *sei,* was der andere *scheine*; >>Meister Arouet *sagt*: ich weine und Shakespeare *weint.*<< (335).[444]

The familiar opposition of Voltaire and Shakespeare as the representatives of the neo-classical French and the Romantic Nordic (for want of a better attribute; the translation from Herder's "Nordic" to German is as uneasy as Thomas Percy's to the Anglo-Saxon) is present, and one might expect Hegel to refer to the most prominent representative of that opposition, Lessing, but he can only be traced through what must be seen as a reference to the 17th "Literaturbrief": "Aber ums Sagen und Scheinen gerade – und nicht um das natürliche wirkliche Sein – ist es in der Kunst zu tun. Wenn Shakespeare nur *weinte,* während Voltaire zu weinen *schiene,* so wäre Shakespeare ein schlechter Poet" (335).[445]

Lessing's genial definition of genius, as not being natural but only seeming to be so and at the same time providing the spark for another genius, is at the basis of Hegel's construction of the unity of the ideal and its reality, a unity which he sees brought forth through action. The problem he is trying to solve is the dichotomy between the ancient and the modern, nature and art, or the heroic and idyllic: a dialectic, the synthesis of which brings forth a representation that is neither naked imitation nor bombastic fantasy; this argumentation runs parallel with his synthesis of character in the heroic and idyllic ages, which also serves this kind of *mimesis,* a method which appropriates some of the ancients, not to imitate them, but to infuse the moderns with enough heroic ingredients to escape the dullness of mere realistic representation.

Hegel's examples of the limitations of painting are of course reminiscent of *Laokoon* and he also finds an ambivalent example in James Macpherson's *Ossian,* which he notes may well have been invented by the adapter, although he claims Macpherson still achieves the ancient *unity of place and character* – cer-

---

[444] "In this matter too Goethe and Schiller provide a striking contrast. Goethe is less 'pathetic' than Schiller provide and has a rather intensive manner of presentation; in his lyrics especially he remains more self-reserved; his songs, as is appropriate to song, make us notice their intention, without fully explaining it. Schiller, on the contrary, likes to unfold his 'pathos' at length with great clarity and liveliness of expression. In a similar way Claudius in Wandsbecker Bote (i, p. 153) contrasts Voltaire with Shakespeare: 'the one is what the other brings into *appearance.* M. Arouet *says*: "I weep", and Shakespeare 'weeps'" (235).

[445] "But what art has to do with is precisely saying and bringing into appearance, not with actual natural fact. If Shakespeare only wept, while Voltaire brings weeping into *appearance,* then Shakespeare is the poorer poet" (235, my translation). Lessing again, for direct comparison: "Because *genius* can only be fired by *genius*; and the most easily by one who seems to have everything from nature and is not intimidated by the perfection of art" (my translation). "Denn ein *Genie* kann nur von einem *Genie* entzündet werden; und am leichtesten von so einem, das alles bloß der Natur zu danken haben scheinet, und durch die mühsamen Vollkommenheiten der Kunst nicht abschrecket" (*Werke V* 72).

tainly a different criterion from the three unities of the French neo-classicist school (359-360). The unity of place and character has to be produced; Hegel sets up a dialectic of humanity and nature and finds that humans have to form their environment for their own purposes, an activity which tends to the particular, whereas at the same time nature provides humans with the primary means of living. So a balance has to be struck that takes into account the practical and natural needs and desires of humanity. In aesthetic terms, Hegel equates these with the practical prose of life, on the one hand, and the idyllic golden age where nature functions like an edenic mother, on the other. Each of these situations is, however, undesirable on its own; preferable is a third, a middle way:

> Am geeignetsten für die ideale Kunst wird sich daher ein *dritter* Zustand erweisen, der in der Mitte steht zwischen den goldenen idyllischen Zeiten und den vollkommen ausgebildeten allseitigen Vermittlungen der bürgerlichen Gesellschaft. Es ist dies ein Weltzustand, wie wir ihn schon als den *heroischen,* vorzugswiese idealen haben kennenlernen (367).[446]

This "third way" is by no means reactionary or regressive, but an ideal: "ein Weltzustand" that Hegel has described as "heroic" through his analysis of Greek drama, but which in modernity it is not to be achieved through *mimesis*, the representation of reality which was possible among the ancients, but more through Shakespeare's method, perfected by Goethe and Schiller, of representing the *ideal* in art: "Die Kunst als Darstellung des Ideals muß dasselbe in allen den bisher genannten Beziehungen zur äußeren Wirklichkeit in sich aufnehmen und die innere Subjektivität des Charakters mit dem Äußeren zusammenschließen" (371).[447] It is precisely this merging of the subjective and objective that is crucial for my argument, for it is an explicit presentation of a method that makes possible a modern literature of originality that thrives on intertextuality, a national literature that can be universal, can be world literature.

Although Hegel uses the term "external reality", it should perhaps be stressed that he is not referring to his own time and space, or rather not only that, but to the way in which those can be joined with the "heroic" to produce a work of art. This cannot be achieved by writing another *Oedipus Rex* or a modern bourgeois drama, but something in between, which retains enough of the former to give the latter a dynamic of the "heroic". Although Hegel also care-

---

[446] "Therefore what is most fitted for ideal art proves to be a *third* situation which stands midway between the idyllic and golden ages and the perfectly developed universal mediations of civil society. This is a state of society which we have already learnt to recognize as the Heroic or, preferably, the ideal Age" (260).

[447] "Art by being the representation of the Ideal must introduce it in all the previously mentioned relations to external reality, and associate the inner subjectivity of character closely with the external world" (263). A.W. Schlegel's review on *Hermann und Dorothea* also calls the age of the ancient Greeks heroic (*Sprache* 54).

fully notes the necessity of historicising with regard to time, place and outlook when writing a work that takes place in the past in another "world"; he condemns extremes of both faithfulness and appropriation: "Man kann diese entgegensetzte Forderung so ausdrücken: der Stoff solle entweder *objektiv* seinem Inhalt und dessen Zeit gemäß oder er solle *subjektiv* behandelt, d.h. ganz der Bildung und Gewohnheit der Gegenwart angeeignet werden" (373).[448]

These lines are nothing new for readers of Friedrich Schleiermacher's famous dictum on translation requiring either moving the reader to the author or vice versa, with the slight difference that Hegel is referring to original writing and the fact that he prefers *neither*: "Die eine wie die andere Seite, in ihrem Gegensatze festgehalten, führt auf ein gleich falsches Extrem [...]" (373). This does not mean, however, that Hegel does not accept the use of previous material; on the contrary, he is laying down the rules for appropriating it with the greatest artistry. Characteristically, he lays down three "Gesichtspunkte" for his dialectic and synthesis:

> *erstens* das subjektive Geltendmachen der eigenen Zeitbildung,
> [(i) the subjective stress on the contemporary civilization]
> *zweitens* die bloß objektive Treue in betreff auf die Vergangenheit,
> [(ii) purely objective fidelity in relation to the past]
> *drittens* die wahrhafte Objektivität in der Darstellung und Aneignung fremder, der Zeit und Nationalität nach entlegener Stoffe
> [(iii) true objectivity in the representation and adoption of foreign materials distant in time and nationality] (374/265).

These three points demonstrate very clearly the method of appropriation as it was practised in Germany by Goethe, for example, and indeed by others elsewhere. Hegel, on the other hand, theorises with hindsight and again picks up familiar strands in the three following sections on each of the above points. All three, it should be noted, are translatable to the discourse on translation, because they demonstrate the three main strategies that have been applied in translation: appropriation, which in modern jargon would be referred to as functionalistic, that is, reader-oriented; foreignisation, which focuses on the original itself; and the third, a synthesis of both, which has probably been the practical result of many a translation through the centuries, despite polemics for or against the first and second points.[449] Luther's "Sendbrief vom Dolmetschen" is a case in point, wherein he stresses the authority of the Hebrew originals above the Vulgate and

---

[448] "These opposite requirements may be put in this way: the material should be handled either objectively, appropriately to its content and its period, or subjectively, i.e. assimilated entirely to the custom and culture of the present" (265).

[449] Goethe's own three versions of translations in the Chapter "Übersetzungen" of the *Divan* fall into this structure (*Werke 2* 255). In fact, Goethe applies the distinction of genre into the three "Naturformen der Dichtung"; "Epos, Lyrik und Drama" (187).

interpretations of Catholic scholars (to whom he refers in very derogatory terms), on the one hand, and the native language on the other, which in turn reinforces the *translation* and its evangelical function. Luther wanted to have it both ways and certainly did.

Hegel, however, did not have a translation to defend, but a lecture to deliver, a lecture on the aesthetics of original writing, in this case the representation of the material at hand for the author. He defines his thesis statement thus: "Die bloß *subjektive* Auffassung geht in ihrer extremen Einseitigkeit bis dahin fort, die objektive Gestalt der Vergangenheit ganz aufzuheben und die Erscheinungsweise der Gegenwart allein an die Stelle zu setzen" (374).[450] It becomes clear further on in the section that Hegel's idea of "past" is not simply an historical concept, but rather a textual one: it refers to history as retained in texts, and even focuses on texts as historical events rather than the events themselves. The examples are all literary, from the Bible through Hans Sachs to Shakespeare and Racine, and Hegel's concern is the way in which texts are interpreted through rewriting; the movement is translational and the subject is one of the most common problems of translation: how the other text should be represented, in terms of time and/or space, in the subjective space of the present, which in Hegel's context is the German-speaking cultural sphere of the early nineteenth century.

It is also clear from the start that Hegel does not approve of his thesis statement and he very soon serves up the most common antithetical example of the German aesthetic discourse since Bodmer and Breitinger started rebelling against Gottsched – the terrible French neo-classicists:

Von dieser Art war der sogenannte gute Geschmack der Franzosen. Was sie ansprechen sollte, mußte französiert sein; was andere Nationalität und besonders mittelaltrige Gestalt hatte, hieß geschmacklos, barbarisch und wurde verachtungsvoll abgewiesen. Mit Unrecht hat deshalb Voltaire gesagt, daß die Franzosen die Werke der Alten verbessert hätten; sie haben sie nur nationalisiert, und bei dieser Verwandlung verfuhren sie mit allem Fremdartigen und Individuellen um so unendlich ekler, als ihr Geschmack eine vollkommen hofmäßige soziale Bildung, Regelmäßigkeit und konventionelle Allgemeinheit des Sinnes und der Darstellung forderte (375).[451]

---

[450]   "The purely *subjective* interpretation in its extreme one-sidedness goes so far as to cancel the objective form of the past altogether and put in its place simply the way that the present appears" (265).

[451]   "This sort of thing was exemplified in the so-called classical good taste of the French. What was to please had to be frencified; what had a different nationality and especially a medieval form was called tasteless and barbaric, and was rejected with complete contempt. Therefore Voltaire was wrong to say that the French had improved on the works of antiquity; they have only nationalized them, and in this transformation they treated everything foreign and distinctive with infinite disgust, all the more so as their

Even Hegel gets a little polemical when discussing the French, and as we have seen, the topos had by then become a commonplace. Even the standard metonymical presence of Voltaire is in place, as is, to be sure, Shakespeare's as an antithetical example: "Die Franzosen haben sich deshalb am wenigsten mit Shakespeare vertragen können und, wenn sie ihn bearbeiteten, das gerade jedesmal fortgeschnitten, was uns an ihm das liebste sein würde" (376).[452] Although Hegel is describing what almost all directors of Shakespeare might do, he is merely repeating a fixed dialectic in his aesthetic discourse. What is most interesting in his argumentation is the obvious element of rewriting, itself couched in neo-classical terms of imitation.

As might be expected, Hegel also divides this kind of subjectivity into three aspects, the synthesis of which may be interpreted simply as banality. This is the danger of "nationalising" the foreign so fully that it becomes common, and Hegel is of the opinion that art should exactly "von dieser Art von Subjektivität gerade befreien" ["free us from this sort of subjectivity"] (377/268). His example of Kotzebue as the ultimate practitioner of such subjective banality is perhaps apt in a German-speaking context, but not quite so well chosen when one considers that Kotzebue was not only very successful in Germany but also one of the most translated dramatists into English in the early nineteenth century, and several of his plays ran simultaneously on the London stage at the time. So banality seems to transcend subjectivity into the general no less than what Hegel considers to be "art".[453]

Hegel's antithetical point under the heading of "Wahrung der historischen Treue" also makes use of the opposition of the French and German traditions, con-struct(ur)ing both, the latter even partly through harping on a difference which was distilled out of Shakespeare – yet another translation without an original. The main difference in this section is of course the thesis that the Germans, as opposed to the French, take much more note of the foreign as it appears, are much more open to the "Zeit- und Nationalcharakter" in each case, and let them remain as they are. There are only two concrete examples in the short section: Friedrich Schlegel and Herder. From the former, Hegel claims, "ist die Vorstellung aufgekommen, daß die Objektivität eines Kunstwerks durch eine solche Art der Treue begründet werde" ["the idea has arisen that the objec-

---

taste demanded a completely courtly social culture, a regularity and conventional universality of sentiment and its representation" (266-267)

[452] "This is why the French have been least able to come to terms with Shakespeare, and when they put him on the stage cut out every time precisely those passages that are our favourites" (267).

[453] It seems to be possible to posit kitsch in both the general and individual; the general in the way in which it appropriates universal feelings (love, sorrow, etc.) cheaply for representational purposes, and the individual in the way in which it appropriates individual markers such as traditional parts of a culture (clothing, etc.).

tivity of a work of art should be established by this sort of fidelity"]; his translational view is apparent in the term "Treue" or "fidelity", which is perhaps not surprising coming from the brother of one of the best-known translators of Shakespeare into German. Herder is noted for his "instigation" to study the folk poetry of foreign nations, "und man hat es für eine große Genialität gehalten, sich ganz in fremde Sitten und Volksanschauungen hineinzudenken und zu - dichten" [and it was taken to be great genius to think oneself into foreign customs and the insights of foreign peoples, and make poetry entirely out of them"] (379/270). Hegel claims, however, that this approach can never be anything but "something outside the ken of the public" and he rejects it as the opposite extreme of the first kind of subjectivity.

"Die wahrhafte Objektivität des Kunstwerks"[454] represents Hegel's synthesis and weaving of the strands he has been discussing. This section expresses my thesis of a translation without an original in Hegel's own terms, not as translation but as originary production for the literature of the nation.

Hegel begins with an example of failure, Goethe's *Götz*. Although it does retain the historical truth and epochal colour without sacrificing the subjective grasp of the present, the work fails because it is trivial: "Aber die Nähe war so groß und der innere Gehalt zum Teil so gering, daß sie ebendadurch trivial wurden" (381).[455] Hegel is obviously hard to satisfy, and he notes that the weaknesses of Goethe's play become evident when staged; it is rather to be read than seen, which seems to echo Goethe's own words about Shakespeare (and Bloom's about Goethe) (382).[456]

Apart from the pitfall of triviality, there is the methodological problem of appropriating the past: the past as a previous mythology, history, literature. Hegel notes that the heritage of the ancients is so ubiquitous that every schoolboy knows the Greek gods, heroes and historical figures, and that "wir können deshalb Gestalten und Interessen der griechischen Welt, insoweit sie in der Vorstellung zu den unsrigen geworden sind, auch auf dem Boden der Vorstellung mitgenießen" ["because the figures and interests of the Greek world have become ours in imagination, we can take pleasure in them too on the ground of imagination"] (382/272). Only the identification through education is described here, but there seem to be levels of identification in Hegel's system of appropriation, which at times are contradictory to say the least. For example, after stating the obvious on the Greek heritage in humanistic education, he continues and says: "es ist nicht zu sagen, weshalb wir es nicht mit der indischen oder ägyptischen und skandinavischen Mythologie ebensoweit bringen können"

---

[454] The sub-heading: "The true objectivity of the work of art" is not in Knox's translation.

[455] "But the nearness was too great and the inner content of the material in part so slight that, just for this reason, they were trivial" (271).

[456] As noted earlier on, the conception of the "unstageability" of *Hamlet* and *Faust* possibly comes from A. W. Schlegel (*Sprache* 94).

["there is no saying why we should not be able to get so far with Indian or Egyptian or Scandinavian mythology too"] (382/272). The similarities are to be found in the general – in god, the belief in a god or gods – whereas the difference is in the particular and remains foreign through the distance in time and space. This is to say that one can accept a belief in foreign gods, but not the gods themselves.

He claims that the same applies to customs, laws, etc., because they have no relevance to the modern reader, and gives a definition of the nationally historical:

> Das Geschichtliche ist nur dann das Unsrige, wenn es der Nation angehört, der wir angehören, oder wenn wir die Gegenwart überhaupt als eine Folge derjenigen Begebenheiten ansehen können, in deren Ketten die dargestellten Charaktere oder Taten ein wesentliches Glied ausmachen (383).[457]

This includes the factor of education: the construction of identity through the knowledge of history and literature, the act of which is more important than the ties of geography and tribe: "Denn auch der bloße Zusammenhang des gleichen Bodens und Volks reicht nicht letzlich aus, sondern die Vergangenheit selbst des eigenes Volks muß in näherer Beziehung zu unserem Zustand, Leben und Dasein stehen" (383).[458] In short, the nation is not made of land and people, but culture, more precisely the cultural ties provided through history and literature *as available*. New historical information thus cannot simply be fed into a national literature, even if it stands closer to the people in question in both space and time than, say, the Trojan war. Hegel's example of the *Niebelungenlied* shows that even "native" heritage has to be propagated through several channels of distribution, through the repetition of an educational system, rewriting and re-publication, re-interpretation – methods which are first and foremost translations into the present:

> In dem Niebelungenlied z.B. sind wir zwar geographisch auf einheimischem Boden, aber die Burgunder und König Etzel sind so sehr von allen Verhältnissen unserer gegenwärtigen Bildung und deren vaterländischen Interessen abgeschnitten, daß wir selbst in den Gedichten Homers uns weit heimatlicher empfinden können (383).[459]

---

[457] "History is only ours when it belongs to the nation to which we belong, or when we can look on the present in general as a consequence of a chain of events in which the characters or deeds represented form an essential part" (272).

[458] "After all, the mere connection with the same land and people as ours does not suffice in the last resort; the past even of one's own people must stand in closer connection with our present situation, life, and existence" (272-273).

[459] "In the *Nibelungenlied*, for example, we are geographically on our own soil, but the Burgundians and King Etzel are so cut off from all the features of our present culture and its national interests that, even without erudition, we can find ourselves far more at home with the Homeric poems" (273).

The difference is canonical, and even if Bloom would in this case argue that this simply reveals the fact that the *Iliad* is miles better than the *Niebelungenlied*, the other fact remains that the propagation of the former is intended and it is in most cases translative. Hegel's notion of "national interests" is noteworthy in this context, but perhaps most significant of all is the fact that after two hundred years of national literatures, Homer no longer occupies this canonical position in practice, for he is hardly read anymore except by specialists and literary enthusiasts.

The other example Hegel takes for the failure of using "native" material as opposed to classical is concrete, namely that of Klopstock's changing the mythological figures in his odes from Greek to Nordic, discussed above. Hegel joins here in the choir of German critics who have since Goethe's personal judgement in the twelfth book of *Dichtung und Wahrheit* nodded in agreement without examining the subject any further. Hegel repeats the argument, thereby contradicting his own remark (quoted above) on the possibilities of adopting Indian, Egyptian or Scandinavian mythology for poetic purposes. How else are such elements to be introduced if not through practice or translation? The example of Shakespeare might be seen as the successful introduction of a dramatist and his world into another cultural sphere through the intellectual discourse we have been following here, but then again, the translations were what gave it its true dynamics: prior to Wieland's versions, the discourse was only for English-speaking specialists; after them Shakespeare became German, as Friedrich Gundolf (and many others) would see it.

And this is exactly Hegel's argument in what follows; it is not possible to use the obscure myths referenced by Klopstock because "die Kunst ist nicht für einen kleinen abgeschlossenen Kreis weniger vorzugsweiser Gebildeter, sondern für die Nation im großen und ganzen da" [art does not exist for a small enclosed circle of a few eminent *savants* but for the nation at large and as a whole"] (383/273). This statement demonstrates the tension between the general and the particular which Hegel has so painstakingly drawn up.[460]

Hegel continues his dialectical tension when he discusses "[die] echte [...] Weise der Objektivität und Aneignung von Stoffen aus vergangenen Zeiten" ["the true artistic mode of portraying objectivity and assimilating materials drawn from past epochs"] (*Ästhetik I/II* 384/*Aesthetics I* 273). His premise is that what he refers to as "Nationalgedichte" always contain what belongs to the history of the nation in question. Examples cover a wide span, from Homer through the Greek dramatists, the Spanish *Cid,* Tasso, Camões, Shakespeare and

---

[460] It is also reminiscent of Goethe's judgement on Herder in the tenth book of *Dichtung und Wahrheit:* "daß die Dichtkunst überhaupt eine Welt- und Völkergabe sei, nicht ein Privaterbteil einiger feinen gebildeten Männer" ["all poetry is a gift to the world and to nations, and not the private inheritance of a few refined and cultivated men"] (*Werke 9* 408-409/Smith 365).

Voltaire. Even the Germans have by Hegel's time stopped using foreign material for "national epics", in contradistinction to Bodmer and Klopstock, who wrote from biblical material. This again seems to contradict what he has said about the Greek heritage which, in contrast to the Bible, seems to be part and parcel of German education. Then again, he also notes that it is no longer fashionable for nations to have their own Homer, Pindar, Sophokles and Anakreon, which raises the question of what he really thinks can be adopted, and, more importantly, how.

The question, and the answer which Hegel gives, have to do with his ideal of representation and lead to a discussion of the artist and true originality. Both the question and the answer are relevant, for the method he implies in the former is to be applied by the practitioners in the latter; these two are not dialectical oppositions, but rather two sides of the same coin, rather in the way Ben Jonson said of Shakespeare "the poet's made as well as born" in an indirect translation from the Latin of Lucius Annæus Florus.[461] To return to Hegel's answer: after claiming that national poetry needs native history and elements to become what it aspires to, he instantly admits that this is not possible: "Nun kann sich aber die Kunst nicht allein auf einheimische Stoffe beschränken und hat sich in der Tat, je mehr die besonderen Völker miteinander in Berührung traten, ihre Gegenstände immer weiter aus allen Nationen und Jahrhunderten hergenommen" (385).[462] So far, so good, but the artist who is able to take himself into the foreign world is not the greater genius, but rather the one who is able to use the particular of the foreign to achieve the human, the general.[463] Hence, and despite what he has said earlier, the first commandment is "unmittelbare Verständlichkeit", and as Goethe had done before, Hegel notes that Shakespeare had always given his different materials an English national character – although he differs with Goethe regarding the Romans, whom he sees as retained in Shakespeare's works (385).

What this all adds up to is further discussion on Goethe's failures and successes in the adoption of foreign materials: his essay on Philostratus' description of paintings and, more importantly, the *West-östlicher Divan*. According to Hegel, Goethe fails in the first instance to rewrite Philostratus' *Imagines* because such ancient subjects are and will be foreign to the readership. Goethe's reworking of oriental poetry is, on the other hand, a success that manages to transcend obscurity and introduce something new and vital at the same time.

---

[461] Apparently one English translation is: "Each new year consuls and proconsuls are made; but not every year is a king or a poet born." This has sometimes been changed to „the poet is born, not made".

[462] "But art cannot restrict itself to native material alone. In fact, the more that particular peoples have come into contact with one another, by so much the more has art continually drawn its subject-matter from all nations and centuries" (274).

[463] This shows perhaps that Harold Bloom has been influenced by Hegel.

Hegel's description of Goethe's method needs to be quoted at length, for it shows an insight that supports the whole argument of this book:

> Dagegen ist es Goethen selber in einem weit tieferen Geiste gelungen, durch seinen >>West-östlichen Divan<< noch in den späteren Jahren seines freien Inneren den Orient in unsere heutige Poesie hineinzuziehen und ihn der heutigen Anschauung anzuzeigen. Bei dieser Aneignung hat er sehr wohl gewußt, daß er ein westlicher Mensch und ein Deutscher sei, und so hat er wohl den morgenländischen Grundton in Rücksicht auf den Charakter der Situationen und Verhältnisse durchweg angeschlagen, ebensosehr aber unserem heutigen Bewußtsein und seiner eigenen Individualität das vollständigste Recht widerfahren lassen (386).[464]

Hegel does not define any further what he means by "morgenländischen Grundton" [eastern keynote], but perhaps he is referring to Herder's early concept of translation, of what should be translated.[465] But Hegel is not speaking of translation, nor even adaptation, for it is obvious that he and most other critics see Goethe's rewriting as "original". Such is the tone in what Katharina Mommsen claims in *Goethe und die Arabische Welt* is the "grundsätzliche Erklärung des Orientalisten Lentz" [the basic explanation of the orientalist Lentz], which she refers to thus:

> Unsrer [der Orientalisten] Hilfe bedarf man nicht, um die Herkunft irgendwelcher von Goethe verwendeter östlicher Motive nachzuweisen. Was der Dichter an Orientalischem las, war in abendländischer Sprache abgefaßt oder in solche übertragen. Ob in diesen Quellen zutreffend berichtet oder richtig übersetzt worden war, ist sowohl für das Verständnis wie für die Beurteilung dessen, was Goethe daraus gemacht hat, unerheblich...(13).[466]

---

[464] "On the other hand, in a far deeper spirit Goethe has succeeded, in the later years of his free inner inspiration, in bringing the East into our contemporary poetry by his *West-östliche Divan* [1819] and assimilating it to our vision. In this assimilation he has known perfectly well that he is a westerner and a German, and so, while striking throughout the eastern keynote in respect of the oriental character of situations and affairs, at the same time he has given its fullest due to our contemporary consciousness and its own individuality" (275).

[465] For a detailed study on "das Ideal in der "tonbewahrenden" Übersetzung" [ideal of preserving the tone in translation] in Herder's translation theories, see A.F. Kelletat, *Herder und die Weltliteratur* (47-56). Note also Hölderlin's ideas about "Grundton" above.

[466] "One does not need the help of us [orientalists] to show the origins of some oriental *motifs* used by Goethe. What the poet read of oriental origin was written in an occidental language or translated into it. Whether these sources were accurate reports or correct translations, is for our understanding and the evaluation of what Goethe has made out of it, insignificant" (my translation).

This is the same argument that Richard Farmer delivered about Shakespeare's sources being translations and the product hence *original*. It is certainly strange to see the world of the sources and the translational work almost erased in a word, "insignificant". Whatever the sources, everything the genius Goethe did has to be subsumed under his "originality". No matter what Goethe himself intended, it seems most probable that this view comes from the critics who think he was "wary" of influence; the paratexts with the *Divan,* in contrast, openly acknowledge the foreign sources and actually underline the foreignness of the texts, even to the extent of delivering a chapter on translation.

Perhaps the "tone" is Goethe's after all, or as Edward Said put it rather irreverently in his *Orientalism,* the *West-östlicher Divan* was based "on a Rhine journey" (19). Nevertheless, like Goethe himself, Hegel is very much aware of the foreignness of the source and he is discussing exactly how the appropriation can be executed so that it is original and yet universal. And despite what he has said before about the mistaken appropriations of the foreign, he is now certain that Goethe has found the way to do it successfully, not only in the case of oriental poetry, but also Greek drama:

> In dieser Weise ist es dem Künstler allerdings erlaubt, seine Stoffe aus fernen Himmelstrichen, vergangenen Zeiten und fremden Völkern zu entlehnen und auch im ganzen und großen der Mythologie, den Sitten und Institutionen ihre historische Gestalt zu bewahren; zugleich aber muß er diese Gestalten nur als Rahmen seiner Gemälde benutzen, das Innere dagegen dem wesentlichen tieferen Bewußtsein seiner Gegenwart in einer Art anpassen, als deren bewundernswürdiges Beispiel bis jetzt noch immer Goethes >>Iphigenie<< dasteht (*Ästhetik I/II*. 386-387).[467]

The foreign can be "subsumed" by a kind of inner "subjectivisation" of the material, even if – perhaps only if – it retains outward historical markers such as myths and customs. But this also implies that markers of genre and form can have a decisive influence on the execution of the borrowing from the foreign source; they can provide the modern, national or "subjective" content with the necessary sublimity without being anachronistic or too foreign, if and only if the translators and authors have managed to translate the form into the target language. But before we return to this subject, Hegel's discourse has to be followed to its ultimate goal of the artist's originality.

---

[467] "In this way the artist is of course allowed to borrow his materials from distant climes, past ages, and foreign peoples, and even by and large to preserve the historical form of their mythology, customs, and institutions; but at the same time he must use these forms only as frames for his pictures, while on the other hand their inner meaning he must adapt to the essential deeper consciousness of his contemporary world in a way in which the most marvellous example hitherto is always there before us in Goethe's *Iphigenie*" (275-276).

He rounds off his discussion on appropriating the foreign with a short overview of the genres and how they impose different demands on the method: lyric poetry needs little historical information, the example is Petrarch and Laura (but then again, I would argue, the sonnet form itself provides the historical information); the epic requires the most historical information (which, however, needs to be "intelligible"); and the drama is the most problematic, for although the historical reality needs to be retained as a frame, it must not stand in the way of the drama. Hegel names here an example of Shakespeare's failure: his historical dramas, which the pedants want to see with each small historical detail, something the rest of the world cannot bear. Hegel even repeats Goethe's judgement, that these plays are rather to be read than seen on stage (which, as we have seen, is also Hegel's judgement of *Götz*) (388/276).

Hegel's conclusion, after citing a number of examples from Greek drama, is that anachronism is not only allowed, but necessary. He thus states openly that the foreign object in terms of time and/or space can be subsumed by the subject to create a work of art of true objectivity, if the author is allowed "zwischen Dichtung und Wahrheit zu schweben ["to hover between *Dichtung und Wahrheit*" (Knox 279)],[468] or as he adds: "Hiermit sind wir zu der wahren Aneignungsweise des Fremdartigen und Äußeren einer Zeit und zur *wahren Objektivität* des Kunstwerks durchgedrungen" (391).[469]

The route to this true objectivity leads through the higher interests of the spirit and the will so that the truly human can transcend all external characteristics and achieve the true pathos, "den substantiellen Gehalt einer Situation und die reiche mächtige Individualität, in welcher die substantiellen Momente des Geistes lebendig sind und zur Realität und Äußerung gebracht werden" ["the substantive content of a situation and the rich, powerful individuality in which the fundamental factors of the spirit are alive and brought to reality and expression"] (391/279). This and only this can produce the objective art that addresses our subjectivity: "Dann spricht auch das Kunstwerk an unsere wahre Subjektivität und wird zu unserem Eigentum" (391).[470]

The question of how to come to "our property" – how to create it – has informed Hegel's interest in the Chapters I have been discussing; his analysis of the appropriation of sources to create a true work of art is, I think, exemplary for what I have termed translation without an original, particularly in the focus on Shakespeare and Goethe. As a matter of fact, Hegel's use of Goethe goes far be-

---

[468] Knox uses here the title of Goethe's autobigraphy, which may well have been Hegel's intention, but, on the other hand, he may well have been referring to the concepts of poetry and truth in general; or both.

[469] "All this said, we have now penetrated to the true mode of appropriating what is strange and external in a past period, and to the true objectivity of art" (279).

[470] "In that event the work of art speaks to our true self and becomes our own property" (279).

yond the example (as we have seen, some of the intertextualities border on being quotes) and his general drift of thought with respect to method is in tune with Goethe's theory and practice.[471]

What Hegel's discourse also shows is the way in which a literature makes its entrance to the canon: by defining first through discursive strategies what elements, native and foreign, belong to a canonical work, and then producing works accordingly. This method focuses first on creating a national canon that can compete with the "international" one and produce works that are truly canonical. Such a process requires that extant forms, figures and narratives (in a broad sense) be taken into account, for the nature of the canon is to absorb only what can be *interpreted* as equal to what is already in it.

It is, therefore, necessary to look at Hegel's interpretation of the person who is able to produce the canonical work, a work of true objectivity, for he or she, like the beholder, is a subject, and a very special one at that, the key to Hegel's understanding of originality. Again, most of the discourse is rather derivative in content, although the master's talent of putting previously expressed thoughts into a system that is itself a challenge to any criticism is not to be underrated. But the two most remarkable elements are his judgements on the national with regard to genre and productive temperament and the surprising conclusion in his canonisation of original artists.

Hegel views the artist as an object in order to describe his or her subjectivity, and he divides his discourse into the expected triad or "Gesichtspunkte" in which we:

> *erstens* den Begriff des künstlerischen *Genies* und der *Begeisterung* feststellen, *zweitens* von der *Objektivität* dieser schaffenden Tätigkeit sprechen und *drittens* den Charakter der wahren *Originalität* zu ermitteln suchen (393).[472]

Hegel's idea of genius and enthusiasm is not exactly storm and stress, quite the contrary. First he differentiates "fancy" (*Phantasie*) from "passive imagination" (*Einbildungskraft*) by stating that the former, but not the latter, is creative, and then he is on his way to defining the artist as a maker in the classical sense

---

[471]   The text seems to contain many echoes of Goethe's and Schiller's theories. Mommsen notes: "Als Hegel seine *Vorlesungen über die Ästhetik* hielt, hatte er bereits den *West-östlichen Divan* gelesen. Dadurch findet man bei Hegel manche Formulierungen, die an Goethesche Wendungen anklingen" (322). "When Hegel gave his Lectures on Aesthetics, he had already read the *West-östlicher Divan*. Due to this, a lot of Hegel's phrasing is reminiscent of Goethe's" (my translation).

[472]   "[...] *first*, we establish the Concept of artistic genius and inspiration, *secondly*, we discuss the objectivity of this creative activity, and *thirdly*, we try to discover the character of true originality (281).

of the poet who creates something out of external reality.[473] This he does by re-verting to the familiar three points (within point one above) and notes first that for creative activity "das *Auffassen* der *Wirklichkeit*" ["grasping reality"] is nec-essary, a reality which encompasses both the external appearances of things and the inner qualities of humans. Secondly, creativity must do more than simply absorb reality. It should also be able to pinpoint the "anundfürsichseiende Wahrheit und Vernünftigkeit des Wirklichen" ["absolute truth and rationality of the *actual* world"] which is supposed to be expressed; this demand for reason and truth is the philosophical approach that is necessary to produce a work of art that shows intellectual consciousness and ability, without being philosophical in its expression. Hence Hegel rejects all naive ideas of spontaneity: "Es ist deshalb eine Abgeschmacktheit, zu meinen, Gedichte wie die Homerischen seien dem Dichter im Schlafe gekommen" (395 & 396/282).[474]

What the artist does (makes) is to give the material and its "Gestaltung" his own subjectivity.[475] The artist's sensibility, then, absorbs the external world, analyses it for its philosophically reasonable and truthful content and then ex-presses it with his own subjective and unmistakable imprint as a work of art. This straightforward analysis of the creation of a work of art is supported by a closer look at the artist and his abilities. Again Hegel reverts to his formal prin-ciple of three points, discussing talent and genius as two different sides of the same coin. He seems to be close to Herder when he notes that talent and genius are innate qualities; as Herder says of language in the *Abhandlung*, Hegel asserts of thought, stating that humans are born with the ability *as humans,* as a species, to think, to believe in a god, and only need education to give language form.[476] With art the situation is different, yet at the same time not so different; the artist has a specific talent, genius, but this, too, requires a very natural sensibility, so that experienced beauty can be made into expressed beauty:

> Wie die Schönheit selber die im Sinnlichen und Wirklichen realisierte Idee ist und das Kunstwerk das Geistige zur Unmittelbarkeit des Daseins für Auge und Ohr herausstellt, so muß auch der Künstler nicht in der ausschließlich geistigen Form des Denkens, sondern innerhalb der Anschauung und Empfindung und näher in bezug auf ein sinnliches Material und im Elemente desselben gestalten. Dies künstlerische Schaffen schließt deshalb, wie die Kunst überhaupt, die Seite der Unmittelbarkeit und

---

[473] Knox uses the terms "'capacity ', 'fancy'" for *Phantasie*, both within inverted commas, and for *Einbildungskraft* he uses "passive imagination". In both cases the original German is also given, within parenthesis. I follow him in this, although it might be debated.

[474] "It is therefore an absurdity to suppose that poems like the Homeric came to the poet in sleep" (283).

[475] The masculine is used in key with Hegel's own use and the gender of the German word *Künstler*.

[476] Herder's essay on the origin of language is discussed in the second volume of this work.

Natürlichkeit in sich, und diese Seite ist es, welche das Subjekt nicht in sich selbst hervorbringen kann, sondern als unmittelbar gegeben in sich vorfinden muß (398).[477]

This alone, according to Hegel, describes the genius and talent with which the artist is born, and it is necessary to ask what aspect of immediacy and naturalness is included in artistic creativity, what it is that the subject must find as immediate and given in itself. Hegel answers through a comparison: "In ähnlicher Art sind auch die verschiedenen Künste mehr oder weniger nationell und stehen mit der Naturseite eines Volks im Zusammenhange" (398).[478] Unsurprisingly, perhaps, this is followed by a number of stereotypical versions of the various genres different peoples are able to produce according to their natural abilities, particularly, however, in the production of folk poetry, where Goethe, as usual, appears as the German representative. Hegel's tension between what seems to be the Herderian organic principle of nations and the influence of the environment is not resolved by the third and final point with regard to genius and talent, wherein he simply states that the difference between the real artist and others is the fact that the artist learns the necessary techniques with greater ease.

After striking an uneasy balance between the activities of fantasy and what he suddenly refers to as technical execution (which includes, it appears, talent and genius), Hegel comes to the third productive element, that of enthusiasm (*Begeisterung*), or inspiration in Knox's translation. The dialectic in this case is truly elemental, based on the opposition of inspiration aroused through the senses and through intention, both of which Hegel rejects for his synthesis: "Die wahre Begeisterung deshalb entzündet sich an irgendeinem bestimmten Inhalt, den die Phantasie, um ihn künstlerisch auszudrücken, ergreift [...]" ["Thus true inspiration takes fire on some specific material which the imagination seizes with a view to expressing it artistically ..."] (402/287). Inspiration, then, requires a certain content to be aroused, and Hegel does not hesitate to ask the question this (syn)thesis surely raises in this context, namely "in welcher Weise solch ein Stoff an den Künstler kommen müsse" ["In what way must such a material come to the artist?" (402/287). Certainly not from the artist's inner self, Hegel claims, noting that some of the Pindaric odes were written to order. But

---

[477] "Just as beauty itself is the Idea made real in the sensuous and actual world, and the work of art takes what is spritual and sets it out into the immediacy of existence for apprehension by eye and ear, so too the artist must fashion his work not in the exclusively spiritual form of thought but within the sphere of intuition and feeling and, more precisely, in connection with sensuous material and in a sensuous medium. Therefore this artistic creation, like art throughout, includes itself the aspect of immediacy and naturalness, and this aspect it is which the subject cannot generate in himself but must find in himself as immediately given" (284).

[478] "Similarly the different arts too are more or less national, connected with the natural side of a people" (284).

Hegel is not advocating patronage, merely deconstructing a myth, and he is quick to come to the artist who in latter-day discourse had given rise to many such ideas, due to his writing from "nature".

> Die Stellung des Künstlers ist nach dieser Seite hin von der Art, daß er eben als *natürliches* Talent in Verhältnis zu einem *vorgefundenen* gegebenen Stoffe tritt, indem er sich durch einen äußeren Anlass, durch ein Begebnis, oder wie Shakespeare z.B. durch Sagen, alte Balladen, Novellen, Chroniken in sich aufgefordert findet, diesen Stoff zu gestalten und sich überhaupt *darauf* zu äußern (402-403, emphasis in text).[479]

The essence of the artistic subject in Hegel's construction is the way in which it tackles the material it finds, the way in which it reacts to the demand for expression in the material, to give it form and make it into a true object of art. This is of course no reproduction of the material in the most banal sense of imitation; to achieve the true objectivity of art it is not enough to represent objects by faithful imitation alone. As Hegel is quick to note, such a criterion would make even Kotzebue an objective poet, for in his works we find "die gemeine Wirklichkeit durchweg wieder" ["commonplace reality ... over and over again"] (404/289). No, the artist must go into the deep structures of his material, grasp its substance as a whole. Goethe himself, claims Hegel, was not fully able to do this as a young poet, even if he did represent reality with vividness. Without what Hegel calls "ein echter Gehalt" ["genuine substance"], however, this is not enough to achieve the true beauty of art (404).

Going into the substance of the material is also not enough, for even if the artist has subsumed it into the innermost parts of his mind (*Gemüt*)[480] it must unfold to "conscious clarity" (*bewußten Klarheit*). When this is not achieved in a serious attempt, then the pathos of the work can only hint at the inherent possibilities without having the energy and intelligence to express the nature of the content in full. Such are, for example, folk songs, which in their simplicity may hint at deeper feeling but are not able to express it. The exceptions prove the rule, as Goethe's "Schäfer's Klagelied" and the rewriting of Herder's translation of the Danish "Erlkönig" are named as successful candidates. The problem is that this kind of poetry can very easily "zur Barbarei der Stumpfheit herunterkommen" ["sink to the barbarism of an obtuseness"], which is a neat underlining of the whole Hegelian argument: even material that is "given", such as folk poetry, can only become artistic in the hands of an artist such as Goethe (405/290).

---

[479] "From this point of view, this sort of position that the artist is in is that he enters, with a *natural* talent into relation with an available *given* material; he finds himself solicited by an external incentive , by an event (or, as in Shakespeare's case for example, by sagas, old ballads, tales, chronicles), to give form to his material and to express himself in general on *that*" (288).

[480] Knox translates *Gemüt* with "heart" which I find too narrow.

By the time Hegel himself finally defines the true objectivity of art, he has formed his materials into a philosophical work of art which he can express with a sentence of sublime length and endurance of thought:

> In dieser Beziehung können wir, dem Begriff des Ideals gemäß, auch hier von seiten der subjektiven Äußerung die wahre Objektivität dahin feststellen, daß von dem echten Gehalt, der den Künstler begeistert, nichts in dem subjektiven Inneren zurückbehalten, sondern alles vollständig, und zwar in einer Weise entfaltet werden muß, in welcher die allgemeine Seele und Substanz des *erwählten Gehalts* ebensosehr hervorgehoben als die individuelle Gestaltung desselben in sich vollendet abgerundet und der ganzen Darstellung nach von jener Seele und Substanz durchdrungen *erscheint* (406, my emphasis).[481]

Subject and object are rarely so intertwined and at the same time fully independent of each other; the artist must be so taken with the authentic content that he transports it in and out of himself completely, along with his own subjectivity, for this object represents not only a subjective and artistic transformation of selected material, but also the identity of the artist, whereby Hegel is quick to eliminate all ideas of a metaphysical or divine essence; the work of art acquires its identity in the artist and vice versa. Hence nothing can be left within; everything must be taken and transformed and delivered. The subjectivity of the artist is retained in the work of art and, furthermore, it can only unfold in the work itself:

> Denn das Höchste und Vortrefflichste ist nicht etwa das Unaussprechbare, so daß der Dichter in sich noch von größerer Tiefe wäre, als das Werk dartut, sondern seine Werke sind das Beste des Künstlers und das Wahre; was er ist, das *ist* er, was aber nur im Inneren bleibt, das *ist* er nicht (406, emphasis in text).[482]

Through the unity of the subject and object, of the artist and the work of art, Hegel posits his idea of originality. The crossing of the general and the particular, real originality is based on the identity of the subjectivity of the artist

---

[481] "In this connection, keeping to the essential nature of the Ideal, we may affirm as follows what true objectivity is, even here as regards subjective expression: from the genuine subject-matter which inspires the artist, nothing is to be held back in his subjective inner heart; everything must be completely unfolded and indeed in a way in which the universal soul and substance of the chosen subject-matter appears emphasized just as much as its individual configuration appears completely polished in itself and permeated by that soul and substance in accord with the whole representation" (290). Again, I find Knox's use of the word "heart" mildly inappropriate.

[482] "For what is supreme and most excellent is not, as may be supposed, the inexpressible—for if so the poet would be still far deeper than his work discloses. On the contrary, his works are the best part and the truth of the artist; what he is [in his works], that he *is*; but what remains buried in his heart, that *is* he not" (291).

and the true objectivity of the work of art: "Wir können diese Einheit als den Begriff der echten *Originalität* bezeichnen" (407).[483]

Before Hegel analyses this construct in its final version, he, true to his methodic principles, discusses "Manier", manner in the sense of individuality and style, elements that represent the thetic and antithetic in his final discussion on originality. As he is obviously less interested in these elements, he only discusses them briefly, apparently to differentiate them from the synthetic result, that of originality.

It must be said that after Hegel's painstaking construction of the artistic subject and its identification with the notion of originality, the result is a little disappointing. First he rephrases his thesis quoted above: "Die Originalität ist deshalb identisch mit der wahren Objektivität und schließt das Subjektive und Sachliche der Darstellung in *der* Weise zusammen, daß beide Seiten nichts Fremdes mehr gegeneinander behalten" (411, emphasis in text).[484] The discussion that follows, however, is mainly preoccupied with what is not original. First he attacks what he sees as a vain attempt at humour where the artist abuses his subjectivity and the content in order to put himself in the limelight, a failure that may be "extremely impressive" but in the end lighter than it appears. Shakespeare is of course the example of one who has both great and deep humour, and Jean Paul also represents flashes of genius which are, however, also accompanied by the banality of ordinary sampled humour. When referring to irony, which he does not think much of, Hegel uses the opportunity to attack Romantic linguistic mysticism, which believed that the poetic lay in the "unsaid" and remained "concealed". For this purpose he uses Friedrich Schlegel as the metonymical representative: "So wurde z.B. in Friedrich Schlegels Gedichten zur Zeit, als er sich einbildete, ein Dichter zu sein, dies Nichtgesagte als das Beste ausgegeben; doch diese Poesie der Poesie ergab sich gerade als die platteste Prosa" (413).[485]

Finally, Hegel refers once again to Goethe, and his failure in *Götz* to produce the work of art he might have achieved, and he finishes his discussion on originality and indeed the first part of his aesthetic lectures (as prepared by the editors) by reiterating his synthesis on originality and offering a canon that is surprisingly small, and some would say reactionary: "Keine Manier zu haben

---

[483] "We can describe this unity as the essence of genuine originality" (291).

[484] "Thus originality is identical with true objectivity and links together the subjective and factual sides of the representation in such a way that the two sides are no longer opposed or strangers to one another" (294).

[485] "So, e.g., in F. von Schlegel's poems at the time when he imagined himself a poet, what is unsaid is given out as the best thing of all; yet this 'poetry of poetry' proved itself to be precisely the flattest prose" (296).

war von jeher die einzig große Manier, und in diesem Sinne allein sind Homer, Sophokles, Raffael und Shakespeare originell zu nennen" (416).[486]

After such an anticlimactic end to the construction of the artist's original subject, one might be tempted to reconsider Hegel's theorisation, for that, in its grand sweep and detailed argumentation, was hardly a negation of the possibility for modern artists to become original. Perhaps this was simply a rhetorical nod to the everlasting authorities of the classical canon (Shakespeare now unquestionably included). And the fact remains that Hegel used Goethe above all as an example in his discussion, both his failures and undeniable successes; so strong is the tendency in the text to refer to Goethe that he must be seen as the ideal artist being constructed, or as the model, one who succeeded in constructing the subject Hegel synthesises.

There is a broader perspective, however, which needs to be discussed. The individual, particular artist has been represented by Hegel as a generator of the particular from the general, and at the same time what the artist creates must achieve true objectivity. Concretely, this has implications on several levels in the current context:

a) the movement from the general to the particular in the form of the work of art,
b) the determination of the particularity of the general, i.e. of the mimetic sources of the work (environment or reality, history, texts, tradition),
c) the identity of the work of art with the artist.

All these points refer to the discussion above, with regard to ideas on *mimesis*, the discussion on the canon and the German synthesis into a national literature worthy of inclusion in the canon. They need not be discussed in detail, serving only as concluding remarks.

In point a) the translational movement has been noted, even in the case of Bloom's ideas of a "strong author", whose strength seems to be the fact that he can subsume, devour or absorb the material he finds appropriate to use. The same can be said of the German authors discussed, although their bold definition of Shakespeare as a paradigm for the "Nordic", the natural, the modern, served explicitly as an incentive to imitate not Shakespearean works but Shakespearean art.

Point b) reflects the narrowing down of the "general" as a source for the particular artist and the particular work of art; this is the moment when the "uni-

---

[486] "To have no manner has from time immemorial been the one grand manner, and in this sense alone are Homer, Sophocles, Raphael, Shakespeare, to be called 'original' (298 emphasis in text). This characteristic of having no characteristic has already been noted in Lessing's theorisation. See also Hume's similar idea on national character in the second volume.

versal" can become national, even if it is originally foreign. Hegel's assertion that Greek mythology has been made national through education, even more so than originally "Germanic" myth, is a good example. However, the determination of the particularity of the general functions, also with hitherto-unknown foreign materials, if, and only if, they are subsumed into the national and subjective; again Hegel provided an example with the *West-östlicher Divan*. He does not, I think, resolve the inherent contradictions of these arguments. What both include, nevertheless, is the need for a translational movement, and indeed previous translation in most cases, for the Greek mythology is of course translated (as is the Germanic or the Oriental) and then simply rewritten or intralingually/intersemiotically translated, to use Jakobson's terminology.

Point c) is the most interesting in Hegel's argumentation, for it tackles problems of subjectivity that are rarely addressed in translational contexts – not even almost two centuries later, as Bloom's ideas of originality show best, with the almost metaphysical "power of thought, [...] that it triumphantly survives translation" (*Canon* 52). Perhaps he should have said it survived *through* translation. As has been shown, Bloom is certainly not alone, perhaps due to a stress on the objecitivity of the work of art, a stress that disentangles – or at least has tried to disentangle – the subject of the artist from the object of art. At the same time, Bloom, along with many other critics, even those who focus on the text itself or its reception, never want to and never can get fully rid of the artistic subject (Bloom would not be interested, although he does not go as far as Hegel in erasing the difference between the subject and the object). As we have seen, Hegel (unlike Heidegger) does not revert to any "verborgen" or hidden (invisible?) element in the work of art, but sees it concretely as the enfolding of a subject into a work of true objectivity. And in this process he sees the subject as a transformer of the material "vorgefunden", forming the material into what it will become in its true objectivity.

Again the translational movement is conspicuous in this moment of what is considered as an opposite of translation, and there of course exists translation that achieves its goal in the retention of as much of the objectivity of the work of art as is possible; this does not mean, however, that the transformer is a non-subject, but rather an interpreter capable of retaining an objectivity of the work of art through his or her artistic subjectivity as a *translator*.

On the other hand, one might apply Roland Barthes' thesis in "The Death of the Author" and simply deny the subjectivity of the author and therefore of the translator as well, making the identity of the work the same as the reader's and his or her interpretation. Barthes' well-known and to this day controversial thesis, that

[a]s soon as a fact is *narrated* no longer with a view to acting directly on reality but intransitively, that is to say, finally out of any function other than that of the very practice

of the symbol itself, this disconnection occurs, the voice loses its origin, the author enters into his own death, writing begins (125),[487]

can easily be applied to translation; it is indeed a description of the loss of origin in translation, automatically assumed since the emergence of the author as an originator, a text personified, the owner of material and moral rights to his or her work.[488] What Barthes does is condemn the *authors* to the Limbo of translation, writing in the second degree. This is perhaps the reason for the outcry against this famous essay, the thesis of which is an intentional antithesis to the bourgeois conception of writing, which requires the subjectivity of the owner and author, added to which must be the moral message, the connector that Barthes denies it: for it was through invention of the application of morals in literature, the desire of "acting directly on reality", that a myth of the origin of voice was constructed; this became possible in Europe with the emergence of native-language texts and the printing medium, the market that was able to evade the central ideological control of a church that had previously been able to manage the act of writing in most aspects.[489]

This development, as briefly depicted above, is interesting, but it is more important to consider the implications one can infer by examining these two antithetical formulations of subjectivity and textual production with regard to originality and translation. Their examination is certainly valid, for Hegel and Barthes represent two ends of a spectrum, not only in an ideological sense but also in a temporal one. Leaving the temporal element out (although one might consider the "timelessness" of an epoch, in this case a version of "modernity"), the question is really whether the two are as antithetical as they seem, or if there is a possible synthesis that does not devalue either thesis, but revalues them, with a new perspective and formulation.

In working through Hegel's aesthetic theory on the construction of subjectivity and originality, we have constantly come across his stress on the subject

---

[487] "dès qu'un fait est *raconté*, à des fins intransitives, et non plus pour agir directement sur le réel, c'est-à-dire finalement hors de toute fonction autre que l'exercice même du symbole, ce décrochage se produit, la voix perd son origine, l'auteur entre dans sa propre mort, l'écriture commence" (61).

[488] The loss of origin as described here is also one of the objectives of conference interpreters who interpret simultaneously, whereby the loss should occur exactly in the moment they mediate reality with their own voice.

[489] Native-language texts of the Middle Ages were in many cases beyond the moral control of the Church. This was perhaps partly due to patrons who supported such texts in defiance of the Church, or more often, simply because texts such as the medieval romances served as a subcultural medium of entertainment. This might explain the lack of sexual and other morals in many of the romances, a fact that has even brought twentieth-century enthusiasts such as Loomis, for example, to proclaim their indignation at the low moral content.

unfolding through the reworking of extant material. For Hegel, the subject speaks with the material which then disappears in the true objectivity of the work of art, which is identical with the subject.

Barthes, conversely, claims that not only for Mallarmé, but

> for us too, it is language which speaks, not the author; to write is, through a prerequisite of impersonality (not at all to be confused with the castrating objectivity of the realist novelist), to reach that point where only language acts, 'performs', and not 'me' (126).[490]

This claim, which sometimes metonymically signifies the whole of poststructuralism, ideas of the dissolution of the subject and so on, sets the entire focus on the language produced, and sees it as self-sufficient, or at least as the creative source of writing, as opposed to the voice of speech. This again might be in discord with Derrida's observations in *Of Grammatology*, were it not for the qualification earlier in the essay that in "ethnographic societies the responsibility for a narrative is never assumed by a person but by a mediator, shaman or relator whose 'performance' – the mastery of the narrative code – may possibly be admired but never his 'genius' (125).

It is in this figure of the mediator that I find the lost subject Seàn Burke seeks and finds in his "Reconstructing the author", an introduction to his reader, *Authorship: From Plato to Postmodernism* (xv-xxx).[491] Leaning on Heidegger and Nietzsche, he wants to retain the author as a kind of "who?" in the plurality of postmodern discourse. This is of course a legitimate objective, but he fails to face the "foundational" problem, so bound is he to the (literary) authorial discourse he wants to deconstruct. It is rather in the "mediator" that the subject can unfold in the Hegelian sense, whereby one might attribute this activity to a mass of people, beyond literature, for it is the moral mediating function of the aesthetic with its high priest the "author" that is dead, and the act of communication in its various facets has taken over the role of the literary aesthetic with a number of communicators in the authors' place.

The new role of the literary mediator can then be defined as that of a communicator *par excellence*, of an eloquence that retains its individuality in the language it expresses. Individuality within plurality has always been located in language; the subjective poet of modernity is the most lyrical and expresses his or her alterity by being linguistically distinct from the rest. It has been the objective of modernist poetry to be individual through language and not content or

---

[490] "[…], comme pour nous, c'est le langage qui parle, ce n'est pas l'auteur ; écrire, c'est, à travers une impersonnalité préalable – que l'on ne saurait à aucun moment confondre avec l'objectivité castratrice du romancier réaliste –, atteindre ce point où seul le langage agit, « performe », et non « moi »" (62).

[491] The term is of course not new, but it is an attempt at a definition which encompasses the subjects of author and translator. A translation of Horace by inversion.

personality; even novelists, prose writers have often been considered original due to their "lyrical" prose: poetic prose, which is individual through language and not content or plot. The subject can only determine its difference from others through language, the same code everybody uses within a linguistic area. So in the final analysis, the mediators of the global world, be they active in the banal hegemony of modern communication or the minority activity of literary production, are its translators.

Table of Contents Volume II

Index of Names

Flachsland, Carolina, 233
Florus, Lucius Annæus, 287
Foster, Idris L., 189
Fowler, Alastair, 197, 200
Franklin, Thomas, 257
Fränzel, Walter, 225-227
Friedell, Egon, 270
Friedrich II, 226
Friedrich, Caspar David, 89
Friese, Wilhelm, 110
Frisi, Paolo, 246, 260
Frost, Robert, 22
Fry, Michael, 16
Fukuyama, Francis, 63
Gabriel, Gottfried, 56-57
Gadamer, Hans-Georg, 33
Garrick, David, 112, 151
Gaskill, Howard, 25
Gautadóttir, Fjóla, 9
Gautadóttir, Selma, 9
Gautason, Jakob, 9
Gellner, Ernest, 14
Genette, Gérard, 27-28, 57-59
Genseric, 188
Gentzler, Edwin, 7
George III, 121, 209
Gérard, François, 89
Gerstenberg, Heinrich W. von, 232, 261, 267
Geulen, Christian, 15
Gigon, Olof, 60
Gildon, Charles, 149
Gloucester, Robert of, 152
Goethe Johann Wolfgang von, 27, 66, 73-74, 76-83, 89-90, 199, 221, 229-230, 232-247, 250, 254-255, 259, 266-273, 276-281, 284, 286-291, 293-294, 296-297
Goldsmith, Oliver, 156
Göransson, Johann, 169
Gottsched, Johann Christoph, 223-228, 234, 236, 238, 282
Gower, Earl, 103
Grainger, James, 125
Grammaticus, Saxo, 131, 187
Gray, Thomas, 25, 92, 112-115, 124-127, 152, 156, 190, 202, 209, 254
Greenblatt, Stephen, 29

Gregory, Lady Augusta, 99
Grimm, Gunter E., 220-221
Grimm, Jacob, 164-165, 169
Grímsdóttir, Guðrún Ása, 161
Groom, Nick, 92, 116, 122-123, 127-128, 132, 135, 137-138, 141, 153-154, 157-158, 162
Gualter, Archdeacon of Oxford, 181
Guattari, Félix, 18
Guðmundsson, Böðvar, 131, 187
Gundolf, Friedrich, 227, 244, 266-269, 286
Gunnlaugsdóttir, Álfrún, 9
Guthke, Karl S., 79
Hagemann, Susanne, 9
Haller, Albrecht von, 224
Hamann, Johann G., 232, 239
Hammond, Carolyn, 160
Hammond, James, 126
Hammond, Martin, 261
Handke, Peter, 62
Hanmer, Sir Thomas, 146
Hannah, Jean, 166
Hardt, Michael, 14
Harnes, Michel de, 185
Hart, James, 88
Hart, Kevin, 72-73
Hastings, Adrian, 16
Haugen, Einar, 156
Havelock, Eric A., 33
Haywood, Ian, 94
Hazlitt, W.C., 207
Hegel, Georg W.F., 52, 63, 73, 81, 231, 241, 246-247, 250, 270, 273-300
Heidegger, Martin, 7, 44-56, 62-63, 72-73, 298, 300
Heinesen, William, 73
Heinsius, Daniel, 220,
Hellmuth, Eckhart, 15
Henry VIII, 148
Henryson, Robert, 205
Herder, Johann Gottfried, 8, 27, 35, 49, 51, 79-80, 89, 92, 101, 137, 221, 224, 232-233, 236-240, 246-247, 254, 260-270, 272, 276-277, 279, 283-284, 286, 288, 292-294
Herodotus, 43, 50, 207, 242
Heusler, Andreas, 153, 216, 219, 223-224, 227-228, 234

Hickes, George, 132, 167
Hitler, Adolf, 96
Hjelmslev, Louis, 170
Hobsbawm, Eric, 14, 16
Hofstadter, Albert, 45, 47-50
Hogg, James, 74
Hölderlin, Friedrich, 23, 27, 89, 221, 229, 242-245, 288
Hölty, Ludwig Christoph Heinrich, 234-236
Hönig, Hans, 7
Holmes, James, 7
Holz, Arno, 26
Home, Henry, Lord Kames, 93
Home, John, 87, 93, 111-113, 251
Homer, 8, 21, 25, 28-29, 31-33, 40, 42-43, 60-61, 83, 88-89, 91-92, 106, 116-121, 145, 206, 221, 232-239, 241-243, 286-287, 297
Horace, 33, 37-44, 48, 55, 163, 217-218, 247, 249, 255-256, 258, 277
Howard, Henry; Earl of Surrey, 22-23, 221
Huber, Thomas, 216
Humboldt, Wilhelm von, 49, 239
Hume, David, 91, 93, 102-103, 106, 121, 199, 215, 224, 248, 254, 265, 297
Hurd, Richard, 138, 143-144, 153-154, 198, 248
Hutcheson, Francis, 254
Hutten, Ulrich von, 160, 215
Huxley, Aldous, 66
Huyssen, Andreas, 19, 71
Hyde, Douglas, 99, 105
Ibsen, Henrik, 72
Ingres, Jean-Auguste-Dominique, 89
Irmscher, Hans D., 263
Jakobson, Roman, 21-22, 27, 88, 243, 298
James V, 146
James VI, 102, 109
Japhet, 101
Jerome, St., 20, 67-68
Jerusalem, Karl Wilhelm, 83
Jervas, Charles, 74
Jiriczek, Otto L., 97, 100-102
Johnson, Samuel, 68, 76-77, 90, 93-94, 97, 100, 103-108, 119-120, 123-124, 126-127, 129, 136, 138-140, 146-147, 166-167, 197-200, 204, 207, 225, 262

Jones, William, 164-167, 172, 188
Jonson, Ben, 73-74, 149, 287
Joyce, James, 16, 41, 68, 73
Junius, 126, 136
Kaiser, Gerhard, 266
Kames, Lord, see Home, Henry
Kamuf, Peggy, 46
Kant, Immanuel, 18-19, 52, 56-57, 73, 215, 224
Kaufmann, Walter, 43
Keats, John, 44, 53
Kedourie, Elie, 215
Kelletat, Alfred, 236
Kelletat, Andreas F., 9, 69, 233, 242, 288
Kelly, Louis G., 28
Ker, W.P., 150-151, 194, 276
Keysler, Johann G., 158
Kidd, Colin, 16, 98, 116, 190
Kirchmayer, Thomas, 216
Kissinger, Henry, 15
Klopstock, Friedrich G., 87, 89, 126, 160, 215-217, 223-224, 227-237, 243-245, 266, 286-287
Klotz, Christian A., 255-256, 258-259
Kohlmayer, Rainer, 7
Knebel, Karl L., 242
Knútsson, Pétur, 9
Koch, J.A., 89
König, Gustav, 233
Koerner, E.F. Konrad, 165
Kotzebue, August von, 283, 294
Kristeller, Paul O., 223
Kristeva, Julia, 32, 57-58, 78
Kristjánsson, Jóhann R., 9
Kristjánsdóttir, Bergljót S., 98
Kundera, Milan, 62
Kußmaul, Paul, 7
Lacan, Jacques, 8
Laing, Malcolm, 25, 98
Laing, Samuel, 98-99
Lange, Samuel G., 224
Langland, Robert, 150, 152
Lamport, F.J., 90
Langton, Bennet, 126
Laplace, Philippe, 9
Lavater, Johann C., 270
Leersen, Joeep, 96, 175, 232
Lefevere, André, 7, 20, 25, 28

Index of Subjects

Académie française, 15, 30
Adequatio, 53, 55, 231
Aeneid, 21, 116, 182, 205, 258
Aesthetics, 52-54, 68-69, 73, 71, 75-76, 80-81, 87, 92, 123-124, 127, 135-139, 141-146, 150, 164, 173, 184, 200, 201-202, 204-205, 209, 216, 221, 223-230, 233-234, 246-247, 249-251, 254-255, 257, 261, 263, 265, 272-274, 276-278, 280-286, 291, 296, 300
Alexandrine, 23, 152-153, 185, 220, 224, 227-228
Alliteration, 150-153, 177-178, 185
Anapest, 152, 178
Antiquarian, 88, 96, 141, 152, 253
Ash of Yggdrasill, 189
Avant-Garde, 277
Babel, 22, 27, 31, 46, 64-65, 70
Ballad, 21, 27, 88, 137-138, 146, 294
Barbarian, 240, 253, 294
Bard, bardic 78, 89, 92, 95-96, 106, 108, 112, 115, 127, 130, 139-140, 149-150, 160, 174, 176, 178, 210, 229-230, 232, 267, 272
Belles lettres, 111, 113, 145, 196-197, 200
Beowulf, 129-130, 150-151
Bible, 22, 24, 28, 31-32, 45, 63, 67, 71, 88, 109-110, 111, 113-114, 143, 165, 207, 215, 234, 260, 282, 287
Blank verse, 22-23, 120
Book of Mormon, 26
Caledonians, 162
Canon, 67-79, 198, 246, 271, 273, 298
Celts, Celtic, 8, 93-94, 97, 99-101, 104-106, 108, 110, 112, 115-117, 123, 127-128, 131, 132-133, 136, 138, 141-143, 153-195, 230
Cethegi, 38
Christian, Christianity, 30, 32, 110, 122, 162-163, 177, 179, 218, 255, 275, 277-278
Colonialism, 28, 40, 95, 119, 172, 195
Colophon, 184
Comedy, 148-149

Comparative-historical linguistics, 156, 158, 164-166, 168-170, 172, 196, 205
Concessio, 74, 123, 136-137, 139-141, 144, 153, 193
Couplet; heroic couplet, rhyming couplet, 23, 88, 98, 120, 220
Court poetry, 134
Cultural nationalism, 15, 203
Cultural sphere, 37, 67, 244, 282, 286
Dactyl, 125-126
Danelaw, 189-190
Darraðarljóð, 124
Deconstruction, 13, 18, 35, 59, 73, 159-160, 182, 190, 247-248, 256, 258, 263, 294, 300
Der Junge Werther, 78-79, 83, 89-90, 183, 229
De vulgari eloquentia, 29-30
Diaspora, 116
Dionysian, 36, 133
Diplomatics, 90
Distich, 125
Dithyrambic, 264
Dróttkvæði, see Court poetry
Druid, 98, 106, 115, 162-163, 171, 187-188
Edda, 88, 98, 130, 156, 161-162, 169, 178, 182, 187, 189, 230-231
Editing, 27-28
Egil's saga, 131, 135, 177, 191
Elegy, 114,125, 126
Eloquence, 28, 197, 199, 300
Empathy, 7
Enlightenment (*Aufklärung*), 8, 15, 89, 91, 93, 110-111, 113-114, 120, 197, 216, 226, 266
Epic, 21-22, 25, 40-41, 53, 75, 87-88, 90-91, 94, 100, 105, 112-114, 116, 119-120, 122, 132-133, 137, 149, 151, 154, 183, 205-206, 220, 232, 234, 236-242, 253, 263, 275, 287, 290, 299
Epigone, 116, 174-175,
Equivalent, equivalence, 22-23, 41, 92, 152, 158, 220, 230-231, 243, 248
Erlkönig, 27